*The Early Greeks*

# The Early Greeks

## R. J. HOPPER

*Emeritus Professor of Ancient History, Sheffield University*

**BOOKS**
10 East 53d St., New York 10022
*(a division of Harper & Row Publishers, Inc.)*

© by R. J. Hopper 1976

Published in the U.S.A. 1977 by
HARPER & ROW PUBLISHERS, INC.
BARNES & NOBLE IMPORT DIVISION
ISBN 0–06–492978–7
LC–76–20894

Printed in the United States of America

# CONTENTS

# ILLUSTRATIONS

# PREFACE

IN A PERIOD of increasing specialization it may be felt presumptuous that one writer should attempt to cover the whole span of this book. Nonetheless, for reasons given in the Introduction, such a task must be attempted. The result tends to show an inadequacy of contact with primary sources and a dependence on those intermediate publications which sum up the results of detailed scholarship. Inevitably there is a time-lag, and generalizing statements can be overtaken by new knowledge. This is something which must be accepted if fragmentation of theme is to be avoided and the pursuit of knowledge is to be justified by the process of making it available to a wider public outside the various groups of specialists. The alternative, the sort of work to which a number of writers make contributions, has its well-recognized disadvantages, above all in the field of Prehistory, but also in no small degree in the case of the history of Archaic Greece.

An effort has been made wherever possible to present the evidence of archaeology, written sources of a more strictly historical character, and literature, as some sort of amalgam. Here again the disabilities of the non-specialist become very apparent. The choice of chapter headings is a matter of the author's personal judgement. Only to a limited degree can the chapter divisions be chronological.

Problems of book length and publication costs inevitably limit the extent to which sources may be quoted and references given to the relevant literature. For the same reason material objects referred to in the text cannot be fully illustrated. It has been felt that an extensive separate Bibliography in a work of this sort is a luxury which can be replaced by a select list of general works, and references to a limited number of periodicals.

The author would like to thank all those (too numerous to mention individually) who have helped in the formation and correction of his ideas; and particularly the publisher's reader for his criticism of earlier versions of the text; and Mrs Susan Loden for her infinite patience.

# INTRODUCTION

IN A BOOK such as the present, entitled *The Early Greeks*, there can be little dispute concerning a terminal date for the period involved. The middle of the sixth century saw the consolidation to a large extent of the *polis* system. It also saw the development of the power and prestige of Sparta, and the beginnings of the cultural and political greatness of Athens which would find its highest point of attainment in the fifth century BC. At the same point took place the advance of the Persians to the Aegean, an event which turned mainland Greek interest to Persia, and Persian interest to Greece. It led at a later date to the Ionian Revolt, to Greek involvement in the affairs of Asia Minor and to the Persian invasions of Greece. These invasions stimulated Athenian greatness, the development of her political system in contrast to that of Sparta, and in effect produced the eventual clash, to come in the Great Peloponnesian War. There can be no doubt that there is a clear dividing line in the mid-sixth century. The question of the early beginnings is quite another matter.

How far back must the origins of the Greeks be carried? George Grote could say: 'I begin the real history of Greece with the first recorded Olympiad of 776', and adds: 'I may appear to be striking off one thousand years from the scroll of history.'[1] The advance of archaeology and philology has made such ruthless surgery impossible, and has introduced many controversial matters, including the date of the coming of the Greek language or of an early component of Greek to the land which thus became Greece: an issue which could call into question the title of this book, since its theme is thus carried back far beyond the earliest contemporary evidence for the written use of the Greek language in the eighth century BC. In effect the Ventris–Chadwick decipherment of the Linear B tablets is here accepted as indicating the use of primitive Greek or a component of Greek from the earlier fourteenth century in Crete and from an uncertain date on the mainland. There follow the problems connected with the manner in which this Indo-European language was introduced, the routes its speakers followed from their original homeland in southern Eurasia and the links they had with other users of Indo-European languages such as the Hittites of Anatolia. There is then the problem of date: was the entry effected in the period of Neolithic culture in the southern Balkans, or during the Early Bronze Age, at the end of Early Bronze II or at the transition from Early Bronze III to the Middle Bronze, or at both periods of Early Bronze? Were there successive incomings: warlike invasion and peaceful penetration? In any case, what were the nature and affinities of the languages spoken earlier, and how far did elements of them survive?

As well as this matter of language there is the possibility of the survival of pre-Greek ethnic elements in Early Iron Age and Classical Greece, to influence the make-up of the population. Consequently something must be said (but briefly) on the Early Bronze cultural background, since the view is accepted here that the Neolithic did not see the coming of Greek-speakers. With the latter part of the Middle Bronze there is introduced the question of the influence of Crete on the mainland, and subsequently, in the Mycenaean period, the contact of the mainland with Crete, and especially Knossos, because of the presence of Linear B tablets there in the Late Minoan II-III A period. The strikingly elaborate economic and administrative system of the mainland palace centres in the Late Bronze (Mycenaean) period can be seen as an extraneous element superimposed on the simpler and more primitive Middle Bronze culture, and this latter may have to some degree re-emerged after the disasters of the end of the Bronze Age to form an element of the Early Iron culture of Greece, to which was added a new intrusive element. In the latter part of the Late Bronze Age there is the question of relations with other regions of Europe.

The preoccupation with material remains ranging from the spectacular to the trivial might seem to have little to do with the more traditional literary-historical aspects of early Greece. Indeed some might be tempted to quote sourly another observation of Grote: 'I really know nothing so disheartening or unrequited as the elaborate balancing of what is called evidence – the comparison of infinitesimal probabilities and conjectures all uncertified – in regard to these shadowy times and persons.'[2] None the less these lengthened perspectives and controversial issues cannot be neglected in themselves, and they are closely involved with the traditions held by the Greeks, since in this early period (of the Late Bronze Age) was placed the Greek Heroic Age and the episodes which the Greeks made the foundation of their chronology: Herakles, the siege of Troy, the Returnings (*nostoi*) of the heroes, and the coming of the Dorians and return of the Herakleidai, besides a number of events purporting to take place in Greece before the expedition to Troy, such as the dynastic struggles in the Peloponnese and the expedition of the Seven against Thebes. The archaeological and the traditional cannot be separated, but have to be looked at together in a sensible fashion.

The following account begins (Chapter 1) with a description of the geographical background, which cannot be neglected as a factor in the development of the Greek way of life. Then the period of Bronze Age culture on the mainland, its development, zenith and decline are clearly important for the subsequent history of Greece. A considerable influence *was* exerted by Bronze Age Crete on the Middle and Late Bronze culture of Greece; the Linear B tablets at Knossos, in the earlier fourteenth century, in turn, seem to show that there were primitive Greek-speakers there. There is a temptation to devote a special chapter to Minoan Crete, but on consideration it seemed that the Cretan connection could best be treated in the context of the mainland. After all, so much which characterized Minoan Crete seems wholly alien to later Greece, despite the efforts of scholars to detect 'continuity'. There is also the practical consideration that such a chapter would have to be disproportionately long if justice were to be done to the problems of Minoan Crete, including those of the Theran eruption and its effects.

On the other hand the Greeks, from the period of the Homeric poems onwards, took a particular interest in Crete: not only Crete of the earlier Iron Age, but also, in a remoter period, that of the ruler called Minos. Consequently Chapter 2 is devoted to Crete in mythology. This is followed by Chapter 3, concerned with the Bronze culture of the Mainland and the Aegean, leading to the great days of the Late Helladic (Mycenaean) period, the background, from the modern standpoint, of the Greek Age of the Heroes; this is important, despite what Grote[3] has to say of it.

The following chapters have been given titles which seem to the author to sum up successive stages or aspects of Greek experience. Chapter 4, 'Obscurity and Recovery', deals with the decline at the end of the Bronze Age and the slow recovery marked by the development of the 'Geometric' culture, the settlement of the western coastland of Anatolia and the early development of the *polis* with its governmental, economic and social structures. Chapter 5, 'Expansion and Innovation', looks at exploration, colonization proper and the contact of the Greeks with the eastern Mediterranean and the Orient. This chapter has been written in rather general terms, as a useful preliminary to Chapters 6, 7 and 8, dealing with the period from the late eighth century, through the seventh, to the mid-sixth. In this period the material remains steadily increase, and the literary evidence, though often scant or late, does make it possible for the modern student to feel that he is dealing with something approaching true history. The greater detail in these chapters involves a certain degree of repetition and elaboration of the material in Chapters 4 and 5. The titles given might be queried. None the less the period and themes treated in Chapter 6, 'The Beginning of Consolidation: Tyrants and Hoplites' are greatly concerned with the phenomenon of tyranny and the emergence of the Classical form of land warfare. Furthermore the seventh century saw the first clear emergence of the Greek city-states, their frontiers expanding to meet those of their neighbours. In this process of development it has to be admitted that Sparta and Athens stand somewhat apart. Hence the title of Chapter 7: 'The Abnormal States'. Chapter 8, 'The Foundation of Classical Greece', is the easiest to define, with the development of Spartan leadership, the rise of Athens, and a new factor, the appearance of the Persians.

As far as is possible, from the period of the Homeric poems onwards archaeological and literary evidence have been closely combined, but for the latter it is painfully apparent, again in the words of Grote, that: 'We possess only what has drifted ashore from the wreck of a stranded vessel. . . .'[4]

# CHAPTER 1

# THE GEOGRAPHICAL BACKGROUND

The essential heartland area from the standpoint of the present narrative is the southern portion of the Balkan peninsula, to a great extent cut off from the area to the north by mountain masses. It has an extension eastwards through eastern Macedonia into Thrace: a strip of fertile land of varying width marked off on the north by the Bulgarian mountains, which allow easier north and south communication at their eastern end, in the region of the narrow passage between the Aegean and the Black Sea. There are crossing places in the northern barrier, principally from Bitola (Monastir) to Florina, from Skopje to Salonica along the valley of the Vardar; further east from modern Bulgaria by way of the Struma and Nestos Valleys and other subsidiary routes to modern eastern Macedonia and Thrace. Where Mount Rhodope (the Bulgarian Mountains) declines to the course of the Maritsa (the ancient Hebros) and to Turkey in Europe with its capital at Edirne (Adrianople), there is easy access from the Black Sea to the Aegean.

South of this barrier (in effect the boundary of modern Greece) there are confused mountain masses, of which the greatest is the north–south backbone range of the Pindos, cutting off western Greece north of the Gulf of Corinth, that is Epeiros, Akarnania and Aetolia, from the east. The traveller from Salonica southwards is also soon made aware of the great mass of high land east of the Pindos and north of the course of the Thessalian Peneios, culminating in the massif of Mount Olympos. Through it the valley of the River Haliakmon gives difficult access from north-western Macedonia to the sea and the mouth of the Vardar. Further south there is the route across the Pindos from Ioannina in Epeiros via Metsovo to Trikkala and the plain of Thessaly. There is another from Agrinion in Aetolia up the valley of the Acheloos via Karpenision to the valley of the Spercheios and Thermopylai; there is a third from southern Aetolia via Naupaktos, Amphissa, Delphi and Livvadia to Thebes in Boeotia, joining at Livvadia the main route from the plain of Thessaly through eastern Lokris and Boeotia and ultimately across Mount Kithairon to Attica. From Boeotia two routes lead through the Megarid to the Peloponnese: the one hugging the eastern sea coast, in antiquity involving the difficult Scironian Way; the other passing down through the backbone of the Megarid, starting at Plataia in Boeotia. From Doris in central Greece a route to the Gulf of Corinth west of Amphissa follows the valley of the River Mornos.

A similar spectacle of confused mountain masses is presented by the Peloponnese, separated from central Greece by the Gulf of Corinth, but linked with it by the isthmus. The mountains of the Peloponnese, running out to the four southern capes, are not exceptionally high (the highest mountains of Greece are in the seven thousand to ten thousand-foot range), but they are steep, and make the country relatively difficult of access. On the north and west there are coastal strips of tolerably level ground. From the north, in ancient Achaea south of the gulf, there is no natural route of importance inland to Arcadia. On the west there are three: up the valley of the Alpheios to western Arcadia; through a gap north of Kyparissia to southern Arcadia; and from the Bay of Navarino eastwards through Kalamata and the Langadha of Taygetos to Sparta and northern Lakonia. Otherwise high land divides Triphylia, Messenia, Lakonia and the Argolid from Arcadia.

It must be borne in mind that modern traffic requires well-engineered roads or railways, the former following the easier hill slopes, the latter the valleys (witness the route from Kalamata to Megalopolis). They do not in many cases follow the most direct route available to pack animals and the 'well-girt' man, and so conclusions on ancient communications should not necessarily be based on the modern map. A commonplace of historians is that the mountain system of Greece produced a fragmented country of small plain areas, some with access to the sea, others enclosed, drained by rivers or underground channels. Geography does not always explain everything: why Athens, for instance, and Attica came ultimately to form one unit, and Boeotia did not.

The geography of the land shows in innumerable cases a defensible crag, at times so inaccessible as to seem most inconvenient (a good example is Arcadian Orchomenos). This served for a community as a defence-point and a centre of government and sometimes of cult, dominating the surrounding area, and, as an 'acropolis', forming the nucleus of the *polis* or city-state community. The acropolis *pār excellence* was that of Athens; the citizen community which surrounded it formed the greatest Greek *polis*. In the case of Athens the *polis* of the Classical period came to comprise a considerable territory, united to form one unit, bounded by the sea and the range of Mount Kithairon between Attica and Boeotia. In the case of Boeotia, on the other hand, the process of union did not reach the obvious geographical boundaries, and this area remained divided among a number of *poleis*, mostly small, which Thebes sought to dominate. The same was in some measure true of the Argolid and certainly of Arcadia.

A glance at the map of Greece and the Aegean will show the islands east of mainland Greece as the clear continuation of the mainland mountains: an outer arc shutting in the Aegean and the sea north of Crete, stretching from Cape Malea via Kythera and Antikythera to Crete, and from Crete via Kasos and Karpathos to Rhodes. The sea area thus bounded, at all times of importance, was in the period covered by this book the outstanding one for cultural contact and exchange, linked by Rhodes and the southern coast of Anatolia with Cyprus and the Near East, and southwards from Crete with Libya and Egypt. Later, when Rome was dominant, the main line of trade shifted further south, and the Aegean became less important, despite the great cities of the western Asia Minor coast. In the Aegean itself there are other island chains from Cape Sounion south-east to Kos and Rhodes; particularly important in this area were the rival island states of Paros and Naxos. Further north the arc of Andros, Tenos and Mykonos (neighbour of the sacred island of Delos), leading to Ikaria and Samos, represents an important route to Asia Minor. Another, not so clearly defined, leads from Kyme in Euboea (the Aegean port of Eretria) by way of Lemnos and Imbros to the Hellespont (Dardanelles).

Greece, with its land barriers and its Aegean sea lanes, in which seafarers seem to be beckoned on from one island to another, therefore looks like the pre-eminent nurse of sailors. This is a commonplace of modern Greek historians. In part it is correct. Around 700 BC the poet Hesiod is clearly reconciled to seafaring in his *Works and Days*, though for him the sea is a hostile element, as it remained for all Greeks at all times. As he says: 'If ever you turn your misguided heart to trading and wish to escape from debt and joyless hunger, I will show you the measure of the loud-roaring sea.'[1] His poor views of it, based on no extensive travels, are repeated in the next generation (in the sixties of the seventh century) by one who had fared further and worse: the adventurer Archilochos of Paros, who talks of 'the bitter gifts of Lord Poseidon').[2] Hesiod mentions 'fifty days after the solstice' (i.e. July–August) as 'the right time for men to go sailing'.[3] He makes no mention of the *meltemi*, a wind in the Aegean, which can make the summer seas dangerous enough. Earlier in the year, he suggests, 'another time for men to go sailing is in Spring when a man first sees leaves on the topmost shoot of a fig tree as large as the foot-print that a crow makes ... this is the Spring sailing time'.[4] All travellers in Greek lands know how late the silver fig-tree branches produce their tender green leaves. In all, the safe season for sea travel is very limited, and the dangers from storm, as from rocks, are always considerable. Thus is explained the Greek preoccupation with poor drowned sailors cast up unburied on an alien shore.

On land also it was not always perpetual summer. Apart from the prosaic references to storms of rain and wind, and to the havoc done by storm water, there are the poetic references: Zeus, as Lord of Olympos, is 'the cloud-compeller'. For Sophocles man is not only 'the power that crosses the white sea, driven by the stormy south wind, making a path under the surges that threaten to engulf him', but one also who 'has taught himself . . . how to flee the arrows of the frost, when 'tis hard lodging under the clear sky, and the arrows of the rushing rain'.[5] Anyone who has seen the sea fog rolling in, or experienced the icy mist on a high mountainside, understands the truth of the Homeric observation:

When the South wind on the mountain crests spreads mist, no friend of shepherds, but to thieves better than the night, and one can see as far as a stone's throw. . . .[6]

Attica traditionally enjoyed a clear light atmosphere conducive to quick wits, or so the Athenians said. In contrast the climate of Boeotia was heavy, and so were the Boeotian wits. Climate in many respects was a regional matter, but in general it was far from ideal. In fact it might be suggested that the ancient Greeks were a great people (or *some* of them were) partly because of the hardiness engendered by their climate. Where the climate was more favourable and the land more fertile, as in Ionia, they seemed to show fewer of the sterner virtues. The Greeks of Greece proper endured the rain of winter (snow in the north and on high land) and the drought of summer, and they knew that 'dust was the twin brother of mud'.[7] It is to be suspected that the idea that the Greeks spent so much time out of doors in public (and so developed their communal life) because of the benign climate is largely nonsense. Modern writers talk of the stoas as refuges against heat and rain; ancient writers speak perhaps more of the warm blacksmith's shop. If the Greeks resorted to public places it might well have been to avoid constricted domestic quarters, bugs and raucous wives, rather than to enjoy the climate. One advantage, however, they did have: they were spared the long dark winters of northern climes.

The Greeks of Greece from an early date spread out east and west in the Mediterranean. Their homeland was set between the Adriatic and the Aegean. There is a natural tendency to concentrate on the Aegean, the direction of the so-called 'older' civilizations; and this is reinforced by the impression that each of the two peninsulas, Balkan and Italian, turns its back on the other. Culturally, it must be admitted, Greece looked east, but not entirely so in a geographical sense. It is true that on the Adriatic side the most backward region (in Antiquity) of the western Balkan peninsula faces the coast of Italy, which is harbourless except for Ancona. On the other hand from the straits of Otranto south to the Ionian Sea the case is different. It was to the west that the colonizing Greeks went at an early date, though they may have traded earlier with the east. In any case colonization implies exploration. From the Gulf of Corinth northwards there was a relatively easy coasting passage via Thiaki (? ancient Ithaka) or Kephallenia to Corfu (ancient Kerkyra), and a relatively short passage across to the heel of Italy. Some may have struck boldly across to southernmost Italy and to Sicily through the Ionian Sea. Some of their' earliest journeys were to Ischia, north of the Bay of Naples, and perhaps as far as Elba. Later they travelled to Corsica, to the southern coast of what is now France, and to the Mediterranean coast of Spain, so getting experience of wider and rougher seas, though the land, in modern times at any rate, is more reminiscent of southern and eastern Greece than some of the other regions in which they ultimately settled.

On the other hand to the east of Greece, in the Aegean, there are the seemingly enticing chains of islands across to the Asiatic shore, marking routes followed by many Greeks in the 'Dark Age' after the dissolution of the Bronze Age civilization of Greece. They settled on the western coast of Asia Minor from Lesbos southwards, on the islands and the mainland, to Caria and Rhodes. Here again they were subjected to special influences of geography. Their settling-places, at first probably numerous but small, were often divided by natural barriers, though not very serious ones. The land on which they settled was for the most part fertile, and so they prospered. The fact that large rivers such as the Hermos (Gediz) and the Maiandros (Menderes) flowed down from the interior meant communication with their eastern neighbours, and therefore possibilities of trade, but also danger of attack and domination by interior powers, while the rivers with their alluvium were a menace to the harbours of the coastal settlements.

In the course of time, from the seventh century onwards, for various reasons to be explained later, these Greek cities of Asia Minor engaged in colonization on their own account: at a later date, therefore, than the cities of Greece proper, who had started their colonizing activity in the eighth century. Colonists from Greece and western Asia Minor at varying periods settled on the coast of Macedonia and Thrace, and were thus introduced to a barbarous land full of natural resources, far better watered and forested than Greece, with heavier rainfall. One coming from the southern Aegean or the kind climate of the Gulf of Smyrna would not find it attractive. Thus Archilochos in the earlier seventh century sourly described Thasos with its jagged hills as 'the backbone of an ass, full of wild woods'.[8] Anyone who has endured the pouring spring rain of Thasos day after day must feel sympathy for those Greeks who left their (generally) warmer south for these northern regions richer but less kindly; but the difference should not perhaps be exaggerated.

From the north-eastern Aegean the narrow seas of the Hellespont, the Propontis (Sea of Marmara) and the Bosphorus led to the Black Sea. It was and is no light matter to penetrate the 'Narrows', which were eventually settled by Ionians, especially from Miletos, and by Megarians from Greece. This direction came to be regarded eventually as the route of the Argonauts, fraught with dangers. It may be that penetration of the Black Sea area by ship had to wait on the improvements in marine construction which may have taken place at the end of the eighth century BC. If there was settlement of any part of the Black Sea coasts earlier than the seventh century – and this is unlikely – it would have been by land. In penetrating to the Black Sea the Greeks were thereby introduced to a large open stormy sea, which they found 'inhospitable' (*axeinos*), and so sought to placate it by calling it 'hospitable' (*euxeinos*). Here their geographical experience was broadened by encountering the great rivers, such as the Danube (the Ister, a name known in the seventh century), and by settlement on the rich soil of the western Black Sea and southern Russia, fertile beyond the imagining of the Greeks who stayed at home. In southern Russia they came to the fringes of the steppe, and met the settled Scythians (with whom they eventually effected an interesting cultural amalgam) and heard tales of the nomad Scythians, and others more wonderful relating to the great spaces of the Eurasian steppe (so different from Greece). There were gold-digging ants, griffins and Arimaspians, to delight the heart of Herodotus in the fifth century. On the south coast of the Black Sea the Ionian Greeks and the Megarians settled on the Pontic littoral, marked off by mountain ranges from the Anatolian plateau to the south. Here again there was a climatic contrast to a good deal of Greece and western Asia Minor: it was a rainy area (and in the east subtropical), with a misty overcast atmosphere. Their chief centres (still the chief towns of Pontic Turkey) were at Sinope, Amisos and Trapezos. Amisos had relatively easy access to the plateau, and Trapezos was the terminal of an important route to the interior of eastern Anatolia, and on to the Middle East. In this Pontic strip were rich supplies of timber, fruit and other natural resources.

Just as the Pontic coast of Asia Minor presented contrasts to Greece, so did the southern shore bordering the Mediterranean, once past the mountainous bulge of Lykia, in which the Greeks succeeded in planting only one colony, Phaselis, to the north of Cape Gelidonya. Coastal Pamphylia and the area to the east of it, Cilicia Campestris (Cilicia of the Plain), separated from Pamphylia by Cilicia Aspera (Mountainous Cilicia), present a fertile aspect in modern times, especially to the east of Antalya and round Adana. There is access from the interior by three routes, but they were not easy in ancient times, and from time to time this area was controlled by powers that held the sea rather than the interior. While the immensely impressive remains of Roman cities, as at Perge, Aspendos and Side, show that the period of maximum prosperity was in the earlier Roman Empire, there were a number of Greek colonial foundations, which tradition ascribed to an early date, established among the native peoples, and of mixed character.

From Rhodes along the southern coast of Asia Minor, by sea rather than by land, and passing by way of Cyprus, was an important route to the north-eastern corner of the Mediterranean, to the Amanus Pass, to the Amuq Plain and the middle Tigris and Euphrates. Further south were the coasts of Syria and Palestine, with routes inland through which the older civilizations of the Near East might be reached, and ultimately Mesopotamia. This area was the meeting-place and mingling-place of Mediterranean and Near Eastern cultures, of Greeks and Semites, and earlier of Egyptians and Hittites. Another route, already mentioned, was from Trapezos south-eastwards to Armenia (Urartu), and to north-western Persia, the route past Ararat used ever since. From the later sixth century there was a road through Anatolia from Ephesos and Sardis; this was the Persian Royal Road to the capital at Susa. How it compared for use with the southern sea route it is difficult to judge, but Greek contacts with the interior (and particularly with Phrygia) were perhaps greater than is sometimes believed, even before the period of Lydian domination in the seventh and sixth centuries.

It is justifiable to believe that these considerations of geography, outlined here for the early Iron Age and the Classical period, were valid at all times, since they depend on major physical factors. There is no reason to think that temperatures and rainfall, or prevailing winds, differed grossly in any period of antiquity from the present, even in remote antiquity, though it is to be regretted that pollen analysis has not made a greater contribution to our knowledge. On the other hand it is easy to see that even if rainfall remains much the same, water-conservation and soil-conservation must vary according to the degree at different times of afforestation and soil erosion. In some matters the effects of rainfall are apparent now and must have been in antiquity: thus the heavier rainfall of the western side of the peninsula, in central Greece and the Peloponnese, results in heavier tree cover. East of the Pindos and in the eastern Peloponnese (except for Parnon and Taygetos) the tree cover is much reduced and the land denuded. Again in the north in Macedonia, there are more trees producing both timber and fruit. This seems to be due to the heavier rainfall, with the consequent abundance of water, so apparent in the regions of Verria and Edessa. Yet in this, as in the drainage of marshes and the development of irrigation, account has to be taken of recent developments: a century ago or less a good deal of northern Greece must have looked very different. But the rivers must have looked much the same, larger with more abundant water in the north, and showing for much of the year in the south the same trickle wandering amid a sea of stones as now.

It is to be assumed that in terms of tree cover, water-conservation and erosion Greece paid heavily for the Greek Bronze Age, with its intensive occupation and wide use of timber both for fuel and for timber-framed mud-brick buildings. In the early Iron Age, with less intensive occupation, it is likely that the tree cover had time to restore itself, just as it did, for example in the Lavrion region of Attica, during the Turkish occupation of Greece. It would subsequently suffer a gradual attrition once more in the Archaic, Classical and Hellenistic periods. Such attrition was attended by renewed denudation, offset by hillside terracing, as in Attica and elsewhere. How far contour-ploughing on the hill slopes was adopted to resist erosion it is difficult to say. It is certainly true that the primitive plough drawn by animals was more suited to this technique than modern agricultural equipment.

There is one final point: in Classical antiquity at any rate, as in modern times in Greece and Turkey, there was and is the problem of the goat: at once a great asset to humanity in terms of milk, meat, skin and hair, and ruinous to the vegetational cover of the land. How far this was true of the Bronze and earlier Iron Ages it is impossible to say.

## CHAPTER 2

# CRETE AND THE GREEKS

Since the discovery of Minoan Crete by Sir Arthur Evans and others it has been impossible wholly to leave the island out of consideration. It has become clear that its Bronze Age culture exerted an important influence on mainland 'Greece'. It seems best, however, to leave an account of this influence to Chapter 3 and the problems of Middle and Late Bronze Age 'Greece', and to include something on Linear B documents and the presence of Greeks in Crete in that chapter, as a peripheral rather than a central theme. It must be admitted that what might be called 'Linear A Crete' seems to have relatively little relevance to Greece after the Mycenaean period, however much scholars may toy with the idea of 'continuity'. Consequently Crete of the palaces has been omitted from this book, except in so far as it seems strongly relevant to the Mycenaeans.

On the other hand the later Greeks had a profound conviction of the early importance of the island, which must have stemmed from dim memories of Minoan culture rather than from Crete of the Iron Age. It is under this aspect that Crete is considered here.

The earliest Greek literature, the Homeric epic, was probably written down, after the introduction of the alphabet, in the eighth century BC, the end-product of a long period of oral composition which might go back to the Bronze Age. In the *Odyssey* Crete is a land of very diverse population and an island of great wealth, ruled by King Minos in Knossos. In the *Iliad*, in the Catalogue of the Ships, the list of the Greeks who went to Troy, the Cretans are led by Idomeneus, grandson of Minos, and Meriones. In this passage Crete is called 'hundred-citied', and among those mentioned are Knossos, Phaistos and Miletos, homonym of the city of Asia Minor described as Carian 'of barbarian speech' in the *Iliad*. It may be added that Gortyn 'with its walls' is also mentioned: not a Bronze Age centre, as far as can be judged by the existing remains on the acropolis, but important in the Archaic period, and later the capital of Crete under the Romans; it provides an example of one of the later elements in the Catalogue. The eighty ships of the Cretans at Troy were

9

not much inferior in number to the hundred led by Agamemnon of Mycenae and the ninety led by Nestor of Pylos.

The passage from the *Odyssey*, like the other references to Crete in the epic, formed the core of later comment. Thus Strabo, the Augustan geographer, explains the Kydonians and Eteocretans (True Cretans) there referred to as original natives (autochthonous) and the rest as incomers. He interprets the adjective *trichaikes*, applied to the Dorians, as a reference to their helmet crests rather than to their characteristic three-tribal division. It is a good example of the interpretation of Homeric terms which later writers attempted, not always with success. In the same passage of the *Odyssey* Minos is named as King of Knossos and described as 'the nine-year king, the familiar of Zeus'. *Enneoros*, 'of nine years (or seasons)', is difficult to interpret. Minos *might* be thought of as king for a period, and then replaced, or as renewing his powers every nine years. It is clearly on this epic reference that Strabo based his description of Minos as a lawgiver, divider of the island into three parts with a city in each, and two of these he names as Knossos and Phaistos (the third is lost from the text). He also describes Minos as imitator of Rhadamanthys, an ancient lawgiver, and explains *enneoros* in the sense that for nine years Minos went up to the cave of Zeus (? on Ida) and brought down thence the commandments (*prostagmata*) of Zeus. Another epic passage used by Strabo is the sequel to *Odyssey*, XIX: 172, in which Odysseus in disguise claims to be Aithon, brother of Idomeneus and so grandson of Minos, and in this feigned character relates how Odysseus on his way to Troy put in to Crete, 'at Amnissos, where there is the Cave of Eileithyia, a difficult anchorage'[1] – a reference, in effect, to what was originally a coastal Minoan site and to a cave already a centre of cult in Minoan times.

Late writers like Strabo clearly used earlier material which can be carried back into the eighth century and to the epic, but it is sometimes difficult to distinguish between these genuinely early elements and later literary confections. Some of the latter are readily detectable. The complexity of mythological detail, bringing about contradictions in chronology, produced in later writers two Cretan rulers of the name of Minos. Of these the first was a son of Zeus and Europa (daughter of Phoinix), brother of Rhadamanthys and Sarpedon. He was a lawgiver in his life and judge of the dead thereafter. He was given a son, Deukalion, and a daughter, Ariadne. A complicated and clearly artificial story connected him and his brothers with Asterios (as his successor), the grandson of Doros (eponym of the Dorians) and great-great-grandson of the older Thessalian Deukalion who survived the flood. The elaboration was intended to explain the diversity of population which the epic ascribed to Crete. A second Minos appears as grandson of the first, father of another Deukalion and another Ariadne. This effort to keep the mythological record straight in terms of generations need not be taken seriously: the epic and Hesiod knew of only one Minos. The two figures of the same name, however, served to resolve the contradiction felt by Strabo and others between the just lawgiver and the oppressive tyrant of other legends connecting him with the 'bull from the sea', the Minotaur and Daidalos.

The fully elaborated story was that Minos, offering a sacrifice to Poseidon, prayed that the god would send a bull from the sea as victim. When his prayer was answered Minos did not sacrifice the splendid animal but replaced it with another. Accordingly the god made the bull furious and caused Pasiphae, the wife of Minos, to fall in love with it. Her wanton fancy she gratified with the aid of the cunning craftsman Daidalos, an exile from Athens of the Erechtheid clan. In this case again, but for different reasons, Greek myth believed in two persons of the same name. One was a craftsman who first developed lifelike sculpture, the other a builder and engineer. In fact the name looks very like a personification of the verb *daidalein*, 'to use cunning workmanship'. To Daidalos, obviously in the second capacity, the *Iliad* ascribes a work at Knossos. Hephaistos, the smith god, sets on the shield of Achilles a representation of 'a dancing place [*choros*], like to that which once in broad Crete Daidalos wrought for fair-tressed Ariadne'.[2] 'Dancing place' is the usual translation, but the description is of a *dance* of young men and maidens like the Crane Dance on the early sixth-century François Vase.

In the second century AD the rather careless and frequently muddled guidebook-writer Pausanias tells the tale of Daidalos, the fugitive from Athens, 'who made images for Minos and his daughters as Homer signifies in the *Iliad*'. Homer does nothing of the sort. This garbled version *might* refer to the non-Homeric story of the cow (quaintly portrayed on a Pompeian wall-painting, suitably supplied with wheels) which Daidalos made for Pasiphae to facilitate the gratification of her desires; but it is more likely that the explanation is provided by another passage of Pausanias, where he remarks: 'The Knossians have too the *choros* of Ariadne which Homer mentions in the *Iliad*, wrought on white stone.'[3] This comes in a context of statues made by Daidalos and preserved in various Greek centres, and it is clear that Pausanias thought *choros* meant not 'dancing place' but a relief of dancing figures, to which his other reference applies; possibly he was right. In the story the union of Pasiphae and the bull produced the half-human half-taurine monster the *Minotauros*. The Minotaur lived, according to the Augustan writer Diodorus of Sicily, in the *labyrinthos*, a term which that writer also applies to an Egyptian tomb, 'which', he claims, 'Daidalos saw in Egypt and imitated in Crete for Minos'.[4] This is a palpably artificial story to connect the use by the fifth-century historian Herodotus of the word *labyrinthos* to describe an Egyptian, partly subterranean funerary structure with Crete, Minos and Daidalos. Between the earlier and the later writer comes Callimachus, the third-century Alexandrian poet, who mentions in one of his poems, 'the winding structure of the tortuous labyrinth', together with Pasiphae, the Minotaur and the Cretan adventures of Theseus. The Homeric epic makes no mention of it. It was thought of, in fact, as a maze, and appears, like the Minotaur, on coins of Knossos. Modern scholars, it must be noted, have then connected *labyrinthos* with the word *labrys*, which Plutarch claims is the Lydian word for an axe and is associated with the statue of Zeus of Labraunda in Caria. This axe is the double axe and it appears carried by Zeus on Carian coins. Herodotus does not mention Crete in connection with the labyrinth, and no ancient writer connects *labrys* and *labyrinthos*. Yet Herodotus was a native of Caria, and the Carians were traditionally associated with Minos, Minos with Crete and Knossos and Knossos with bulls. The word *labyrinthos* shows the termination -*nthos*, which some scholars have regarded as pre-Greek. In all there is more than enough scope for conjecture.

Further legends connected Minos with Greece and the West. Minos, it was related, carried out military activity in the Aegean and laid siege to Megara between Attica and the Isthmus of Corinth, a story with a folk-tale element about it. There was in the Megarid a place called Minoa (the name also appears elsewhere in Greek lands), which may have been the genesis of the connection with Minos, but the association with Athens is not so easily explained. This story appears to have been very common in Attic literature, for the good reason that it concerned the Attic hero Theseus, and it is treated at some length by Plutarch in his *Life of Theseus*, in which, in his usual manner, he mentions the permutations of detail, and shows how the story of the Minotaur was rationalized by the fourth century BC. The son of Minos, Androgeos, visited Athens and was there murdered. In consequence of this and of natural disasters indicating the wrath of the gods, Athens, under its king, Aigeus, was forced at intervals to send in reparation seven youths and seven maidens to be devoured by the Minotaur; the moderate rationalizers explained that their fate was not so grisly as this, but the extreme rationalization turned the Minotaur into an overbearing noble called Tauros. This tribute continued until Theseus, son of the Athenian ruler, went to Crete, won the heart of Ariadne, slew the monster and escaped from the maze with a clew of thread given him by Ariadne, who then escaped with him from Crete. The rationalizers made the labyrinth a prison, and made Theseus slay Tauros or defeat him in athletic contest!

Ariadne, in the various versions of the tale, suffered a variety of fates. In the epic, described as the daughter of 'baneful' Minos, she did not get very far, 'For Artemis slew her in sea girt Dia by reason of the witness of Dionysos'.[5] Dia is the island off present-day Iraklion; the meaning of the reference to Dionysos is quite obscure. In a fashion the hand of the rationalizer is to be seen again, for in one version Ariadne dies in childbirth, but in Cyprus. The best-known alternative version is of her desertion in Naxos by Theseus, to be reserved for a more distinguished association with Dionysos. On his return to Athens Theseus and his companions put in to Delos and there he 'danced with the young Athenians a dance that, in memory of him, they say is still preserved among the inhabitants of Delos, consisting in certain measured turnings and returnings, imitative of the windings and twistings of the labyrinth'. And this dance ... is called among the Delians the Crane Dance.'[6] As noted above, it appears, with the ship of Theseus, on that splendid example of Attic black-figure pottery of the earlier sixth century, the François Vase.

One element in the sequel involved Daidalos, who was cast into prison or prevented from leaving Crete. He and his son Ikaros therefore fled, either making themselves wings, or more prosaically by ship. An Athenian version of the story claimed that they fled to Athens, and Minos in pursuit was carried by storm to Sicily. According to the other version Daidalos and Ikaros fled to Sicily, in this case, too, pursued by Minos, who (in both versions) perished at the hand of Kokalos, ruler of Kamikos in Sicily, or of his daughters. Ikaros was drowned in the sea which bears his name, while in Sicily and elsewhere in the West Daidalos carried out great engineering works. In attendance on Minos, or following after him, was a great expedition of all the Cretan cities except Polichni and Praisos. This force landed at the site of Minoa and besieged Kamikos, but failed to take it. Consequently the Cretans attempted to return home, but were cast by storm on the coast of south-eastern Italy (Iapygia) and there founded Hyria. This story is told as early as the mid-fifth century BC by Herodotus, who adds that as a result of this disaster Crete was depopulated, and subsequently resettled by a new population including Greeks. These were the Cretans of the period of the Trojan War, and once again on the return from Troy the island was depopulated of humankind and animals by plague and famine, to be repopulated once again. To this story Diodorus adds that the Cretan expedition founded Minoa and Engyon in Sicily, and that these Cretans were joined later by others from the expedition to Troy.

Minos himself, it was said, was buried in Sicily at Minoa, in a tomb of double form, the front portion being a temple; there is a faint suggestion of some such structure as the so-called Temple Tomb at Knossos. His bones were sent back to Crete (as a political gesture) between 488 and 480 BC by Theron, tyrant of Akragas. Phalaris, an earlier tyrant of the same city, presented to the temple of Athena at Lindos in Rhodes a bronze mixing-bowl inscribed: 'Daidalos gave me as a friendly gift to Kokalos'. A final and variant episode is worthy of mention. It appears in the account of Plutarch, in his narrative of the flight of Daidalos to Athens pursued by Minos. He tells of an expedition secretly prepared by Theseus against Crete, the destruction of the son of Minos and the acceptance of Ariadne as pro-Athenian ruler of Crete – one of the sillier stories!

As a contrast to the picturesque detail of Plutarch it is instructive to quote the sober words of the Athenian historian Thucydides, of the later fifth century BC: 'The first person known to us by tradition as having established a navy is Minos. He made himself master of what is now called the Hellenic sea, and ruled over the Cyclades into most of which he sent the first colonies, expelling the Carians and appointing his own sons as governors; and thus did his best to put down piracy in these waters, a necessary step to secure the revenues for his own use.'[7]

As early as 700 BC and the *Odyssey*, in terms of surviving literature, the Greeks therefore showed a conviction of the importance of Crete. It was regarded as a centre of craftsmanship, and as a place of curious associations: Zeus was born in Crete and his tomb was shown there – hence the conviction that 'the Cretans are always liars'. In the *Hymn to the Delphian Apollo* (of the seventh century?) the god, seeking priests for his oracular shrine, abducts Cretan seafarers to serve him there. A good deal can, of course, be ascribed to the importance of Iron Age Crete in terms of material culture and institutions, an importance perhaps greater than scholars are willing to admit. The participation of Cretans in the foundation of Sicilian Gela could also be advanced for the link with the West. Athenians had been interested in Sicily since the time of the Persian War of 480–479 BC, an interest which culminated in their two expeditions to the island during the Great Peloponnesian War. Therefore they were interested in Sicilian legends, and it seems likely that Sophocles' *Kamikioi* and Aristophanes' *Kokalos* were concerned with the story of Minos, the contemporary enemy of their own Theseus.

Not everything, however, is thus explained. It is true that the interpretation of Greek legend has an insidious charm which must be resisted; the same problem will arise again for Mycenaean Greece. It is a matter of controlling rashness and using good sense. Does the western expedition from Crete to Sicily incorporate memories of western connections for the Minoans, connections which have been carefully argued on archaeological grounds? Leaving aside the problem of the suggested presence in Crete of the volcanic glass liparite, found in the Aeolian Islands, the available archaeological evidence is relatively weak for Minoan connections and stronger for Mycenaean ones, but in the particular context the distinction is possibly unimportant. Again, can the legend of the disaster overtaking Minos and the Cretan expedition be taken to conceal a real disaster to Minoan power in Late Minoan I B or in Late Minoan II? Might the tale of Theseus' naval attack hide the process whereby Greek-speaking people were established at Knossos? If these suggestions seem as far-fetched as the association of Crete and the explosion of the volcanic Thera (Santorin) with the story of the destruction of Atlantis, the suggestion cannot be excluded that the early Greeks learned of events in Bronze Age Crete, with, it might be argued, the Egyptians as intermediaries, and then with their mythopoeic attitude bent the narrative to their own purposes. It is hard not to be impressed by the epic references, and even more by Herodotus' story of the two depopulations of the island, in view of the fact that material evidence has been interpreted to suggest something of the sort in Late Minoan I B and Late Minoan III.

## CHAPTER 3

## PREHISTORIC GREECE

### THE EARLY AND MIDDLE BRONZE AGES

For the southern Balkans a problem arises as to the ethnic origins of the peoples who developed the Late Bronze Age culture of the region. There is the additional problem involving the title of this book – *The Early Greeks*. It does not appear that the observations of physical anthropology are helpful in identifying 'Greeks'. Indeed the term 'Greek' is not particularly adequate, less so than, for instance, 'Cretan'. It should, of course, be 'Greek-speakers', since ultimately the language identifies the people and their basic culture in a somewhat rough and ready way, for want of something better. It is essential therefore to tackle the language question *first* and then the process by which it was introduced. Something must be said as briefly as possible on the material cultural characteristics of those periods when 'Greek-speakers' may have penetrated to the area which is, in modern parlance, 'Greece'.

*The Linguistic Problem*

A consideration of Minoan Crete and the Linear B tablets found at Knossos shows that there are two questions: that of the decipherment, seeming to reveal an early form of Greek or a component of Greek, and that of the date of the tablets. It has been accepted, for the present account, that the decipherment can be agreed, with reservations on detail, and that the date of the Knossos tablets lies around 1375 BC, when they were baked in a conflagration. The point should also be made that similar tablets (and other uses of the same script) are forthcoming on the mainland in contexts of various dates down to the late thirteenth century BC. The Linear B script might be described as a cousin of Linear A, the latter as yet undeciphered. Linear A has not so far been found on the mainland, with the exception of isolated signs on imported objects. The relationship of the two in Crete is obscure.

It is not easy to explain the inadequacy of Linear B for the rendering of

16

primitive Greek. It has been suggested that it developed over a considerable period in Crete side by side with Linear A – 'It has been demonstrated that the date of borrowing of Linear B signs for Linear A cannot be as late as the latest [Late Minoan I] examples of the latter. This is some support for the view of Furumark and Pugliese Carratelli that the date of origin may lie as far back as the sixteenth century'[1] – but it is not made clear what language it was originally used to record, if this original development took place before the arrival of Greek-speakers in Crete. There is a temptation, when so much is obscure, to suggest that Linear B was taken to the mainland, perhaps by refugees from the eruption of Thera or some other disaster, and there developed and adapted, to be taken back again to Crete. The alternative is to believe that there were Greek-speakers in Crete at a date earlier than is generally supposed.

Whatever may be felt on this issue, if the decipherment of the Linear B tablets is accepted, Greek or a component of later Greek must have been present in the Aegean some time before 1375 BC, probably in Crete around 1450 BC, at the beginning of Late Minoan II or earlier. Unless it is assumed that Greek-speakers came to Crete from some other direction than the mainland, then they must have been present in the latter area before 1450 BC. It is unlikely that they arrived in Greece and Crete simultaneously. Some considerable time must in addition be allowed for the evolution of the social and economic system reflected in the Knossos tablets, since this cannot have been taken over wholly from the native Cretans. As far as mainland Greece is concerned, there are no signs of violent intrusion between the end of Early Helladic III (c. 1900 BC) and the destruction manifest in the Late Helladic towards the end of the thirteenth centuty BC. The suggestion that this latter destruction in Crete and on the mainland marks the appearance of Greek-speakers has not found general acceptance. The alternative is to place the incoming at the end of Early Helladic III, and an earlier incursion at the end of Early Helladic II, though nothing can be said of any connection between the two of a linguistic or ethnic nature.

This incoming of speakers of a component or components of early Greek has to be traced from the Indo-European homeland lying to the north of the Black Sea, where the original speakers of what became a large group of related languages were nomads ranging over a considerable area. The Greek-speakers have to be related also in their movements to those using other Indo-European languages, Thracian, Phrygian, Illyric, and especially to those who spoke the Luvian and Hittite languages of Anatolia, the western portion of which stood in close geographical relationship with mainland Greece. Proto-Luvian and Proto-Hittite are seen by philologists as being closely related and in contact with one another in the process of their differentiation, so that they must have been brought into Anatolia by the same western route, since there is no clear archaeological evidence for the suggested entry of the Proto-Hittites from the east. It is reasonable to attempt to connect this incoming with the record of Troy, given the position of that city. One suggestion is that the sackers of Troy I were the Proto-Luvians in the first half of the third millennium BC, a hypothesis very difficult to establish. Then it is suggested that these Indo-European Luvian-speakers were spread over western Anatolia by a subsequent incursion signalized by the destruction of Troy (Early Bronze Age) II g and other centres. In western Anatolia place-names showing the elements -ss-, -nth-, -nd- are regarded by some philologists as being Luvian. They also appear in Greece and Crete (Korinthos, Parnassos, Kerinthos, Amnissos). That there was a connection between western Anatolia and Greece is accepted in Greek saga, as in the story of the migration of Pelops the Phrygian to Greece before the Trojan War, and the dispatch of Bellerophon to Lycia. Sober judges of the philological evidence are prepared to accept the presence of a limited number of Luvian-speaking immigrants (influencing place-names) in Greece, if not in Crete. The extreme view, that Luvian was the principal language of central and southern Greece, entering the area in the twentieth century BC and attended by the introduction of Minyan ware related to the grey wares of western Anatolia, appears untenable.

Despite all efforts at conjecture, the present archaeological record is such, especially in Thrace and eastern Europe, that the passage of the Indo-European-speakers is obscure in detail. Equally obscure is the identity of the destroyers of Troy I, of Troy II g, and of some sites in mainland 'Greece' at the end of Early Helladic II, with the added puzzles, in the case of Troy, of the apparent continuity of material culture to and including Troy V, and the difficulty of accounting for the upsurge of Troy VI, which, in the opinion of the second excavators, started at a date when in 'Greece' a further penetration of incomers, apparently of modest material culture (the Middle Helladic), seems to have taken place, though their identity as Greek-speakers is a reasonable deduction from subsequent developments, not a proved fact.

Greater certainty on these questions will perhaps be obtained through extended archaeological and linguistic work relating to eastern Europe and western Anatolia. It may be said that at the end of the Middle Bronze the picture is one of a cultural continuum, in general terms, covering both sides of the Aegean and Crete. In 'Greece' (which could now logically be written as Greece) there must have been in process of formation a rich amalgam of surviving Neolithic elements, elements of the (non-Greek-speaking) bearers of the culture of Early Helladic I and II, of the incomers at the end of Early Helladic II, of those who followed at the end of Early Helladic III, possibly of elements from Anatolia and of others at times from Crete. These combined, it is reasonable to assume, to produce the complex society and organization of the Mycenaean world. There is always uncertainty, however. It is as well to bear in mind that the amalgam may have been an imperfect one, or the various elements may have remained separate (some more advanced, and some less), like the Franks, Greeks and Slavs of medieval Greece. Indeed the Classical Greeks believed in the separate existence of diverse ethnic elements side by side, and thought particularly of the Pelasgians in this connection. On this obscure state of Greece follows the Late Bronze Age, its inception heralded by the richness of the shaft graves of Mycenae.

### The archaeological problem

Something more needs to be added from the archaeological standpoint to explain what has been said in the previous section on the Early and Middle Bronze Ages in relation to the linguistic problem.

The long and complex Neolithic development in mainland Greece must have made some contribution to the subsequent amalgam of cultures in the area, and elements of it may have emerged from time to time later. Nothing more specific than this can be said.

A whole series of sites, from Thrace and Macedonia south to the Peloponnese and out into the Aegean (to link with Crete), provide the material for the study of Early Bronze culture in its three divisions (I, II and III). As in the Near and Middle East, it is an impressive culture in contrast to the following Middle Bronze. This is especially true of Early Bronze II, strikingly represented also in Troy II, and especially in Troy II g. There are a number of important sites, such as Eutresis and Orchomenos in Boeotia, showing connections with Troy (as at Orchomenos) and the Cyclades (as at Eutresis). Another important site is Krisa (Kirrha) in Phokis. There are remains at Thebes, to some extent obscured by later (Late Bronze) palatial structures. In the east-central area Euboea (Lefkandi), Attica (Aghios Kosmos) and Aegina seem to suggest relations with the Aegean and western Anatolia. Of prime importance in the north-eastern Peloponnese is Lerna, with its 'House of Tiles' and complex wall, and the round building under the Mycenaean palace at Tiryns. These sites and other parts of the Peloponnese are clearly of great moment for the question of incomers. These are taken as penetrating *from the north* to the south, and probably from across the Aegean. In this connection the western area north of the Gulf of Corinth is one which is of considerable interest in this early period. The theory has been tentatively put forward that the region west of the Pindos might have afforded a land route for the intrusion of Greek-speakers (as traditionally it did for the later 'Dorians') coming southwards and crossing the Pindos into central Greece; hence the importance of Lianokladhi in the Spercheios Valley. This would not exclude the possibility that others took the route southwards on the eastern side of the peninsula or crossed the Aegean from the north-east.

For a western route the finds on Lefkas are intriguing. They merit description in detail. Thirty-three round tumuli stand over circular stone platforms, with burials in the platforms, in the mounds and sometimes just outside, in the Nidhri Plain. It appears that the dead were burned on these stone platforms, but not completely consumed, and the remains were placed in individual graves. The first of these graves were built in the platforms and later ones in the mound or near it. The individual graves were cists of slabs or dry-stone walling, *pithoi* or plain pits which may have contained sarcophagi of wood. Something of a parallel is provided by tumulus burials in Messenia (in *pithoi*), which are generally dated to the Middle Helladic, but might be earlier.

There is a serious problem of date arising in connection with the Nidhri Plain burials. Two groups have been distinguished: the group of the 'family graves' and that of the 'royal graves'. While the former are Middle Helladic, the latter, in view of the occurrence of 'sauce-boats' and other Early Helladic pottery, seem to belong to Early Helladic II. It is difficult to put them into the Middle Helladic. A certain doubt on the dating of this second group, which seems to show direct connections with 'Aegean culture of the second Early Helladic phase',[2] is greatly to be regretted, since these burials in tumuli, in chambers or pits, seem to have analogies not only with the Messenian burials mentioned above but also (admittedly in rather general terms) with the shaft graves of Mycenae and Lerna – the former representing so spectacular a development at a late stage of the Middle Helladic. But there are important differences, as for instance the circular stone platforms in Lefkas; and even if we accept the Early Helladic II date of the 'royal graves', it would be rash to regard them as prototypes of the burials in Messenia, Mycenae and Lerna, and also to relate them too readily to what have been suggested as similar burials in the north-west, in Albania, where the intention is to derive the Messenia-Argolid burial practice from the north-west with a view to identifying the origins of those using it: as incomers, in fact (and Greek-speakers), from the north-western direction and not by way of the Aegean. It is an attractive idea, and a promising line of research if this is directed to the crossing-places of the Pindos such as the Spercheios Valley. Light may also be cast on the problem when the grave enclosures, circular platforms and cist graves found at Vrana near Marathon are fully published.

The somewhat confused and inadequate picture given by the archaeological evidence suggests a number of interesting points for the Early Bronze: the existence on a number of sites of fortifications, though it is on occasions unclear whether these are established against land or sea attack; there are also the two apparent episodes of violence, in some cases evidence at the end of Early Helladic II and in other cases at the end of Early Helladic III. There is also peaceful penetration in some instances, indicated by changes in cultural equipment but with no evidence of violent intrusion.

It is not easy to evolve a simple pattern to cover all this. It *can* be suggested that when the end of Early Helladic II on a site is marked by destruction and little or nothing follows, Early Helladic III levels have been eroded. The main issue, however, is harder to explain. There seem to be two periods when there were incomers, at the end of Early Helladic II and at the end of Early Helladic III. It can reasonably be suggested that if newcomers at the end of Early Helladic II forced themselves in at some place, they were peaceably admitted through consciousness of weakness in the case of others. Alternatively they were repelled, and like the children of Herakles in Greek tradition, returned in a later generation. It is less easy to believe that later arrivals at the end of Early Helladic III were welcomed by their forerunners who came at the end of Early Helladic II. It is important to understand the chronological perspective involving something like one hundred and fifty years, and to realize that with such an interval of time a complex process may be oversimplified by modern historians. It is also a nice point whether the various incomers represented different ethnic or dialect groups. If we take account of the coastal settlements, it must be agreed that the sea was important, and equally, if we note the fortifications, that danger of attack was considerable. There were undoubtedly present over a considerable period in the eastern Mediterranean bands of marauders and groups of migrants seeking the weak points of settled communities, as happened later, in the Late Bronze Age. The pressure they exerted was continuous, and their inroads, marked by destruction, might seem simultaneous at a number of sites, since no detailed chronology is available, though in reality they could be separated by a generation or more. Whatever the uncertainties, the older simple picture of the coming of these 'Greek-speaking' intruders at the end of the Early Helladic III is no longer confirmed in an obvious manner by the archaeological evidence. Equally it is by no means clear that Grey Minyan pottery is diagnostic of their coming.

The character of the Middle Bronze Age (Middle Helladic) in Greece in material terms is seemingly undistinguished in comparison with Early Helladic II. It is revealed (inadequately) by finds from both habitation sites and cemeteries. On some sites the transition from Early to Middle Bronze is unmarked by the destruction apparent on others. As seen above, the latter phenomenon has been taken to indicate the violent intrusion of a new element of population, but even where no such break is clearly demonstrated, changes in cultural equipment have been observed. The simplest explanation, to repeat what has been said earlier, is that, as in Early Bronze (Early Helladic) II, some communities resisted and some yielded; some were destroyed, and others were taken over perhaps by infiltration; some may have been bypassed. It was a complex and untidy process, continuous over a considerable period, and perhaps not wholly to be distinguished from the events involving some sites at the end of Early Helladic II.

The archaeological problems may be considered first. An important part of the material remains is represented by the pottery, and especially by the grey 'Minyan ware'. A former simple view of the Middle Helladic period regarded this pottery as being characteristic of it, and as having been originally brought to the Greek mainland by the incomers mentioned. As has been seen in relation to the linguistic problem, these incomers were taken to be Greek-speakers, and so grey Minyan ware was regarded as being characteristic of this language group. The situation is now seen to be far from simple. First the pottery in question surely belongs to a much broader category of 'grey ware', in evidence over wide areas of time and space from Iran westwards, and found in western Anatolia both in Bronze and Iron cultures. Grey Minyan proper is characterized by a peculiar texture and by at least one very striking shape, the 'chalice' with a thick, horizontally grooved stem. If such a pottery type is given a special significance it must be clearly identified; it is doubtful whether excavators have always done this. Furthermore, it is not now so apparent that Grey Minyan is necessarily something new and inspired by an external tradition at the end of the Early Helladic. It, or something like it, appears in Early Helladic contexts, and the possibility must be considered that it was developed in mainland Greece as one example of a very widespread pottery technique. In any case no pottery which might be antecedent to it has so far been found in those regions through which Indo-European-speakers would have passed south in their progress (if it was direct) from their original homeland.

It will be useful also, in this context, to say that the *megaron*, basically a rectangular building with a porch before it, is not characteristic in any special sense either of the north or of Indo-European-speakers. This type of structure, showing considerable variation in detail at different times, reaches its full development as the central unit of the Mycenaean palaces in the Late Helladic period. In a simple form it appears in mainland Greece in the Neolithic B of Thessaly, and in Early and Middle Helladic. It also seems to appear in Anatolia at Beycesultan, possibly at the end of the Chalcolithic (after *c.* 3700 BC), in levels VIII, IX and X (*c.*2200–2000 BC), and could also be seen in the sanctuaries of the Middle Bronze period on the same site. Levels VIII, IX and X are, indeed, taken to follow a supposed Indo-European invasion, placed between Early Bronze II and III – a suggestion not uninfluenced, perhaps, by the interpretation of events affecting Troy II *g* – but it is doubtful if the idea is justified. The *megaron* type of structure is present at Troy before the destruction of Troy I and Troy II *g*, and in mainland Greece before the destruction which on

22

some sites marks the end of the Early Helladic II. It therefore antedates a possible invasion of 'Indo-European-speakers' (unless this is put back to the Late Neolithic). It would be rash also to regard it as being indicative of other wide-ranging cultural connections. The same type of rectangular building with porch is found, for instance, at Tepe Gawra in Mesopotamia, east of Nineveh. It is represented in the very earliest (Uruk period) level, which precludes its derivation from Anatolia. Equally, however, it is unnecessary to derive its Anatolian and Greek mainland appearance from the Middle East. It is a simple functional type of building, in its earliest form developed to meet a widespread need based on a particular social and administrative structure. A parallel has been seen in the headman's house among the modern Kurds, with its porch roof of logs and brushwood supported by two wooden pillars.

In general a study of the archaeology of the Middle Helladic leaves an impression of a culture either poorly represented in the surviving remains or poorly explored. There is no clear evidence of events in the north, though at Argissa (in Thessaly) there was destruction by fire at the end of the Early Helladic. South of Thessaly there are similar obscurities, exemplified, for example, by the mound of Lianokladhi in the Spercheios Valley, where there is present what seems to be grey Minyan ware in an ambiguous Early Helladic–Middle Helladic context. Something similar is apparent in Lefkas, in the Nidhri Plain burials. If in some cases there is no clear division between Early Helladic and Middle Helladic, in others, as for example at Eutresis and Krisa, there is none between Middle and Late Helladic.

In central Greece there are problems: what, for instance, is the explanation for the poor representation of Early Helladic III in Attica, where there follows, none the less, a number of important Middle Helladic sites, as at Brauron, Aphidnai, Eleusis and Marathon (Vrana)? At the latter site recent excavation, it is suggested, has produced Middle Helladic 'palatial' remains, and while it is claimed that the other sites named show little contact with the Aegean and Crete, Cretan Kamares ware appears at Marathon. In the eastern Peloponnese finds at Corinth show the dangers of conclusions from imperfect archaeological evidence: there are no indications of occupation in the city area later than Early Helladic II, but matt-painted (Middle Helladic) pottery is forthcoming from the North Cemetery. There are also indications of destruction and burning at Korakou nearby, at the end of the Early Helladic. Centres of importance at a later date have obviously suffered through such later occupation, as far as the earlier levels are concerned. There can therefore be no clear picture of the Middle Helladic state of Tiryns or Mycenae, but there are remains of houses, and the grave circles at Mycenae are of very great importance: grave circle B contains late Middle Helladic burials, and one grave in circle A yielded the latest Middle Helladic pottery. Lerna (stratigraphically Lerna v) provides not only the earliest horse bones (like Troy vi), but also clear evidence of contact (not necessarily direct) with Middle Minoan Crete, the outstanding source of influence on the Late Middle Helladic. Still in the Peloponnese, the Middle Helladic occupation of Lakonia seems important, and Kythera should now be an important link with Crete. In the west of the Peloponnese, south of the entrance to the Gulf of Corinth, the 'Teichos Dymaion' ('the fort of the Dymaeans', so called from the Classical Achaean state of Dyme), near Patras shows an Early Helladic settlement ending in burning, and followed by Middle Helladic occupation at what would seem to be an important crossing-point from western central Greece to the Peloponnese. Further south, at Koryphasion at the northern end of the Bay of Navarino, there is, dating from the end of the period, the earliest known *tholos* tomb on the mainland, in an area which seems to have had a particular connection with Crete, whence the *tholos* (domed or beehive) form may have been imported. It is worth noting that there was early occupation on the sites of the two later 'national' centres: at Delphi a quantity of Middle Helladic sherds has been found; and at Olympia, in the sacred enclosure, Middle Helladic apsidal houses, and, outside, indications of Middle Helladic occupation following on Early Helladic.

It was to be expected that in the Middle Bronze the Cyclades would be of importance, especially as a link with Crete. A resurgence in Middle Cycladic is indicated after a decline (as in Early Helladic Attica) at the end of Early Cycladic ii. Of major interest is the settlement of Phylakopi ii in Melos, which makes clear the intermediary function the island performed between Crete and the mainland. There Grey Minyan and Kamares ware meet (as on the mainland at Lerna), and eventually Cretan influence becomes dominant. Another clearly important site is that of Aghia Irini in Kea, on a large and important harbour inlet. Again there is a meeting of Grey Minyan and matt-painted wares from the mainland and a limited amount of Kamares ware from Crete. The most striking feature is the temple with an inner shrine and terracotta figures (vaguely Minoan in dress), one of which may be a cult figure, the others worshippers, though the exact character of the building in Middle Helladic is uncertain. The settlement continued to be prosperous until its total destruction by an earthquake (probably the effect of the Thera eruption), when Late Minoan i b and Late Helladic ii pottery styles were in use. It is difficult to believe that other sites similar to Phylakopi and Aghia Irini do not await discovery to supplement the rather poor and scrappy evidence otherwise forthcoming from the Aegean Islands.

The population of Middle Helladic Greece lived in houses with a rectangular main unit and open porch, sometimes with an apsidal end. The oval form also occurs. Some communities were without defensive walls, others possessed them: there is a nearly complete fortification at Malthi in the western Peloponnese; what might be a defensive wall (or terracing?) on the Aspis at Argos; and another wall on the Deiras nearby. There are others at Aegina, Rafina (Attica) and Ano Englianos (Pylos). In some cases Middle Helladic walls are obscured by later remains, and not every wall, it has been pointed out, need certainly be a fortification: some may well have been used for terracing. If all the indications are taken together, fortified towns on the mainland seem to have been relatively less common in the Middle Helladic than in Early Helladic II. Is it to be concluded that the period was more settled after earlier population movements? Was there little wealth to attract marauders? Or were these people of the Middle Helladic redoubtable defenders of their possessions? The possession of little wealth *might* be indicated by the absence of valuable grave goods, but this could in turn be explained by the absence of a custom of making such offerings. And have the more important burials been found long since and robbed? Again, in the Cyclades, the coastal sites of Phylakopi on Melos and Aghia Irini on Kea were fortified on the *landward* side: an attractive suggestion is that the intention of seafaring men was to leave their families and possessions safe from neighbours' depredations. The whole problem is obscure by reason of the inadequate evidence.

They buried their dead (with the paucity of grave goods already mentioned) in cist graves or *pithoi*, in a crouched or extended position in the cists. There is a gradual development in the grave form, and it is reasonable to see the type of cist grave (rectangular, with pebble floor, some kind of side walling and a covering of slabs) as a simple forerunner of the shaft graves of Mycenae. The pottery development is complex: Grey Minyan and monochrome matt-painted, Argive black Minyan, yellow Minyan, polychrome matt-painted and early Mycenaean, the latter influenced by Cretan pottery styles and the reversal in them from light on dark to dark on light decoration.

## THE LATE BRONZE AGE

### *The material remains*

The final stage of Bronze Age Greece is commonly called Mycenaean because of the manifest importance of that centre. It is dated in some measure, but not exactly, in parallel with Late Minoan Crete, and the latter in turn by the expulsion of the alien Hyksos from Egypt and the establishment of the New Kingdom, the Egyptian Empire. Late Helladic I may roughly be dated 1550–1450 BC; Late Helladic II, 1450–1375 BC; and Late Helladic III, 1375–c. 1125 BC. The latter is subdivided into Late

25

Helladic III A (1375–1300 BC); Late Helladic III B (1300–1225 BC); and Late Helladic III C (1225–1125 BC). The latter part of Late Helladic III C, sometimes called Sub-Mycenaean, is the bridge (to use a dubious metaphor) to the Early Iron Age. It need hardly be said that the dates are approximate and subject to modification.

Several points need stressing. The first is the close connection with Crete indicated by the presence of Cretan pottery in Greece, and the evidence, already mentioned, that the Cyclades, and especially Melos, formed a meeting-place of the two cultures in a way that Kythera, despite its settlement by the Minoans, seems not to have done. There is also the modification of Middle Helladic pottery to follow the fashion in Crete, which was to produce the finest dark-on-light pottery. Other objects of Cretan manufacture, some in precious metals, also appear in Greece, as gifts, trade objects or booty. The close link between Greece and Knossos in the Late Minoan II–III A I periods, when the Linear B tablets at Knossos seem to indicate the presence of Greeks there, has already been mentioned in Chapter 2. The conviction of the later Greeks that there was some peculiar relationship between Knossos under King Minos and parts, at any rate, of the mainland may also be mentioned (see Chapter 2). It is not surprising, therefore, that Evans (who did not have the benefit of the now generally accepted decipherment of the Linear B tablets) believed that Crete exercised some kind of suzerainty in Greece.

In some respects the supposed influence of Crete and the basic contrast between the modest and undistinguished Middle Helladic culture and the impressive Late Helladic are felt to be marked by the shaft graves at Mycenae; a form of burial which occurs not only at Mycenae, but at Lerna also, though little remains there of their form and very little of their contents. Essentially the shaft grave was a development of the Middle Helladic cist grave: a cutting in the rock or subsoil, lined with dry-stone walling. On the walling rested horizontal timbers, which in turn supported reeds or brushwood and a layer of clay. Thus the soil cast back did not fill the whole grave, and a sort of chamber was formed. The same type of burial occurs in Anatolia, as in the 'royal' tombs of Alaca Hüyük, which vie with the shaft graves of Mycenae in the interest and splendour of their contents, though they are far earlier (Early Bronze II).

The shaft graves at Mycenae occur in two groups: the first now inside the great fortification walls and surrounded by a double circle of vertical slabs. Originally this group was outside the walls on the slope of the acropolis, and was subsequently enclosed when the walls were extended to take in the graves in the thirteenth century. The original disposition was made clear by the discovery, outside the walls, of another group of shaft graves covered by a shallow burial mound with a stone edging, so that the term 'grave circle' is appropriate enough. In both grave circles – the one denominated A and excavated by Schliemann, who believed he had found in it the grave of Agamemnon of the Homeric *Iliad*, and the more recently excavated Grave Circle B – it was apparent that the separate graves were indicated by marker gravestones, sculptured in relief, or (in cases where they are now plain) with painted decoration.

The associated pottery in the case of grave circle A suggests a date at the end of the Middle Helladic and the beginning of the Late Helladic. Sherds in the surrounding stone edging of grave circle B (grey, black and yellow Minyan, and matt-painted) suggest a date late in the Middle Helladic period. Ever since the first discovery of grave circle A there has been a powerful impression of the wealth and technical skill here represented. It *could* be argued that the impression is fallacious and that the Mycenae shaft graves are exceptional amid the generally modest burials of the late Middle Helladic period. On the other hand it must be borne in mind that they come at a time of transition to the days of Mycenaean greatness, and it is hard to avoid the belief that much else has been lost: witness the two destroyed shaft graves at Lerna, and there may have been others elsewhere. The contents of the Mycenae shaft graves are diverse: there are objects clearly of Minoan manufacture; others which look like imitations; and others which appear alien. It is not easy to reach decisions on the origins of some of the objects, as, for example, the two types of thrusting-sword. Most impressive are the funerary masks of gold (with their indications of individual personality); the inlaid daggers; the silver 'siege' vase; the duck vase in rock-crystal; the curious vessel in silver in the form of a stag; and the gold lion's head libation vessel. If there is no easy identification of some of the objects, others, of Minoan or Minoanizing character, have an obvious connection with Crete.

The question constantly arises how these mainland people (it would be risky to call them Greeks with total assurance) obtained the objects in some instances, and the gold and craftsmen to make them in the case of others. Did they make plundering raids on Crete, or take advantage of earthquake disaster and disorder in Crete to make their way to Egypt to serve as mercenaries and help to expel the Hyksos, and then return laden with their reward? Or were they themselves fugitives expelled from some other region? Again the expulsion of the Hyksos from Egypt has been suggested: a historical parallel to the mythical arrival at Argos of Danaos and his fifty daughters pursued by the fifty sons of Aigyptos. It is on the whole better to avoid this ingenious interpretation of Greek mythology and heroic saga, but some scholars are determined to stress the Egyptian connection, instancing the supposed example of mummification in one of the burials, the supposed Egyptian technique of the crystal duck-vase, the ultimate origins of the inlaid dagger technique, the pin with a female figure holding swags terminating in lotus(?) flowers, the 'cup of Nestor' with its Egyptian hawks, and above all the gold face masks. These are the most suggestive objects for an Egyptian connection, but something like them is known from other times and places. Short of suggesting that the wealth of the shaft graves came ultimately from some source of economic prosperity – and this would be difficult *at this juncture* in the history of Mycenae – the best explanations seem to be plunder, trade, princely gifts and immigrant craftsmen. How far some objects have Anatolian origins or affinities is a problem yet to be properly debated.

It is generally, if vaguely, agreed that those buried in the Mycenae shaft graves were members of ruling and so 'royal' families. The rich contents would seem to indicate this, as would the august or forceful character impressions given by some of the masks. The term 'shaft grave dynasty' has been used. Similar great families of warrior-rulers must have existed elsewhere to match the beliefs of the later Greeks expressed in their mythology, perhaps associated with mercenaries. Further down the social scale the 'commoners' were buried in cist graves. There were other burials near shaft circle A when it lay outside the walls, indicating a certain social hierarchy.

There were at Mycenae other forms of burial-place, associated by ancient writers with the great figures of Greek heroic saga, especially those concerned with the Trojan War. Greek legend and the possibility of knowledge handed down from the Bronze Age will be discussed later in this chapter and in the next. Here it is a question of the material structures. There are a number of large *tholos* tombs, constructed of corbelled masonry in ever-decreasing circles and surmounted by a capstone. They are constructed in hillsides and approached by a passage-way or *dromos*. Some of them have a side chamber. The finest is the 'Treasury of Atreus'. On the basis of a typological study these *tholoi* have been classified into three groups stretching in date from *c.* 1510 BC to 1300 BC or later (the date of the 'Treasury of Atreus' is disputed). The earliest date, *c.* 1510 BC, therefore places the earliest of them tolerably close in time to the later grave circle A, with little margin for any process of evolution. The shaft graves were on occasions reused (for as many as four successive burials). Reopening cannot have been very convenient. In one shaft of grave circle B there was constructed a chamber of stone, but this appears to have occurred something like two hundred years later than the other graves and displays affinities with chamber tombs of northern Syria. It is not, therefore, a transitional stage between a shaft grave and a built tomb, though *in theory* there is a possible development from rectangular chamber to circular, the most economic form in terms of area. It is better to suggest a derivation from the vaulted tombs of Crete, especially since they are now known to have been used at a later date than Early Minoan, and an example has been found in the vicinity of Knossos. In an area which, it is suggested, had a close connection with Minoan Crete, namely Messenia in the western Peloponnese, a small tholos tomb has been found near Koryphasion, at the northern end of the Bay of

Navarino, containing chiefly Middle Helladic funeral gifts. It is the earliest yet known of the *tholos* type.

The great tholoi of Mycenae, particularly the 'Treasury of Atreus', excel in size and monumental character. These have been empty since antiquity, but it is clear from those on other sites that the burial procedure went thus: the dead person was laid out in state on a bier with the funeral offerings about him; the tomb was closed; and some form of funeral feast was held outside in the *dromos*. When the tomb was needed for another burial it was opened and fumigated. The remains of the previous occupant were pushed to one side, buried in the floor or placed in a side chamber. The idea may have existed that when the flesh had mouldered the spirit had also dwindled away to nothing. Thus remains could accumulate, and the contents of such *tholoi* can represent a very considerable succession of burials. The practice outlined here also brings it about that, while there could be some possibility of stratification, it would be dangerous to draw conclusions on certain issues, on wife or servant sacrifice, for instance. The *tholos* tombs have also been exposed to official or clandestine robbery. It is to be wondered how soon they were robbed in cases of well-known and rich burials, as the tombs of the pharaohs of Egypt were. They were liable to collapse, and in general it may be said that their contents are never fully preserved. How far the burials were remembered in antiquity for what they were is a nice problem. There is evidence of ritual in some cases, conducted outside in the *dromos* (but not at Mycenae?), but it is very doubtful if such ritual was connected with the great names of heroic saga.

If there has been a tendency to talk of a 'shaft grave dynasty' there is also an inclination to speak of a '*tholos* tomb dynasty'. It is probably unjustified, since this type of burial structure became standard for the ruling class on the mainland. In any case at Mycenae the long stretch of time from *c.* 1510 BC to perhaps *c.* 1250 BC seems likely to have covered more than one dynasty. In fact does each of the great *tholoi* represent a ruling family?

Elsewhere in Greece *tholoi* occur in some numbers. In close proximity to Mycenae damaged *tholoi* have been found at Prosymna (the site of the Argive sanctuary of Hera), and especially at Dendra, not very far from Mycenae, where the contents of a royal tomb (showing three successive periods of burial?) escaped the attentions of tomb robbers, while another (of Late Helladic III A 1 date) produced a Mycenaean bronze cuirass of a type known from the Linear B tablets. These are lesser tombs in terms of size than those at Mycenae. Of others known, the 'Treasury of Minyas' at Bocotian Orchomenos is of major dimensions, with its gigantic lintel stone and side chamber, the roof of which is finely decorated with linked spirals. It has lost its dome, and so has another at Vapheio in Lakonia, south-east of modern Sparta, in the floor of which a rich treasure, including the Vapheio gold cups, escaped robbery. The western Peloponnese has produced others, which have suffered from robbery and collapse: the most important are at Peristeria and Routsi, of the Late Helladic I–II period. Others occur at Volos (ancient Iolkos) in Thessaly. Of particular interest are those in Attica: in the country in south-eastern Attica, on the hill of Thorikos (where the *tholos* is associated with two other tombs, one with possible indications of later cult); and north-west of Athens at Menidhi near Parnes. These are taken to be earlier than the examples (including one of a Mycenaean princess) found on the north slope of the Areiopagos in Athens itself, which seem to belong to Late Helladic III A.

Side by side with the *tholoi* appear the chamber tombs of what might be called the middle class. They replace the cist graves of the Middle Helladic, and are basically rectangular chambers hewn out of the soft rock, frequently with additional side chambers. They were used for the burial of generation after generation of Mycenaeans, in some cases from Late Helladic I to Late Helladic III, so that there is a certain amount of stratification, but liable to disturbance.

The shaft graves, the *tholoi* and the chamber tombs, chance finds and closed deposits of pottery have produced the material (to be added to that from private and public buildings) which permits an assessment of the artistic achievement of the Mycenaeans. Of particular importance is the pottery, which shows the progressive stylization of decoration and the evolution of patterns and of shapes. The appearance of such pottery in datable contexts outside the mainland and Crete, in Egypt and the eastern Mediterranean, coupled with the study of closed deposits, has provided an essential absolute dating framework. A good deal of work remains to be done. There are those who would reject the Late Helladic I, II and III scheme and its subdivisions, and replace them by site-names (for example, 'the Zygouries period'), which are less liable to suggest a spurious accuracy. There is a danger also of subjective stylistic judgements and of circular chronological arguments. Provided, however, that margins of accuracy of a quarter-century or somewhat more are borne in mind, the system serves well enough.

The burials contain imported materials. There is gold, a metal probably imported. Semi-precious stones occur, particularly skilfully bored beads and amber. The use of bronze presupposes the availability of copper, which was certainly imported from Cyprus, though Egyptian tomb paintings show what may be Mycenaeans bearing ingots like those known from Cyprus and elsewhere – and would Mycenaeans of the mainland offer such to the Egyptians if they imported copper themselves from Cyprus, or are they other than Mycenaeans? Tin was imported, but it is unclear whether from east or west. There is ivory from Egypt or the eastern Mediterranean, and ostrich eggs: They all argue widespread trade connections. So does the presence of Mycenaean (Late Helladic) pottery abroad, though a problem there arises. While in Kythera, Miletos and Ialysos (in Rhodes) it is clear that the Mycenaeans from *c.* 1400 BC (or even *c.* 1500 BC) replaced the Minoans in these settlements abroad, elsewhere the presence of Mycenaean pottery may indicate not settlement but native importation. Whether or not this is true, it is very apparent that a Mycenaean predominance manifests itself in the Aegean and the eastern Mediterranean from the fifteenth century, with its apogee in the fourteenth, with a common pottery style (or *Koine* as it has been called), even if of local manufacture, at a number of centres. How far this pottery penetrated to the west is uncertain. It certainly did to southern Italy, and probably to Malta. The question of the contact with the Lipari Islands and the import of volcanic liparite seems no longer as clear as it did once for Crete and the mainland. Amber was certainly imported, at certain periods, but did it come by way of the Adriatic or indeed from the Baltic necessarily? It is no longer possible to quote megalithic tombs, or Stonehenge or faience beads as indications of contacts with the far west.

The evidence so far discussed – burials and the objects found in them – has been given priority, since it presents a full spread in time from the sixteenth to the thirteenth century BC. This is not in general true of the most obvious memorials of Mycenaean greatness, the fortress palaces. These were subjected to change and modification as the generations passed, and while it is possible in certain cases to detect earlier remains within the Middle and Late Helladic periods, the bulk of what is visible belongs to the last stages of the palaces in the thirteenth and early twelfth centuries BC, so that a stretch of something like three and a half centuries lies between the first major impact of Minoan culture and the downfall and end of Mycenaean greatness, a good deal of it ill represented in terms of building structures other than tombs. In the case of Tiryns there would appear to be three detectable periods, the last of Late Helladic III date. At Mycenae a Middle Helladic wall might represent part of the original citadel, or be a simple retaining wall. In the case of Athens, Thebes and Volos the palaces were later overlaid, and at Thebes and Athens the fortification walls were swallowed up by later building. In Athens and Volos very little indeed of the palaces remains. The palace of Thebes is overlaid by the modern town and is currently being very fruitfully excavated. The top of the citadel of Mycenae has suffered from later occupation; so has Tiryns, but to a lesser degree. The best-preserved palace site is Pylos, as far as its plan is concerned; but it covers only a limited time before its destruction. There was a Middle Helladic settlement on the hill, but this was swept away. A fragmentary portal and wall on the north-eastern part of the hill are said to be of Late Helladic I date. There is also the south-western building, said to have been twice

31

destroyed by fire. The main part of the palace dates between *c.* 1300 BC and *c.* 1200 BC.

Mycenaean palaces occur at sites which are centres of Greek heroic saga. This is the case for Mycenae, Tiryns, Athens, Thebes and Volos (Iolkos), all of which are associated with great figures of saga: Mycenae with Agamemnon, Tiryns with Herakles, Athens with Theseus, Thebes with Oedipus, Iolkos with Jason and the Argonauts.

The palace at Ano Englianos in Messenia mentioned above is commonly called Pylos, for most scholars attribute it to Nestor and his father Neleus. Two areas well known in saga, the region of Lacedaemon (Lakonia), the kingdom of Menelaos, husband of Helen, and the region of Kalydon, associated with Atalanta, Meleager and the boar-hunt, have not so far produced palaces, but in the case of Sparta there is the Vapheio tomb, which must be a royal grave. Somewhere nearby there should be a palace, since there are *tholoi* near the palaces of Mycenae, Athens, Pylos and Iolkos.

The palaces of Tiryns and Pylos demonstrate most clearly the palace structure, with lower courses of stone blocks and with mud-brick and bonding timbers, covered with plaster, above. The main unit is the large hall or *megaron*, which can no longer be connected specifically with the advent of newcomers from the north. At Pylos and Tiryns it is obviously an elaboration of a more simple structure with a long history. It has porch, vestibule and hall, with a central great hearth. Above the hall at Pylos there seems to have been a chimney and a clerestory arrangement supported on four columns. There was certainly a second floor, where it is probable that the women lived. Fronting the hall was a court with an entrance gate. At Pylos there are also a bathroom and one or two private open-air courts, an archive room, pantries and corridors and, behind the great hall, an oil storeroom with ranges of jars. There was probably another storeroom on the first floor; and a separate great wine store and workshops are indicated. At right angles to the main hall at Pylos there was another *megaron* unit (but with no hearth), approached from a large vestibule which also gave access to a maze of rooms in the south-western building, including what looks like a substantial corner tower. Another such strong-point seems to have existed on the right of the entrance to the court fronting the great hall. Thus the palace, with its massive south-western wall, was at least partly fortified, but there are no indications of such massive buildings as at Mycenae, Tiryns or Athens.

Tiryns has a great defensive enclosure which lies to the north of the palace hill, reminiscent of the vast enclosure wall round the site of Gla in Boeotia, in what was once Lake Kopais. At Mycenae the striking feature of the citadel, apart from the rising series of walls, are the 'houses', some of them certainly annexes of the palace, and in one or more cases (the 'Citadel House' and the 'House of Columns') probably parts of the palace descending the acropolis slope. The greatest feature of Mycenae are the splendid fortification walls, in their last construction including the Lion Gate. The same pattern of fortification, to force the attacker to present his unshielded side to the missiles of defenders, appears again at Tiryns and probably at Athens. Nothing can be said of the walls at Thebes, and little on the (as yet) confused remnants of the palace. At Gla the vast circuit wall has within it a curious series of structures: a succession of rooms, quite unlike the normal Mycenaean plan, facing a large enclosed space with a gate. The site was occupied for only a relatively short time in the thirteenth century and then abandoned.

An important series of houses appears at Mycenae below the citadel and not far from it, in the extensive lower town, in which grave structures were mixed with buildings for the use of the living. Such 'lower towns' surround or adjoin all Mycenaean palace centres. These buildings at Mycenae were extensive and well constructed. They have yielded a considerable amount of material, including ivory and lead, and may have been the centres of craft activity. One of them has, somewhat tendentiously, been called the 'House of the Oil Merchant', by reason of the large number of oil jars found in it. In fact, however, these houses, like the wine and oil stores incorporated in the palace at Pylos, may have been centres of palace commercial activity, rather than of private enterprise.

Elsewhere (including, it may be noted, Olympia and Delphi) there are the houses of lesser folk, differing little from those of other periods. There are no totally separate shrines except in the island of Kea (at Aghia Irini), and no hilltop sanctuaries have so far been discovered.

It seems tolerably clear that Late Bronze Age Greece from southern Thessaly southwards, and east of the Pindos, was a highly developed country in terms of settlement and communications. The palace centres seem to be the residences of rulers of varying degrees of importance and wealth: the rulers of Mycenae *look*, to judge from their stronghold, as if they were greater than those of Tiryns or Berbati-Dendra not far away. Or were these latter vassal centres? If they were not, but were in fact the strongholds of independent princes, a number of problems arise, particularly concerning the sources of their wealth, and the whole complex of governmental and economic organization. Linear B tablets have been found at Pylos in particular, and in some measure at Mycenae, on the acropolis and in the houses mentioned above. If there was in fact a record room at Mycenae, as there was at Pylos, it looks as if it has been swept away, but it may well be that the tablets were used at diverse points in the palace and its annexes, as at Knossos, and that more may yet be found. At Thebes there is every hope that this will happen.

The evidence of the tablets complicates an already complex and in some respects puzzling picture. They are concerned only with day-to-day administration. None the less the terminology employed for this and for military organization, from the *wanax* or ruler downwards, is not easily interpreted; but once the decipherment is accepted it is clear that there was an elaborate system, as at Knossos in the period of the Linear B tablets there, with incomings and outgoings of materials, and all kinds of activity involving entitlements and duties. There seems also to have been local government (and coastal defence?), integrated with a central administration from the palace. There was other economic activity, demonstrated by the tablets and the material remains. The evidence for commodities stored, such as perfumed oils, cannot have related only to the needs of the palace itself. The existence must be assumed of a commercial organization, and even one with overseas connections. This is a picture very different from that of a simple heroic age.

The cultural background is in some measure illuminated by such fragments of wall-paintings and pictures on gems and seals as have survived. In many aspects of its art, and the general setting of its palace life, Mycenaean Greece is odd. A Minoan transported from the great days of Knossos to the mainland would have found the *megara* with their great fixed hearths somewhat strange, and the vestibules, courts and gates different in some details from those he knew at home. He would, on the other hand, have found the frescoed walls familiar enough in technique, though the style he would note as being more formal and stylized than that of the best and more naturalistic of the Knossian. The colourful monkeys robbing birds' nests, the cats stalking birds, the impressionistic plant life are missing. Mycenaean fresco-painters give in many respects a curiously childlike impression: an unnaturally striped boar, quaint trees like tennis-racquets, a frozen procession of casket-bearing ladies. Indeed there are many problems of imitation and dating and style, not helped by the very fragmentary state in which the frescoes have survived. Again there is nothing in Crete like the Pylos horses, the strange surrealist painting of the lyre player and his attendant bird, or the curious and intriguing pictures of battle scenes between wild and woolly savages (reminiscent of those on the silver shaft-grave *rhyton*, the silver 'siege' vase mentioned above), and neat warriors well equipped with long thrusting swords and boar's-tusk helmets. On the other hand again, the formalized griffins of the Knossos throne room appear with other animals at Pylos. Again at Pylos the Minoan native would have found the horns of consecration familiar. In Tiryns of the thirteenth century the ladies in their long flounced dresses and Minoan locks parade with their jugs and toilet boxes on the walls, in a style similar to but more formal than the Knossian. Smaller art objects, such as gems and signet rings, which might come from plunder or be gifts or collector's pieces (like the seal cylinders from Thebes) would seem familiar enough to a Minoan in technique and style.

There is, however, a real problem of identification for the modern observer. For example, there is the splendid ivory group found at Mycenae in a so-called cult room: did the group identify the cult room or the reverse? The ivory group must not be over-identified as 'two goddesses with a divine child', or even as 'two princesses with a royal child'. They are, in fact, two well-dressed women and a child. They illustrate the possibility of conjuring up an arguable but uncertain religious background. Rings and gems, likewise, may have come from Crete as spoil, or they may have been part of a collection of *objets d'art*, or they may be mainland copies. There is no reason why collections of Minoan art objects should not have existed. After all the kings of Assyria later collected, or at any rate assembled, furniture decorated with ivory carving in their palaces. There is the perpetual difficulty that verbal comment and explanation are lacking, despite the decipherment of the Linear B tablets, for the odd representations. How do we explain the strange crocodile-headed creatures which appear on a Mycenaean fresco at Tiryns, done in white, black, blue, yellow-brown and dark-red on a blue ground? Whether they are ass-headed monsters or Ta-urt demons, they appear not infrequently in Minoan contexts, and are seemingly of religious significance. Do they represent a similarity of belief and iconographic background, or just a liking for this exotic art type, like our own *chinoiserie* or the decorative use of the Pompeian style? When figures appear wearing the conventional Minoan loin-cloth, is it to be believed that this really was worn in the chilly atmosphere of, say, Volos, or is this the equivalent of the heroic nudity of Roman emperors or the togas of British statesmen?

On the other hand, there exists a sufficiency of material objects of which the purely artistic value is low and the religious association is strong, since they occur in what must be cult contexts. These seem to make clear that there were links in cult and religious belief between Mycenaean Greece and Crete. There are also significant major monuments, such as the Lion Gate at Mycenae, where the relieving triangle over the gate is filled with a slab decorated in relief with a pillar on a base flanked by two felines (lions or lionesses or some other ill-identified animals). The pillar is similar to smaller model pillars found in Crete, which *may* have a cult significance. Flanking animals appear in Crete with a female figure between them, sometimes on a mountain base. The same arrangement with a central female figure appears also in archaic Greek art as the 'Mistress of Animals'.

It is not unreasonable, therefore, to seek a connection between the pillar and the goddess, and between the Cretan representations and the Mycenaean, to discover something more than a mere imitated coat of arms. It also seems likely, it may be added, that there was a continuity of sanctity, in some way, on some sites at least, between Mycenaean times and later periods. It can fairly be suggested that Athena and Hera of the

Archaic period (associated like the Bronze Age goddess with something like a bird epiphany) may in certain cases be a descendant of a Mycenaean female deity, herself having some connection with Crete. Apart from the cave and hilltop sanctuaries which are very numerous in Crete, the palaces of that island seem to indicate that shrines or chapels were on a very minor scale. It has been customary to say that on the Mycenaean mainland, in the palaces, cult practices were carried out at the hearth in the *megaron*: witness the portable altars, and what appears like a libation channel beside the location of the ceremonial chair (?) in the *megaron* at Pylos. On the other hand the same palace complex does show some kind of cult place. There has also recently been discovered, in the 'Citadel House' at Mycenae, a shrine of some complexity, with remarkable terracotta figures and terracotta snakes; and there is the shrine at Aghia Irini in Kea with its figures of deity (?) and worshippers. There is little point in guessing what it may all mean. The Linear B tablets on the one hand seem to reflect a religious organization as complex as the administrative, with 'key-holders', 'sweepers' and 'slaves of the god', of which the significance is totally obscure; on the other hand there seem to be present some indications of Olympian deities in Mycenaean Greece, as in Knossos; the evidence is there, but not as clear or as cogent as might be wished.

Thus from the sixteenth century BC there is on the mainland a culture strongly influenced by Crete – though it must be borne in mind that the links are partly represented by a mainland presence in Crete at Knossos in Late Minoan II. At first the Minoan imprint is vivid and fresh; later it becomes somewhat stale, with conspicuous differences in frescoes and vase-painting. Mycenaean influences spread far abroad, but one overseas connection disappears: there is an absence of amber in Late Helladic III. On the other hand it has been demonstrated by clay analysis that Late Helladic figured pottery reached Cyprus and beyond. Cyprus was an island rich in copper, which was exported abroad, as the undersea excavation of the Yassiada ship off the south coast of Anatolia indicates. It was also an important area of Mycenaean culture, and a producer and importer of pottery and other objects in the Mycenaean style, such as the silver cup from Enkomi inlaid with bulls' heads in gold and *niello*. It must also have passed on Mycenaean influences to the southern coast of Asia Minor and to the coast of Syria. At Ras Shamra (Ugarit) was found an ivory lid with a goddess (?) flanked by goats and wearing a very Mycenaean-looking skirt. The same site also produced a gold libation bowl, on which the King of Ugarit appears hunting splendid bulls which owe something to the Minoan-Mycenaean tradition.

There is much that is puzzling. It has been pointed out already that the most important monuments and remains of the Mycenaean culture belong to the thirteenth century, a century which also saw interesting events in Troy. From the archaeological examination of these monuments and sites a number of events can be very reasonably guessed at, if not established with certainty. The first is the destruction of the palace at Thebes somewhere around 1300 BC. Next in order are major events at Troy. Troy VI was destroyed round about 1300 BC, possibly by an earthquake. The subsequent rebuilding (Troy VII *a* 1) has been well described by its American excavator:

The houses, for the most part small, were numerous; they were crowded closely together, often with party walls, and they seem to have filled the whole area inside the fortification, where they were superposed over the earlier buildings, as well as the considerable spaces that had previously been left open. Another distinctive feature is the presence in almost every house of large *pithoi* or storage jars . . . sunk deeply beneath the floors. . . .

One, or at the most two, generations would seem to be a reasonable estimate of the duration of the settlement. It came to its end in a devastating conflagration that swept over the entire citadel and reduced all the houses to ruins. Under the masses of stones that fell into the streets inside the South Gate were found remnants of the skeletons of two human victims of the catastrophe, which has the appearance of the handiwork of man. The crowding together of a great number of small houses within the fortress and the installation of innumerable huge storage jars to lay up a supply of provisions are factors that suggest preparations for a siege, and the final holocaust was the usual accompaniment of the capture, sacking and burning of an ancient town.[3]

The date of the destruction of Troy VII *a* 1 has been placed *c.* 1250 BC, or even earlier. The dating is based on the finds of Greek Mycenaean pottery and its local imitations, and is something less than satisfactory. Some misgivings must be felt in particular about the continued presence of what is called 'Grey Minyan' ware; and 'Grey ware' might be a more accurate description. A good deal about the date and fall of Troy VI and Troy VII *a* 1 has been called into question. The city was not abandoned as a result of this disaster; a remnant remained to continue the existence of the settlement: this stage is called Troy VII *a* 2, and seems, from pottery finds, to have continued for some time, until evidence appears of a cultural break and the arrival of new people with affinities (as suggested by their pottery) with eastern Europe. These may have later become the Phrygians, who ultimately settled in Anatolia. There is, however, a serious issue here. The dates here given are those commonly but not universally accepted, based on the views of Blegen, the second excavator of Troy. Much depends on the dating of Late Helladic III B, especially in relation to its successor, Late Helladic III C, and on the presence of pottery from the latter period at Troy VII *a* 1.

At Mycenae a significant event took place around the mid-century. The houses outside the citadel were burnt. It is clear from the smashed oil jars that this destruction was effected by either external foes or internal insurgents. The buildings were never restored, if the pottery indications are rightly interpreted. There followed an improvement of the fortifications of the citadel, including the carrying of the great wall round the outside of the grave circle A, the formation of the existing enclosure over the grave circle, and the improvement of the great gate. This work, like the construction of the 'Treasury of Atreus' (which some would put at this date and not earlier), *might* be described as prestige construction. Other works were unequivocally defensive – the extension of the wall circuit, and the securing of access by an underground passage to a spring outside the fortifications. Similar access to springs was made at Athens and at Tiryns. At Athens also the Mycenaean postern gate on the northern side of the acropolis was blocked, and to this period belong the great fortification wall at Gla and other fortifications in Boeotia, Phocis and Thessaly. On the Isthmus of Corinth a wall (near that constructed in the sixth century AD to protect the Peloponnese against barbarian attack) seems to belong to this period, and would presumably be intended to defend against attack from the north.

Despite these preparations, which cannot have been carried out overnight, disaster overtook Mycenaean Greece at the end of the Late Helladic III B. There was severe destruction at Krisa in Phocis, Gla in Boeotia, Zygouries in the Corinthia, at Mycenae, Tiryns, the Menelaion in Lakonia, Pylos and Nichoria in Messenia. Some sites were abandoned (Pylos, Eutresis, Berbati, Prosymna). It is not easy to estimate what happened in Iolkos (Volos in Thessaly) or at Athens, because of later occupation. There are some indications that eastern Attica was relatively unaffected, as was the Aegean (western and southern), since sea passage remained open, as imported objects seem to indicate.

Only Mycenae was occupied in any considerable measure after this, but with symptoms of decline. There was a dispersal of population to what have been called less dangerous areas, such as Achaea, and Kephallenia; and refugees seem to have travelled as far as Cilicia and Cyprus to augment Mycenaean influences in these regions. The date of this disaster (it looks like *one* event, though it could in reality be a succession) is generally placed somewhere in the last two decades of the thirteenth century. The fire which destroyed the palace at Pylos baked the archive of Linear B tablets, which can thus be taken to record transactions on the eve of disaster. There are some indications of defensive preparation, and possibly mobilization, but we cannot tell the nature or direction of the attack. The fortifications and the Isthmus wall do not preclude the co-operation of dissident internal elements with an outside enemy. In general scholars reject the suggestion of an attack from inside the Mycenaean world, as, for instance, from Crete, Rhodes or the Cyclades. If the attack came by land it must have been from either the north-west or the north-east. If it was seaborne it *could* have come from the north-east; hardly from the east through the southern Aegean; nor from the south or west. An attack from Libya is *just* possible.

The latter part of the thirteenth century and the early part of the twelfth were a time of troubles. This is clear from Egyptian records, the general import of which is undisputed, even if names and details are arguable. In 1223 BC there was an attack by the Libyans and Ekwesh (or Qwesh) on Egypt. There was another Libyan attack on Egypt in 1194. The archives of the Hittite Empire cease around 1200 BC. The reason was the great land and sea raids of 1191, in the reign of Rameses III, which destroyed the Hittite power, disrupted the eastern Mediterranean and threatened Egypt. There are, thereafter, indications of a new people at Troy. In Egyptian reliefs strange Sherden warriors appear with slashing swords and new helmet forms. It is tempting to quote as another indication of military activity and new forms of equipment the 'Warrior Vase' of the late thirteenth century, found on the acropolis of Mycenae. It shows a file of marching warriors, to whom a woman bids farewell with a gesture of mourning. It is altogether appropriate that it should have survived from a time when death and destruction were frequent, and when many a warrior set out never to return. Are these mercenaries from the varied peoples circulating at this time?

These disturbances were not in every case mere raids. The great land raid of 1191 BC, for instance, was a migration of whole tribes with women, children, animals and wagons: the equivalent of the later movement of barbarian tribes.

There were in this period undoubtedly migrations of peoples who ultimately settled in and influenced the culture of the eastern Mediterranean at the end of the Bronze and the beginning of the Iron Age. As far as Mycenaean Greece is concerned the mechanics of its destruction are totally obscure. More than one group of invaders may have been involved at different times and in different places, and in any case the events may have covered a number of years. Efforts to establish connections with the north, by a study of weapon typology in particular, have attained no conspicuous success. The question of the origins of the attackers remains 'archaeologically unanswerable', as does the problem of their eventual settlement.

It is easy to believe that a highly organized civilization such as that of Mycenaean Greece could be thrown into disorder by internal strife and raids from outside, resulting in the economic and social decline evident in Late Helladic III. The depopulating effects of epidemics cannot be discounted, and there were shifts of population in Greece and to areas abroad. Some Mycenaeans no doubt went marauding themselves. In this way the population of certain areas declined. How far other factors played a part, such as over-cultivation or the ruthless destruction of tree cover for building purposes and fuel, it is impossible to say, but it is useful to hold the possibilities in mind. More will be said on this subject in the following chapter.

## The heroic saga

The study of Bronze Age Greece does not depend wholly on material remains. It has already been pointed out that the later Greeks had some ideas about what modern scholars would call their Late Bronze Age past, which the Greeks called their Heroic Age. Some of their ideas were no doubt the product of a fertile imagination. Once, before Schliemann's discovery of Troy and Mycenae, there was a tendency to consider every idea they had on this early period to be a literary creation – thus, in the words used by Grote of himself, 'striking off one thousand years from the scroll of history'.[4] It is now clear that things were a good deal different. The Greeks had their folk memories; they could see round them the ruins of a remote greatness; works of Bronze Age art may well have survived. In the absence of writing from the end of the thirteenth century to the eighth, there could have been oral tradition in story form, and oral poetry, the forerunners of the written epic, which produced the Homeric poems written down in the eighth century when alphabetic writing became available. More will be said later on the Homeric poems in their proper context.

A certain element in the Greeks' story of their remote past was pure folk tale, and the more distant figures clearly lack any element of verisimilitude. On the other hand, certain events were made the kernel of heroic saga: at the very centre was the episode of the Trojan War. Preceding this was an earlier expedition of the semi-divine hero Herakles against Troy, connected with a curious conviction that there was something special and odd about the construction of its walls. It was believed that a great expedition of the Achaean Greeks was mounted against Troy to recover Helen, wife of Menelaos, King of Sparta, who had eloped with Paris, son of Priam, King of Troy. The great hero of the expedition was Achilles, coming from Phthiotis in southern Thessaly, on the fringe of the heroic world. A Catalogue of the Ships of those who went to Troy was given in Book II of the *Iliad*, one of the two great early poems in epic hexameters which have been preserved to modern times. It is generally agreed that the Catalogue has a Boeotian bias, and the expedition itself sailed from Aulis in Boeotia. The expedition was led by Agamemnon, King of Men, who possessed the greatest power among the participants in the expedition and made the greatest contribution to it. He gives ships to the Arcadians, and attempts to pacify the wrath of Achilles by an offer of towns in the Peloponnese. Later legend, such as that used by Aeschylus in the *Oresteia*, made Agamemnon King of Argos. The *Iliad*, on the other hand, knew that he ruled over Mycenae 'rich in gold', and gave Argos, and Tiryns hard by, and much else, to Diomedes. The territory of

40

Agamemnon was an extensive one, and stretched to the Gulf of Corinth. It is interesting to note the comment of the late fifth-century Attic historian Thucydides, in his preamble to the history of the Great Peloponnese War. In considering the magnitude of the expedition to Troy (which he accepts as a historical reality) he observes: 'Now Mykenai may have been a small place, and many of the towns of that age may appear comparatively insignificant, but no exact observer would therefore feel justified in rejecting the estimate given by the poets and by tradition of the magnitude of the armament.'[5]

The brother of Agamemnon was Menelaos, King in Lacedaemon. His fame was scarcely less great than that of Agamemnon, since he was the husband of Helen. From her earliest childhood the fatal beauty of Helen had given trouble: Theseus had carried her off, and she had been recovered by her brothers Kastor and Polydeukes. She naturally had many suitors, and because of her beauty they agreed that those who failed to win her, would, as it were, guarantee the husband in possession. Menelaos won her. It is difficult to see why: a good enough warrior, he must always strike the reader of the *Iliad* as indisputably dull. Perhaps it was felt that the sequel was thus more credible. Ultimately, of course, he got his reward, for, wedded to a daughter of Zeus, it was his destiny to live immortal in the Elysian Plain. But before that Helen was to flee with Paris to Troy (later it was suggested that only a wraith got so far), and thus fulfilment of the suitors' oath was required. They went under the leadership of Agamemnon, some very unwillingly, like Odysseus.

Thus the myth-making genius of the Greeks sought to explain the concept, firmly accepted even by rational men like Thucydides, of an association of Greek states in a great enterprise against a foreign city. It must be admitted that modern explanations (assuming the reality of the expedition) are hardly more satisfactory. It is difficult to see the importance of Troy, located where it was. It might have been suitable for the rearing of horses (an epic epithet for the city) or sheep (to promote a wool trade), but it was hardly suitable to control entrance to the Black Sea, or the Hellespontine crossing from Europe to Asia, as a stage in a tin trade route from Bohemia. The point is, perhaps, worth making that the site at Hissarlik excavated by Schliemann was *Troy* in the conviction only of the Classical and later Greeks and the Romans, and the visitor to Troy must wonder whether its remains equal its great reputation in antiquity. It is possible to deny the historicity of the great expedition, and to say that the tradition is a romantic elaboration of memories of marauding raids. Thucydides, indeed, himself hints at this. *And* the names of the heroes are the names of common men in the Linear B tablets. But there is still the problem: why choose Troy as the objective of the expedition?

A still greater problem is the concept of an association of states: from southern Thessaly southwards to the Gulf of Corinth and east of the

Pindos (with the exception of Ithaka, the island kingdom of Odysseus, in the west), the Peloponnese, Crete, Rhodes and the adjacent islands. There is the choice of postulating *either* an emergency association for a specific purpose – such as to nip in the bud and at a distance some threat to the associated states – *or* an empire with a wide-ranging policy of dominance. The *Iliad* seems to represent a curious compromise: Agamemnon is an unsure *primus inter pares*, coping, sometimes unsuccessfully, with turbulent fellow-rulers, certainly not vassals of a subordinate sort, just as Zeus is faced with similar problems in dealing with *his* associates. On the other hand he gives ships to the Arcadians (though this is a matter of logic if they are ever to ge to Troy across the seas) and seems to have Peloponnesian cities in his gift. It is reasonable to seek evidence elsewhere of such a Mycenaean empire. As Thucydides points out, the classical term which the Greeks used to designate themselves, 'Hellenes', was used in the epic only of the followers of Achilles from Phthiotis. Otherwise the terms used are 'Danaoi' (now agreed to have no connection with the Danauna of Egyptian records), 'Argeioi' and 'Achaioi' (with whom have been equated the Egyptian Ekwesh or Qwesh). In the imperial Hittite records at Boğaz-köy there are a number of references to 'Aḫḫiya' or 'Aḫḫiyawa', which have, with disputed philological validity, been equated with 'Achaioi'. To judge from these references, this power was of considerable size, located somewhere in the Aegean overseas from the mainland, but apparently with interests on it, and having relations of varying degrees of friendship or the reverse with the Hittites.

It has long been a matter of debate how the geographical terms appearing in the Hittite archives are to be interpreted and located, including the River Seha. It is also natural to ask, if Troy was of importance, whether it figures in the Hittite archives. Equally it is puzzling that there appears to be no reference to the Hittites in the list of the Trojan allies in the *Iliad*. Few scholars have been willing to accept Aḫḫiya as being located on the Greek mainland, as a term for a Mycenaean empire. A more plausible site could be Rhodes, which is conveniently near the Anatolian mainland. Since in Greek tradition, from the period of the epic on, there is an assumption of a relationship between Greece and Troy, with guest friendships, and an apparent absence of difficulty in communication, there has been a temptation to think of the Trojans as akin in origins, culture and language with the Greeks, and even to think of a state of Aḫḫiya-Achaea as straddling the area from north-western Anatolia into Thrace. It is an attractive theory, but it involves a reorganization of Bronze Age Anatolian geography too great to be credible, and some unconvincing interpretations of archaeological evidence. The location of a state whose rulers could be of importance in Hittite protocol, of which it could be said, 'The Kings who are of the same rank as myself, the King of Egypt, the King of Babylonia, the King of Assyria, and the King of Aḫḫiyawa',[6] is a major puzzle.

The Trojan War was the centre of Greek saga. In terms of *generations* the Greeks organized their heroic tales back into the dim past of the venerable ancestors, and forward into the semi-historical sequel to the capture of Troy. An example is Minos: Minos begat Deukalion, and Deukalion Idomeneus, and Idomeneus participated in the expedition to Troy. And there is the well-known statement of Thucydides, which sounds like the conversion of two generations into years: 'Sixty years after the capture of Ilion the present-day Boeotians were driven out of Arne by the Thessalians. . . .' Since the historian goes on to mention a subsequent period of twenty years, it may be that he is using some other form of calculation, but the 'capture of Ilion' is the fixed point. Within the many interrelated cycles of myth, the Greeks attained a remarkable degree of consistency from the generation before the Trojan War, in co-ordinating fathers, sons and grandsons of the different cycles, though some problems defied them. A good deal was no doubt contrived by later scholars, but there is no reason to reject everything on that account.

Apart from the earlier expedition against Troy, there were also expeditions against other cities. The woeful tale of Oedipus, which was the end-episode of an early cycle relating to Thebes, gave rise to the expedition of the Seven against Thebes, which brought together heroes of the generation before Troy, Adrastos, King of Argos, and his associates, including Tydeus, an exile from western Greece. Their failure to capture Thebes was remedied in the next generation by their sons, the Epigonoi, among whom was Diomedes, Tydeus' son, who went to Troy as leader of the Argives. The west, from which direction Tydeus came, was the scene of another famous enterprise, the hunt of the Kalydonian boar. Yet another expedition which was placed before the Trojan War was the voyage of the Argonauts in quest of the Golden Fleece, though the *real* circumstances which gave it its detail and direction certainly derived from a period long after.

Many other adventures had to be fitted in, like those of Amphitryon, the putative father of Herakles, and the adventures of the great hero himself, some of which are mentioned in the *Iliad*, when the garrulous old Nestor tells of Herakles' wars with Nestor's father Neleus and his own brothers. Neleus, who came from Thessaly to the western Peloponnese, was an example of another type of story, of the heroic migrant, whose descent was sometimes from a god by a mortal woman, a story which concealed his obscure origins. Another adventurer of the same sort was Pelops the Phrygian, associated like his father Tantalos with Asia Minor, coming to the Peloponnese to win a wife in a folk-tale contest. He established, so it was believed, a Pelopid dynasty at Mycenae. The story represents this dynasty as the successor to another, the Perseid dynasty of Eurystheus, a rival of Herakles.

Thus the greatest Bronze Age centre, Mycenae itself, is involved in tales of dynastic succession and strife, as the grim story of the curse of Pelops and the sins of the house of Atreus suggest. Herakles is linked with the Argolid as baron of Tiryns, and with Eurystheus, who is his taskmaster in the Labours, and afterwards drives out his children, the Herakleidai. Thucydides tells the story in his account of the history of the early Greeks. In a short passage the historian has contrived to pack in a great deal of early Greek folk tale and saga right from the birth of Herakles, favoured of Zeus and Athena, and Eurystheus, favoured of Hera, onwards. Like much of Thucydides' account of the early period of Greece, it is clearer in general principle than in particular detail. Much is probably derived from intellectual argument rather than from traditional information. Given the story of the arrival of Pelops, and his establishment in power, this would plausibly happen to one coming with resources to a poor country, as the historian suggests. Thucydides is concerned to explain such a story as rationally as possible, and modern scholars have to do the same. It would be unwise to fit this concept in detail into the archaeological record, but it does suggest a suitable picture of dynastic strife and change, which may have ended in the exiled Heraclids bringing barbarian aid into Mycenaean Greece, and in the end overthrowing its Bronze Age culture. It also suggests relations between Asia Minor and Greece, as with the story of Bellerophon, who is sent from Argos to Lykia in south-western Asia Minor in the second generation before the siege of Troy, in which his grandson Glaukos takes part.

Likewise the other stories present a picture of strife and movement and adventure which is plausible enough. The characters in them are centred on specific sites: the Seven and the Epigonoi at Thebes; Herakles, not only at Tiryns and Mycenae, but in some of his adventures at the Pylos of Neleus and Nestor in the western Peloponnese; the stories of Pelops and Atreus and their family at Mycenae or Argos; the story of the Kalydonian boar at Kalydon in Aetolia; the Argonauts at Iolkos in south-eastern Thessaly. If we add Theseus and his exploits, centred, in part at any rate, on Athens, it will be seen that each coincides with an important centre (archaeologically) of Mycenaean culture. As yet no centre is known in Aetolia to match the cycle of Kalydon, but one may yet be found – Pylos after all remained undiscovered until recently. There is no palace site in Lakonia either, to supply a residence for Menelaos and Helen, but there may be one still undiscovered somewhere in the vicinity of the Vapheio tomb, which produced the splendid Minoan gold cups. The position of Ithaka is also obscure. Odysseus is leader in the *Iliad* of the Kephallenians. It is not clear that modern Thiaki is ancient Ithaka, and while the cult of Odysseus in the cave at Polis Bay is obviously ancient and important, there is no trace of a palace, apart from the ambiguous remains at a site called Tris Langadas.

There is, however, a sufficient amount of coincidence between saga and Mycenaean remains to justify some hard thoughts about the reality of the saga stories and the possible historicity of their heroes. To match the great quantity of minor and not so minor legend there is the increasingly well-filled map of minor Mycenaean sites detected by careful surveys, which show the highly developed and populous state of Mycenaean Greece, and the existence of something like princedoms and baronies of varying magnitude. A picture of them is given in that curious document already mentioned, the Catalogue of the Greek Ships and their captains who went to Troy. It is not the same as a catalogue of Classical Greek states. It begins, oddly, with Boeotia and ranges over an area which does not include southern Italy or Sicily or anything of the mainland coast of Asia Minor, despite evidence of Mycenaean connections with these regions, and the subsequent association of the epic with Ionia. Miletos is non-Greek and on the Trojan side. The vindicators of Menelaos' honour come from the Ionian Islands, from central Greece up to and including southern Thessaly and Euboea, from the Peloponnese, from Crete (of mixed race), from Rhodes and from some other islands of the Dodecanese. Many of the places named were unimportant in Classical times. Even though this document (which some believe to have survived from Mycenaean times) has a strongly Boeotian character, and details an expedition which sailed from Aulis, Agamemnon is nevertheless its leader. It is thus tempting to speak of a Mycenaean confederation, and even to envisage some kind of feudal organization. Agamemnon appears as the leader of a set of sometimes recalcitrant chieftains, holding his position because his forces are greatest. 'He stood out,' says the Catalogue, 'among all the heroes because he was best, and led by far the most people.'[7] However much, it must be said, the organization which seems to emerge from the Linear B tablets, with the *wanax*, the *lawagetas* and the rest, *does* sound like some kind of feudal system within a state (and, incidentally, very different from the Homeric picture), it is perhaps best to avoid using terms like 'feudal' and 'empire' for the system pictured in the *Iliad* or suggested by the Hittite records. Even so, Agamemnon not only provides ships for the Arcadians but offers Achilles towns not in his personal kingdom as a peace offering.

There is one more thing. It will be seen that a temptation to take serious account of the Greek mythographers' succession of generations is difficult to resist, at any rate for the post-Trojan War period. It will be well, therefore, to point out that these chronological constructions and equations are not always convincing, as the fairly central theme of the Heraclids shows. Eurystheus, the favoured of Hera and taskmaster of Herakles, expelled Herakles' children from the Peloponnese after their father's death, and pursued them to Athens, where they were welcomed by Demophon, son of Theseus. Theseus himself was of the pre-Trojan

45

War period, but sufficiently near to it to carry off Helen when she was a child, and to be expelled in consequence by the Dioskouroi, her brothers, when they came to rescue her. This was one version of the story of how Theseus lost his throne and was replaced by Menestheus, who led the Athenian contingent to Troy and was given, perhaps, too big a notice in the Catalogue of the Ships. But Demophon succeeded Menestheus: so if he welcomed the Heraclids and defeated and slew Eurystheus, as the story said, this must have been after the Trojan War, and if the ill-fated Hyllos and the other Heraclids first attempted to return three years after their expulsion, this must have been after it too. But Eurystheus, who was slain in Attica, was replaced in his kingdom by Atreus; and this would make Atreus post-Trojan War, a war in which his son Agamemnon commanded!

In other words, the sequence will not work, however many adjustments may be made. The key, of course, is Athens. Euripides wrote a play called the *Heraclidae, The Children of Heracles*, in which Demophon figured as a champion of the oppressed. He also wrote another play, the *Supplices*, in which Theseus, the father of Demophon and champion of 'democracy', supported the suppliant Argive women, the bodies of whose husbands lay unburied before Thebes after the expedition of the Seven. In another play (*Iphigenia at Aulis*) Euripides gives the son of Theseus, not Menestheus, as the leader of the Athenians at Troy. In other words, tradition could be made to serve special purposes. Athens must appear as the champion of the oppressed and be linked to great events of earlier Greece, even if this did do violence to chronology. But take the interventions of Athens away, and there is no serious flaw in this chronicle of feuds round Mycenae.

With regard to material remains it is not difficult to see in the *megara* at Mycenae, Tiryns and Pylos the sort of great hall where the suitors foregathered in the tale of the *Odyssey*, and even the hall of Alkinoos in fairy-tale Phaiakia, to which his daughter Nausikaa directs Odysseus.

. . . go up to the city of the Phaiakians, and ask for the house of my father Alkinoos, high of heart. It is easily known, and a young child could be thy guide, for in nowise like it are builded the houses of the Phaiakians, so goodly is the palace of the hero Alkinoos, but when thou art within the shadow of the halls and the court, pass quickly through the great chamber [*megaron*], till thou comest to my mother, who sits at the hearth in the light of the fire, weaving yarn of sea-purple stain, a wonder to behold. Her chair is propped against a pillar, and her maidens sit behind her. And there my father's throne stands close to hers, whereon he sits and drinks his wine, like an immortal.[8]

The mixture of the sexes implied in this passage is perhaps more characteristic of later Ionia than of Mycenaean Greece, and *megara* no doubt survived in primitive Ionia, but for the rest this description would fit the Mycenaean *megara*, especially that at Pylos, with the place in it for the ruler's seat. The creators of the *Odyssey* dimly knew of splendid heroic palaces which had at one time existed, and gave such a building to Menelaos at Sparta. In this palace went on that splendid life of feasting and enjoyment appropriate to the heroes.

Phaiakia was a sort of fairyland, and the Phaiakians were especially favoured of Zeus. In consequence the palace of Alkinoos was particularly splendid. King Alkinoos there kept state not inferior to that of the gods on Olympos, for whom Hephaistos also deployed his skill. It would not be possible to parallel all the details given in the epic. The surviving remains afford no such walls of bronze or statues of gold and silver, and some of the phrases are clearly stereotypes of the oral epic. There is the memory, however, of a former joyous and opulent life, contrasting in many respects with contemporary conditions when the poem took form, but incorporating some details of Dark Age Greek society. It has also been suggested that details did come down, in popular memory or oral poetry, of the material background and equipment of the Mycenaean Age. A close enough parallel, it has been said, for the house of Odysseus in the *Odyssey*, can be found in the 'House of Columns' at Mycenae. There is the tower-shield on an inlaid shaft grave dagger paralleled by that given to Ajax in the *Iliad*. The boar's-tusk helmet and even the Mycenaean bathtub are known from material remains and the epic. And if there were memories, there were also the survivals of actual objects from the Late Bronze Age. That Bronze Age burials were found later is clear from the story of the discovery of the bones of Theseus on the island of Skyros and their conveyance back to Athens, and of the recovery of the bones of Orestes from Tegea. Survival of objects from a distant past is basic to Herodotus' story of what he saw in the temple of Apollo Ismenias at Thebes, or at any rate the *belief* that such *could* survive. Herodotus thus describes a series of tripods:

I myself saw Kadmeian [Cadmean] characters engraved on some tripods in the temple of Apollo Ismenias in Boiotian Thebes, most of them [the *characters*] shaped like the Ionian. One of the tripods has the inscription following:
  'Amphitryon set me up, coming from the far Teleboians.'
This would be of about the age of Laios, the son of Labdakos, the son of Polydoros, the son of Kadmos. Another of the tripods has this legend in the hexameter measure:
  'I to far-darting Phoibos was offered by Skaios the boxer, when he had won at the games – a wondrous beautiful offering.'
This might be Skaios the son of Hippokoon; and the tripod if dedicated by him, and not by another of the same name, would belong to the time of Oidipous, son of Laios. The third tripod has also an inscription in hexameters which runs thus:
  'King Laodamas gave this tripod to far-seeing Phoibos, when he was set on the throne – a wondrous beautiful offering.'
It was in the reign of this Laodamas, the son of Eteokles, that the Kadmeians were driven by the Argives out of their country, and found a shelter with the Encheleans.[9]

The cynic might readily say that if Herodotus could believe all this he could believe anything. But it is essentially the same problem that we have with folk memory in general – when there is no corroborative evidence, how do we rate its credibility? It is important to bear this dilemma in mind, but something of value can be derived from such documents and their ancient interpretation. There is no reason to believe that the objects Herodotus saw or the inscriptions they bore were actually from the fourteenth or thirteenth centuries BC. Cadmean letters were, as Herodotus' comparison with Ionian shows, archaic Greek not Linear B signs, though the term 'Cadmean' is also used in connection with Bronze Age Greece. The tripods were probably of the eighth-century Greek type, and even if the inscriptions might well be forgeries, they might *possibly* belong to the seventh or even the eighth century BC and indicate (as does Herodotus' comment) an interest in the remote past, in genealogies, and in movements and displacements of people, individual persons (under the guise of the expulsion of a hero for blood guilt) and communities as well. So here Amphitryon, husband of Alkmene and putative father of Herakles, goes from Tiryns to Thebes in Boeotia. The Cadmean expulsion refers to the story of the departure of Kadmos and Harmonia from Thebes to Illyria, where their tombs were shown – a symbol of those movements which the Greeks were convinced took place for some generations on either side of the Trojan War. These movements were also the vehicle of cultural diffusion. The period of these tripods coincided with the rise of the written epic, when interest in the heroic past was strong (as is demonstrated by the appearance of hero cults). Tradition claimed that the bodies of those who attacked Thebes with Polyneikes (five of the Seven) were buried at Eleusis after their recovery from Thebes by Theseus at the instance of Adrastos; and recent excavation at Eleusis has revealed the presence of early *seventh-century* graves; *not*, it is to be hoped, ones surviving from the Bronze Age.

While it is true that there are some traces of cult observances associated with Bronze Age *tholoi*, it is important to note that when a cult of Agamemnon came into being at Mycenae it was at this same period of the rise of the written epic, though it was *not* located in the town or on the site of a grave circle or at the great *tholoi*, but some distance away near the modern road down to the plain. In consequence a well-known passage of the second century AD guide-book writer Pausanias should be ascribed to Roman antiquarianism rather than to folk memory, however happily it seems to fit with the discovery of the grave circles. He says:

Parts of the circuit wall are still left, including the gate, which is surmounted by lions. These also are said to be the work of the Kyklopes, who made the walls of Tiryns for Proitos. Among the ruins of Mykenai is a conduit called Perseia, and there are underground buildings of Atreus and his children, where their treasures were kept. There is a grave of Atreus, and graves of all those who on their return from Ilion with Agamemnon were murdered by Aigisthos after a banquet which he gave them. The tomb of Kassandra is disputed: the Lacedaimonians of Amyklai claim it is at Amyklai. Another tomb is that of Agamemnon; another is that of Teledamos and Pelops. The two last are said to have been twin children of Kassandra who were murdered by Aigisthos in their infancy after he had murdered their parents . . . But Klytaimnestra and Aigisthos were buried at a little distance from the wall; for they were deemed unworthy to be buried within the walls, where Agamemnon himself and those who had been murdered with him were laid.[10]

The reader of Pausanias becomes painfully aware that Greece was full of well-authenticated monuments of the Heroic Age. The Roman tourist wanted them; the Greek guide would produce them. That ancient grave monuments *were* discovered is certain, but the allotment of famous names is quite another matter. In the passage mentioned we know that Pausanias is referring to the *tholoi* and the great walls and the Lion Gate. He could hardly be referring to the grave circles, which had not yet been discovered. If the original grave-markers survived it is hard to explain why the burials had not been plundered, and there are very human reasons why it should be thought that the righteous Agamemnon deserved to be buried inside the walls, and his murderers outside. In any case the earliest literary tradition, existing in the *Odyssey*, makes no references to Klytaimnestra, who appears for the first time in the Aeschylean tradition. The passage is thus a good illustration of the discretion which has to be used in matching up the material remains and the heroic tradition. But something survives to stimulate and puzzle the modern scholar.

The later Greeks, and the Romans, did believe that written records might come down from the Heroic Age and the siege of Troy. Hence the story of how the account of the Trojan War was written by Diktys of Crete, who went to Troy with Idomeneus. This account, it was said, written on lime wood or on paper made from lime bark, was found when the tomb of Diktys was burst open by an earthquake. The account was written in Phoenician characters. The earthquake took place in the reign of Nero, and he commissioned experts to interpret the record, who discovered it to be the work of Diktys, on the Trojan War. It must be wondered if this was not a find of Linear A or Linear B tablets converted to bogus historical purposes! The characters, however, were Phoenician and therefore different, it may be concluded, from 'Cadmean'.

Pausanias, in the passage on Mycenae, refers to the returning home or *nostos* of Agamemnon. After the theme of the Trojan War, the Greeks were greatly concerned with the *nostoi* or 'returnings home of the heroes'. Some, indeed, did not return, including the greatest, Achilles, who was slain at Troy; and there was that most tragic figure, the Greater Ajax, who committed suicide. Some perished at sea, like the Lesser Ajax, who died for his impiety. Others got home only to be murdered by usurpers, as Agamemnon was. Or seeking to escape this fate and their unfaithful wives, others set out again. Menelaos, after some wanderings, reached home with Helen (or recovered her in his wanderings) and lived happily thereafter, as Telemachos found when looking for his father. In the same poem old man Nestor is back in Pylos after an uneventful voyage. In contrast Odysseus, who wandered for ten years, returned to deal with his wife's suitors, and then set out again.

It is clear that these traditions represent a considerable elaboration, some of it wholly artificial, intended to explain the later establishment of colonial cities and provide them with founders. But there is still a core of tradition that echoes the disorder and dispersal which would follow a great expedition and the disintegration of a civilization. It seems reasonable, despite all the garbled chronology and later accretions, to relate it to what is known from archaeology and the Egyptian records.

Following on the returns (or failure to return), the Greeks believed that another series of events took place. There is a prosaic and factual-sounding account in the Athenian historian Thucydides in which he mentions the *nostoi*:

Even after the Trojan War Hellas was still engaged in removing and settling, and thus could not attain to the quiet which must precede growth. The late return of the Hellenes from Ilion caused many revolutions, and factions ensued almost everywhere; and it was the citizens thus driven into exile who founded the cities. Sixty years after the capture of Ilion the modern Boeotians were driven out of Arne by the Thessalians, and settled in the present Boeotia, the former Kadmeis; though there was a division of them there before, some of whom joined the expedition to Ilion. Twenty years later the Dorians and the Heraclids became masters of the Peloponnese; so that much had to be done and many years had to elapse before Hellas could attain to a durable tranquillity undisturbed by removals.[11]

This, the Greeks believed, was the Return of the Herakleidai, the Children of Herakles, to recover their lost heritage at something like the fifth attempt. They led the invasion of a new Greek element, the Dorians, to disrupt a Greece already unsettled but reorganized, and after Agamemnon's death, by his son Orestes, as Pausanias related: '... Orestes, son of Agamemnon, made himself master of Argos. For he dwelt near; and, besides the kingdom he inherited from his fathers, he had added a large part of Arcadia to his domains, and had succeeded to the kingship of Sparta.'[12] Here an effort is clearly being made to reconcile the Bronze Age importance of Mycenae with the Iron Age prominence of Argos, and to suggest the continuance of the wide domains of Agamemnon. Pausanias continues:

When Orestes died, his son Tisamenos succeeded him. . . . It was in the reign of this Tisamenos that the Heraclids returned to the Peloponnese. Their names were Temenos and Kresphontes, sons of Aristomachos: the third brother Aristodemos was dead, but his children came with their uncles. In my opinion their claim to Argos and the kingdom of Argos was perfectly just: for whereas Tisamenos was descended from Pelops, the Heraclids were descendants of Perseus. They declared that Tyndareos had been driven out by Hippokoon, but that Herakles slew Hippokoon and his children, and handed over the country in trust to Tyndareos. They told the same story about Messenia, how that it also had been given in trust to Nestor by Herakles, after he had captured Pylos. So they drove Tisamenos out of Lacedaemon and Argos, and expelled the descendants of Nestor from Messenia. These descendants of Nestor were, first, Alkmaion, son of Sillos, son of Thrasymedes; second, Peisistratos, son of Peisistratos; and, third, the sons of Paion, son of Antilochos. With them was also expelled Melanthos, son of Andropompos, son of Boros, son of Penthilos, son of Periklymenos. Tisamenos went with his army and his children to the country which is now called Achaia. Where Peisistratos went, I know not; but all the rest of the Neleids went to Athens, where they give their names to the house of the Paeonids and the house of the Alkmaeonids. Melanthos even came to the throne, from which he had driven Thymoites, son of Oxyntes, the last Athenian king of the house of Theseus.

This passage contains a rich store of links between the leading states of Archaic and Classical Greece, the claims of great Athenian families to heroic ancestors, links through the Neleids of Athens with the founders and ruling families of Asia Minor states, and the basis of Argive claims to leadership in the Peloponnese.

The disturbances which are here incorporated in saga as the Return of the Heraclids and the Dorian invasion, a great period of transition in the early history of Greece, were once connected by scholars with the destruction at the end of the thirteenth century. Few would now accept this view of the idea of an 'invasion' as the Greeks saw it. There is little evidence of incomers; hence the more acceptable theory of a raid or raids which brought destruction and temporary dislocation. Incomers there were, but they must have come later, and their arrival belongs among the events of the early Iron Age, which will be taken up in the next chapter.

# CHAPTER 4

# OBSCURITY AND RECOVERY

The glories of Bronze Age Greece left their mark, even if dim and distorted, in the minds of later men. The poet Hesiod, at the beginning of the seventh century, in his *Works and Days*, tells of the races of men, and in the series, from gold to iron (which, as a concept, may have been derived from the Orient), he places fourth a generation 'which was nobler and more righteous, a god-like race of hero men . . . the race before our own'.[1] These were the men who were the heroes of the Late Bronze Age saga, of a period which Hesiod contrasted with his own, of which he says: 'For now truly there is a race of Iron, and men shall never rest from labour and sorrow by day and from wasting by night.'[2] The violence and confusion of the Late Bronze Age are also echoed in the passage of Hesiod in which he mentions two episodes of saga, the expedition of the Seven against Thebes, and the very core and centre of Greek heroic myth, the expedition to Troy (see Chapter 3). Somehow the remembrance of disturbances, migrations and dynastic strife came down to Hesiod's day, helped and embellished, no doubt, by the oral epic. There was clearly a difficulty felt in reconciling the violence with the 'nobler' aspect of the heroes. The events remembered or imagined formed ultimately a connected whole involving several generations before the central Trojan War, and the war itself, followed by the saga of the 'returnings home of the heroes' (the *nostoi*) or their dispersion to other lands. These themes of Greek saga have been considered in Chapter 3. The sequel, which was in Greek legend the dividing line between the heroic past and the beginnings of the unheroic present of the Greeks, was formed by the return of the Herakleidai, the coming of the Dorians and the Ionian migration to Asia Minor, three descriptions of events which require a great deal of qualificatory comment.

The archaeological dividing line, as far as one can be determined, is, first, the destruction of Mycenaean centres somewhere round the end of the thirteenth century BC. This was the initial severe blow to the Bronze Age civilization of Greece (see Chapter 3 above), and ushered in a period of transition characterized by some recovery after the first disaster, followed by more destruction leading to the preliminaries of the Iron Age. No period of Greek history (assuming 'Greek' is rightly used here and earlier) presents more problems to the archaeologist and historian. The story of the return of the Herakleidai and the Dorian invasion was one of profound importance for the future ideas of the Greeks, whether or not the reality matched the belief, since it was linked with the concept of the division between 'Dorians' and the 'Ionians' or non-Dorians of the Classical period. There is hardly a sector of Greek life into which this distinction did not eventually penetrate.

In such a concept, in some measure based on dialect and partly political, it is not surprising that myth-making was summoned to the aid of history to explain and enlarge the differences, and to carry them back to the very beginnings of the post-Mycenaean period. Greeks, it was believed, were present in Greece in the 'Heroic Age'; in fact their presence was essential to such an idea. In the Homeric picture of the Heroic Age Greece is restricted on the west and north, covering much the same areas as that indicated by Bronze Age archaeology. Within this region dwelt Greeks distinguished by the name of the city they inhabited, or called (in the epic, and subsequently on occasion) 'Achaioi' or 'Argeioi'; the first name arises from a remembrance of the heroic importance of Phthiotic Achaea in Thessaly, or perhaps of Peloponnesian Achaea in the migration period, when tradition claimed that it played a part (as source and recipient) in the movements of displaced people; the second from a combination of the legendary (heroic) importance of Argolis and the later (eighth-century) distinction of Argos. On occasions there are other ethnic terms, such as Cadmeans, and the names of peoples somehow conceived as alien and more 'primitive' who were supposed to be present in early Greece, as for example the Pelasgoi and the Leleges, the latter also associated with the Carians and Asia Minor. Most of these ideas must have had some root in fact, even if they were distorted by time and embellishment, and it is likely that a memory survived of remnants of pre-Greek peoples.

Immediately on the borders of this epic world were other dimly conceived peoples in whom the Greeks of the period of formation of the epic took a certain interest from a distance. They are to be seen in the *Odyssey* in the references to the mainland barbarians over against the island of Odysseus (whichever island Ithaka was); and the Homeric references to the oracle of Zeus at Dodona in Epeiros, and to the Selloi as priests of the oracle, overlap into this outside area. The legend of the Dorians in its various ramifications necessitated placing them part in and part out of the area of 'heroic' Greece: they were mainly outside, but the

*Iliad* put Dorians in Crete and in the Dodecanese at the time of the Trojan War (influenced by various beliefs and purposes to be considered later), and Thucydides says of them: '. . . there was a division of them there before [i.e. before the preliminaries of the 'Dorian invasion' proper], some of whom joined the expedition to Ilion.'[3] The later Greeks of various periods drew a complicated picture of the movements of the Dorians. In a remote period, they claimed, the tribes who 'returned' as the Dorians led by the descendants of Herakles (the Herakleidai), were an element who *had* been within the bounds of 'heroic' (or 'epic') Greece, but had been pushed northwards into Thessaly by the 'Cadmeans', the Bronze Age Greeks (in modern terms) of central Greece. They then crossed over the Pindos, the mountain backbone of central Greece, to Epeiros, the remote and backward region of the west. At this time, it was believed, these tribes were called Makednoi. In due course they burst out of these backlands into the 'Achaean' or 'epic' world, led by a clan which had been driven out of this 'heroic' world by reason of dynastic struggles. They had made a number of attempts at return, and had at last succeeded, at a date related to the Trojan War, which the later Greeks worked out with some accuracy; and this 'return' they also related to the events and heroic personalities of the three generations after the return from Troy. It is possible to conceive of the return of the Herakleidai as something like the action of some banished noble or expelled ruler of the Roman or Byzantine periods, leading a tribe of barbarians against the civilized world.

It is tolerably clear that the Herakleidai were connected in the legend, through Hyllos, son of Herakles, with the Hylleis, one of the tribal divisions of the invaders. Later they were thought of as an élite, and thus distinct from a mixed horde indicated by the second tribal name, the Pamphyloi ('of mixed race'). The significance of the third tribal name, Dymanes, is obscure. The legend therefore accepted the idea of a mixture of tribes. The story that they were pushed north at an early stage, like the exile of the Herakleidai, was a necessary part of the tradition that the Dorians and their leaders were Greeks, like the Achaioi with whom they ultimately came into contact, or at least spoke Greek of a sort.

It is to be noted that for various reasons the Greeks were concerned with the incoming of *an* element of the Greeks, for political reasons, as pointed out already, and for reasons of dialect shortly to be discussed. They were not concerned with the appearance of the *original* Greeks. They avoided the problem, making Hellen the eponym of the Hellenes, and Doros, Aiolos and Ion, variously related to him, and Achaios, the eponyms in their turn of the main branches of the Greek race divided by dialect: Dorian, Aeolian, Ionian and Achaean. And, of course, the Athenians claimed autochthony, that they had always been in Attica; in effect, too, the same thing was suggested of the Arcadians. They thus avoided one of the main preoccupations of modern scholars, the date and manner of the initial entry of the Greek-speakers, discussed above in Chapter 3. On the other hand they did concern themselves with a subsidiary issue, the question of incomers at the end of their 'heroic' age, to become eventually the Dorians. Modern scholars have endeavoured to explain certain phenomena by a suggestion that some Greek-speakers remained behind in the northern area of the southern Balkans, to emerge thence at or after the end of the Bronze Age and to add a new element to the composition of the Greeks. The later Greeks thought otherwise and postulated an expulsion and a return, as outlined already. Both ideas seek to explain the development of a divergent dialect or dialects, and accept the principal that the Dorians were *Greeks*. The basic difference of opinion concerns the way the process of incoming took place.

The tradition took the future Dorians north and west, and brought them back from the north-west. Those who evolved the tradition were influenced in their ideas by the Classical pattern of Greek dialects and their interrelations, and by the fact that certain regions of Greece were regarded as being wholly 'Dorized' (though this was something not easy to define accurately), some partly and some not at all. There was also the question of the relationships between the dialects of the Aegean Islands and of western Asia Minor and those of Greece proper. Similar considerations of dialect also influenced the narrative in relation to the route they took into Greece and the way they occupied it. A main factor in determining the traditional route was the location of possible crossing-places of the Pindos range (accepting a land route) and of the Gulf of Corinth (involving ships). In central Greece there was a tiny region on the borders of Phokis called Doris. How it got its name is unknown, but the Spartans, as the Dorians *par excellence*, came to regard it as their 'mother state'. There was also a conviction that, though the obvious way into the Peloponnese was by way of the Isthmus of Corinth, the invaders did not go that way: indeed they were advised against it by their guide, one Oxylos, an Aetolian, grandson of Thoas, related through his mother to the Heraclids. So they were made to cross the Gulf of Corinth by sea. It happened that there was a place on its northern shore called Naupaktos ('where the ships are put together'), and, whatever the source of the name, it was a good departure-point for the legendary crossing. Led by Oxylos they crossed to the southern shore, and the route they took thence and their ultimate areas of settlement (marked by dialect, institutions and traditions) conditioned other elements of the story. The later Greeks also knew that when peoples move they may push others before them.

Such matters influenced the story of the 'Dorian invasion'. It must be stressed here again that 'Dorian' is not a wholly satisfactory term of description for what is in effect a very complicated matter of dialects, institutions and customs varying very much in detail and involving Greek

55

states ranging from corrupt and mercantile Corinth to austere and warlike Sparta, and Sparta's greatest enemy, Argos.

Passing reference has already been made to a celebrated passage of Thucydides on this 'invasion', which shows the combination of tradition with the penetrating intellect of a great historian unique in antiquity. In it Thucydides refers in succession to the dispersion after the Trojan War and the city-foundations which traditionally ensued, to the 'Dorian invasion' and its forerunners, to the 'Ionian migration' and to one sphere of Greek colonization, but *not* wholly Peloponnesian or Dorian (a warning that Thucydides' generalizations can show distortion).

Here it is necessary to consider more closely a factor which strongly influenced the tradition, as is apparent from Thucydides' reference to Boeotians and Thessalians in connection with the Dorian invasion: the question of dialect differences. The study of the local divisions of the Greek language is made difficult first by the limited amount of material available in the case of many dialects, and second by the relatively late date of the bulk of it. Written texts can go back only to the middle of the eighth century approximately, the date of the first surviving use of the Greek alphabet. A considerable gap of time separates this from the date of the Linear B tablets and a much earlier form of Greek. Despite the inadequacy of the syllabary to render the language, it is possible to conclude that all Linear B tablets known up to the present employ a similar dialect, which has to be related to the later forms. The later dialects (of the Archaic and Classical periods) can be classified and philologically distinguished or related. Such a classification was made in antiquity: a threefold division, of Dorian, Aeolian and Ionian, to which were made to correspond the eponyms Doros, Aeolos and Ion. It was also held that the location of some dialect-speakers differed in early antiquity from that obtaining later. Thus Herodotus claimed that originally there were Ionians in Achaea (the southern coast of the Gulf of Corinth) and also in Boeotia; at the time of the first attempt of the Herakleidai to return under Hyllos it was Achaeans and *Ionians* who marched out against them. Pausanias asserts that before the return of the Herakleidai the Argives spoke the same dialect as the Athenians. In general it is not irrelevant to point out that Herodotus uses the term 'Iones' diversely, for the inhabitants of Ionia, for those of Attic descent and those who celebrated the Apatouria festival, and, as the other passages show, for the pre-Dorian inhabitants of the Peloponnese. It has, indeed, been suggested that the Hebrew 'Yawan' and the other oriental versions of this name (from the early Greek form 'Iawones') relate not to the Ionians of western Asia Minor but to the earlier settlers of the southern coast and, it might be added, to the Greeks of Cyprus.

This confusion of terms was part of the larger problem that although the Greeks were vaguely conscious of prehistoric ethnic differences and, being members of individual city-states, were strongly conscious of differences of dialect, customs and social structures, the terminology available to express them was inadequate. There was also the complication of reconciling divergent and contradictory claims made by Greek states. These problems are nowhere better illustrated than by a passage of Herodotus on Athens, where he attempts to list, but not to explain, the diverse names of the Athenians, based on myth relating to the 'venerable ancestors', as they have been called, to the link, true or false, between Attica and Ionia, and to Athenian claims to autochthony. The task of reconciling diverse traditions was an unenviable one. It is illustrated in this passage of Herodotus by the reference to the Pelasgians. The Athenians are here identified with them; elsewhere they are a more primitive, alien and potentially hostile people. They illustrate that belief in the diversity of ethnic character and origins of those who formed the Greek amalgam. It is well illustrated by another passage of Herodotus, like the foregoing the more interesting because of its relatively early date before scholars of the fourth century BC and later had been at work. This is a complex passage referring (in terms of Greek belief) to the aboriginal Arcadians, as is clearly stated, and to the inhabitants of the disputed territory between Argos and Sparta called Ionians: another group of aboriginals, indicated as such by this specialized use of the term 'Ionian' to denote the pre-Dorian inhabitants of the area before they were assimilated by the Argives from the north and the Spartans from the south. The Achaeans in this passage were the subjects of Tisamenos, son of Orestes, displaced from the eastern Peloponnese and in turn displacing the original Achaeans to Attica. In modern parlance all these would be called Mycenaean Greeks. The same is true of the Aetolians, characterized by Herodotus as immigrants by reason of their dialect and the incoming or return of Oxylos with the Dorians.

This tolerably simple picture is complicated by the small pockets of other 'immigrants' whom Herodotus seems to regard as incomers at the same period. The Dryopians seem to have some connection with southern Thessaly and the region of Mount Oita (Dryopis). It has already been noted that the Spercheios Valley is a significant passage-way into east-central Greece. They were subsequently scattered in various widely separated areas, in the eastern and western Peloponnese and in Euboea; in the latter island they were recognized as being distinct from the other Euboeans. Legend connected their dispersion with the Dorians through Herakles in defiance of mythical chronology. The Paroreetai ('the mountain-side people') of this same passage appeared in Triphylia in the western Peloponnese, according to Herodotus, and are described by him elsewhere as 'Minyan' inhabitants from Lemnos. The term 'Minyan', through Minyas and the Minyai of Orchomenos in Boeotia and their opponent Herakles, goes back to the pre-Trojan War period in saga.

What is meant here is doubtful, but it is worth pointing out that in Greek belief there was a connection between the Tyrsenoi or Tyrrhenoi, the Etruscans of Italy, and Lemnos; and that the well-known odd Lemnian relief and inscription, and some curious Etruscan-looking figures found in Italian excavations on the island, give cause for thought. Among the Sea Peoples the Tursha have been connected with the Etruscans, through the name Tyrsenoi, and it is not too imaginative (if the Tursha–Tyrsenoi identification is correct) to think of pockets of Tursha settled in Lemnos and in Greece. However this may be, there was current the idea of distinct ethnic groups connected with the population movements of the Late Bronze Age, and matching the Carians, Leleges and Pelasgians of an earlier (?) period.

Modern scholars have classified the Greek dialects into two basic groups (in part regional): East Greek and West Greek. East Greek is divided into two main groups: Achaean (from the early ethnic term 'Achaioi', for Greeks in the epic) and Attic-Ionic. Achaean is subdivided into Aeolic and Arcado-Cypriot. West Greek comprises the Doric dialects and a subgroup called North-west Greek. Thessaly, Boeotia, the island of Lesbos and Aeolis in north-western Asia Minor were basically Aeolic-speaking, but West Thessalian and Boeotian are influenced by North-west Greek, and the Aeolic of Aeolis by the East Ionic of Ionia to the south. The dialects of Arcadia and Cyprus form the other subgroup of Achaean. It is agreed that the original basis of the two, before their separation in the Late Bronze Age movement of population from the Peloponnese to Cyprus, must go back at least to Late Bronze Age times. It may be noted here that tradition asserted early (post-Trojan War) settlement on the southern coast of Asia Minor also, and in fact Pamphylian shows some connection with Arcado-Cypriot. The Attic-Ionic group comprises Attic, the West Ionic of Euboea, the Central Ionic of the Aegean islands and the East Ionic of Ionia and the off-shore islands of Chios and Samos. Whatever the Athenians might assert, Attic is regarded as showing some influence of Doric. Doric covers most of the Peloponnese, excluding Elis and Arcadia, and includes Megara. In the Aegean the islands of Melos, Thera, Crete, Rhodes, Kos and the coast of Caria used Doric dialects, as did Phaselis on the coast of Lykia. The north-western subgroup comprised Aetolia, Phokis, Lokris and Elis. The spread of the various dialects to the Adriatic (Akarnania and Kerkyra), to the west and to other fringes of the Greek world was the result of the colonization process.

A theory formerly held, that the speakers of the Ionic and Achaean dialects came into Greece in successive waves, is no longer acceptable, despite the indications of incomers at the end of Early Helladic II and Early Helladic III. Also, as will be seen later, the idea of a 'wave' of Doric-speakers hardly fits the material evidence. The wave theory would imply the existence of differentiated dialects of Greek already formed *outside* the area at an early date. It has been pointed out that if this had been so the speakers of these dialects would probably have moved in divergent directions. In fact the Greek language was an amalgam of elements effected in the area consequently becoming 'Greece', and there the initial differentiation into East Greek and West Greek took place. It seems to have been philologically proved that ancient Arcadian and Aeolic (at the stage of the Greek language represented by Linear B) were related, but the relationship was not total. There is thus an indication of two prehistoric dialects. On the other hand Attic-Ionic can be shown to be a later development. The reference in Herodotus and Pausanias mentioned above (pp. 57–8) must relate to the Greek spoken before the Dorizing of the Peloponnese and the modification of Thessalian and Boeotian by North-west Greek.

It can now be seen on what geographical and dialectal bases the later Greeks elaborated the picture of the 'Dorian invasion'. It was conceived as a penetration by *land*, necessitating the crossing of the Pindos to central Greece, and then a movement south. Ships were necessary for the passage of the Gulf of Corinth at an early stage, and for the crossing of the Aegean to Crete, Rhodes and Kos, a movement which was placed *before* the Trojan War: an oddity in the story of the Dorians which does not appear to have worried Thucydides, and was unnecessary to explain the dialect picture. On the other hand it added to the prestige of the Dorians and later to that of the great Dorian state of Argos. The dialects of the Boeotians and western Thessalians had a tincture of North-west Greek, and therefore the Boeotians and Thessalians were conceived as being pushed out in front of the Dorians proper. In effect this phenomenon could be explained as the addition of a Dorian element to the pre-existing population.

The Dorians proper could not take the obvious route to the Peloponnese by way of the Isthmus of Corinth since the Thessalians and Boeotians were established across it. Because of the Thessalians, their forerunners, they could not descend into Thessaly by the route over the Pindos via modern Metsovo. There was a route further south in central Greece by way of Karpenision, past Mount Timphrestos, through the Spercheios Valley to Malis. The Boeotians, however, blocked their way south-eastwards; so they had to turn south through Doris and the valley of the River Mornos to the Gulf of Corinth, and westwards to take ship at Naupaktos to cross to Molykrion or Rhion. All this was indicated to the later Greeks by the observed facts of dialect and geography. It was observed also that the dialects of Aetolia and Elis were akin. So the story was elaborated that Oxylos guided the invaders, persuaded them to cross the Gulf of Corinth by sea and diverted them from the territory of Elis, which he coveted and obtained as a reward for himself. When the

Dorians had crossed the Gulf of Corinth the main attack, it was believed, was directed to the east and south of the Peloponnese, under the leadership of Temenos, to Argos, whence Tisamenos, the son of Orestes, was displaced into Achaea, displacing in turn 'Ionians' from Achaea into Attica – some of the refugees referred to by Thucydides in the passage mentioned above (p. 56). The second objective, under the leadership of Prokles and Eurysthenes, the sons of Aristodemos, was Lakonia. Another band, in the legend, went south-west to Triphylia and Messenia under Kresphontes. Some modern scholars have been disposed to reject this element of the 'invasion', and among the Greeks there was a conviction that the Dorizing process in this area was incomplete, or was never effected until much later by the Spartans in their eighth–seventh-century westward aggression. Relations with non-Dorian Arcadia were regarded as being strong; hence the story that Kresphontes was dethroned as 'a friend of the people', and that his sons were slain, except Aipytos, who was saved by his Arcadian grandfather Kypselos and was restored by the Arcadians and Heraclids from Sparta and Argos to his Messenian kingdom.

There was also a tradition that Corinth and Megara were not Dorized initially but later, and that Megara had been part of the kingdom of Attica. So the Dorians could not make for the eastern Peloponnese either by the Isthmus or by way of the coastal strip of Achaea. They had to cross Arcadia. Arcadia, however, was certainly not Dorized, as its dialect showed, and so a convenient marriage of the daughter of the Arcadian Kypselos to the son of Aristomachos facilitated the passage of the invaders.

Part of the later Attic propaganda was that Attica had been the base of displaced 'Ionians' (i.e. pre-Dorian Greeks), who from there made their way across the Aegean. They founded, it was claimed, the cities of Ionia, which shared some institutions with Attica, and claimed ancient rulers descended from the Neleid dynasty of Pylos in Messenia. This necessitated the story (already mentioned in Chapter 3) of the flight of Melanthos, grandson of Nestor, to Athens, being driven out by the Dorians. In Athens he replaced in the kingly office the descendant of Theseus, and repelled an attack on Attica which must have been thought of as an attack of Dorians from Boeotia. In the next generation Kodros, his son, repulsed another attack from the south at the cost of his life. Both stories served to confirm the claim of Athens to be untouched by the Dorians.

The whole account adopts the idea of an expedition, the last of a number attempted, but combines with it the admission that the process was spread over generations and was a piecemeal affair. Some elements are more palpably contrived than others, to support the pretensions of certain Greek states such as Athens, Argos and Sparta. It can in general be described as logically thought out. The process *could* have taken place in this way; the reality might well be another matter.

The arrival of 'Dorians' or any other incomers, however named, is difficult to establish from archaeological evidence of a clear and decisive sort. The material remains which might be relevant are restricted in amount and not easy to date with exactitude. It is clear from expert studies that the assessment of evidence, and especially issues of date, can be something of a subjective matter, affected by the degree of caution or the opposite natural to the writers concerned. Above all it is obvious that in Thessaly (and some areas to the south), in Macedonia, in the Balkans further north and in eastern Europe, a great deal more excavation needs to be done before the evidence will permit anything like firmly agreed conclusions. It is also apparent that eastern (eastern Mediterranean) synchronisms with Late Helladic III B and C allow some considerable variations of dating at crucial points, so that, in using the evidence of pottery, there is the problem of the degree of contemporaneity indicated for Late Helladic III A and III B, for Late Helladic III B and III C and for Late Helladic III C and Sub-Mycenaean, the latter term not now in favour as a chronological division. The historian must require the archaeologists to come to terms on these issues, which involve an important aspect of Late Bronze Age Greece – the decline of Mycenaean civilization and the beginnings of the transition to the 'Iron Age'.

An early stage in the study of the material evidence (or what seemed to be evidence) was strongly influenced by the Greek tradition to produce a simple picture of Dorian incomers, destroyers of the Bronze Age culture of Greece and heralds of the 'Iron Age', associated with iron weapons and tools and forming part of a movement of barbarians from the northern Balkans and the Danube. This was the general theory. There were held to be certain objects which were diagnostic of the Dorians' presence: long pins and violin-bow and arched fibulae or safety-pins appropriate to the simple woollen clothing of these incomers who dressed differently from the Mycenaeans. Also, at a time in modern scholarship when the Mycenaean pottery and the following geometrically decorated styles (Proto-Geometric and Geometric) were still imperfectly understood in the matter of date and development, the latter fabrics seemed to present a radical break with the former in the character of the decoration, and especially in its organization on the surface of the pottery, which also showed taut profiles contrasting with the preceding Mycenaean. Thus pins, fibulae and the geometric decoration of pottery were identified with the Dorians. The pottery decoration showed discipline and order, and was therefore appropriate to an ethnic group which produced the Spartans. Attempts, not very successful, were made to derive this linear decoration from the north.

61

It was recognized from the beginning that human remains ascribed to these incomers could not be identified; but this was to be expected, since the Dorians were by definition only retarded relations (speaking another dialect of Greek) of the Greeks already in Greece. In the north-west, at Dodona, the oracle centre of Zeus (mentioned in the Homeric epic) yielded numbers of bronze figurines not unlike those moulded or painted on Geometric pottery. It was felt for this and other reasons that there might be some Dorian connections with Zeus (a 'northern sky-god') and Dodona, and with Apollo, who was connected with the north through the Hyperborean maidens, who came to his island of Delos and were buried there. In Dorian Sparta Apollo took over the older pre-Dorian god Hyakinthos to become Apollo Hyakinthios. The whole made a neat and tidy pattern, but it has not stood the test of much increased, even if still inadequate, knowledge.

In matters of religion the decipherment of the Linear B tablets has given cause for thought, on the question of continuity in the case of the Olympian gods. In similar fashion a simple selection of pottery from the Athenian Kerameikos (the Potters' Quarter) will demonstrate that there is no complete break between Late Helladic III C (Sub-Mycenaean) and the following Proto-Geometric and Geometric pottery. The other supposed Dorian diagnostic objects also present difficulties. That long dress-pins were not particularly 'Dorian' is demonstrated by a story of Herodotus, telling of the ancient enmity of Athens and Aegina, and how the widows of the men who did not return from a military engagement surrounded the one survivor and stabbed him to death with their dress-pins. The gist of the story is that in fact the terms 'Dorian' and 'Ionian' in this context are artificial. This does not exclude the need to explain the appearance of these long pins where and when they do appear, if they are not forthcoming in earlier contexts.

In addition to these considerations the uneasy thought was always present, from the earliest stages of modern study, that Attica, traditionally untouched by Dorian influences, was the outstanding exponent of the Geometric style.

Cognizance must be taken of an increased amount of material forthcoming in recent years, and of the conclusions based on increasingly detailed study. It is sensible to look at the material and the conclusions based on it under three heads. The first is represented by certain clear evidence and undeniable deductions based on it. The second comprises evidence which is to some extent negative, so that conclusions may be undermined or reversed as new archaeological discoveries are made. The third is concerned largely with material objects of which the origins and affinities are always likely to be uncertain, and conclusions based on them are likely to be a matter of subjective judgement and hopeful conjecture.

Under the first head may be considered certain events involving

Mycenae and other centres, about which positive statements can be made, even if causes and dates are obscure. Something has been said already on this subject in Chapter 3. There is first the destruction seen at Mycenae, to be dated about the middle of the thirteenth century BC, and involving buildings, the 'houses', including the 'House of the Oil Merchant', outside the acropolis, but not, it is generally felt, involving the acropolis itself. This destruction, undoubtedly the result of hostile action, could have been caused by foreign attack, or by hostilities with another Mycenaean state, or by internal strife. What was destroyed was not restored. It is tempting to regard this event as serving a warning of what was to come, which prompted the ensuing improvement of fortifications and preparations against siege, seen not only at Mycenae but also at Tiryns, Athens and elsewhere, but not very obviously at Ano Englianos in the western Peloponnese. Such preparations, it may be added, did not necessarily envisage a single attack from a specific direction or by a specific enemy. Any indications of a single direction of attack are weak. It is better to suppose an apprehension of troubled times and of attack from any direction. The construction of a wall at the Isthmus of Corinth would seem to indicate an attack feared by land from the north, as did the wall erected in the same region in the sixth century AD; but the intention and the danger might be much more complex, as could be suggested by the action of the Peloponnesians in 480 BC in erecting such a wall in the face of land *and sea* attack by the Persians.

Then at the end of Late Helladic III B (in the late thirteenth or early twelfth century) destruction came to many Mycenaean centres, apparently at one time; but there could well have been several episodes within a limited number of years, though not distinguishable as such in the archaeological record. There is no indication of the attackers' origins. There is certainly no evidence that they stayed in Greece. If they did, their physical characteristics and their equipment must have been largely the same as that of those who represented the Mycenaean culture. *If* there was an oppressed element among the Mycenaean population, this element might have made common cause with the invaders, like some of the peasantry in the later Roman Empire. On an analogy drawn from the same period it is possible to suggest a destructive raid or several raids, which could come most suddenly and unexpectedly from the sea (a possibility not excluded by the isthmus wall), like the attack of the Herulians on Athens in AD 267. But it is unlikely that so many centres could have been destroyed in this fashion. In terms of direction, the suggestion of attacks coming from the west or south is to be rejected, though an attack by the Libyans cannot wholly be excluded. It also seems unlikely that they came from the east, since Lefkandi, in Euboea, the eastern coast of Attica (Perati) and the southern Aegean seem to have been unaffected, and retained communications with the eastern Mediterranean, unless it is assumed (as has been suggested) that this area was already dominated by the intruders. An attack by land from the north seems most favoured by the current historical theory, by way of the mainland, with which must be coupled the northern Aegean Sea. One effect of the attack was that some centres, such as Ano Englianos, never recovered. On the other hand Mycenae did, and the 'Granary' was constructed inside the Lion Gate, and pottery was manufactured, in the so-called Granary and Close Styles, which show that life went on and that some attempts were made to revive Mycenaean culture. It is to be supposed that this was done by a surviving native remnant.

A final destruction, which at Mycenae involved the Granary, came in about 1150 BC. It is agreed in connection with the earlier destruction (and it may well be true of the later one also) that there was a flight to peripheral areas of Greece, to Kephallenia and to Achaea, and further afield to Cyprus, where there is evidence of destruction in the early twelfth century, which may have been caused by these migrants in company with others. In any case it is believed that a dialect of Mycenaean Greek was carried to Cyprus to form one part of the later Arcado-Cypriot group. So much is generally agreed, but there is no evidence to connect 'Dorians' with these events.

Somewhat less well substantiated, because the supporting evidence in most cases is negative, is the decline in material culture apparent to an increasing degree as the second half of the twelfth century wears on. The same low cultural level characterizes the eleventh century. It seems also that population was reduced. The process could have been initiated by external attack and aggravated by disorder. Natural causes such as climatic changes and epidemics cannot be discounted. From the second half of the twelfth century settlements are very poorly represented, except in the case of Iolkos (Volos), where there are some substantial stone structures. Pottery for the most part appears to continue the Mycenaean tradition, which seems to indicate the continued existence of a Mycenaean element of population. There is also a limited amount of alien hand-made pottery, which could be taken to indicate an intrusive element. The replacement of inhumation by cremation, where this is apparent, may well have no significance, since the burial rite over a period shows relatively frequent changes later. On the other hand burials in slab-lined cist graves and in unlined graves cut in the subsoil become common (as a replacement of chamber-tomb burial), and such graves are represented in some numbers on Salamis and in the Kerameikos cemetery of Athens. Such cist graves can be paralleled in the north-west, in Epeiros, and may be the clearest indication of incomers in the period after c. 1150 BC, towards the end of the twelfth century and in the eleventh.

Weapons and small objects represent a third category of 'evidence', most difficult to assess. It is hard to know how to evaluate the occurrence of certain weapon types, swords and the like: how to explain the appearance of parallels elsewhere, the most important in the Urnfield culture of eastern and central Europe; and how to establish the mechanics of interchange between these areas and Greece. The same is true of the long dress-pins mentioned earlier, which *could* indicate the presence of incomers; but such pins could have *either* northern *or* eastern connections. Arched fibulae may show northern affinities or may be a development within Greece itself. There are also problems of dating.

Two things seem to be well established: first, there were no close links with the northern Balkans and the Urnfield culture, though the cemetery at Vergina seems to indicate that Macedonia did have such a contact; second, it is also apparent that Greece was impoverished in the twelfth and early eleventh centuries. Access to supplies of bronze or its constituents was cut off both in the north and in the east. The overwhelming preponderance of tools and weapons is of iron at a time when, in the Urnfield culture, bronze metallurgy was still in its heyday, and may have continued at a high level until the eighth century. It has therefore been concluded that iron-making did not come from the north, as was formerly thought. Its origins, it is now agreed, were in the east, but it seems likely that the lack of bronze occasioned the development of iron-working in the southern Balkan peninsula, perhaps in Macedonia, where, at Vardar-oftsa, there are indications of the industry. In general the latter part of Late Helladic III c (Sub-Mycenaean) and the period characterized by Proto-Geometric pottery (*c.* 1050 BC to *c.* 900 BC) were backward in terms of material culture. The elusive Dorians are not much in evidence: the cist graves are the best indication of possible incomers or of a reversion to the burial practice of the Middle Bronze. It is unfortunate for Athenian tradition that such graves appear in some numbers in Attica, which would seem to support the modern suggestion of a 'Doric' influence on the Attic dialect.

It is to be wondered whether archaeology will ever solve these problems. Yet the Doric-speakers *are* ultimately present in Greece, and the fact of their penetration by the routes suggested in Greek legend (or by something like them) must be accepted, though they need not have come in archaeologically detectable waves. If they were backward pastoralists, like the modern Vlachs, there is no reason why they should not have penetrated seasonally to more southern areas (though hardly as far as the Peloponnese) over a considerable period, and on occasions have taken to forceful aggression by reason of pressures on themselves from the north. This process could not have taken place to any great extent while strong states existed in Mycenaean Greece, but when these were shattered the possibilities of penetration were increased.

In this particular connection thought has recently been given to setting these events, relating to Greece, in a wider context involving the north and east. The first objective must be to identify the destroyers of the Mycenaean civilization. The period described above, of the building of fortifications in Greece, is also the period of the Land and Sea Raids, or the beginning of them. There are indications that famine may have played a part in these disturbances, and it is interesting to recall that Herodotus mentions a famine which occasioned the migration of the Tyrrhenians from Lydia to the west to settle in Italy, according to Lydian legend.

In this story of Herodotus allowance can be made for the garbling of a tradition concerning an event in the distant past. Otherwise here is an excellent example of a people set in motion by natural disaster, to match the marauding 'northerners' and 'Sea Peoples' appearing in the Egyptian records. The Ekwesh attacked Egypt with the Libyans in c. 1232 BC, and the record of Pharaoh Merneptah gives their names (here in modern and controversially vocalized form) as Ekwesh, Teresh or Tursha, Lukku, Sherden or Shardana, Sheklesh or Shakalsha. There are problems in the identification of the Ekwesh, and the Lukku, but scholars have been greatly tempted to identify the Tursha with the Tyrrhenians, the Shardana (who earlier appear as Egyptian mercenaries) as Sardinians, and the Sheklesh as Sicels. It is also tempting to connect the Tursha with the story of Herodotus above. Later there took place the great Land and Sea Raids of 1183 BC, which destroyed the Hittite Empire and brought turmoil and destruction to the eastern Mediterranean and threatened Egypt. These rovers (with their wives, children and possessions) were made up of the people called by the Egyptians Peleset, Tjekker, Sheklesh, Denyen and Weshesh. Most of them can be cautiously identified as tribes connected with Cyprus and the southern coast of Anatolia. The Peleset or Puleshti, coming originally from Anatolia and with some tincture of Mycenaean culture, settled in southern Palestine to become the Philistines of the Bible.

They were a mixed horde, 'People from all Lands', gathered by land and sea routes. There is no reason why Mycenaean Greece should not have been affected by the destruction they spread in the initial stages of their gathering. Mycenaean Greeks must also have joined them in their raids, just as they made their way to Cyprus, but there are difficulties in identifying them with the Ekwesh.

Given that the fall of Troy, which is not relevant to the present theme, and the destruction of Mycenaean Greek centres can be ascribed to these movements of the early twelfth century, there then follows the problem of accounting for a second destruction which put an end to the period of limited recovery at Mycenae marked by the construction of the Granary. There is also the question of Troy VII b, in which the appearance of 'knobbed ware' (*Bückelkeramik*) has commonly been taken to indicate an intrusive element of population, explained as the Phrygians, who were Indo-European-speakers and after a period of semi-nomadism formed the Phrygian state with its capital at Gordion. It has recently been doubted whether the feature giving the name to this pottery is really new; on the other hand the pottery of Troy VII *b* does show other details which connect it with Roumania and suggest the movement of a fresh element of population southwards. This may well have set others in motion, and among them a movement of Greek-speakers from the north-west who inflicted further and final damage on the remnants of Mycenaean civilization. This process would begin at the end of the twelfth century, corresponding closely enough with the traditional date for the coming of the Dorians, and continue later. There would follow, in the archaeological record from *c.* 1050 BC, the period characterized by Proto-Geometric pottery and its appearance in Asia Minor on the site of Old Smyrna, which again fits well enough with the traditional date of the Ionian city foundations.

A recent study has summed up the process from the archaeological standpoint, and placed it in a context of events covering a much wider area. There was a time of troubles beginning in the late thirteenth century BC, with many confusing shifts of population and raids, possibly caused originally by climatic changes, over-population and dearth, which destroyed the relative stability of the earlier thirteenth century BC in the eastern Mediterranean and in the regions to the north. Already in the thirteenth century there may have taken place the infiltration of 'northerners' as pastoralists, mercenaries and adventurers, introducing items of their equipment. In the first decades of the twelfth century there were attacks from various directions, 'quite possibly including a raid from as far as the middle Danube and the (equally important) return of the raiders, loaded with spoil and captive craftsmen'.[4] Some such theory is necessary to explain the relationship of weapon types from Greece and from eastern and central Europe. Apart from the movements of population, already mentioned, to the eastern Mediterranean, to settle in Cyprus and join the Sea Peoples, it is not unreasonable to place in this period other movements to Sicily, Sardinia and Italy, the Shardana perhaps to Sardinia, the Sheklesh to Sicily and the Tursha to Italy, even as the Peleset (Puleshti) settled in the eastern Mediterranean to become the Philistines. These are risky but justifiable conjectures. Further north new people came to Troy VII *b*. As for the incomers into the former Mycenaean area, it is suggested that:

A combination of factors, but chiefly . . . the refugee movement from the Aegean, provided the irritant that set the cist-burying inhabitants of Albania and Greek Epirus travelling south into the political vacuum left by the break-up of the Mycenaean order, or else settling permanently where formerly they were seasonal visitors. They may have been accompanied by some returning refugees (or their descendants), in whom we may see a 'Return of the Herakleidai'. Such men would have kept fresh the memory of that lost Mycenaean world of grandeur and prosperity.[5]

With the events which the Greeks interpreted as 'the Return of the Herakleidai' and the ensuing population displacement in Greece itself, they connected a movement to Asia Minor. It has already been seen, on the evidence of the *Iliad* followed by Thucydides, that there was a convenient belief in a pre-Trojan War settlement of Dorians in Crete and in Rhodes and some other islands of the Dodecanese. The problem here, already explored, lies in the definition of 'Dorian' in terms of dialect and institutions. It would not be possible clearly to disprove the assertion (what, in any case, in terms of serious history, as opposed to myth, would 'pre-Trojan War' mean?). On the basis of what has already been said on the Dorian problem the probability lies in the direction of much later political pretensions of Dorian states wishing to establish a participation in the Trojan War and in early overseas settlement. The idea is easier to explain than in the case of earlier links indicated in the heroic saga between Greece and Asia, such as the coming of Pelops from Phrygia and the going of Bellerophon to Lykia, where a propaganda intention is difficult to explain.

Another early movement *in* rather than *to* Asia Minor was associated with the Trojan War and its immediate sequel. The Greeks were concerned to explain the settlements on the southern coast of Anatolia, in Pamphylia and Cilicia, such as Aspendos and other settlements to the east. These, they believed, were of considerable antiquity, and they knew them to be of mixed Greek and native character, as was apparent from the use of the native languages of Lykia and Pamphylia (seen on coins) and the bastard Greek of Soloi. There were simple legends of foundations, as of Aspendos from Argos and of Side from Kyme in Aeolis, but there was also an awareness of a more complicated situation. This is most strikingly illustrated in the story of Mopsos, son of Manto, daughter of Teiresias, by either Apollo or a Cretan Rhakios. He was a seer, as befitted his descent, connected with the oracle of Klaros near Kolophon in Ionia, and victorious over Kalchas, the Greek seer at Troy, in a contest of divination. Migrating from Klaros to southern Asia Minor, he became the founder, among other cities, of Mallos on the River Kydnos in Cilicia. He also appears in the city name Mopsuhestia ('Hearth of Mopsos') on the River Pyramos. The same legendary figure was made a Lydian under the name Moxos; the story of his origins and activities clearly indicates a vague awareness of complex ethnic relations, which are not difficult to justify and clarify, in some measure, through modern discovery. It could be argued, if rather rashly, that his Cretan descent from Rhakios might hark back to Minoan relations with Asia Minor. More intriguing, his name has been detected (in the form MPS) in the Old Phoenician version of the bilingual inscription found at Karatepe in eastern Cilicia north of Adana.

In the case of the regions of the western coast, Caria, Ionia and Aeolis, and the off-shore islands of Samos, Chios and Lesbos, it was believed that settlement had taken place four generations after the Trojan War. During that war the inhabitants of western Asia Minor were the allies of the Trojans and the victims of Greek depredations. The list of Trojan allies in *Iliad* II includes Larissa (in Aeolis), but its inhabitants are Pelasgian, just as further south the Carians who hold Miletos and the region of the Maiandros and Mount Mykale are 'of barbarian speech'. The passages of Thucydides' *History* relevant for the settlement may be recalled. It is to be noted that in these passages Thucydides gives a special position to Athens and Attica, following, as befitted an Athenian, the tradition which took displaced Peloponnesians into Attica to give Athens a king from Messenian Pylos and a large accession of population, then to be led by some of that king's descendants to Ionia.

Herodotus, who was an admirer of Athens but not an Athenian, gives in some detail an account of the settlement of Asia Minor as it emerged in its completed form. It reflects some ideas different from those implicit in the tradition developed at Athens. In connection with events in the mid-sixth century after the defeat of Kroisos of Lydia by Kyros (Cyrus) of Persia, he describes in order the Ionians, Dorians and Aeolians of Asia Minor, taking the Ionians first. It is interesting to note his description of Ionia as an attractive region, which might well have been a factor in inducing the migration, and, in addition, his observation on Aeolis. It is to be observed that nothing is said by Herodotus concerning the effects, in terms of interior communications, imposed on the coastal cities of Aeolis by the mountainous country to the east. Equally there is no mention of the advantages and dangers to Ionia of the river valleys giving access to and from the interior – the valleys of the Hermos, Kaÿstros and Maiandros in particular. In this second case, however, it might be argued that the whole theme of Herodotus in this portion of Book I is a clear enough illustration of both advantages and dangers, in relations with the Lydians and Persians.

The historian lists the Ionian cities of Asia Minor in four dialect subgroups within East Ionic: Miletos, Myous and Priene in Caria; Ephesos, Kolophon, Lebedos, Teos, Klazomenai and Phokaia in what he calls 'Lydia'; actually Erythrai over against Chios also belongs to this group, but since it shares a subdialect with Chios the two are grouped together; the other large Ionian island, Samos, is placed in a dialect category by itself. These city-states met at the Panionion on the northern side of Mount Mykale, sacred to Poseidon of Helike in Peloponnesian Achaea, for at Helike, as Herodotus explains, 'the Ionians took refuge on their defeat by the Achaian invaders'. It is also claimed that the twelve

Ionian states of Asia Minor were intended to match in number the twelve old Ionian states on the southern coast of the Gulf of Corinth. This is palpably a fiction. The origin of the Ionian Poseidon from Helike *sounds* convincing, but contrasts with the later (Athens-fostered?) association of the Ionians with Apollo and the sacred island of Delos, as typified by the *Hymn to the Delian Apollo*. Later, as it appears from Thucydides, the festival of the Panionia declined in importance, and so did the Ionian significance of Delos stressed by the historian with quotations from the *Hymn*, to be replaced by a festival at Ephesos, the Ephesia.

South of Ionia, and next in Herodotus' account, was the Dorian Pentapolis (once a Hexapolis until the expulsion of Halikarnassos), comprising the three cities of Rhodes, Lindos, Kameiros and Ialysos, and Kos and Knidos, with their centre in the temple of Apollo at the Triopion, near Knidos.

Finally, in northern Asia Minor there were the twelve cities of southern Aeolis (the area of Mount Ida and its settlements were not included): Kyme Phrikonis, Larisa, Neon Teichos, Temnos, Killa, Notion, Aigiroessa, Pitane, Aigaiai, Myrina and Gryneia – except for Kyme not distinguished names. Smyrna was originally the twelfth, until its seizure by exiled Kolophonians and its addition to the Ionian group, not, apparently, attended by admission to the Panionia.

It may be noted here that an awareness is apparent in the mind of Herodotus (based no doubt on a consideration of local tradition which he must have known well) that the picture was really a more complicated one. There was the question of what constituted 'pure-bred' Ionians, and how far a supposed origin in Athens and the keeping of the Apatouria festival were diagnostic of the Ionian; and so it was necessary to find a reason why Ephesos and Kolophon did not celebrate it. Herodotus makes no secret of his rejection of the idea that those whom Attic tradition regarded as displaced from Achaea into Attica and from Attica to Ionia were the Ionians *par excellence*.

In the passage in question some important points are stressed: the motley nature of the emigrants; the particular character of the migration (no accompanying women); and the violence characterizing the Carian settlement (the tradition on which Herodotus must have been well informed). He goes on to point out that the Ionian kings (in whom Athens staked a particular claim) were 'either Lykians of the blood of Glaukos, son of Hippolochos, or Pylian Kaukones of the blood of Kodros, son of Melanthos; or else from both these families'. Both figures, Glaukos and Kodros, go back to the Heroic Age, while the Kaukones are one of those 'ancient peoples' of fictitious or real wide distribution like the Pelasgoi, Leleges and Dryopes. The Arcadian Pelasgoi, Abantes, Minyai, Cadmeans and Dryopes of the passage in question are not easy to identify; to judge from another passage of Herodotus, they must represent for the historian (the Dryopes possibly excepted) elements of the pre-Dorian population of Greece.

This is a strong contrast to the Athenian story, in which Ionian city-founders were sons of Kodros, who when Medon, his son, or Akastos, his grandson, were life-archons, led settlers to Ionia: so Androkles was the founder of Ephesos and Andraimon of Lebedos. In another case Oinopion, as founder of Chios, is described as a son of Theseus. Alternatively, where other traditions were too strong to be overridden, it was asserted that a Kodrid had taken a detachment from Athens to join others from elsewhere, at the foundation or later. It was all very convenient, when Athens started to develop, at the beginning of the sixth century, or even earlier, the idea of herself as the 'mother' of the Ionians: when Solon, the Athenian lawgiver, spoke of Attica as 'the oldest Ionian land', and the father of the Athenian tyrant Peisistratos gave his son the name of the son of Nestor, the Neleid ruler of Messenia. It was even more convenient still after 480–479 BC and the repulse of the Persian invaders of Greece, when Athens became the champion and leader of the Ionians. As in the case of almost everything else in early Greek history, the true position was somewhat different.

In addition to the observations of Herodotus there exist a multitude of statements by later writers, in particular Strabo and Pausanias, which contrive to suggest a picture very different from the simple Athenian version. In addition efforts have been made by modern scholars to establish connections between states and areas of Greece proper and those of Asia Minor by the study of names (personal and place-names) and cults. Similar efforts have been made to determine ethnic connections and something of the process of settlement by the study of dialects and institutions, especially tribes and festivals. A certain amount of this material is official but late, drawn from inscriptions. The problem is the interpretation of the material and the establishment of its validity for the early period. In the case of the literary material concerned with the settlement of western Asia Minor – and the same would be true of other issues such as colonization and the history of the late eighth and seventh centuries in Greece – there is no reason why there should not be a real tradition of events coming down through writers of early lyric and elegiac poetry such as Archilochos of Paros, Mimnermos of Kolophon, and Kallinos of Ephesos, by way also of early geographical writers like Hekataios of Miletos and the writers of 'city foundations' (*ktiseis*), to Herodotus and historians of the fourth century such as Ephoros and those of the Hellenistic period concerned with chronology. In this way authentic detail could filter down to Strabo and Pausanias. The chain of tradition is valid enough, but its length and the varying acumen and judgement of its transmitters made it very liable to corruption. Frequently, it is clear, institutions and names, of which the true explanation

71

is unknown, gave rise to palpably artificial explanations: as on the origins of the Thrakides of Chios, or the origin of the name Samothrace (some of the Samians expelled from Samos by the Ephesians settled in the island near the coast of Thrace and it so acquired its name). Some details may be suggested by later historical events.

A particular problem is the ambiguity of terms such as 'Ionian', used by Pausanias for non-Dorian and frequently pre-Dorian Greeks. Pausanias, clearly influenced by Athenian claims, connects Achaeans and Ionians through Ion, and uses 'Achaean' for the pre-Dorian inhabitants of Argos and Lakonia. He also distinguishes 'Ionians' from Athenians. Carians are clearly indicated by Thucydides as the primitive inhabitants of the Aegean Islands, expelled thence by Minos. Similarly in Strabo and Pausanias Carians are a widespread 'original' people of western Asia Minor. It is to be suspected that the later Greeks knew little of the natives the Greek settlers found in possession, though they knew there were such natives; Myous and Priene were wrested from them, and they were present on the sites of Kolophon and Lebedos; at Teos they mixed with the Greek settlers. If they knew little of the other natives, they did know of the historical Carians and found their name useful to extend throughout the western coast in connection with earlier times. It is doubtful if Thucydides' reference to 'Carian' graves on Delos means that the Classical Greeks had any serious archaeological way of defining 'Carian'.

There are also the Leleges. They appear in Strabo side by side with Carians and 'Cilicians' (Kilikes) in north-western Asia Minor. They are described at Ephesos, by Pausanias, as 'a section of the Carian race'.[6] They were, again, a convenient name for primitive natives and their material remains; otherwise it is difficult to see the reason for the distinction between 'Carian' and 'Lelegian', or why the latter should be carried over to Greece proper, as when Pausanias remarks that Lakonia was formerly called Lelegia. It has been pointed out above (pp. 57–8), in connection with the Pelasgians, that the conviction existed of a diversity of primitive peoples in Greece proper, and it is clear that this was extended to Asia Minor, but rested only on a slight basis of knowledge. As for groups associated with ancient tradition and a specific centre, such as the Minyai of Orchomenos, the details of their affinities and movements defy explanation.

The ultimate impression, given particularly by the study of names and cults, is that there are few valid criteria by which to check the traditions. It has already been pointed out that if the celebration of the Apatouria festival is accepted as diagnostic of 'Ionian' or Attic origins, it is difficult to explain the absence of this festival from Ephesos and Kolophon. Consequently only the broadest conclusions are even to be considered. The chief of these is that the migrants to western Asia Minor were a mixed lot. This is baldly stated by Strabo when he describes Chios as founded by a 'mixed mob' (*symmikton plethos*). There are certain other conclusions to be drawn from the numerous detailed references. There was clearly an urge to assert an earlier settlement than the 'Ionian', and to connect this with Crete, and with the Trojan War or an earlier period. In the latter case the aim is to secure the prestige of heroic antiquity; the former assertion seems to rest on a vague conviction among the Greeks of the early importance, political and cultural, of the island of Crete. So Cretans under Rhakios were 'the first Greeks to arrive' at Kolophon; then Rhakios was linked with Manto, daughter of Teiresias, the nearby oracular site of Klaros, and Kalchas. The purpose is even more transparent in the case of Miletos. In the words of Pausanias: 'When Miletos had put into their shores with a host of Cretans, both the land and the city took their new names from him. Miletos and his army came from Crete fleeing from Minos son of Europa.'[7] A pre-Trojan War event therefore, and a supposed relationship of Miletos in Caria with Miletos in Crete. The connection of the eponym of the city in Caria with Crete is made more explicit by Strabo, who quotes from Ephoros: 'Ephoros says: Miletos was first founded and fortified above the sea by the Cretans, where the Miletos of olden times is now situated, being settled by Sarpedon, who brought colonists from the Cretan Miletos and named the city after that Miletos, the place formerly being in the possession of the Leleges; but later Neleus and his followers fortified the city.'[8] The final remark obviously reconciles two traditions, and the Neleid foundation or fortification fits in with the pretensions of leading Milesian oligarchic families of the fifth century BC. It would be tempting to regard these accounts of early Cretan settlement at Kolophon and Miletos as true tradition, in view of the possible Mycenaean settlement at Kolophon and the undoubted Minoan and Mycenaean fortified settlement at Miletos. On the other hand Cretans appear elsewhere in less convincing contexts. Teukrians (Trojans) come from Crete and bring the name of Ida from Crete to the mountain of the Troad. Despite the quoted authority of Kallinos of Ephesos, of the seventh century BC, it is wise to believe that the name of Ida suggested the connection. Similarly Pausanias ascribes the foundation of Erythrai to Erythros the Cretan, together with a hotch-potch of Lykians, Carians and Pamphylians whom he is hard put to it to explain; and again, at Chios, Cretans led by Oinopion are joined by Abantes and Carians. Despite the temptation in the case of Miletos, it is better to be cautious and to ascribe these supposed Cretan connections to similarities of names and the tendency to seek a foundation date and cultural connections as early as possible for an important city.

A further widely manifest feature is the suggestion, distinct from any version of an Athenian participation, of direct migration from the Peloponnese: this *might* be Argive counter-propaganda: so, Klazomenai is founded by emigrants from Kleonai and Phlious in the north-eastern

Peloponnese, displaced by the Dorians. This may be part of the wide-ranging Argive claims which will be discussed later in connection with the so-called 'Heritage of Temenos', a claim related to the Herakleidai. Here it may be noted that Strabo mentions Heraclid and Argive colonization of Lindos, Ialysos and Kameiros by Tlepolemos from Argos, of Kos by the sons of Thessalos the Heraclid, and of Crete, the Rhodian cities, Halikarnassos, Kos and Knidos, by Dorians from Megara, and Althaimenes the Argive. This may well be Argive propaganda, but it hardly trespasses on the region claimed by Athens. On the other hand a suggestion of emigration direct from the western coast of Messenia, recorded by Mimnermos of Kolophon, seems to do so.

The evidence of dialect (considered earlier) *could* indicate a simple pattern of migration. On the other hand the study of names and cults, if valid, shows a mixed settlement, as at Priene (with some settlers direct from Messenia), Ephesos (with a local and oriental element as in the cult of Artemis), Kolophon, Chios and Erythrai; and a quite extraordinary mixture in the case of Samos, of elements from the Argolid, Thessaly, Boeotia and possibly Arcadia and Aetolia – tending to raise grave doubts about the method producing such a conclusion. The study of dialects and institutions to produce 'ethnic' indications is far from satisfactory, and vague in the extreme. Miletos, Myous, Priene, Teos, Klazomenai emerge as 'Ionian'; Samos, Magnesia on the Maiandros, Pygela, Erythrai, Smyrna and Phokaia as 'uncertain'; Melie as Boeotian; Ephesos as 'Ionian', on the basis of the calendar, the existence of the four-tribal system indicated by the appearance of the (Attic and Ionian) Argadeis, and despite the absence of the Apatouria festival; Kolophon, too, lacks the festival, but is saved as 'Ionian' by its dialect. The results are not very convincing. It is to be debated whether the early traditions – if they existed in detail – were quite so clear on geographical and *polis* divisions in mainland Greece as later writers were, and whether these divisions were as clearly marked in early Greece as later. And, indeed, not all were so clearly defined even in the Classical period: witness the disputed territory between Argos and Sparta, or between Attica and Boeotia, such as Eleutherai and Oropos.

There are further points which may be made. There are the indications of violence between the settlements, as in the case of Smyrna, formerly Aeolic and then seized by Kolophonians. Here it should be noted that Mimnermos of Kolophon mentioned the relations of the two cities in his *Smyrneis* and in his *Nanno*, quoted by Strabo as the basis for his account of the foundation of Kolophon by Andraimon of Pylos and for the history of Smyrna. Strabo obviously gives the 'official' Ionian version, and if the reference in this quotation from Mimnermos to 'grievous pride' relates to the Leleges, as Strabo believed, this is an example of violence against the natives at the initial foundation, which also appears elsewhere. Other

violence was between communities of the Greeks, who are thought to
have shown early the *hybris*, the arrogant aggressiveness, which they also
displayed later. Samos was wrested from the Samians by Ephesos, and
later recovered. Melie on the northern slope of Mount Mykale was
destroyed, probably by her neighbours rather than by the Ionian League,
in about 700 BC or in the early seventh century, as excavation appears to
suggest (but this may be a misdating). Vitruvius, the writer on
architecture of the first century BC, in narrating the foundation of the
Ionian cities, ascribes it to Athens, prompted by the Delphic oracle, and
to Ion as leader, but also to the 'common counsel of all Greece'. Among
the thirteen colonies he names Melite, which was possibly the Carian
name Hellenized as Melie (which appears in this form in Hekataios'
*Genealogies*). According to Vitruvius, Melie was destroyed by 'the
common counsel' of the Ionian settlements on account of the *adrogantia* of
its citizens. This *adrogantia*, it has been suggested, may have consisted of
attacks on shipping using the Samos Channel, and especially on Milesian
ships. The supervision of the altar of Poseidon Helikonios, formerly in the
charge of Melie, passed to Priene, and the territory of Melie was divided
between Samos, Miletos, Priene and Kolophon. It may be noted here
that a series of inscriptional documents of Hellenistic date (dealing with
the boundaries of Priene and the Samian territories on the mainland)
refer to these events, and contain references to earlier historians
(including Ephoros, Theopompos and Douris of Samos) and to a treaty of
the seventh century. Similar material must lie behind the later Greek
knowledge of events going back at any rate to the early seventh century.

There are also indications of repeated attempts at settlement in
different places, as in the case of Klazomenai, in the narrative of
Pausanias: 'When the Ionians were come, a roving band of them sent for
a leader, Parphoros, from Kolophon, and founded a city under Mount
Ida. They soon abandoned it, however, and returning to Ionia founded
Skyppion in the land of Kolophon. Once more flitting of their own accord
they quitted the territory of Kolophon, and took possession of the land
which they still occupy, and here they built on the mainland the city of
Klazomenai; but afterwards for fear of the Persians they crossed over to
the island.'[9]

There are other indications of successive groups of settlers. Thus at
Teos settlers come first from Orchomenos; there follow 'Ionians', led by
the great-grandson of Melanthos and then 'not many years after'
(Pausanias) men from Attica and Boeotia, the former (oddly in terms of
chronology!) led by the grandsons of Melanthos. In some cases a
succession of settlers is propounded in order to fit in with the Athenian
foundation or participation claims. For example Phokaians come from
Phokis, but they cross to Asia under Athenian leadership, and settle 'by
an understanding with the Kymeans'; then they are not admitted to the

Ionion confederacy 'until they should get Kings of the race of Kodros'.[10] These they then get from Erythrai and Teos. In the same fashion the 'Ionians' who later founded Klazomenai get a leader from Kolophon.

In summing up what emerges in general from the tradition it may be said in the first place that the settlers were conceived of as being a mixed lot. They were far from being regarded universally as assembling in Attica and departing thence to Asia Minor. The extreme Athenian claim is represented by Thucydides. This is toned down elsewhere, as in Vitruvius and in Pausanias, where the migration is connected with the quarrel of Medon and Neleus, sons of Kodros, and their appeal to the Delphic oracle. Neleus departs to Asia with the other sons of Kodros, 'taking such of the Athenians as chose to follow them, but the bulk of their army was composed of the Ionians,[11] 'Ionians' here being non-Dorian Greeks. Kingship, the tradition agrees, was the form of leadership, the office surviving later, as in Athens. Thus there were kings (*basileis*) of the family of Androklos, at Ephesos, possessing kingly insignia and privileges, and at Chios and Priene. There was an *archon basileus* at Miletos. In an inscription from the Panionion on Mount Mykale the term king (*basileus*) is linked with that of president (*prytanis*), which appears in a number of Ionian states at a later date. It may be that the sacral representatives of the states of the league meeting at the Panionion were called *basileis*. Tombs of some early leaders were shown, round which legends concentrated. These incomers sometimes ejected the previous inhabitants (Carians, Leleges and Kilikes) – it always seems to be assumed that there were previous inhabitants – and sometimes combined with them. An 'oriental' element is clear from the cult of Artemis at Ephesos, and perhaps for this reason Pausanias, describing the early inhabitants of the site of Ephesos as Leleges, adds that 'the bulk were Lydians', and that an element of them, 'those around the Sanctuary', came to terms with the Athenian leader Androklos and his 'Ionians'.[12] He also comments on the 'pre-Ionian' (i.e. pre-migration in this case) date of the oracle at Didyma. In terms of dates the later Greeks assumed an early migration, since they related Ionian foundations to the Trojan War, its sequel, and to a succession of Athenian royal figures down to the eleventh century. None the less there was also a conviction of repeated attempts at settlement, additions to original settlements and changes and modifications in Asia Minor itself, for which the framework of the tradition was formed by the later important cities of Asia Minor, though account was taken of other and minor settlements. It seems to be generally inferred that the Ionian confederacy was early in existence.

This traditional account is to be supplemented by the evidence of archaeology. This has serious limitations in the present theme. First and foremost there is the question of pottery finds. The pottery fabrics involved are Late Helladic III C of the twelfth and early eleventh centuries, the latter part of it formerly called Sub-Mycenaean, followed by Proto-Geometric, commonly dated from 1050 BC to 900 BC, though some would modify the commencing date downwards, while some categories of Proto-Geometrics are taken to continue well beyond 900 BC. Proto-Geometric is followed by full Geometric, developing until the last quarter of the eighth century. The importance of Late Helladic III c (and Sub-Mycenaean) is that it is involved with the problems of the end of the Bronze Age, in Greece, the Aegean and western Asia Minor. Proto-Geometric, given the dates ascribed to it, is likely to be part of the material evidence for the Ionian migration.

The study of Proto-Geometric pottery is relatively recent, and began with Attic Proto-Geometric, well known from the Kerameikos Cemetery. This pottery is clearly in some ways a development from the preceding Late Helladic III c, but it is characterized by high excellence in shapes and by the quality of the black glaze paint used to decorate it with linear patterns, including pendant concentric semicircles. Athens and Attica seemed at first, and still seem, to be the prime centre of its development. As knowledge of this pottery fabric increased to include that produced at other centres from Thessaly to Crete, there was a tendency to detect Attic export, or at least widely diffused Attic influence, *presumably* conveyed by specimens of the Attic fabric. The next step was to suggest that Attic traders were the intermediaries, who were thereby indicated as travelling far and wide, and to postulate a revival of trade in the eleventh/tenth century BC. It was not unreasonable to strengthen this theory (which rested in effect on Attic pre-eminence in Proto-Geometric) with the tradition of the part claimed to have been played by Athens in the Ionian migration. Objections could be raised in relation to this supposed early revival of trade both by sea and by land, and the magnitude of the trading contacts need not be exaggerated. It could have taken place by short stages north and south from Attica and across the Aegean (as island evidence might suggest). It is in a measure to be modified by the discovery of what seems to be an independent development in Thessaly at Iolkos (Volos), but hardly to be totally rejected.

This pottery fabric is, in any case, obviously of importance for the Ionian migration. Its presence on Ionian sites may seem to help in dating this process, but the origins of settlers are hardly likely to be established by it. Some Proto-Geometric found in western Asia Minor is an imitation, and from the Late Mycenaean period onwards there is the perpetual controversy as to how far Greek pottery from burials or other sources indicates the presence of incomers or imports by the natives.

In the matter of the 'natives' there is the problem of establishing their presence archaeologically, through native pottery fabrics, such as 'grey ware', continuing a long tradition of the Bronze Age, and through the identification of native structures: of discovering, in fact, the kind of evidence which Strabo mentions in connection with the Leleges: 'Throughout the whole of Caria and in Miletos are to be seen tombs, fortifications and traces of settlements of the Leleges.'[13]

It is possible from the evidence of historic Caria to identify 'Carian' structures on a number of sites in the south of western Asia Minor, including Melie, but to extend this exercise to the more shadowy peoples is likely to present as many problems as Thucydides' 'Carian graves' on Delos. A major issue is the question as to what population the Greeks really found when they arrived in Asia Minor, to match the expulsions and combinations of the traditional account. A good deal of the debate on the topographical issues centres on the Hittite Boğaz-köy records, the location of Aḫḫiya, Arzawa, Assuwa and the Lukka lands, with all the problems of the chronology of these documents (are some of the fifteenth rather than the thirteenth century BC?), all of which is relevant to Mycenaean relations with Asia Minor. But between these Late Helladic III A, B and C times and the Ionian settlement comes the period of disaster and decline: the great raid which put an end to the Hittite Empire must have had its effect, and so must the incomers who seem indicated by the evidence at Troy VII B. How far was western Asia Minor depopulated, suffering in Late Helladic III C the same decline as mainland Greece? To what extent and when was there a break in occupation between the latest Mycenaean and the earliest Proto-Geometric? How did repopulation take place to produce what might be called the Proto-Phrygians, Proto-Lydians and Proto-Carians? It may be said at once that some of these problems are never likely to be completely solved, others not for a long time, for while the material from organized field research multiplies rapidly, an enormous amount remains to be done on often difficult terrain or terrain hampered by waterlogging, as at Miletos and Iasos.

The Mycenaean evidence is anything but satisfactory, and up to the present confirms the view that there was a considerable gap in Mycenaean connections southwards from Troy, with Lesbos outside the Mycenaean sphere of influence, and Chios dubiously within it. Finds of sherds may indicate only casual contacts. The point may be made that, as distinct from such casual contacts, 'settlements can be expected only on a maritime site, easily provisioned from the sea, and easily defensible against land attack'. Miletos was such a site. Apart from this, the excavators of Iasos on the Carian coast claim (1970) to have found evidence of structural remains going back as far as Late Helladic III A and even much further, with sherds as early as Middle Minoan, imported and imitations. There was a settlement on Kos, and one of Late Helladic III C at Emborio on Chios, preceded by a little Late Helladic III B. There is a recent claim for a settlement near Erythrai and for another as far north as Pitane in Aeolis, but neither claim is supported by detail.

There is the problem of cemeteries which lack associated settlements.

The outstanding example is Rhodes (except for traces at Lindos). There are other cases such as the Mycenaean tombs on the Halikarnassos peninsula (Late Helladic III c and earlier), and at Müsgebi in Caria (Late Helladic III A–B and some c), showing strong affinities with Rhodes and Kos. They illustrate the strong element of chance in discovery. Little is forthcoming from Lesbos and Samos; nothing from Phokaia; some sherds from Smyrna and Klazomenai; some Late Helladic III A 2 from Ephesos (Ayasoluk), and some sherds from Milas and Knidos. What is called 'Sub-Mycenaean' has been found in a deep sounding at Sardis, and a 'Sub-Mycenaean' cemetery has come to light at Çomleki between Milas and Bodrum. The *tholos* tomb containing some Mycenaean pottery at Kolophon seems to be in a category by itself. The evidence is clearly uneven and inadequate to support any far-reaching conclusions, including the location of the Mycenaean kingdom of Aḫḫiya in view of the intensification of finds southwards. The same inadequacy of evidence characterizes the issue of continuity or discontinuity between Late Helladic III and Proto-Geometric. Discontinuity seems to be established (with some sort of violent break) at Miletos after Late Helladic III c, but probably not for long, at Kos (after Late Helladic III c), probably in Rhodes and probably also at Iasos since 'the Protogeometric is inserted into a Mycenaean level' there.[14] At Emborio in Chios there was a break, but the date is uncertain. It is to be noted that there is something similar in the Aegean Islands: discontinuity in Melos and Paros in Late Helladic III c; possible continuity in Delos as a religious centre (?); some continuity from Late Helladic III c, but also some dislocation, as it has been called, in Naxos, though the evidence is less than satisfactory. None the less, despite the poor evidence for some sites, it is not unreasonable to suggest a period of disruption (however caused) and decline in the eleventh century BC. It is to be noted that in Crete also there were disturbances in Late Minoan III c, caused by incomers and/or internal strife, which could be coupled with the tradition of Cretans emigrating to Asia Minor.

There followed thereafter the Proto-Geometric period, which must indicate a revival, and was the era of the Ionian migration. The tradition said nothing of the route taken by the migrants across the Aegean, though Thucydides speaks of Athens 'sending out colonies to Ionia and most of the islands'.[15] Strabo, on the authority of Pherekydes, puts the Aeolian migration before the Ionian, which *might* suggest a coastal route through the north, but this is unlikely. The leading authority on Proto-Geometric, discussing its presence in the islands – sherds on Delos and Kea and a 'megaron' on Naxos – suggests: 'The link between Naxos and both the Dodecanese and East Attica must surely involve other islands as well, and the evidence of Miletus does suggest that the first movement of the Ionian Migration passed through the Cyclades at the time of transition to

Protogeometric, but no clear picture of the situation at the end of Late Helladic III C is yet available—for example, the Proto-Geometric pottery of Naxos from the little that is known about it, seems to be related not so much to that of Attica as to that of the area to the north including Thessaly.'[16] The connection here mentioned is interesting for its resemblance to the Boeotian–Thessalian element in the colonizing tradition, but it also serves to underline the inadequacy of the evidence for the islands.

Proto-Geometric pottery is present in some quantity at Miletos. It belongs to the period mentioned above, i.e. transitional from Late Helladic III C to Proto-Geometric in Attica: a date around 1000 BC would not be far out. It is a local ware and is said to show affinities with Attic Proto-Geometric. There is a quantity also at Old Smyrna associated with native grey ware, which decreases in volume as time progresses. Again there are affinities with Attic. Proto-Geometric has been found in Rhodes and Kos – the Proto-Geometric *skyphos* (drinking-cup) type in the latter case recalls the type found in Argos. There are cemeteries at Iasos and on the Halikarnassos peninsula, and the pottery has appeared at a number of sites: at Pitane in Aeolis and at Phokaia, Teos and Müšgebi, but hardly at all in Lesbos, Chios and Samos, which might be a matter of chance. In a deep sounding at Sardis pottery has been found in a style inspired by Proto-Geometric. This indicates its penetration inland, but it would be pointless to connect it with the tradition of a Heraclid dynasty at Sardis, lasting, according to Herodotus, 505 years and preceding the Mermnad dynasty founded by Gyges.

The finds of this pottery give indications of a resumption of contacts between Greece and Asia Minor. It covers a considerable period, and therefore provides dates only within wide margins down to 900 BC or somewhat later. It does not *necessarily* indicate the presence of Greeks. At Iasos, for instance, the excavators ascribe the cremation and inhumation burials in cists of various sorts and pithoi seemingly to Carians; at least they ascribe the clay and bronze tomb furniture 'to a local Carian production'. There is still the problem of incomers or, alternatively, of native importers and imitators. At least some of the material, however, must indicate the presence, even if transient, of Greeks.

When the excavations at Miletos have finally been completed the history of the development of what had been and was destined to be an important community will be revealed. Meanwhile the clearest picture of the earliest type of Greek settlement is presented by the excavation of Old Smyrna (across the gulf from the Hellenistic, Roman and modern city), now embedded in the silt of the Meles, but originally a peninsula connected to the mainland by a narrow neck or causeway. The English excavator of the site points out that it resembled the description in the *Odyssey* of the city of the Phaiakians: 'Thereby goes a high wall with towers and there is a fair haven on either side of the town, and narrow is the entrance, and curved ships are drawn up on either hand of the mole, for all the folk have stations for their vessels, each man for himself.'[17]

The first tiny settlement at Old Smyrna contained small houses of one room, rectangular or oval in plan, built of mud brick, with a fenced yard. One such house, of oval shape, is well preserved in its lower courses, and has been dated to the end of the tenth century BC. A wall circuit belongs to the ninth century, and so do larger rectangular houses. It is unlikely that from this early date other more pretentious buildings remain undiscovered in the unexcavated areas of the site. The primitive shrines would exactly resemble the houses. It has been calculated that this settlement originally possessed space enough within its walls, but by the eighth century its population had increased, so that, in the words of the excavator, a roomy village had become a slum town. This first phase has been dated from c. 1050/1000 BC to c. 750 BC, from Proto-Geometric to all but the latest stage of Geometric. It ends with a burnt layer, which has been ascribed (with no certainty) to the taking of Smyrna from the Aeolians by the Ionians of Kolophon.

This earliest phase of Old Smyrna suggests a number of conclusions: for instance that the initial settlements were small, and therefore the first settlers were in small bands (otherwise sea transport would have been difficult) and were joined by others later; that there were many of these small settlements, some of which may be indicated by casual finds of Proto-Geometric pottery. It is suggested that the immigrants found the country underpopulated but not unpopulated, so that there were natives to supplement the labour of their own small numbers, and that initially land was abundant. Thus they could multiply in numbers, and the natives with them, so that the later Greeks' belief in expulsions of the natives might be based on later, *not* initial conditions. It has also been conjectured that the incomers formed an 'aristocracy' and eventually established themselves in the country, in farm houses, as well as in the *polis* settlements. The Meliac War is not to be dated too early. To judge from the burials which belong to the settlement before its destruction, this took place in about 700 BC. This is the opinion of the recent excavators, but it means bringing the end date of Proto-Geometric pottery down too far. On the other hand 850 BC seems too early. The war was probably, as observed above, an example of the subordination or elimination of smaller communities by the larger: what has been called a 'crystallization' which formed the historic cities of Ionia. Something similar no doubt took place in Aeolis; and in the area of contact between the two the adding of Smyrna to Ionia marks the attainment of an equilibrium. It is not to be supposed that the Ionian League and the Panionion came into being at an early date, though the altar of Poseidon Helikonios may have done, or that the league conducted the Meliac War. It is more likely that the Ionian cities, which had not been greatly affected by the development of the Phrygian kingdom in the interior, drew together after the destruction of the Phrygian kingdom by the Kimmerians (Gimirrai) and the rise of the Mermnad dynasty of Lydia, with its aggressive disposition.

The ninth and eighth centuries in western Asia Minor were a period of development from small beginnings. In the seventh century the polis development took place *pari passu* with mainland Greece, producing oppressive aristocracies and tyranny, and in the second half of the century notable cultural advances, despite barbarian attack and Lydian aggression.

# CHAPTER 5

# EXPANSION AND INNOVATION

The half-century or so which saw the production of the two objects about to be described was one of crucial importance for the Greeks. The objects themselves bear the clear indications of this importance. The first is a clay cup found in the island of Ischia off the western coast of Italy. It is an imitation of a late Geometric Greek pottery style from Asia Minor, and it bears an inscription in an alphabet of consonants and vowels (though no distinction is made as yet between long and short vowels), not in a syllabary like the Linear B system of the Mycenaean period. The ultimate origins of this alphabet lay with the Phoenicians at the eastern end of the Mediterranean. The second is the *lekythos* or perfume bottle of Tataie, one of a large group of such with gradually modified shapes, which was found at Cumae in the Italian Campania, a Greek settlement on the mainland opposite Ischia, placed on a low hill quite near the shore. It was made at Corinth on the isthmus in Greece proper; it probably contained perfume, which may have come from the Orient, though this is by no means certain. The presence of Greek (or imitated-Greek) objects, ideas and people in the western Mediterranean and the clear links with the eastern Mediterranean are the key-notes of the two important themes of this chapter: Greek colonization and the oriental contacts of the Greeks. It may be added that in no aspect of Greek activity or culture have there been greater advances in knowledge in recent years, or, indeed, greater demonstrations of our ignorance.

## THE GREEK COLONIES

To take colonization first. Why did it happen? The *Odyssey* and the *Works and Days* of Hesiod have already given us the necessary hints. Even after a period of 'settling down' the Greek earth, what there was of it, and Greek skills were not equal to supporting a growing population. And despite the poverty of the land, population did increase, a mark of optimism and thankfulness, but not necessarily related to hard facts. Children were troublesome when it came to feeding more mouths from land which could not be so easily increased, or when it came to dividing an inheritance. Also there was the provision of dowries for daughters, though there was always a solution to the problem of unwanted daughters: they could be abandoned on the hillside, and those who did not perish might be taken up as slaves if it was considered worth the trouble to rear them. It is not hard to see that in these conditions wasteful and uneconomic division of land might result, or litigation. It has already been noted that Hesiod knew all about this, and liked the courts less than his brother Perses. It is better to have only one son: that is his advice, not always easy to follow, since sons were not so willingly disposed of as daughters. They could be useful as sources of labour when young; the trouble started when they grew up and their father died. Furthermore it has been shown abundantly already that most parts of Greece were very vulnerable to failures of the harvest; and it was not a land where many could build up a reserve. Thus there was a strong incentive to go elsewhere. This had already happened in the migration to Asia Minor, and it is probable enough that this was so spread out over a long period that it is not to be distinguished sharply from the dispersion which followed in the period of colonization proper. Asia Minor and the Aegean Islands were the obvious places of settlement, not too far, and not greatly different from the homeland, but as time passed all the suitable sites were occupied, and Greek *polis* exclusiveness tended to exclude the stranger or place him in an inferior position. So later emigrants went further afield.

Economic pressure was not the only reason for colonization. It is certain that some found life dull at home, and sought adventure elsewhere. Some drew swords too quickly in a quarrel, shed blood and so had to flee abroad. The adventurer is later personified in that great figure of the seventh century, Archilochos of Paros, whom the Greeks most admired after Homer. A member of the upper class (but possibly a bastard), he took part in the Parian colonization of Thasos, the rich island in the northern Aegean. There was a good deal of strife in that sea on issues of trade and expansion, and in the north existed a veritable El Dorado region in Thrace, though it was not to be fully developed until later. The pathetic fragments of the poetry of Archilochos show the man as one suited to an age of uncertainty and a life of adventure: living for the present, drinking and whoring, possibly taking his place in the stocks, used to a hard life on shipboard, losing his shield in battle on the mainland against the savage Thracians and taking it as a good joke. In the character spectrum of the Archaic Greek noblemen he may be placed at the adventurous and unscrupulous end rather than at the other, that of the gentleman with his *arete* or sense of honour. Archilochos himself speaks of his contemporary, 'Golden Gyges', the King of Lydia, and such adventurers knew of the wealth of the East (that is, the wealth of Anatolia and the eastern Mediterranean) and of the opportunities there, if they could muster a band of companions. They could then carve out a principality or serve as mercenaries, like the Carian 'Bronze Men' who came from the sea to Egypt in the seventh century, or like Antimenidas, the brother of the lyric poet of Lesbos, Alkaios, who at a later time saw service with the Babylonians and brought back with him from the East a sword splendidly decorated in gold and ivory, having wrought a great deed in slaying a mighty Goliath-like oriental champion. His brother greeted him on his return: 'Thou hast come from the bounds of the earth, having the ivory hilt of thy sword bound with gold.'[1] Some of this activity, undoubtedly, had gone on at quite an early date, but it should be noted that it attained its full dimensions in the later eighth century, and continued well into the sixth: the Age of Adventure it might be called.

Some, then, went abroad for economic reasons, to find an easier life, some for adventure. There was also a third reason, which can be guessed from what has gone before. There was a likelihood of oppression arising from the aristocratic quest for wealth and power. There were the poor men who sought to avoid the harsh rule and crooked judgements of Hesiod's princes. Most, no doubt, would fain behave like their oppressors if they in turn could be top dogs in a new *polis*. There were also men of the ruling aristocracy who had somehow gone down in the scale. In some cases, it is clear, the aristocracies which replaced the early kings became narrower, more violent and more oppressive as time passed, like the Penthelidai at Ephesos and the Bacchiadai at Corinth. Such oppressive and narrow aristocracies would be only too glad to see the back of discontented commoners led away somewhere else by disgruntled aristocrats. The *Odyssey* makes the position clear: the worst fate short of death is to be a landless man and to serve another; to wander for trade or piracy was bad enough, only to be accepted, Hesiod says, when all else fails. There are wanderers in the *Odyssey*, real or pretended; for instance a displaced man might be a bastard excluded from a share in his father's estate. For men who were not born adventurers, or traders who felt an urge to vie with the Phoenicians, the ideal was a fertile land in which to settle. That there were such lands men had heard vaguely, and the description of them had lost nothing in the telling, like that land of Cockaigne where the Cyclops lived: 'They plant not aught with their hands, neither plough: but, behold, all these things spring for them in plenty, unsown and untilled, wheat and barley and vines, which bear great clusters of the juicy grape, and the rain of Zeus gives them increase.'[2] The inhabitants of such lands might be lawless and violent, but this could be dealt with: Odysseus was a match for the Cyclops. The great thing was fertile land away from Greece and the men in possession.

85

And so the great period of colonization begins, during which men went in all directions in the Mediterranean, but north, west and south rather than east, as settlers. The movement must have begun in the early eighth century BC, and continued into the sixth, but the peak was in the late eighth and in the seventh, a period of major importance in Greek history and culture. Local pride might give even earlier dates, but these need not be credited.

How did these emigrant Greeks know where to go? If we look at the picture of Greek colonial settlement as a whole, and take account of the traditional and archaeological information available, it must strike us that some areas failed to attract settlers *at first*, though they seem desirable enough. Thus northern Greece, Macedonia and Thrace, did not receive the earliest colonies, though they were in the Aegean area. It is perhaps reasonable to conclude that the local inhabitants were an obstacle; they certainly were later. The Black Sea region lagged behind also, and it emerges only gradually as the objective, as in the developing story of the Argonauts. And thus, it might be felt, the Black Sea was only gradually and at a relatively late date penetrated by the Greeks. It was not a very attractive sea, with its leaden waves. There were, indeed, claims of very early or quite early city foundations on the southern coast of it, but so far these claims have not been supported by excavation finds. There *could* have been early overland travel from the Aegean to this coast, but it is a reasonable suggestion that the sea passage from the Aegean to the Black Sea remained for long difficult, and necessitated a progressive occupation of sites on its approaches. The Greeks could know all about these difficulties, as they were a matter of Aegean knowledge, but this does not quite explain why the earliest settlements in the Mediterranean were in the west.

It might be suggested that winds helped. We hardly ever hear of Greek sailors being blown north or east. It was to the west that storms bore them, to become explorers whether they would or not, like that lucky Samian Kolaios, who, years after the initial colonization, was blown clear out through the Pillars of Herakles to a region where men were guileless and unsuspicious of traders, and whence he returned, a rich man with a splendid cargo of silver from the region of Cadiz (Tartessos, as we may guess). It was in his opinion, and in that of Herodotus that it was a god who took him, and so when he and his companions came back a splendid offering was made in the temple of Hera at Samos, one of those shrines of special importance in the period in question. It is thus described by Herodotus: 'The Samians took a tithe of the gains to the sum of six talents and made themselves a bronze mixing-bowl of the Argive type; and around about it in a line were the heads of griffins. And they dedicated it in the temple of Hera and set under it three bronze figures over life-size, of seven cubits, in a kneeling position.'[3]

It is worth diverging from the present theme to look for a moment at this memorial of a great adventure. The tripod cauldron of the Geometric period had had its day. From the East, as will be seen later, came splendid great vessels which required separate supports. Some of these had ring-handles and attachments; others had a decoration in the form of animal heads. It was this latter type that the Greeks imitated, decorating the cauldrons with the fierce and furious heads of beaked griffins, which could also be moulded in clay, as in the famous 'Griffin Jug' in the British Museum. The griffin attachments of many such bowls have survived to provide some of the most attractive and impressive works of Archaic Greek bronze work done by the *cire-perdue* process. It was such a cauldron that was dedicated for Kolaios and his friends, on a great base of kneeling figures. It is interesting to note that a small ivory figure of a kneeling youth found at Samos will give some idea of what these supporting figures were like. Thus there is, in this story, in some fashion a link between farthest west and farthest east in the Mediterranean, an illustration of the movement characteristic of this age.

Kolaios was but one of many who had this adventure down to the Classical period and beyond: St Paul was one of them, but he did not get so far. Once again the greatest of them all is Odysseus, blown westwards into a fairyland outside ordinary experience, for while in strict truth the direction of Odysseus' adventures is quite unclear, somehow the conviction grows on the reader of the poem that they must be located in the west. Leaving aside the storm-carried mariner, we may believe, first, that at any rate the central Mediterranean had been in some measure penetrated in the Mycenaean period, but it is difficult to assess the value of 'memories' as an encouragement to sail west. Some such memories may have survived. However this might be, the sailing itself was not too difficult. Those who, from the east, made for the Isthmus of Corinth (rather than attempt to sail round dangerous Cape Malea at the tip of the Peloponnese) need not be very intrepid sailors to push gradually westwards: the spirit of a Columbus was certainly not necessary, nor his resolution. It was easy to creep on out of the Corinthian Gulf northwards to Thiaki and Kerkyra (Corcyra, Corfu), where the crossing was possible to southern Italy, which might be seen in the distance on a clear day. From southern Italy the sailor could make his way down to Sicily. It might also be suggested that some went straight across to Sicily through the Ionian Sea, for the first settlements seem to have been in Sicily, not in southern Italy. This looks like furthest first. The same seems to be true of the Italian settlements, among which the earliest are farthest north on the western coast, at Ischia and Cumae. These settlements seem determined by the need for bases to trade with Elba and the Etruscans in metals. In the case of Sicily the main reason is certainly the occupation of the areas of greatest fertility in corn.

Knowledge of the west might come from the storm-driven sailor or from the cautious or not so cautious explorer, or explorer-trader. When he returned, *if* he returned, his gratitude might take him to Delphi, to the shrine of Apollo, if he were a mainland Greek, just as Kolaios as a Samian went to the sanctuary of Hera in his island. He might well make a dedication, though it could possibly be too early for it to bear an inscription. Later all the great shrines of the gods would be full of dedications, of grateful individuals and of communities, of athletic victors and of princely houses, some small objects and some large structures, some cheap and some costly like the gold bowl dedicated by the Kypselidai at Olympia, some recording obscure events, and others landmarks of Greek history, such as the Persian helmet captured at Marathon from the Persians and dedicated by the Athenians at Olympia; or the helmets from the same site, one of which is in the British Museum, taken from the Etruscans at the battle of Cumae by Hiero the Sicilian tyrant. They were the records of events, and the pabulum of historians like Herodotus. They were indispensable to those who studied specialized themes like the Olympic victors or the history of specific cities. They made the great religious shrines of Greece veritable record centres, a stimulus to pride, imagination, and on occasions to bitter enmity, when one city displayed spoils taken from another or a boastful and triumphant epigram of victory. Before the use of the alphabet and writing, such inscribed memorials, including those of grateful adventurers, would be non-existent, but Delphi in particular appears to have served an important purpose as a clearing house of information, for stories of new lands were retailed to the priesthood of Apollo, and passed on to those who sought new homes, to the great credit of the god and his oracle. It thus came about that he could be worshipped in Sicily as 'The God who leads the Way'. In truth the human explorers and traders deserved more credit.

It may be added that the discovery on colonial sites and elsewhere of actual specimens of Greek Geometric pottery, and, more commonly, of imitations, has been taken to indicate early contacts which were more likely to be intentional than accidental. There is much that is uncertain and debated about this evidence, but it may be further observed that the sources of this pottery or of the influences indicated by native pottery decoration seem very diverse: Athens, Corinth, the Aegean Islands and Crete have been recognized: a rather different picture, therefore, from that given by the preponderance in the seventh and early sixth centuries of Corinthian pottery, replaced by that of Athens in the sixth and fifth. It is clear that these explorers and traders to distant lands were a mixed lot (as indeed later traders were), and that some of the contacts were of members of states which later fell behind in colonizing – a fact which is also true of the somewhat different activity in the eastern Mediterranean.

The traditional picture of colonial settlement in Sicily, at any rate, is of a division between Euboean and Dorian colonizing states, the former category so named from the great part played in the colonization of Sicily by the two cities of Euboea, Chalkis and Eretria, and particularly the former. The meaning of 'Dorian' is obvious – a connection with the cities which, in Greece proper, claimed such an origin. It is unlikely that the picture was thus simple: a body of colonists must often have been mixed (as those were who went to Asia Minor), with some participants coming perhaps from states (such as Athens and Aegina) which were not traditionally colonizers; but the division was roughly true and later accentuated by the political split between Dorian and anti-Dorian states, especially in Sicily.

As in the case of the Pontic (Black Sea) colonies the foundation dates of these western settlements could be influenced by local pride. The real dates have to be checked by a combination of archaeology, especially as it involves the earliest pottery, and the indications given by Thucydides in an introduction to his account of the great Sicilian Expedition of Athens launched in 415 BC. In this passage, it may be noted, terms of years are mentioned as between one western colonial foundation and another. It could be suggested that the Greeks who set out westwards were already chronology-conscious, as it might be put, making annual marks or driving nails into a beam, like the later Romans, and so establishing a relative chronology but not an absolute one.

It must be stressed that the dating of these western colonies is the foundation, and a shaky one, of much of the archaeological chronology of early Greece. One or two impressions emerge as likely enough: for example that Ischia (Pithekoussai) and Cumae were early foundations in Italy; and that Naxos was the first settlement in Sicily, for there Apollo Archegetes, the 'Guide and Leader', had an altar. On the other hand recent archaeological discovery does not altogether appear to confirm earlier ideas of the foundation chronology based on Thucydides, whose account seems to rest on the historian Antiochos of Syracuse. Indeed it could be that the Dorian state of Syracuse, founded from Corinth, gave itself a priority in foundation after Naxos in keeping with its greatness in the Classical period, and thus the dates of foundation of other cities were adjusted downwards to fit the foundation date of Syracuse, which was 734 BC. Those who take this revised view would date the foundation of Sicilian Naxos to 757/6 BC, and that of Hyblaean Megara to 750 BC. This is a complicated subject, but one, it must be stressed, of general importance, not merely an exercise of scholarly research. It is unlikely that it will grossly upset the general framework of chronology, but it pushes back somewhat the dates of the earliest settlements, and therefore of the preliminary explorations. It makes even clearer than before that the Greeks were at least the contemporaries of the Phoenicians in the west, and certainly did not come after them. It also fits in with the early importance of Thiaki on the route west. Most important of all, if true, it would demonstrate the importance of Megara on the isthmus between Attica and the Corinthia in this early western colonization. In early Greece Megara was a rival and hostile neighbour of Corinth, contesting border areas and finally losing to Corinth. Certainly in the west Megara was overshadowed by Corinth. An exercise of the historical imagination, by no means excessive, might suggest that Megara was an early and important link between Greece and the west, not only in her own interests but also in those of Argos and perhaps Aegina, two states which did not participate directly and officially in colonization. Of these Argos was *the* Dorian state *par excellence* before the rise of Sparta in the late seventh and sixth centuries BC, and a rival of Corinth in the Peloponnese. Also, it seems to be suggested by tradition, Argos had some sort of connection with Aegina in the seventh century at any rate. Argos, indeed, had its rich plain, and it can be argued, as for Athens also, that Argos expanded at home in the eighth century, but its rulers might wish to have some part in colonization for other reasons than necessity. Aegina was exceedingly poor and stony in soil, so that it early turned to trade. It is not, therefore, unreasonable to suggest that these two states supported Megara in her ventures, though it must be stressed that this is conjecture and nothing more. It may also be pointed out, in reference to the earlier date given for Chalkidian Naxos, indicating a certain priority in Euboic activity in Sicily, that this fits in with the tradition of Eretrian settlement in Kerkyra, the halfway house between Greece and Italy, before the Corinthians displaced them from this island.

Somewhat later than this Sicilian settlement there took place the colonization of southern Italy, from the 'toe' to the 'heel'. The Chalkidians settled Rhegion (modern Reggio), as they had Zankle across the straits in Sicily. Thus they could bar the way to the western sea for those to whom they were ill-disposed, making more difficult the already dangerous sea passage through the straits, where in course of time Skylla and Charybdis came to be localized. At the other end of the 'foot' of Italy Taras (Taranto) with its splendid harbour was settled by emigrants from Sparta: a picturesque story, as will later be seen, explained this colonial settlement which was unique for the state, with the exception of her association with Kyrene. In fact expanding Sparta was faced with two possible solutions of her population problem, colonization *or* conquest of her neighbours. Taras and the interest which Sparta later took in Kyrene are examples of the first solution, but she did not continue to adopt it, and for obvious reasons. Colonies would, indeed, reduce both tension and population pressure, but they also took away able-bodied men, and these Sparta could not afford to lose in view of her peculiar situation in the Peloponnese.

Between Rhegion and Taras a diverse assortment of Greeks settled: Lokrians at Western Lokroi; above all Achaeans from the northern Peloponnese and some fugitive Messenians at Kroton (later to be the refuge of Pythagoras) and Sybaris, where tradition claimed that all the refinements of civilization were developed, including the chamber-pot. Much later, natives of Kolophon in Asia Minor founded Siris. The sources of wealth of these cities, as in the case of those of Sicily, were corn, cattle and timber. Southern Italy had not *then* suffered so much from denudation as to be the melancholy and impoverished backwater it is now. Over across on the western sea other secondary cities were founded such as Terina and Poseidonia (later Paestum). Part, at any rate, of the purpose of their foundation was commercial, to exploit tracks across the intervening mountains from the Ionian to the Tyrrhenian Sea, in order to bypass the straits. The main reason, on the other hand, must surely have been to occupy the pockets of fertile land on the western coast and thus relieve population pressure. Further north, beyond Neapolis, the settlements of Ischia and Cumae have already been mentioned; they were of extreme importance for contacts with the Etruscans and early Rome, as, for instance, in the transmission to them of the alphabet. It would be tedious to enumerate the many names of participating states and their colonial foundations. Let it suffice to make two points: the Sicilian and Italian cities were never mere outposts of Greek civilization. They were a major element in it, so that Sicilian cities such as Syracuse and Akragas were ultimately larger and more splendid, as their great temples show, than most cities of Greece proper, and Hellenic southern Italy came to be called Magna Graecia. Again it should be noted that southern Italy and Sicily were not exclusively colonized from Greece proper. Kolophonians at Siris have already been mentioned. Gela in Sicily was an early foundation of Rhodians and Cretans; Knidians later settled in the Lipari Islands. Still later, as a sequel to defeat by the Persians, Samians settled at Zankle (Messana). A link, in some measure, between some of the Greeks of Greece proper and these western Greeks was the great festival centre of Olympia, where the foundations may be seen of the 'treasuries' of some of these colonial states lying under the shadow of the Hill of Kronos hard by the ancient temple of Hera.

Further west, before Carthaginians and Etruscans barred the way, was the sphere of the eastern Greeks, the Greeks of Asia Minor, in an area settled later than Italy and Sicily. Massilia (Marseilles) was founded by Phokaians from Phokaia in Ionia in about 600 BC, with daughter colonies at Antipolis (Antibes) and Nikaia (Nice), among other towns. From this southern region of what might at that time doubtfully be called Gaul the Greeks spread into Spain, especially to Emporion ('the Trading Centre'), modern Ampurias on the beautiful Gulf of Rosas, where any Greek would have felt at home, always provided that there was peace with the natives.

So it came about that later, in the sixth century and in the early fifth, when the Asia Minor Greeks were under particular pressure from the Persians, they thought of the west as a place of refuge; Sardinia comes up time and again in this connection, and not always in the minds of eastern Greeks only. Some Phokaians took refuge at Alalia in Corsica, and then, after hostile contact with the Carthaginians and Etruscans, at Velia in southern Italy, the later location of the Eleatic school of philosophers. The land of the Cyclops still exercised its attraction: above all, the Greeks who went to these lands did not have to move out of the climatic belt to which they were accustomed.

Elsewhere, for the most part, they had to do this. Apart from planting a Dorian colony from Thera (with Spartan interest) in North African Kyrene and its subsidiary settlements of Barke and Euhesperides, the Greeks turned to the northern Aegean, the Black Sea (Euxine) approaches and to the Black Sea itself. In the territory of Macedonia west of the River Strymon (the modern Struma), and especially in the three-pronged peninsula which is such a curious geographical feature of its coast, a variety of Greek states from the Aegean established colonies, but pre-eminently Eretria and Chalkis in Euboea, so that the whole region of the three-pronged peninsula came to be called Chalkidike. It must be wondered what dynamism, coupled with restricted arable land at home and local rivalries, led to the great activity of these Euboean cities, involved also (in the late eighth century) in a war over the plain between them, called the Lelantine Plain: and so the war was called the Lelantine War. Tradition maintained that it divided many of the states of the Aegean area into two camps and took on the form, in some measure at any rate, of a colonial war. This is unlikely, but there is every reason to believe that there was a great deal of warlike activity in the Aegean in one way or another in this period of transition, as between island states such as Naxos and Paros. There were plenty of opportunities for adventurers such as Archilochos, who has been mentioned already as taking part in the Parian colonization of the northern island of Thasos beyond the Strymon eastwards.

On the mainland coast of Thrace there were several notable Greek settlements – Maroneia, Abdera and Ainos – but these were planted later. The northern Aegean was, by Greek standards, bleaker than Sicily and southern Italy. The winds could blow cold from the north and north-east. Not very far behind the coast, at some points, lay the great mountain *massif* of Rhodope, though in the east, at the back of Ainos, flat land stretched to the western shore of the Black Sea. It was a savage land of wild animals, including lions (those on the coins of Akanthos are authentic creatures, not just known by hearsay) and wild people. The latter were barbarous and warlike, and always ready to butcher intruding Greeks. On the other hand coast and interior alike were rich in precious metals (exploited by the native tribes, who, when coinage came in, struck great heavy pieces), a temptation to those in quest of wealth, whether individuals or states. There was also much timber, suited for shipbuilding, corn and fine wine. The Greek settlements here were later than in the West, but some of them in Chalkidike and Thrace attained considerable prosperity, as their coins show. Perhaps too there was something about the wild and tattooed Thracians, kin of the even more barbarous peoples beyond Mount Rhodope, which stimulated the Greeks and broadened their minds, so that Thrace became a meeting-place of Mediterranean clarity and northern mystery. And if this seems too fanciful, it is worth while pondering that Abdera in Thrace was later distinguished for its philosophers, and that Stageira in Macedonia was the birthplace of Aristotle!

The Macedonian and Thracian colonies were not founded earlier than the end of the seventh century BC. This is true certainly of the one Corinthian colony in the region, Potidaia in Chalkidike, and probably of the others. Some, such as Abdera, were much later and were founded from Ionia. On the other hand it must be said that only in recent years has excavation been active in the northern Aegean, and new discoveries may give cause for a revision of ideas. Theoretically it is not hard to see why Thasos might be colonized earlier than the mainland: a protective stretch of sea rolled between the Parian colonists and the savage mainland. That this was an advantage is demonstrated by the dangers and disasters suffered by individuals and states who sought to settle in Thrace. Chalkidike and the coast of Macedonia to the west may well have been safer and preferred.

Further to the east the Black Sea approaches, that is the Hellespont, the Propontis (Sea of Marmara) and the Bosphorus, were a region of fairly early activity. It is interesting to note that, like the Euboean cities, Megara looked north-east as well as west, though this north-eastern movement came nearly a hundred years later than that to the west, and under an impulse which cannot be guessed at. The Megarians instructed by Apollo to establish themselves on the Bosphorus settled on the southern side at Üsküdar to found Kalchedon, and were upbraided by the god through his oracle at Delphi for their blindness in not perceiving the incomparable site they had neglected on the northern side at the modern Golden Horn. They repaired their oversight by the foundation of Byzantium, and the wisdom of Apollo's judgement has been apparent ever since in New Rome, Byzantium, Constantinople and Istanbul, even after the transfer of the Turkish capital to Ankara. Anyone who has watched the ships of every mercantile nation moving through the narrow straits between the Mediterranean and the Black Sea is marking the importance of the ancient city and the route it commands. The Megarians were, indeed, early in the field, but it was also natural for the

93

Greeks of Asia Minor to look in this direction if they planned colonies. Tradition made a number of Asia Minor cities, and especially Miletos, active in this region. Here again it is only human that any colonial city which could manage it with conviction would push back its foundation date as far as possible, to equal or surpass the western colonies. Tradition, which might be of this sort, claimed the establishment of some of the colonies on the southern shore of the Black Sea as preceding the occupation of its approaches. It will be remembered that the west provides examples of 'furthest first', but the problem of the Black Sea colonies is a difficult one, not made easier by the fact that archaeological investigation has been very deficient until quite recent years. The excavation which has taken place, it may be added, seems to support a relatively late date.

It is often asserted, and probably correctly, that the penetration of the Black Sea against wind and current was very difficult for primitive ships – this was the danger-fraught route of the Argonauts. In this case, if there was early settlement along the southern coast at such centres as Sinope (modern Sinop), it might be supposed to have taken place overland. And it might further be suggested that such early settlements were destroyed by the irruptions of the barbarous Cimmerians in the earlier seventh century, so that they had to be refounded. It is a problem which can be solved only by the discovery of further archaeological evidence. For the moment it looks as if all Black Sea settlements are late, that is of the seventh century, and late in it too.

Eventually the Asia Minor cities, and especially Miletos, planted a great number of colonies on the Black Sea coasts, to exploit the resources of these areas: the southern coast was rich in fruit trees and timber; it is worth remembering that the town of Kerasos may have given us the word 'cherry'; the eastern end enjoyed a subtropical climate, though the poisonous honey culled from azaleas by the local bees was a mixed blessing; there was also silver, and iron ore, for in this region iron-working was first developed in the district of the legendary Chalybes as far back as the end of the Bronze Age. The towns of the coastal strip had access, too, to the central plateau of Anatolia, over the Pontic mountain barrier. Centuries after the foundation of Trapezos (modern Trabzon or medieval Trebizond) from Sinope Xenophon was to lead the Greeks, who had carried out the Anabasis, from the interior of the Middle East to near Trapezos and their first glimpse of the familiar sea. As we have seen, both before and since travellers to eastern Anatolia, to the region of Lake Van (Urartu, ancient Armenia) and beyond, to Persia, passed by Trapezos, and it may be suggested that along this route from Van to the Black Sea and up the Danube came much fine metalwork to inspire the craftsmen of ancient Europe. Still further on eastwards was Kolchis and the land of the Golden Fleece, with the Caucasus and the Caspian, the region of spells, poisons and Medea. The Greeks also settled on the western and northern coasts of the great sea. It was not always hospitable, but Greek sailors did not necessarily hug the coasts. When they reached these European and southern Russian shores they must have been struck by two things: the limitless fertile earth and the gigantic rivers, especially the Ister, the modern Danube. Herodotus lists and describes the rivers from the Danube to the Don. The Danube drawing its waters from snow and heavy rain he is prepared to mention in the same breath with the Nile: 'The Ister is of all the rivers with which we are acquainted the mightiest.'[4] Other Greeks long before were impressed by it, since it was much greater than their own Hermos or Maiandros. A sherd found in the excavations of Old Smyrna and belonging to a time when the Greeks were setting off in this northern direction bears the name of Istrokles. His father was perhaps a sailor or an explorer.

The colonies on the western and northern sides of the Euxine tapped eventually the great natural resources of corn, and fish, dried and pickled; there was hemp, and skins and furs of all sorts (if the Greeks needed them), and certainly hides, which all Greeks needed in quantity. In return the cities of Asia Minor exported manufactured goods, objects of luxury, textiles and decorated pottery, and wine. The occupation of a very large number of sites by the Asia Minor Greeks and especially by the Milesians eventually produced one of the busiest trade routes of the Greek world, and many others came to share in it. The Aeginetans appear to have traded in this direction. Attic pottery later appears on the southern Russian sites, and in the Classical period the Euxine became a major, or *the* major, source of corn for infertile Greece, and its approaches a major preoccupation of Greek strategy and diplomacy. The occupation took place first, as it seems, in the later seventh century. It continued into the sixth, when Megara planted more colonies there. Something has already been said of the reasons why the exploitation of this rich region did not take place earlier.

Whatever the truth about the settlements of the southern coast, it must be agreed that for a Greek the Crimea was a very distant region. Furthermore, however attractive some of the coast regions may be in terms of weather for one coming from the continental climate prevailing further north, it would be a change for the worse for most Greeks. It should also be understood that during a good deal of the seventh century BC southern Russia appears to have suffered from the turmoil of tribal movements. What led the Ionians to colonize at this rather late date? Some may have wished to escape from political developments similar to those in Greece proper. Others no doubt wanted to get away from the overshadowing power of Lydia inland. It is unlikely that the Ionians were driven abroad by the infertility of their own land; and as far as less-favoured communities were concerned, such as those of Aeolis, there was

Thrace available, in the familiar Aegean. A strong impulse must have come from a desire to trade, since the Ionian cities were particularly well placed to act as middlemen between the interior of Asia Minor and regions overseas, when once the seventh-century turmoil of Asia Minor was over.

In the Euxine region we are as conscious of the contact between Greeks and barbarian peoples as we are in the far west, and even more so, because of the great wealth of material objects which have come from the grave mounds of southern Russia, covering a period of centuries. In the Classical and Hellenistic (post-Alexander) periods in particular we see the splendid productions in metalwork which combine Greek style with native subjects, and which illustrate the mixing of cultures Greek and Scythian. In the same fashion an interchange took place at an earlier date, in the sixth century BC, a period most fertile in contacts between the Greeks and the peoples surrounding them, before they had learned to despise the *barbaroi* as much as they later came to do. The contact of the Euxine region with the Greeks, and especially with the Ionians, is most clearly demonstrated by the presence of East Greek pottery on southern Russian and other Euxine sites, to be replaced later by pottery from Attica, and later still by the stamped wine amphorae of Thasos and Rhodes. Works of art made or influenced by Greeks were carried by merchants or mercenaries even as far as Prussia. It is impossible to exaggerate the importance of the Black Sea in this contact of Greek and barbarian. Nor was it all one way. In the reverse direction, by what route we know not, came the bone plaque with a stylized wolf in the peculiar Scythian style, which was found at the temple of Artemis in Ephesos, from which site we have also the ivory ibex which shows Scythian influence. They might, of course, or at any rate the first might, be relics of the barbarous Kimmerian invaders in the seventh century.

What the attitude of the resident Greeks was to the natives we cannot exactly say: they were probably more adaptable than Ovid when he went into exile at Tomi among the Getae on the western coast of the Black Sea. It happens, however, that a good deal is heard of these northern regions, and of the customs of their inhabitants from Herodotus, since part of his theme is the assault on Europe carried out by King Dareios, the Great King of Persia, in the late sixth century BC in his expedition into European Scythia. It was one of the strangest of expeditions, with Dareios crossing the Danube in pursuit of the nomad Scythians, who retreated before him until he was forced to turn back, when they closed in on his rear so that he barely escaped disaster. The purpose of this expedition has puzzled historians. Dareios could hardly have been attracted by stories of gold; he surely had enough, less hardly won. It would be an odd way to commence a conquest of Europe, which is sometimes suggested as his plan. Rather we must believe that he shared the geographical concept of

Herodotus, and regarded the Danube as flowing south (to match the Nile flowing in the opposite direction, so that the two make a great axis for the Near Eastern world) and forming the western boundary or some boundary of his dominions, beyond which were the nomads of what we would call the Eurasian steppe, a branch of whom had slain Kyros the founder of his dynasty. However this may be, Herodotus gives an account of the Scythians, and appears to think poorly of them except for one characteristic, their mobility, since they had no fixed habitation, which made them at once so invulnerable and so dangerous to invaders like Dareios. They formed the very antithesis to the fixed and stable life of the *polis* and we may suspect that in the back of his mind Herodotus ascribed to this their lack of intelligence in general.

It is evident from the account of Herodotus that the certainty of his knowledge (or the knowledge of his informants) about these northern lands decreased rapidly away from the Euxine shores. He relates much that is proved to be true about the nomad Scythians and about their burial practices, but he clearly lacked, for the more distant parts, the equivalent of an Ibn Fadlan who fourteen hundred years later visited the same regions from Baghdad. Yet it was all to the good. This was a region in which the Greeks could give full rein to their imagination. It has already been observed that the voyage of the Argonauts came to be located in the Black Sea; and there have been those who would place some of the adventures of Odysseus in that sea, under the influence of the Ionian epic tradition; and, after all, Circe was sister of Aietes, Lord of the Golden Fleece. Later on, and further into the interior, they felt that odd people like Aristeas of Prokonnesos might have strange adventures and visit distant peoples 'rapt in Bacchic fury'.[5] They were intrigued by the Scythians, as they were by the Thracians. Both had alien ways and seemed to belong to a quite different world. They told tales of Anacharsis, the wise Scyth, who visited Greece, and of Abaris, who went fasting round the world with his arrow, and taxed the credulity even of Herodotus. They also peopled the vast and distant stretches of these northern lands with even odder creatures: the gold-guarding griffins, the one-eyed Arimaspians and, at the very limits of the world, the Hyperboreans, who sent their mysterious gifts to Delos by way of the Scythians and the Adriatic.

So much for the last in this list of areas of colonization in the proper sense. In all this activity Apollo and his oracle at Delphi played a considerable part, and round his temple in its awe-inspiring situation Greek states had their 'treasuries' in the sacred enclosure, as they had at Olympia. They ranged from Knidos in south-western Asia Minor to Massilia in the far western Mediterranean. Apollo also gained in the process: he and his oracle grew in prestige and moral stature. From being the alien and remorseless god of *Iliad* I, terrible with his arrows, he became the exponent of reason, moderation and self-knowledge, but could not survive the political and moral complications and dilemmas of the Classical period.


## THE GREEKS AND THE NEAR EAST

There still remains the eastern Mediterranean. Cyprus and the coasts of Syria and Phoenicia had long since been areas of maximum cultural and artistic importance. In the age of the revival of culture, that is in the later post-Mycenaean period, this region played a great part, which is reflected in the *Odyssey*. Sidon is a centre of metalworking, and Sidonian women are the great exponents of skill in the production of textiles. As something of a link between this region of the eastern Mediterranean and Greece Crete appears to be of some importance, a centre of far-roving sea travellers. Cyprus was even more important.

In the Near East Assyria was in the ascendant, until by the end of the eighth century its shadow was over Cyprus. The Assyrians were aware of the people they called the Iawana, while the Phoenicians were active in the Mediterranean side by side with the Greeks. Egypt, after being dominated by a Nubian dynasty and threatened by Assyria, shows a revival in the mid-seventh century under the native xxvith Dynasty, with the aid of Greek and Carian mercenaries, the 'bronze men from the sea'. In central Asia Minor on the Anatolian plateau away to the east of the Greek cities, the Phrygians in the region of the River Sangarios had at last settled down from a semi-nomadic condition, which had been theirs since they had come into Asia Minor following on the destruction of the Hittite Empire. Greek tradition knew of King Midas and his wealth (even as a benefactor of Delphi). The Assyrian records speak of Mitta, possibly a title rather than a name. The Phrygians were in contact with the great eastern power, and excavations at Gordion which have revealed extensive buildings and tombs of outstanding importance show that they had attained a high level of technical skill and culture, especially in wood-inlay and metalwork, by the end of the eighth century BC. It is clear that they looked eastwards, not only to the Assyrians in their furthest expansion westwards, but also to the culture area of eastern Anatolia and northern Syria. They may have obtained their alphabetic system of writing from the east independently of the Greeks. There is a bronze bowl from Phrygian Gordion with an inscription scratched on beeswax. The metalwork obviously owed something to the Urartians of the kingdom in the region of Lake Van, now in eastern Turkey, which was also outstanding for its metalwork, like the region still further east in the vicinity of Lake Urmia in north-western Persia. This latter region was in contact with the Asian steppe and also with Urartu and the Assyrians; Urartu itself was in close though hostile contact with Assyria and with the Phrygians and the principalities of south-east Anatolia and northern Syria. They formed a culture complex of the greatest interest and importance for the creation, adaptation and transmission of artistic motives and technical advances over long periods and great distances.

In widely different contexts in Europe and the Mediterranean region have been found objects, of bronze and ivory in particular, which are either original productions of one of the regions mentioned, or the work of expatriate craftsmen, or, finally, imitations by foreign artists, in most cases Greek, though here perhaps it should be pointed out that 'Greek' may mean nothing more than presence in a Greek community. It is not always easy to tell the difference, or to identify the region of manufacture or the source (which may be multiple) of the artistic influences present, which often include renderings which have oriental ideas as their background. From Cumae in Italy comes a fine cauldron now in the National Museum in Copenhagen. Its ring handles are decorated with ox-heads of an impressive and monumental character. Some details of the technique, it is felt by the experts, are neither quite Phrygian nor yet quite Urartian, though akin to both, and certainly oriental. Similar ox-heads have been found at Olympia and Delphi. This idea of a ring handle passing through a moulded attachment is also characteristic of a related group of cauldrons with ring-holders in the form of human-headed birds (sometimes called 'sirens'), of which a considerable number (of the attachments, that is, since they are more likely to survive than the cauldrons) come from Delphi and Olympia, some few from Italy, and some again from the Lake Van region, where they appear to have been originally at home. They vary slightly in type, and again it is sometimes difficult to distinguish between the oriental original and the Greek imitation. The Greeks of this period (of the late eighth and early seventh centuries) retained their earlier enthusiasm for cauldrons. The change from the tripod-cauldron of the Geometric period to the detached cauldron of the following period has been mentioned already (page 87), and so too the Greek predilection for replacing the lions' heads by the necks and fierce beaked heads of griffins, mythical creatures which some hold to be a Greek creation, and others an importation from the Orient. Some of these griffin heads are cast by the *cire-perdue* process; others, some of the earlier ones, appear to be of hammered metal, and filled with some substance which could be poured in as a fluid – another oriental technique. As one scholar has put it, in their cauldron decoration the Greeks were more oriental than the Orient! The griffin attachments are numerous, and of wide distribution, from Asia Minor to Gaul; they are far more common than the prototype with lions' heads, of which the outstanding example, perhaps of Urartian manufacture, was found in the

Regolini-Galassi tomb at Cerveteri in Etruria.

The great chamber tombs of the Etruscan nobility, who had such a passion for funeral splendour, both frescoes and imported luxury goods, especially those associated with feasting and drinking, have yielded many specimens of this oriental or orientalizing work in bronze and in ivory. Once all these objects tended to be lumped together as 'Phoenician', and it may well be true that the Phoenicians, in keeping with the part they play in the *Odyssey*, were responsible for the carriage of some of them from the East to Italy. It may be well to recall too that there was a tradition (see pp. 58, 66) that the Etruscans themselves came from Lydian Asia Minor. Some of these works of art could have been made in Etruria by fugitive craftsmen from the eastern Mediterranean, men who fled from Urartu and Syria when the Assyrians overran those regions in the later eighth century, and some even by the Greeks. A parallel case is the imitation of Egyptian faience scarabs and other small objects in factories in the eastern Mediterranean, at Rhodes and elsewhere, and as far west as Ischia.

A splendid example of eastern bronze work is the conical cauldron support decorated with confronted winged and man-headed creatures, rather like the guardians of Assyrian gateways, from the Barberini Tomb at Praeneste, some distance south of Rome, evidence of Etruscan luxury in Latium. It is in a heavy coarse style, possibly Urartian or Syrian, vaguely reminiscent of late Hittite sculpture, and serves to remind us of other metalwork, in differing styles, which has been found in Cyprus and in various Greek centres. There is, for example, the bronze bowl in the Ashmolean Museum, Oxford, said to be from Olympia, decorated in relief with some engraved detail. Of exceptional interest is another bowl, from a grave in the Kerameikos of Athens, found in a context of Geometric vases. From Olympia again comes a bronze plaque, probably Urartian, certainly oriental, only one of the many objects from the eastern world which recent excavations at the great Greek sanctuary have produced. Further, from the Idaean Cave in Crete there is a whole series of bronze reliefs (in the form of shields with central animal bosses) some of which show oriental motives. Some of them may well have been made on the island by immigrant craftsmen from the same region as those mentioned above in connection with Etruria. Some would suggest they are the work of native Greeks, but it is difficult to believe that the bronze 'gong' from this site, with Gilgamesh rending a lion flanked by two very Assyrian-looking attendants, in much the same style as the cauldron support from the Barberini Tomb, was not made by such a craftsman from Urartu or Syria, even if it served a local Cretan cult.

Finally there is the group of Phoenician bowls, as they are called, of widespread distribution, which includes a number of examples or fragments from Cyprus. One of the finest, in silver covered with a thin layer of gold, comes from a tomb at Praeneste in Italy. These bowls are decorated in a finer and more elegant style than the foregoing, in very low relief with much incision of detail. They produce, therefore, a thoroughly pictorial effect, with figures and landscape and architectural elements used to express some kind of narrative, or a combination of a number of narratives, arranged in concentric bands. The depiction of detail is a curious mixture of Egyptian, Assyrian and other renderings not easy to identify: a mixture which befits the geographical position of the Phoenician cities. It is hard to reject the suggestion that such bowls, combined with memories of the inlaid Mycenaean daggers, inspired the description of the shield of Achilles in the *Iliad*.

These products of oriental workshops can be justified for what they are in many cases, but not in all. Apart from the question of oriental craftsmen working at Greek centres, there is the nice problem of the close imitation, to be distinguished as such only by a specifically Greek rendering of some detail. Objects found at the great centres of religion and resort such as Delphi and Olympia, and at lesser centres such as Ephesos, Samos and Thasos, or in Italy at the Etruscan sites, have presented such problems, which are nowhere better illustrated than by the rather uncouth but powerful ivory carving found at Delphi, representing a human figure 'subduing' a feline: the 'Lord of the Lion' it might be called, and it embodies a common oriental concept which the Greeks took over. For long it was held to be uncertain whether it was a product of an oriental or of a Greek workshop. The discovery of some small extra fragments which belong to its base seems to show that it is Greek, but it is very much on the borderline, and its place of origin is still quite obscure. It may be added that this problem sometimes presents itself later, even at a time when in general it may be said that the Greeks (and this includes their sometimes barbarian craftsmen) had had time to assimilate their oriental heritage. It is true, as will later be seen, that in pottery, in particular, there is little difficulty in recognizing the Greek product which is making use of oriental motives, either at the beginning or when the process of assimilation is completed. They stand out distinctly from the products of Phrygian and Lydian pottery makers and painters. The volume of pottery available for comparison and the finds on Greek sites which sometimes include pottery wasters (rejects), to say nothing of inscriptions, make the expert's task *relatively* easy, though there is still considerable obscurity about the place of manufacture, within the Greek and Italian lands, of quite important vase groups. The problem is vastly more complicated in the case of rare objects of sometimes high artistic worth and in costly materials, found in some mixed or outlandish context.

To sum up: the Near East produced a variety of objects which were widely distributed and imitated in Aegean and Italian lands and in the fringe regions. With such things the Phoenicians, the sea traders of the *Odyssey*, were associated, together with craftsmen of Syria, the region of Lake Van and Phrygia. Bronze work is most in evidence, and other metals were used. It is probable enough that if they were not so perishable objects of wood and ivory would be more in evidence. A surprising number of objects of wood have been found in the great tombs of Gordion in Phrygia, and some at Samos, among other sites, and it is clear that the Phoenicians and Syrians produced masses of ivory carving, sometimes dyed or inlaid with coloured glass: we may recall the Mycenaean *kyanos*, Penelope's chair in the *Odyssey*, of ivory and silver, and the dyeing of ivory in the *Iliad*, though there the craft is ascribed to Lydia and Caria in Asia Minor. It was much admired by the Assyrian kings as the decoration of furniture, and has been found in quantity at Nimroud. Even if it was not imported by the Greeks (though some finds from Thasos, for instance, might indicate that it was), they would see specimens of it when they visited the Near East, where strange monsters, twiformed creatures often confronted about a central floral structure, naturalistic scenes and subsidiary vegetable and floral decoration made up of curvilinear bands sometimes combined with flowers and buds were to be seen not only on small and portable objects of art but also as the decoration of palaces and temples, in paint and stone, as well as in ivory. Of such character, it seems, was King Ahab's 'ivory house' at Samaria. And then there were textiles and embroideries, the speciality of the women of Sidon. It must have been very exciting for those coming from the unswerving rectitude of the Geometric style in Greece.

Much no doubt escapes the modern scholar, and much will be added to his knowledge when more excavation takes place, especially in Anatolia. There it will reveal more of the artistic importance of Urartu, as the excavations at Altın Tepe have done, and the links westward with the Phrygians, and with the forerunners of the Lydian kingdom, the ivory-dyers of the *Iliad*. This is an intensely important area for these cultural connections, especially in the late eighth century and in the seventh. The Ionian Greeks were on the fringe of it. So far it is difficult to decide how much contact they had with Phrygia, but more excavation and more study of the increasing amount of comparative material from Ionia, Phrygia and early Lydia will help to solve the complex problems involved. Many efforts have been made to prove the existence of an overland route eastwards across Anatolia (a forerunner of the later royal road of the Persian kings from Sardis to Susa) as a cultural and trading link.

The point has already been made that the Phrygians may have had contact with eastern Europe and even with the Aegean via the Black Sea, as may regions further to the east and south by the route which later led to Trapezos. But the irruption of the nomad Kimmerians at the beginning of the seventh century destroyed the Phrygian power and threw Asia Minor into a turmoil, from which Lydia emerged as the great power. It is far more likely that the main line of contact of the Greeks with the eastern end of the Mediterranean was by way of the southern coast of Asia Minor, from Samos and Ephesos via Rhodes and Cyprus to settlements on the northern Syrian coast such as Al Mina (ancient Poseideion), one of the gateways to the Assyrianized interior. This seems tolerably clearly demonstrated by archaeology. Likewise for the Greeks of Greece proper, and especially for Corinth at the isthmus, which played an important part in all this, there was the chain of islands across the Aegean to Rhodes, and it has been already made clear that Crete played some part as a stage on the route to and from the East, and later perhaps on the route to Egypt, since it must not be forgotten that this ancient country was also opened up to the Greeks in the seventh century. The presence of sherds from some of the Aegean Islands, followed by those of Corinthian pots, at Al Mina seems to suggest the residence there of settlers and traders from these parts of Greece. This may be so, though in this early period of Greek travel and commerce there was probably the same considerable mixture of origins as later in the Classical period.

This question of eastern trade introduces an important issue. It seems from the *Odyssey* that Crete was important even in the post-Mycenaean period, in the sense that a sea rover might be a Cretan or pass himself off so to be. The Greeks had a firmly rooted idea of the importance of the early Iron Age Cretans; and Apollo, it was claimed, had his Cretan priests at Delphi. There is no denying the importance of the Idaean shields and similar objects found in Crete, which showed links with the Orient. It is reasonable to connect all this with the obviously important position of Crete as a stepping-stone in the island chain from the Peloponnese by the way of Kythera, Anti-Kythera, Crete, Kasos and Karpathos to Rhodes, another island of great importance in this Greek–Oriental connection. In the Peloponnese, at the Greek end, as it were, of this chain, was Sparta, and while Classical Sparta sought to cut herself off from the outside world, the seventh-century state appears not to have done this, for the excavations at the shrine of Artemis Orthia have yielded a wealth of carved ivories, plaques and seals, and objects of bone, which seem to indicate that Sparta also had a part in the 'orientalizing' process, though this need mean no more than that the Perioikoi rather than full Spartiates engaged in the arts and crafts. It is not surprising, therefore, that the presence in Crete in the seventh century of some particularly colourful pottery with decoration incorporating oriental motives and with some interesting shapes, following on after a not undistinguished Geometric style, has led some scholars to ascribe a leadership and primacy in this general development to the Cretans, and to magnify their cultural importance in the Iron Age. It would follow, not unreasonably, that to the Cretans should be ascribed a large influence at Delphi, and even in the West, where Cretans in association with Rhodians founded Gela in Sicily in the earliest seventh century. Sparta also came in later for some of the reflected glory; it could be described as a state not yet militaristically inclined, and possessing a material culture not different from other Greek states. But archaeological finds outside Crete hardly confirm this claim for the island, least of all at Delphi, and while it is not possible to deny to the Cretans skill in pottery and metalwork (whoever these Cretans were, for this is by no means clear), it is not easy to accord them any undeniable primacy in this achievement. It looks, too, as if the Spartan ivories are rather late, and on political grounds almost certainly the work of an inferior class in the state. In fact there is every indication that Corinth was the leader in this connection with the East and an intermediary in trade with the West; witness the importance of the site of Perachora just to the north of Corinth across the gulf. What part Athens played in it is difficult to assess. She is to be regarded as something of a backwater in the seventh century, despite the excellence of her Geometric pottery. The part she played in the earlier development of trade and material culture will be discussed again in Chapter 7. It seems true enough that early in the seventh century she stands out less clearly than Corinth, but the splendid vases of the later seventh century from Vari and elsewhere give reason for caution in drawing too strong a contrast in technical and artistic achievement. This much needs to be said at this juncture on the matter of primacy of achievement in what has come to be called the 'orientalizing' phase of Greek art; more must be said of it later against the general background of seventh-century Greece.

The Greeks did not gain artistic inspiration and material objects alone from this contact with the East. There was also the matter of the alphabet, to which reference has already been made repeatedly. By the seventh century the Greeks were fully possessed of an alphabet of consonants and vowels with overall similarities, but with local differences, the 'epichoric' alphabets. The general version of the Greek alphabet was an adaptation of the system of writing which came into being among the Semitic Phoenicians, derived from pictorial signs. Elements of a system of writing which tried to get away from the clumsy syllabic forms (of which Linear B was one) had appeared earlier, but the Phoenician system was neat and compendious, emancipated from the influence of a professional class of scribes, and suited to the common need for a form of writing which *everyone* might use in all the relations of life. It was also, very naturally, influenced by the nature of the Semitic language of the Phoenicians, which, like Hebrew, possessed a consonantal framework and few unchanging vowels. For the most part in the Phoenician system of writing vowels were understood, as in some systems of shorthand. The Greek language was different, and could not dispense with the representation of vowels, or even, ultimately, with the distinction of long and short vowels. Some of the Semitic sounds were not present in Greek, such as the guttural ' *aleph*, so a series of signs, even if imperfect, was available for vowel sounds. It is clear that the Greeks indulged in experimentation, and could invent letters if they needed them. But the eastern Mediterranean was the place of origin, and contact with the inventors the channel. The great variety of local alphabets may be explained by the assumption of one of two processes: either individual Greeks carried out their own personal adaptations of the Semitic alphabet, and these were transmitted by traders or returning residents to a variety of centres in Greece, or a single adaptation at an eastern Mediterranean settlement such as Al Mina in northern Syria became differentiated when it was taken back to Greece. On the whole the first seems most likely, or a mixture of both. The Greeks, of course, believed that Kadmos the Phoenician had brought letters to Greece at a far-off period of time. The Etruscans in turn got their alphabet (which they passed on to the Romans) from the Greeks. They took it over from the Greeks of Cumae in Campania. A writing tablet from Etruscan Marsigliana shows the alphabetic signs as recited and written in school in the first half of the seventh century. It seems to confirm that the alphabet came to Etruria from the Cumaean Greeks, and suggests that they still retained two 'spare' signs, *xi* and *san*, for which they had no use.

The great achievement for the Greeks was the development of a system of writing which might readily be mastered, and which possessed vowel signs. It has been suggested from time to time that somehow this appearance of vowel signs was promoted by the need to write down quantitative verse, and in particular epic verse. Yet need this be so? Such verse was a matter not merely of vowels but of syllables arranged in a formal pattern, and the musical accompaniment must have had something to do with it. Only to a certain degree did the archaic alphabets distinguish between long and short vowels, and even later the distinction was made only in the case of *e* and *o*, and not in the case of *a*, *i* and *u*. The point might, indeed, be made that the distinction between long and short *e* and between long and short *o* is an early Ionian characteristic (apart from certain odd exceptions such as Paros and Thasos), and Ionia was a region where the use of the poetic elegiac couplet seems first in evidence, and where the epic developed.

Yet *all* the Greeks, though like M. Jourdain they talked prose without knowing it, communicated in their early days in written verse, which they used for epitaphs and inscriptions of various sorts, and for other 'unpoetic' needs (if it is permissible to use such an expression). The question is an obscure one. By far the most important point, however, is that writing became a personal skill, from the middle of the eighth century as far as we can judge. Writing fixed in some degree, but far from completely, works such as the epic poems which had hitherto been a matter of impromptu performance. They now became literature. Writing helped to make eternal the poems we and the Greeks call 'Homeric'; it no doubt also destroyed some of the fire and *élan* of impromptu composition. Most important of all it made possible the writing down of covenants and laws, and the inscribing of dedications to the gods and monuments to men. Appeal need now be no longer to the fallible or prejudiced minds of the aristocratic guardians of the customary law, but to written codes and agreements. The accumulation of historical matter could begin, not least the lists of magistrates and priests and the recording of their years of office (the utility of which the Greeks must have seen among the Egyptians and in the Middle East), perhaps with the main events taking place in them, which formed the background of history and the framework of chronology. The Greeks had no system of universal and absolute chronology, no supreme blessing of BC and AD. Each city evolved, when writing came in, its own system of dating by the yearly magistrates of the community, the length of time some individual had held an important priesthood or the like. Once they were fully established the great festivals such as the Olympic at Olympia or the Pythian at Delphi could help, when the victors' names were listed, and this might be done from the inscribed dedications at the sanctuaries. But the historian's task was a hard one. Nowhere is the problem better illustrated than in that passage where Thucydides dates the outbreak of the great fifth-century war between Athens and Sparta: 'The thirty years' truce which was entered into after the conquest of Euboea lasted fourteen years. In the fifteenth, in the forty-eighth year of the priestess-ship of Chrysis at Argos, in the ephorate of Ainesias at Sparta, in the last month but two of the archonship of Pythodoros at Athens, and six months after the battle of Potidaia, just at the beginning of spring, a Theban force . . . made an armed entry into Plataia.'[6] Add to this the confusion of names and generations, the retrospective confection of forged documents and the uncritical use of the genuine, and it will be clear why some have wondered whether the study of early Greek history is possible to any valuable degree! But without a system of writing there could have been nothing at all, except vague memories.

In this matter of Greece and the East there remains yet one more theme to be explored. This is the opportunity for intellectual contact, for which the evidence is less tangible, not only bringing about the spread of legends about men, deities and monsters, but also the transmission of the accumulated knowledge and experience of the East, hardly 'science' and still less first principles. The more ancient civilizations of these eastern regions had laid up much information, as, for instance, astronomical observations. In the main it was more the stimulus than the matter which produced the physical ideas of a Thales as an alternative to the mythological *Theogony* of a Hesiod. It should be noted that these stimuli were not confined to the observation of eclipses and the use of rule-of-thumb calculation. In particular it should be seen that in the second half of the seventh century the opening of Egypt to the Greeks brought them into contact with a civilization age-old and of tremendous organizational and technical achievement, but set and congealed. From it the Greeks knew how to take ideas on major sculpture and on major building, as well as on the remote past. Egypt in particular came to be regarded as the source of ancient wisdom. The wise Solon travelled there, and from Egypt Plato claimed he had got the story of Atlantis, and perhaps he did – of an Atlantis in Crete. The 'educational' value of the contact with this ancient civilization was the same as that later obtained there by Herodotus in the fifth century, when in many ways the impact was less:

When Hekataios the historian was at Thebes [in Egypt] and, discoursing of his genealogy, traced his descent to a god in the person of his sixteenth ancestor, the priests of [Egyptian] Zeus did to him exactly as they afterwards did to me, though I made no boast of my family. They led me into the inner sanctuary, which is a spacious chamber, and showed me a multitude of colossal statues in wood, which they counted up, and found to amount to the exact number they had said; the custom being for every high priest during his lifetime to set up his statue in the temple. As they showed me the figures and reckoned them up, they assured me that each was the son of the one preceding him, and this they repeated throughout the whole time, beginning with the representation of the priest last deceased, and continuing until they had completed the series. When Hekataios, in giving his genealogy, mentioned a god as his sixteenth ancestor, the priests opposed their genealogy to his, going through this list, and refusing to allow that any man was ever born of a god.[7]

Whether or not the Greeks traced their descent back to gods because of their relatively recent incoming or not, Egypt must have been a highly educative experience to them: to civilians who traded with Naukratis in the Delta (and Ionians had a very considerable share in this), and to mercenary soldiers, like the original 'bronze men' who helped the founder of the xxvith Dynasty to establish himself, or the many others who served the Egyptians, including those, Dorians from Rhodes and Ionians from Kolophon and Teos, who took that romantic journey up the Nile with Pharaoh Psammetichos II between 594 and 589 BC, and scratched their names on a leg of one of the colossi at Abu Simbel to make one of the most exciting of Greek inscriptions. So, too, there was the wisdom of Babylonia. How else did Thales prophesy an eclipse, and make a corner in oil mills and a fortune by foreseeing a good year?

These were important contacts, and the Greeks had the best of both worlds; they were themselves free of the autocratic and theocratic institutions of the Middle East, but they could draw on its accumulated observations. Later on individuals with relatively untrammelled minds could continue the search for general principles. *Historie*, 'inquiry', became a key word of Greek intellectual culture. The pursuit of it became for a time particularly characteristic of Ionia, and when conditions there became less favourable, not so much because of alien domination as by reason of a decline in material prosperity and the presence of internal strife, the representatives of Ionian philosophical thought spread over the Greek world. We should not, of course, exaggerate too greatly what they did, at any rate from the standpoint of science, if indeed we should use that word at all. At first sight their deliberations present an impressive contrast to the *Theogony* of Hesiod, but in their quest for a first principle (such as water, which Thales of Miletos suggested as the primary substance) they were in effect seeking another and non-anthropomorphic type of deity: the world, it was said, 'is full of gods'. As 'scientists' they were tackling the problem from the wrong end, if it was really their concern to understand the physical world in our scientific sense. But they were not as yet really concerned to use their knowledge for practical ends. They were not experimenters as they were in politics, and consequently their importance in the physical and biological sciences was far less than in political science.

# CHAPTER 6

# THE BEGINNING OF CONSOLIDATION:
## TYRANTS AND HOPLITES

The very generalizing character of what has been said in Chapters 4 and 5 and the assemblage together of elements of diverse date from both the written sources and the material remains might well seem unsatisfactory. In fact they can hardly be otherwise. So much is obscure in the written sources (which are rarely contemporary) and in the archaeological evidence. The great strides made in recent excavation should not obscure the fact that publication has frequently failed to keep pace with work in the field, and that dating is often subjective, disputed and vague, while the mechanics of cultural and economic contact and interchange are obscure in the extreme. The objectivity of the study of material remains is not always as great as might be thought. Above all, how far does the surviving material represent a true sample of the original?

All students of the periods down to the latter part of the eighth century are painfully aware of these problems. The eighth century is less dark than the ninth, but it is only with the seventh that a certain confidence can be felt. Not only is there, overall, an increase in material evidence, but there is a feeling that the events of this century were not beyond the knowledge of later antiquity. Much is still obscure but the shape of Archaic Greece is beginning to emerge. On the other hand there is nothing magical as a dividing line in the date 700 BC, and the discussion in the present chapter must in some measure be carried back, at the cost of repetition of what has already been said, and reference forward must be made to events of the sixth century, anticipating what is to be said in Chapter 8. Certain generalizations have already been made concerning the development of the *polis* structure. This can now be looked at more closely with specific reference to named states and their problems: Argos, Corinth, Megara, Chalkis, Eretria, the Ionian cities, Aegean Islands and colonial centres. Sparta and Athens will be dealt with separately in Chapter 7, for reasons which will clearly emerge there. The seventh century saw the development, if not the beginnings, of the hoplite army organization. This process will be noticed in general terms in the present chapter and more specifically and in greater detail for Sparta in the next. The latter part of the seventh century and the earlier part of the sixth were for some states the heyday of the form of government called tyranny. It arose from crises to be studied in the present chapter. Sparta and Athena in a large measure suffered from such crises too, but the outcome was different. The appearance of the phenomenon of coinage is of great importance in this period and will be considered first.

Precious metals had long been used as a special form of wealth, easily adapted as a standard by which to measure values, and to be weighed out, as in the Middle East ornaments were weighed and used in exchange. Gold, silver and *electrum*, the natural or artificial alloy of the two, could be used in this way. In the Homeric poems *talanta* (plural of *talanton*) is the term for the twin suspended scale-pans of a balance; the singular *talanton* was a unit of gold thus weighed. So on the Shield of Achilles in *Iliad* xviii gold 'talents' appear as the prize of wisdom in counsel. There *might* be some memory here of a Mycenaean gold unit of 8·5 grams in the form of pellets, bars or rings. This Mycenaean gold unit is credible enough, though the suggestion that it was the equivalent of an ox is not clearly substantiated. On the other hand the Homeric references here in *Iliad* xviii and elsewhere could be to a unit used in the Dark Age. A lump of silver and tiny ingots of gold which look as if they might have served thus have been found in the late-eighth-century Khaniale Tekke Tomb at Knossos in Crete, but in fact these are most likely to be the stock-in-trade of a goldsmith. They follow no identifiable weight standard. Ingots of bronze and iron could and did function as currency. They were inconvenient as small change or for the traveller, but they were also useful sources of raw material. They could be used like the currency bars or sword blanks of Iron Age Britain, and an iron currency of this clumsy sort was purposely retained by the Spartans in the hope of preventing the concealment of wealth. Long iron rods could be used as spits and as sources of raw metal, and therefore as currency. The name for them was *obelos*, or (in some dialects) *odelos*, and in Attic *obolos*. There was a practice of dedicating such spits in temples. It is illustrated by the story of Herodotus concerning Rhodopis, the famous courtesan of Naukratis, who was ransomed by the brother of the Lesbian poetess Sappho: 'Wishing to leave a memorial of herself in Greece she determined to have something made the like of which was not to be found in any temple, and to offer it at the shrine at Delphi. So she set apart a tenth of her possessions, and purchased with the money a quantity of iron spits, such as are fit for roasting oxen whole, whereof she made a present to the oracle. They are still to be seen there, lying of a heap behind the altar which the Chians dedicated, opposite the sanctuary.'[1] Herodotus' story has been confirmed by the discovery of a piece of the dedicatory inscription at Delphi. These spits must have been of very large size for ox-roasting: actual spits found at the Heraion of Argos and now in the National Numismatic Museum in Athens seem in size suitable ones for sheep. There are also three inscriptions found at the Heraion of Perachora north of Corinth. They record the dedication of a *drachma* (*drachme*) to 'White-armed Hera'. The word means 'a handful' and must refer to a bundle of spits, standard temple equipment to judge from a fourth-century Boeotian temple inventory which refers to cauldrons (for stewing), spits (for grilling) and to the necessary couches and tables for the religious feasts. The date of the Perachora spit inscriptions (on stones forming racks to which the spits were attached) has been much debated: they could be of different dates and suggestions have been made ranging from the eighth century through the seventh into the first half of the sixth.

All this would have been of specialist interest only had it not been for the fact that *obolos* was the word for the smallest Greek standard coin in silver and *drachma* the word for a coin equivalent to six *oboloi*. This fact and the dedications (of which there is evidence, apart from the inscriptions, in the actual spits from the Heraion of Argos) set later Greeks on a course of historical reconstruction associated with the great name of early Greek history, Pheidon of Argos, king and tyrant. Herodotus, the earliest source, narrating the wedding of Agariste, daughter of the tyrant Kleisthenes of Sikyon in the earlier sixth century lists her suitors: 'From the Peloponnese came several: Leokedes, son of that Pheidon king of the Argives, who established measures for the Peloponnesians, and was the most insolent of all the Greeks. . . .'[2]

Herodotus, therefore, associates Pheidon only with measures. On the other hand Strabo (in the period of Augustus) on the authority of Ephoros (fourth-century BC) includes weights and coins: ['Ephoros says that] Pheidon the Argive was the tenth from Temenos, and surpassed his contemporaries in power; whereby he recovered the heritage of Temenos broken into many parts. He invented the measures called Pheidonian, and weights and coined money, silver and the rest.'[3]

Elsewhere he quotes Ephoros as stating that these coins were issued in Aegina. Finally a late lexicographer unites coins and spits: 'Pheidon ruler of Argos first of all men struck coins in Aegina, and having issued coins, he removed the spits and dedicated them to Argive Hera.'[4] Herodotus, it is interesting to note, says nothing of coins or spits: in other words, if he saw the dedication at the Argive Heraion (which incidentally was burned in 423 BC), as he did that of Rhodopis at Delphi, he understood it for what it was, namely temple equipment.

The story of Pheidon and the coins appears to have been invented between the mid-fifth and mid-fourth century; the question of Aegina will be considered later. It seems that the *Constitution of Argos* of the Aristotelian School ascribed only the measures to Pheidon; so do other later sources, but not the weights. The measures are, it is said, either his invention or the object of reform by him. Such a reform can hardly mean a rationalization of weights and measures. It sounds far too advanced a reform to be credited to a ruler of Pheidon's date (in the first third of the seventh century), and even he could not have imposed it on the whole Peloponnese as Herodotus suggests. The thought must occur that the adjective *pheidos* means 'sparing'; and *pheidon*, according to the lexicographer Pollux, was an oil-container, which appears to have poured oil sparingly, 'named from the Pheidonian measures'. These latter, it appears from the *Constitution of Athens*, were smaller than the Attic. So there is Pheidon connected with 'sparing' measures. It may well be that here is a case of pseudo-history based on verbal similarities and nothing more. The tradition has no real value, any more than the dedicatory *drachma* inscriptions can be used to date Pheidon.

In Greece iron spits as currency may well have been replaced by a silver coinage, but the actual development of coinage could not be deduced from the literary tradition given above, or dated by it. Ephoros, it is to be noted, claimed that Pheidon had 'invented coinage, silver and the rest', which is to assume that the gold, silver, electrum and bronze coins of the historian's own day had been present from the beginning. In fact electrum was native in an alluvial form to western Asia Minor, and electrum coins had appeared there before the appearance of silver coins in Greece, where, with dubious exceptions, electrum was not used for coinage. The primacy of western Asia Minor is clearly demonstrated in archaeological terms. A number of primitive pieces have been found there; some were recovered from beneath the earliest temple of Artemis at Ephesos; they are not securely dated. The form they take justifies the use of the term 'coin', which may be defined in very general terms as a piece of metal of acceptable fineness and weight, guaranteed and its issuing agency identified by an impressed device.

The simplest form of coin was a small lump of electrum which had been heated and impressed by crude punches (the punch die) on a striated surface (the anvil), thus at the very beginning setting the tradition for Greek coinage. Next after the most primitive are those coins with punch marks on the reverse and on the obverse (the anvil die), a variety of primitive badges of diverse character including patterns and animals. The most famous example, though not of the earliest group, is the electrum *stater* (standard coin), with a stag and an inscription which seems to name the issuing agent or a deity of which the stamp is the badge or symbol. It may be added that patterns and animals later appear in the punch dies representing the beginnings of a true reverse type. Some of these early electrum coins are very small and must have been difficult to handle. They represent fractions down to one ninety-sixth of the *stater* or standard coin. There is a puzzle here: whether the *stater* and its fractions represented high values or whether the fractions were so small in order to fit in with minor transactions. In that case it is difficult to understand why silver was not used as an alternative. It is unclear who issued these coins: private individuals, conveniently called 'merchants', have been suggested, who, having weighed and tested small lumps of precious metal, wished to recognize these when they returned to the issuer in the process of circulation; or else a state may have produced them (for what purpose will be discussed later). A clear case of a state issue at a somewhat later date is the *stater* with a *phoke*, a seal, the 'canting' type suggesting the name of the Asia Minor city of Phokaia. There are also electrum coins with a lion's head which may stylistically be compared with some lion's heads on Corinthian pots of the latter part of the seventh century. These may well be issues of the Lydian kings: like the Phrygian Midas before him, Gyges the founder of the Mermnad dynasty in the earlier seventh century was associated with the idea of great wealth and his kingdom with gold-bearing rivers. An electrum coin bears the name Walwesh which may represent Alyattes, King (610–560 BC) of Lydia, fourth after Gyges.

The basis of the dating of these early coins is hardly satisfactory. The latest date of the associated objects found at the Artemision of Ephesos is the earlier sixth century; the stylistic comparison of the lion's heads of the supposed Lydian coinage is with Early Corinthian (late seventh century) vase-painting. A reasonable view is that the earliest coinage may have begun around 650 BC and that by 600 BC a number of Asia Minor states were issuing coins. As for mainland Greece there are the indications in the literary tradition that Aegina was the centre for the issue of the earliest Peloponnesian coins. Given the widespread trading activity of the island, including the connection with Naukratis, the trading factory in Egypt, this is reasonable enough. It would be possible to suggest an exchange of silver (from Siphnos or Attica?) and oil (from Attica?) for Egyptian corn. This is the theory. On the other hand the earliest Aeginetan coins are not widely distributed and their dating is a problem. They have a sea turtle on the obverse and a windmill incuse pattern on the reverse, and look fairly advanced. They may have started, it is thought, around 600 BC, but there is no good reason why they should be earlier than the second quarter of the sixth century. The question whether they were circulating in Athens in the time of Solon (in the first decade of the sixth century) will be debated in Chapter 8. The problem of the introduction of coinage to Athens is beset with so many difficulties that no conclusions can be drawn from it concerning the Aeginetan. There is the proverb quoted by Pollux: '*Turtles* overcome the principles of right and virtue', which sounds early and is quoted in a Doric dialect. In view of the comment mentioned on p. 175 on 'Wealth makes the Man', which is placed by Alkaios in the mouth of a Spartan *c.* 600 BC, there is a temptation to ascribe the 'turtle' proverb to the same period, on the grounds that the specific reference to this coinage suggests a date when it was unique. There can be no certainty, however, and in general there is a tendency to put the earliest Aeginetan 'turtles', Athenian 'owls' and Corinthian 'foals' later than was once the fashion. It is easy to see that this question of the date of the earliest coinage of Greece proper is a crux of the first order, connected with the development of major art, and (seemingly) with outstanding economic and social problems.

Before these are considered it is necessary to outline the principal events of the later eighth and seventh centuries BC and consider the personalities involved. It has been said at the beginning of this chapter that from the later eighth century the historian can feel that some of the obscurity of the 'Dark Age' is being dissipated: that some knowledge of events and people (not only of artefacts) which looks something like history seems possible. This is, however, relative: information is often scant and drawn from late sources. After the Homeric poems and Hesiod contemporary literature in what has been called 'the lyric age of Greece' survives only in wretched fragments preserved out of context, and there is a temptation to ingenious conjecture. The problems of chronology are no longer involved only with the neat archaeological approximations of Early, Middle and Late Geometric, but with the dates of individuals and historical episodes which sometimes float unanchored in the ancient tradition and have to be fixed by a laborious assemblage of historical details to obtain what is a more or less convincing picture.

The essential preliminary to the seventh century (with no clear dividing line between) is the second half of the eighth. It in turn rested on the earlier stages of the 'Geometric period'. Something has already been said about this stage of Greek cultural development in the context of purely artistic achievement, and the point has been made that 'Geometric period' (as an alternative to 'Dark Age') relates to the type of decoration seen pre-eminently on pottery. A recent close and skilful study of this pottery and other contemporary objects (mainly from graves) provides evidence for the earlier stages mentioned which is invaluable, always bearing certain points in mind. Of necessity some judgements on decorative details and pottery shapes, and the derivation of such, can be subjective. Furthermore the material for study varies in quantity, and excavation is regionally uneven. Above all quantitative estimates are tricky: how many pots or other objects constitute evidence for 'trade' in the proper sense of that word? How many valuable objects in scarce materials in grave groups are needed to mark an increase in prosperity or a wealthy aristocracy? What in general, even down into the seventh and earlier sixth centuries, is the *magnitude* of enterprises such as the establishment of trading posts or colonies, or the carrying out of military operations? Important examples of these problems will be considered in Chapter 7 in connection with Athens and Attica.

1 Gold death mask (profile) from Shaft Grave V of Schliemann's Grave Circle (A), National Museum, Athens.

2 The Mycenaean late thirteenth-century palace at Ano Englianos (W. Peloponnese). Likely to be Nestor's Pylos. The photograph shows the great megaron and plan of the centre of the palace from the north.

3 The magazine corridor ('Great Casemate') of the latest Mycenaean palace at Tiryns.

4 Tower VIh and east fortification wall of Troy VI (in 1938), from south.

5  Mycenaean stele from Grave V of Schliemann's Grave Circle (A). It is in effect 'a setting out for the hunt' (Marinatos, in Marinatos and Hirmer, *Crete and Mycenae*, Thames and Hudson 1960) or a hostile encounter like that of Laius and Oedipus.

6  Inlaid dagger blade, Mycenaean, *c.* 1500 BC, from Routsi near Pylos. From a *tholos* tomb.

7 Fragment of a fresco from Mycenae with three 'Ta-urt demons'. Observe that it is said to come from a private house.

8 Submycenaean amphora (ht. 24.5 cm.) from the Potters' Quarter (Kerameikos) of Athens.

9 Corinthian Geometric pottery from the site of Corinth. Corinth Museum.

10 A scene of 'lying-in-state' from an Attic standed mixing-bowl in New York, also decorated with a chariot procession and shielded warriors.

11 Bronze bowl from the Kerameikos Cemetery, Athens. Diam.
*c*. 17.5 cm. From Geometric Grave 42 on the south side of the
Eridanos. Possibly North Syrian or Cypriote in origin, 850–830 BC.

12 Conical bronze support of mixing-bowl
of Urartian (Vannic) origin in heavy
Assyrian-influenced style. Found in an
Etruscan tomb at Praeneste in Latium,
Italy (the Barberini Tomb). In the Museum
of the Villa Giulia, Rome.

13 Bronze relief plaque (attachment to
some object of wood) found at Olympia,
Greece. Ht. 15.7 cm. Date *c*. 700 BC.
Later Hittite (Assyrianising) or Urartian.

14 Ivory figure, 'The Lion Tamer', found at Delphi. Ht. without base 19 cm. Oriental subject (Phoenician, Assyrian, North Syrian?) but probably of Greek manufacture, perhaps from an Ionian centre or Rhodes. Date mid-seventh century.

15 Local (?) geometrically-decorated clay cup (imitating a common East Greek type) found in the Austrian excavations on Ischia (Pithekoussai) a forerunner settlement to Cumae. Probably not later than 700 BC and might well be earlier. Scratched reference to The Cup of Nestor (see text).

16 Helmet and cuirass from the 'Cuirass Grave' at Argos.
In Argos Museum.

17 Front view of large griffin head in
bronze (cp. the clay version on the
Griffin Jug from Aegina in the British
Museum). From Olympia (OL 1065).

18 Fragment of finely carved ivory box (best seventh century style) with Athena, Perseus and the Gorgon Medusa (being decapitated). Found in the German excavations at the shrine of Hera on Samos (Samos 6029).

19 Proto-attic amphora, *c.* 675–650 BC, with combat between Herakles and the Centaur Nessos; animals and decorative borders. Note the 'moon-faced lion and panto deer' (Sir John Beazley), and contrast the ordered and monumental style of 20.

20 The 'Nessos Amphora' (so-called from the combat of the
Centaur Nessos with Herakles). Herakles and Nessos
(spelling Netos) on the neck; the three Gorgons on the body
(the presence of Perseus is implied). Transitional to Early
Black Figure, *c.* 610 BC. From the Dipylon Cemetery, Athens.
National Museum, Athens 1002.

21 Orientalizing amphora
from Naxos. Athens National
Museum, 11708. Date *c.* 660 BC.

22 Fragment of Protoargive Krater (mixing bowl) of the first
half of the seventh century (?). The blinding of Polyphemos
by Odysseus and his men.

23 *Above left* Protocorinthian ovoid aryballos (perfume vase) with warriors, *c.* 660 BC. *Right* Early type of spherical aryballos, with flute-player and boy-leaper. Nonsense inscription? Early Corinthian, *c.* 620 BC.

24 Good Early Corinthian (Transitional) jug (olpe) decorated in very neat style with animal friezes. Date *c.* 625 BC. Found in Rhodes. British Museum 60.2-1.18.

25 A portion of the decoration of the Chigi Jug in the Museum of the Villa Giulia. Late Protocorinthian. Procession of horsemen and chariots; hunting scene. From Formello, near Veii. Date *c.* 640–630?

26 Group of Centaur and man in bronze. From Olympia? In the Metropolitan Museum of Art, New York. Said by the Museum to be of mid-seventh century date, but surely much earlier (beginning of seventh century).

27 *Left* Geometric-style ivory 'goddess' (the description is uncertain), from a grave in the Dipylon Cemetery; one of the several figures of the same sort in the grave-group. Ht. 24 cms. The nudity suggests an oriental model, and the material is a link with the near East. Date *c.* 750 BC.

28 *Centre* Statuette dedicated by Mantiklos to Apollo, as an inscription indicates. In Boston (03.997). Ht. 20 cms. The figure originally had a helmet and probably shield and spear. Date 700–675 BC.

29 *Right* Male figure of bronze plate on a wooden core (*sphyrelaton*) found at Dreros in Crete. Ht. 0.80 m. Date 650 BC, or somewhat earlier.

30 Statuette (Ht. 0.75 m.) in limestone (originally heavily coloured) once in
Auxerre, France, and now in the Louvre, Paris. It is in the so-called
'Daedalic' style. Date *c.* 645 BC.

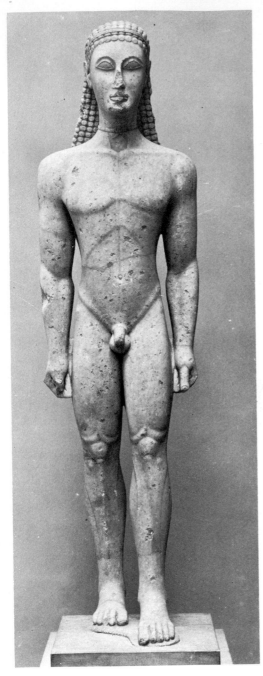

31 Statue of a youth (Kouros), said to be
from Attica (and probably a grave
monument). In the Metropolitan Museum,
New York, no. 32.ii.i. Ht. 1.843 m. It belongs
to the earliest group of this type of figure,
which is to be associated with the gigantic
Sounion Kouros in the National Museum,
Athens. Date *c.* 615–590 BC.

32 Standing female figure in Berlin. Inv. 71,
the so-called Berlin Standing 'Goddess'. From
Attica (Keratea?), and made of Attic marble.
Ht. with plinth, 1.93 m. She holds a
pomegranate, and may be the figure of a
goddess. On the other hand the figure may be
an aristocratic grave memorial. It still retains
considerable traces of original colour, blue,
red and yellow, on the garments. Date *c.* 570.

This *caveat* uttered, it may be said that the archaeological record would seem to indicate the following process of development. The Early Geometric period (900–850 BC) is characterized by parochialism and stagnation, as indicated by the pottery. It seems that merchants seldom travelled beyond their immediate neighbours, and thus differences between local pottery styles are pronounced. Conditions for contact with the Levant and the area of Cilicia were unpropitious because of Assyrian attack. This period of stagnation is followed by one of activity, with an improvement in Aegean communications indicated by the greater homogeneity of pottery styles in Middle Geometric I (850–800 BC). Athens is an important centre, her pottery appearing in Aegina and her influence in the Cyclades, Boeotia and the Argolid. This is the period of developing contact with the eastern Mediterranean and the Levant. Pottery, especially at Al Mina in the last quarter of the ninth century, indicates the settlement of Greeks, even if in small numbers, from Euboea, the northern Cyclades, and, later, Corinth and Rhodes. Much of the pottery was clearly imported for the use of Greeks, not for the natives. This is an important beginning of the contact between Greeks and the Orient, both the coast and the interior. Cyprus must have played an essential part in these contacts, through Cypriot Phoenician merchants, though it is uncertain how far they penetrated into the Aegean. Kition in Cyprus (founded *c.* 925 BC) appears to have been an important centre. It is to be noted that Phoenician activity indicated in the *Odyssey* is difficult to assess in terms of its magnitude and degree of penetration into the Aegean, and into the central and western Mediterranean. Carthage was traditionally founded at the end of the ninth century, but the earliest finds on the site are a century later. Similarly, for the far west the Carmona incised ivories found near Seville, and taken by some as an indication of an early Phoenician presence in Spain, may well belong to the seventh century.

It is apparent that Crete, linked with the Cyclades (but not with Attica), was in some way or other a channel of oriental contacts, whether through Phoenician intermediaries or through resident craftsmen. The contact is indicated by the presence of oriental ivories in the Idaean Cave deposit and by the appearance of curvilinear motifs, including the cable band (imitated from such ivories or from metalwork?). In this connection it should be noted that this 'orientalizing' influence present in Crete does not appear as yet elsewhere; indeed the apogee of the Geometric style is not yet attained. It was attained in the following Middle Geometric II period (800–760/750 BC), when there was an increase in Levantine traffic, and it appears that Attic exports were at their highest point. The implications of this and of the splendid vases of the Dipylon Cemetery in Athens with their silhouette pictures will be discussed in Chapter 7. This was the period when the Greeks, who had turned their attention first to the East, began to explore the West, and probably the northern Aegean also, as a preliminary to colonization. Indeed if the suggested earlier chronology is accepted colonization in the West, apart from Pithekoussai (Ischia) and Cumae in Italy, began in this period in Sicily. It is perhaps safer to see this as the period of pre-colonial exploration ending with the establishment of the most distant colonies, Pithekoussai and Cumae by the Euboeans in the interests of trade. There appear to be increases in population in Attica and in the Argolid. This is the period also of the importation and development of the alphabet in numerous differentiated scripts, some of them, like the Parian, showing curious idiosyncracies.

The point has been well expressed concerning the development from the latter part of this period into the following Late Geometric I (750–735 BC) and II (735–700), the end of which saw the dissolution of the Geometric style: 'The wide variety of epichoric [local] scripts finds some reflection in the wide divergence of Late Geometric pottery styles. We are now entering a period when good communications no longer impose uniformity. In many aspects of Greek life, local pride is becoming an increasingly potent force.'[5] This local pride is perhaps demonstrated by the emergence of a predominant regional centre, where there had previously been a number of scattered smaller centres loosely associated, as seems to have been the case for Attica, the Corinthia, the Argolid and, indeed, Lakonia, which show progress in this respect beyond Boeotia, Achaea, Arcadia and Elis: in short the true emergence of the *polis* discussed earlier. It also meant that such states met at contested boundaries, as did Argos and Sparta, Sparta and Arcadia, Corinth and Megara. These contacts and others elsewhere in the Aegean and western Asia Minor (eastern Greece) take place against the background of the Late Geometric Period 750–700 BC. To the latter part of that period, from 735 BC (to accept the traditional western colonial dates) into the seventh century, belongs the prime age of colonization, the motives for which have been discussed earlier (pp. 83ff). It is natural to see colonial rivalry as another element in the contact of states in Mainland and East Greece. Here starts, in effect, true Greek 'history'. The literary evidence, as pointed out already, is very fragmentary or late: no period has given rise to more ingenious conjecture and study of sources and tradition (*Quellenforschung*, as German scholars call it). It should also be pointed out that, in the colonial field in the west, Corinth is prominent: at Delphi the oracular centre, in Ithaka from around 780 BC and particularly in the west at Syracuse, her own foundation, and on other sites. Corinthian pottery, combined with the account of Thucydides on the Sicilian colonies, forms the backbone of archaeological chronology for the west, applied also elsewhere where the literary tradition is less clear: another source of controversy and uncertainty.

It is useful to look again at some observations made by Thucydides in his review of early Greece in Book I of his *History*. He describes what he believes to be the main developments (in relation to his general purpose) of the late eighth and seventh centuries (in our modern terms), assuring his audience of his critical attitude (as opposed to that of 'most men'), depending, as he does, not on 'poetic lays with excessive ornament' or the 'compositions of chroniclers [*logographoi*] made more attractive to the ear than true', but on the 'clearest data', which he does not define more closely, though his meaning is clear enough. Of the period in question he observes: 'But as the power of Hellas grew, and the acquisition of wealth became more an objective, the revenues of the states increasing, tyrannies were by their means established almost everywhere – the old form of government being hereditary monarchy with defined prerogatives – Hellas began to fit out fleets and apply herself more closely to the sea.'[6]

It is not immediately clear how Thucydides related together an increase of wealth and tyranny, nor is it quite clear how wealth, tyranny and seafaring were connected. He has a good deal to say on sea power. He ascribes to the Corinthians 'modern' shipbuilding and the construction of triremes (which in effect were introduced only much later). Amein-okles, the Corinthian shipwright who made four 'ships' for the Samians, he dates to 721 or 705 BC. It would be tempting to relate these ships to naval warfare, if Thucydides did not go on to say that the oldest sea battle was fought between Corinth and Kerkyra, her unfilial colony, in either 681 or 665 BC. It might be safe to suggest that some improvement in ships did take place in the late eighth century which permitted more efficient navigation, including, perhaps, the penetration by sea of the Euxine. Thucydides continues with comment on 'rich' Corinth (using the Homeric adjective *aphneios*) controlling the isthmus passage north and south and then east and west also, putting down piracy by the use of a fleet. He recognizes clearly the prominence of Corinth in the late eighth century, and seems to ascribe to the city a mastery of the sea, 'a thalassocracy', to use the later term. He follows Corinth in this list by a number of other instances, *not* in the seventh century but in the sixth: the Ionians, Polykrates of Samos and the Phokaians in the western Mediterranean.

There has been a temptation to believe that Thucydides had in mind some established list (unknown to Herodotus) of those states which in succession exercised 'mastery of the sea'. Such a list indeed existed later, preserved from the lost Book VII of Diodorus in the fourth-century AD *Chronographia* of Eusebius, while the details of the duration of each thalassocracy are given in the chronological list, the *Chronici Canones* of Eusebius, best known in the Latin version of Jerome. The states, given in order from the late eighth century are the Rhodians, Phrygians, Cypriots, Phoenicians, Egyptians, Milesians, Carians or (alternatively) Meg-arians, Lesbians, Phokaians, Samians, Spartans, Naxians, Eretrians and

Aeginetans. Some of the later thalassocracies can be connected (as in Thucydides) convincingly with the events of the later sixth century. Others *can* with ingenuity be associated with identifiable events from time to time. None the less the list is a late and bogus confection which can make no special contribution to the history of the late eighth and seventh centuries nor justify any particular stress on sea power in the period. It is more important to note that while Thucydides thus stresses sea power he is at pains to minimize its importance in terms of the character of the ships; they were mostly old-fashioned fifty-oar ships and long boats (*cf.* the Corinthian Geometric mixing bowl in Toronto) until the Persian War of 480 BC, apart from the fleets of Kerkyra and the Sicilian tyrants, and these in effect belong to the same late period. It is true that Thucydides is prepared to admit the value of this early sea power for gain and dominion. Significantly, on the other hand, he goes on to say:

Wars by land there were none, none at least by which power was acquired; such as took place were all between neighbours, and the Greeks did not go out on foreign expeditions far from their own territory to subdue others. There was no gathering of subjects around the greatest cities, nor did they carry out common expeditions on a basis of equality; rather they fought against each other as rival neighbours. At the most in the war long ago between the Chalcidians and the Eretrians the rest of the Hellenic people was divided in alliance on one side or the other.[7]

More must be said of this war of 'long ago' (*palai pote*). Here it is to be noted that Thucydides thinks little of these early clashes, from which he passes by way of the Persian Wars to the Peloponnesian, and the division between Athenians and Spartans, the one state supreme on the sea, the other on land. Thucydides' comment on sea power clearly leads up to the 'thalassocracy' of Athens. It is therefore curious that he says nothing of the development of which Sparta was the supreme exponent, hoplite land warfare. Did he regard its earlier history as unimportant?

In similar fashion he has relatively little to say of the other seemingly important phenomenon of the period under consideration, the appearance of tyranny. It has been seen that he connects it with an increase in wealth. Later he writes: 'In the case of the tyrants in the Hellenic cities, having as their objective their own material advantage and the increase of their house they administered the cities to the best of their ability with a view to security, and [so] no undertaking of note was effected by them except in relation to their neighbours.'[8]

Thucydides then makes an exception for the Sicilian tyrants, meaning their inter-state hostilities, rather than their operations against the Carthaginians and Etruscans. It can properly be argued that here, as in the case of early sea and land activity, his yardstick is a war on a grand scale. None the less it is difficult to avoid the impression from his tone that he regarded events before the fifth century as being on a minor scale. In this he differs from Herodotus, and it is useful for modern historians to reflect how far he might be correct.

The omission by Thucydides of a fuller account of the development of tyranny can be explained by his ultimate preoccupation with military matters and unconcern with earlier political developments. For this it is necessary to turn to Aristotle, whose definition of tyranny echoes that of Thucydides: 'Tyranny is a government by a single person directed to the interest of that person.'[9] Aristotle adds that it is 'the perversion of kingship'. He distinguishes it from another category, again relevant to the seventh and sixth centuries:

There is also a third [type of monarchy] which used to exist among the Greeks and goes by the name of dictatorship [aisymneteia]. This may roughly be described as an elective form of tyranny ... some of the dictators held their office for life; others for a fixed period, or for the discharge of a definite duty. Pittakos, for instance, was elected at Mytilene to deal with the attacks of the exiles commanded by Antimenidas and the lyric poet Alkaios. The fact of the election of Pittakos is attested by Alkaios, in one of his drinking songs, when he bitterly says:

'Pittakos, son of a low-born father they set up as tyrant over their spiritless and ill-fated city, crowding together and shouting aloud their praise.'[10]

There is another illuminating passage in which Aristotle introduces one of the best-known tyrants (and puts him in a special category):

The two forms of monarchical government differ from one another – and differ diametrically – in their very origin. Kingships have grown for the purpose of helping the better classes [epieikeis] against the people [demos]; it is from these classes that kings have been drawn; and the basis of their position has been their own pre-eminence or the pre-eminence of their family, in character and conduct. Tyrants, on the contrary, are drawn from the populace [demos] and the masses [plethos] to serve as their protectors against the notables [gnorimoi], and to prevent them from suffering any injustice from that class. The record of history attests the fact; and it may safely be said that most tyrants have begun their careers as demagogues, who won the popular confidence by calumniating the notables. But though it is true that a large number of tyrannies arose in this way in the days when states were becoming much more populous, there were others, of an earlier date, which arose in different ways. Some of them had their origins in the ambition of kings, who transgressed traditional limitations, and aimed at a more despotic authority. Others were founded by persons who had originally been elected to the highest magistracies, all the more easily because there was a habit, in ancient times, of giving long tenures to public 'craftsmen' and 'overseers'. Others, again, arose from the practice, followed in oligarchies, of appointing a single person to supervise the chief magistracies. In all these ways an ambitious person was given the chance, if he so desired, of effecting his purpose with ease; he had already power in his hands for a start – here as king and there as the holder of some other high office. Pheidon of Argos and a number of others started as kings and ended as tyrants. The tyrants of Ionia and Phalaris of Akragas used other offices as stepping stones. Panaitios at Leontinoi, Kypselos at Corinth, Peisistratos at Athens, Dionysios at Syracuse and a number of others elsewhere began as demagogues.[11]

Aristotle, it is to be noticed, in the particular category to which Pheidon belonged, implies a change: from the support of the 'better classes' (*epieikeis*) against the *demos* to a championship of the *demos* against 'the notables' (*gnorimoi*) by a transgression of 'traditional limitations' (*ta patria*) (cf. Thucydides' 'defined prerogatives'). It should be recalled that while Aristotle here says nothing (except by inference) of an assembly or of the hoplite army, he does so elsewhere, distinguishing the 'rich' (*euporoi*), the 'poor' (*aporoi*) and 'those in the middle' (*mesoi*): 'And of the rich and poor the rich have arms [*hoplitikon*, the equipment of the hoplite soldier] and the poor have not.'

It is to be presumed that Aristotle shared out the *mesoi* between the other two classes. He goes on to make a distinction among the *euporoi* between those who could afford to keep horses and those who could not:

Fourthly there are also differences between the notables – differences based on their wealth and the amount of their property; and these differences appear, for example, in the matter of keeping horses, which can only be done by the very wealthy. Incidentally this is the reason why states whose strength lay in cavalry were in former times the homes of oligarchies. These oligarchies used their cavalry in wars with adjoining states: we may cite the examples of Eretria and Chalkis in the island of Euboea, and of Magnesia on the Maiandros and many other cities of Asia Minor.[12]

In the passage of the *Politics* here quoted Aristotle includes all the elements and developments of the late eighth- and seventh-century political scene, and incidentally shows what Thucydides meant by his association of wealth and tyranny, that the latter was born of a reaction against the former. The developments in question will, for Sparta and Athens, be considered in Chapter 7, and for the other Greek states in the present chapter.

Thucydides, in his comment on the small scale of early military enterprises, mentions as something of an exception (but not in itself outstanding) the hostilities between Chalkis and Eretria in Euboea over the Lelantine Plain between them. He gives no indication of date but speaks of 'long ago' and of the phenomenon that on one side or the other were marshalled as allies 'the rest of the Hellenic people'. This was something more, it is inferred, than a war of neighbours, even if not of great magnitude. It is natural to associate with this war the reference of Aristotle, quoted earlier, to Chalkis and Eretria as cavalry-using oligarchies, citing them alone from mainland Greece, while he names Magnesia on the Maiandros 'and many other cities of Asia Minor' (he might have mentioned Kolophon as a particularly outstanding case).

These Euboean cities seem, therefore, to have held a special position, and indeed the horse-rearing Hippobotai of Chalkis flourished down to their defeat by Athens in 506 BC. On the other hand Strabo in a defective passage refers to the Lelantine War and the agreement preserved in the temple of Artemis Amarynthios to avoid the use of missile weapons. He characterizes the Euboeans as exponents of warfare with sword and thrusting spear, following Homer, which does not necessarily mean hoplite warfare, though on the same or another stele in the temple of Artemis he claims that the forces of Eretria were recorded as three thousand hoplites, six hundred cavalry and sixty chariots. The plain is mentioned in the Homeric 'Hymn to Apollo', the war nowhere except in Herodotus, Thucydides and Strabo. There is a reference in the assemblage of elegiac poetry going under the name of the Megarian Theognis to the fall of Kerinthos (a port on the eastern coast of Euboca) and the laying waste of the vine-clad plain of Lelanton, but this must refer (witness the poet's exclamation: 'Alas for the cowardice!') to another and later occasion. In a well-known fragment of the poet Archilochos (of the sixties of the seventh century) there is a reference which sounds as if the poet had in mind the prohibition of missile weapons mentioned earlier, related by Strabo to the Lelantine War: 'There will be no bows stretched in number nor slings in multitude, when Ares joins the conflict in the plain. It will be the direful work of swords, for the spear-famed lords of Euboea are masters of this battle.'[13] The 'spear-famed lords' represent a Homeric reference. The phrase 'in the plain' refers neither to the Lelantine War nor to a prospect of future conflict on this issue, but means 'on level ground', the proper place of hoplite warfare, as opposed to the rough ground on which light-armed troops used the sling and possibly the bow. There is certainly no compelling reason to connect the reference with Euboea locally; the 'spear-famed lords' of Chalkis were also active in northern Greece. Thus in another fragment of the same poet there is a reference to Torone, an ancient foundation of unknown origins on the Chalcidic promontory of Sithonia, which must have been directly or indirectly a concern of Chalcis.

The date and reasons for the war present problems. It must be placed after the period of association of the two states in founding the colonies of Pithekoussai c. 760 BC and Kyme (Cumae) c. 750 BC. It may be noted that the former colony suffered internal strife (stasis) subsequently, which may have been due to the Chalcidian and Eretrian elements in the colonial population falling out by reason of the war between the founder states. There is not much else that is convincing to date the war. Lefkandi between Chalkis and New Eretria (settled at the beginning of the eighth century) was destroyed or abandoned c. 720–710 BC. In the latter part of the eighth century contact with Corinth, which had been close earlier, was lost. There seems to be a drop in Euboean pottery exports after *c.* 700 BC, but this is unreliable evidence. Hesiod attended (at the end of the eighth century?) the funeral ceremonies of King Amphidamas of Chalkis, who may well have been killed in a battle of this war. It looks as if the end of the eighth century is a suitable period for *the* Lelantine War (for it could be that this was a continuing enmity). Finally it might be argued that the replacement in *c.* 708 BC of the Eretrians by the Corinthians in Kerkyra is to be related to an Eretrian distraction occasioned by the war.

The reasons for this hostile confrontation of two states which previously were amicably associated are obscure. Euboea had its mineral wealth, but few cultivable plain areas – in northern Euboea the region round Histiaia, elsewhere the Lelantine Plain, and the enclosed basin round Dystos. It was not particularly fitted to support a large population. The foundation of Zankle in Sicily *c.* 730 BC from Euboea is ascribed to the incidence of famine, which in Greece could suddenly manifest itself. On the other hand there must have been a considerable drawing-off of population in the last third of the eighth century: Sicilian Naxos was founded in 735 BC from Chalkis and Aegean Naxos; unless it is assumed that these early colonial foundations were very small in numbers (which they could have been, given the limitations of transport) this must have been a large emigration since, soon after, in 729 BC, Leontinoi and Katana were founded from Naxos. Similarly Rhegion was established between 730 and 720 BC by Chalkidians and some Messenians. The war, then, was hardly caused by population pressure. It is not very likely that it arose from trade rivalry, since both states had long traded side by side in the East and in the West. There could be rivalry for domination in the Aegean not unrelated to the northern coasts: Chalkis appears to have exercised hegemony over the northern Sporades and Eretria over southern Euboea, Andros, Tenos and Kea.[13a] Finally it could be suggested that a cause of hostility between the two states was the value of the Lelantine Plain as horse pasture in an island not conspicuous for its abundance of grazing land. On such pasture would depend pre-eminence in cavalry.

Round the two principal antagonists were, according to the tradition mentioned by Thucydides, grouped others. He infers a considerable number: 'the rest of the Hellenic name'. Herodotus gives Miletos as the ally of Eretria, and Samos on the side of Chalkis. He also seems to suggest that Chios supported Miletos and therefore Eretria, and that Erythrai took the side of Chalkis. Plutarch gives Thessalian support (in cavalry?) to Chalkis. It is difficult to omit Corinth from the line-up of states. In view of the dislodgement of Eretrians from Kerkyra by the Corinthians and the services of the Corinthian shipwright Ameinokles to the Samians, she should go on the side of Chalkis, and so her enemy Megara (from whom Corinth had taken Perachora) on that of Eretria. The rivalries could also have penetrated to the colonial sphere: there is the *stasis* at Pithekoussai mentioned earlier, and the expulsion by Chalkidians of a Megarian element from Leontinoi.

The states named were for the most part concerned with maritime activity. Conspicuous by its absence was Aegina, at a later date important as a trading state, but at the probable date of the Lelantine War involved in the Argos–Epidauros group and in hostilities with Athens.

In this wider sense the Lelantine War is not to be regarded as a figment of the imagination of later historians. Nor is it to be taken as a war for a clearly defined period conducted across the Aegean with wide-ranging naval operations. It has been noted that Thucydides believed that these operations and naval activity in general were on a small scale. There is no place for thalassocracies in the true sense. On the other hand his mention of the battle between Corinth and Kerkyra must not be taken too literally to mean that there was none before: his words are qualified by the clause 'that we know of'. There certainly was maritime activity, which had taken the Greeks to their western colonies, to the northern Aegean and to the East. The states named fall into pairs of neighbours, some of whom long remained enemies, though not all (the appearance of tyranny produced some changes): Chalkis and Eretria, Samos and Miletos, Chios and Erythrai, Corinth and Megara. Hostilities were mostly by land, except when an island state was involved; there could be no overall design or plan of campaign. Privateering could take place by sea, attended by the granting or withholding of *asylia*.

The Lelantine War was in effect one aspect of that increasing turmoil generated by the growth of communications with colonies (the battle between Corinth and Kerkyra is a case in point, dated 681 or 665 BC), the quest for new colonial sites and in general the efforts of neighbours to extend or consolidate their boundaries.

The last decade of the eighth century and the first half of the seventh saw continuing and intensified colonial activity on the part of a number of states of mainland Greece, the Aegean and western Asia Minor, the last of which plays an increasingly important part in the seventh century. Some foundation dates, as of Sinope and Trapezos on the southern coast of the Black Sea, are traditionally put too early and require the assumption of refoundation or reinforcement. It is perhaps necessary, in view of the uncertainty of Eretrian fortunes after the Lelantine War, to accept early (eighth-century) dates for the Eretrian foundations of Mende, Methone and Dikaia in northern Greece. On the other hand Chalkis was very active in the seventh century in the region of the three-pronged peninsula of eastern Macedonia called in consequence Chalkidike. Among many other settlements Stageira, the birthplace later of Aristotle, was founded in co-operation with Andros. In a number of cases undoubtedly a native settlement was taken over, as appears to have been the case with

Akanthos. Here Chalkis was a rival of Andros, which might have led to hostilities, but the dispute was settled by arbitration around mid-century, Erythrai and Samos finding for Andros and Paros for Chalkis, which, if correct, indicates that Chalkis and Samos had abandoned the Lelantine War alignment.

It is unfortunate that dates are often uncertain, but enough is known to show the great activity of the first half of the seventh century and especially that of the Asia Minor Greeks. For example in Thrace Abdera was founded by Klazomenai, Maroneia by Chios and Ainos by Mytilene and Kyme in Aeolis. On the Hellespont and in the Sea of Marmara Abydos was established by Miletos, Lampsakos by Phokaia. Above all, as enterprises from mainland Greece Kalchedon and Byzantium were colonies of Megara, entering in the earlier seventh century into an important period of her history. Perinthos on the Marmara was a foundation of Samos, also active on the southern coast of Asia Minor. The improvement in ship-construction indicated by Thucydides' reference to Ameinokles may have permitted an easier penetration of the Black Sea, especially by the Milesians, to settle all the coasts of the sea by the end of the seventh century. In the west Siris on the Gulf of Tarentum (Taras) was established probably from Kolophon (or Achaea), and in Sicily Gela in 688 BC from Rhodes and Crete. Later on, c. 630 BC, Kyrene was founded on the northern coast of Africa from Thera. Right at the end of the century Corinth planted Potidaia in Chalkidike, and Phokaia Massilia and other settlements in the far western Mediterranean. The general background and reasons for this activity have been discussed in Chapter 5.

It has also been pointed out there that at the same period the Mediterranean saw adventurers and mercenaries on the move, like the 'bronze men from the sea' who aided the Egyptian Psammetichos, founder of the Twenty-sixth Dynasty:

. . . certain Carians and Ionians, who had left their country on a voyage of plunder, were carried by stress of weather to Egypt, where they disembarked, all equipped in their bronze armour, and were seen by the natives, one of whom carried the tidings to Psammetichos and, as he had never before seen men clad in bronze, he reported that bronze men had come from the sea and were plundering the plain. Psammetichos, perceiving at once that the oracle was accomplished, made friendly advances to the strangers, and engaged them, by splendid promises to enter into his service.[14]

There thus followed the establishment of the mercenaries at the 'Stratopeda', whence they were removed at a later date by Amasis to Memphis and probably to the site of Tell Defenneh. Later than the period of Psammetichos I, probably c. 615–610 BC, the Greek settlement and trading factory were established at Naukratis. There, according to Herodotus, the Hellenion formed a common religious centre for the

Ionian Chiots, Teians and Phokaians, for the Dorians of Rhodes, Knidos, Halikarnassos and Phaselis and for Aeolian Mytilene. The Samians had a separate temple of Hera, Miletos had one of Apollo and Aegina one of Zeus. There was also, as Chiot dedications show, a temple of Aphrodite. The strong emphasis is on eastern Greek participation, which makes the unique position of Aegina, as the sole privileged mainland state, all the more striking. This can be called the opening up of Egypt to merchants, travellers and mercenaries, the effects of which have been mentioned already.

For the most part only the bare and dry details of these wide-ranging activities have come down, and very imperfectly, to modern times. There is, however, the striking personality, mentioned earlier, of Archilochos, who helps to vivify this aspect of seventh-century life. From his island state of Paros, Thasos off the coast of Thrace was planted with a colony which became of considerable importance for its mines and wine, and for its proximity to the natural resources (and savage inhabitants) of the Thracian mainland. The date of the foundation is given as 720 or 708 BC, and 700 BC is suggested as a date for Archilochos himself. This is too early, and even more so the placing of him as a contemporary of the Lelantine War. Jerome gives as his date 688 BC, and he himself refers to Gyges, the ruler of Lydia and founder of the Mermnad dynasty (of the first half of the seventh century), in terms which might indicate that he was a contemporary. A date towards mid-seventh century is a reasonable one, and his father, Telesikles, could then have participated in either the original foundation of the Thasian colony or a reinforcement of it. Archilochos himself took part in fighting on the mainland of Thrace, and there lost his shield. He suffered hardship in these northern regions (different in climate from his native Paros), hated the wild woodland of craggy Thasos and forgot its vineyards.

As a composer of personal poetry (in the form of trimeters, tetrameters, epodes and elegiacs) Archilochos enjoyed a reputation next to Homer. Despite the extreme fragmentation of his poetry (surviving in grammarians, anthologies and papyri), enough remains to indicate his use of fable and allegory, his indifference to aristocratic convention (he may have been a bastard) and his extreme and uninhibited expression of emotion, attacking, for example, with violent and obscene abuse one Neoboule, daughter of Lykambes, to whom he was once betrothed. He says of himself: 'I am both the servant of Lord Enyalios [the war god], and I know the lovely gift of the Muses.'[15] He was a bold adventurer who had, as he put it, 'the strength of an enduring heart', to suffer hardship and disaster, and to assuage sorrow. His poetry gives striking glimpses of a roving life, of the dangers of travel by sea and of the hazards of life as a fighter. It permits the modern reader to sense the violence, dangers and adventures of the colonial period. The mainland of Thrace and possibly

Thasos, too, were areas of hard battle. What was won was held with difficulty against natives and Greeks. Torone is mentioned, and Naxos, the close and larger neighbour of Paros, and of great importance now and later in the Aegean, as the finds on Delos show. Battered fragments of Archilochos' poetry give glimpses of naval operations, fire and siege warfare and of the peril which hangs above the island 'like the rock of Tantalos'.

Archilochos had an associate, one Glaukos, whose name appears several times in his poetry. By one of those striking chances which happen from time to time, archaeology supplements the literary record. In the Thasos excavation there has been found in the *agora* (market-place) a grave memorial of *c.* 600 BC which recalls, as it has been pointed out, 'the honours paid to founders of colonies'. It reads:

> I am the memorial of Glaukos, son of Leptines.
> The sons of Brentes set me up.

Even more striking is the evidence for a cult of Archilochos on Paros. Around 250 BC a Parian, one Mnesiepes, carried out the construction of a shrine of Archilochos (the Archilocheion), in which the poet was honoured with sacrifices on the instructions of Delphi. The shrine contained a long inscription, of which fragments survive. It gave account of the consultation of the oracle and a biography of the poet containing long quotations of the poems, probably drawn from a transcription of the classical period, not from any Archaic text. Later (around the beginning of the first century BC) comes the inscription of the Parian Gymnasiarch Sosthenes (possibly a descendant of Mnesiepes), and extracts from a longer inscription, the work of a Parian Demeas. It gives the information that Demeas treated the affairs of Paros, and the deeds, piety and zest for his city of Archilochos. Using a list of Parian archons he organized under each archonship events 'lived or described by Archilochos'. It has been suggested that Demeas may also have been the author of the list called the 'Marmor Parium', possibly set up in the Archilocheion. These discoveries illustrate not only the esteem accorded to this great poet, but also the likely nature of the transmission of original material and tradition from the Archaic period to the Classical period and later.

Archilochos mentions not only the seventh-century phenomenon of the mercenary, particularly represented by the Carians, but also the *tyrannis*, a term which he applies to Gyges, King of Lydia, and clearly uses elsewhere to represent an absolute and unrestricted ruler. He thus serves as a bridge to the problem of the tyrant, and in view of the observations of Aristotle detailed earlier the problem of the tyrant is to be approached through Pheidon of Argos.

The supposed alignments of the Lelantine War excluded Argos, despite the fact that in the second half of the eighth century Argos experienced an increase of population (if finds of pottery from local cemeteries are anything to go by), and produced some outstanding Late Geometric pottery, followed in the seventh century by an interesting figure style. Earlier the Argolid was probably composed of scattered villages and small towns, as in the case of the Corinthia and Attica. There possibly took place in the late eighth century a degree of centralization, which seems to be reflected, if with some unhistoric detail, in a passage of Pausanias: 'The Argives of old had stood in almost daily danger of being conquered by the Lakedaimonians, but after they had swelled the population of Argos by destroying Tiryns, Hysiai, Orneai, Mykenai, Mideia and the other petty towns of Argolis they had less to fear from the Lakedaimonians and had at the same time gained a firmer hold over the outlying subject population.'[16] At a later date (in the late seventh century?) they expelled the inhabitants of Nauplion. From the late ninth century and into the eighth there was a tradition (see Chapter 7) of hostility with Sparta. Originally, it was believed, Argos controlled the eastern coast of the Peloponnese down to Kythera and beyond. It has also been suggested that Argos dominated the southern part of Lakonia. It is to be wondered what, at this early date, 'control' or 'dominate' might mean. Certainly in the first half of the eighth century Sparta is said to have conquered the 'Achaeans' of southern Lakonia and settled the area. Helos was subdued around 750 BC and Sparta had access to the sea.

Before and after, the region of Kynouria, with the town of Thyrea (and its territory the Thyreatis), was a bone of contention between Argos and Sparta. Traditionally the two states clashed in the time of the Spartan kings Labotas, Prytanis, Alkamenes (who defeated the Argives), Charillos and Nikandros, both of whom are said to have ravaged Argive territory. There were further hostilities over Thyreatis while King Theopompos, victor of the First Messenian War, 'was still reigning'. A threat, if there was one, from Argos did not prevent the Spartans in the second half of the eighth century from carrying out the conquest of the Messenians, though somewhat earlier, under Charillos, they had failed against Tegea.

It is difficult to avoid the impression that for the greater part of the eighth century Argos was not particularly strong and could embarrass seriously neither Corinth nor Sparta. It is to be noted that subsequent to the hostilities of Nikandros of Sparta and Eratos of Argos in the third quarter of the eighth century the Argives sought to punish Asine for supporting the Spartans, and reduced and destroyed that community (an event confirmed by the absence from the site of pottery later than c. 725 BC and earlier than Hellenistic), but only with considerable difficulty. It may well be that a source of weakness for Argos, as later in her history, was the existence of serfs (*gymnesioi* or *gymnetai*), who, according to

Herodotus, after the disastrous defeat by the Spartans at Sepeia in 496 BC took over the administration until ejected in the next generation, and of perioecic states (i.e. 'dwellers round') which were repeatedly insubordinate. It may be added that the artistic development indicated in the later eighth century, the probable increase in population and the seeming existence of a wealthy aristocracy do not exclude military weakness and internal difficulties. The statement of Pausanias is worth noting, that Argos reached the highest pitch of power in the Heroic Age, but after the Dorian Conquest 'the favour of fortune deserted her'.[17] That there was a reduced and enfeebled kingship seems to be suggested by the same author when he states that Medon, grandson of the Heraclid Temenos suffered reduction in power 'so that he and his descendants had nothing but the title of king'.[18]

A different picture of Argos is given in that assemblage of statements which passed as an oracle and appears in the *Palatine Anthology* and elsewhere:

The best of all land is the Pelasgian plain; best are the horses of Thrace, the women of Sparta, and the men who drink the water of fair Arethusa.

But better still than these are the dwellers between Tiryns and Arcadia of the many sheep, the linen-corsleted Argives, the goads of war.

But you men of Megara are neither third nor fourth nor twelfth nor of any place at all.[19]

Whatever its date, origins and composite nature, it envisages a time when Sparta had not yet risen to military fame, when the Chalkidians ('the drinkers of the water of fair Arethusa') had not lost their military repute, and when the Argives were surpassing them: hardly the eighth century or the sixth, possibly the first half of the seventh, when the Spartans were not particularly successful in the Second Messenian War.

Strongly opposed, also, to the idea of a feeble Argos is the achievement credited to Pheidon, placed by Aristotle in the category of ambitious kings 'who transgressed traditional limitations and aimed at a more despotic authority'.[20] It was claimed for Pheidon that he restored 'the heritage of Temenos': asserting Argive supremacy over Kleonai, Phlious, Sikyon, Epidauros, Troizen and Aegina, 'which had before been so nearly dissolved as to leave all the members practically independent'.[21] A number of traditions exist which justify 'the Heritage': that the non-Dorian Pityreus surrendered the region of Epidauros to Deiphontes, son-in-law of Temenos, and his Argives; that in succession to the descendants of Ajax (Aias) some of these Argives crossed from Epidauros to Aegina, 'and settled among the old inhabitants'; that Troizen was Dorized from Argos (in the Catalogue of the Ships of *Iliad* II the Troizenians are under the command of Diomedes of Argos); that Phalkes, son of Temenos, conquered Sikyon, and Rhegnidas occupied Phlious from Sikyon and

Argos. Tradition claimed also that at the end of the second dynasty of Corinth it was conquered by Aletes and his Dorians. It is interesting to note the legend of Pausanias that Bellerophon of Corinth was vassal of Proitos, King of Argos, though in the Catalogue of the Ships the Corinthians came under the command of Agamemnon. The same idea of an Argive connection with Corinth gave too the later idea that Pheidon's measures had something to do with Corinth, just as his association with Aegina gave rise to the doctrine that he issued coins there. Another tradition to be noted is that of the importance of the Temenion (in the area between Lerna and Nauplion), 'the first point occupied by the Dorians, from which Argos was captured after long battles',[22] a parallel to Solygeion from which, as base, the Dorians captured 'Aeolian' Corinth. This approach by sea (followed in the sixth century by Kleomenes and his Spartans from Thyrea to the Argolid at Nauplion) is difficult to understand as a concept of legend unless it is linked with the presence of Dorians overseas (and thus sea travellers) before the Trojan War: Tlepolemos in Rhodes, and the sons of Thessalos the Heraclid, associated with Argos, in the islands of the Dodecanese, among them Kos, according to another source settled by Argives from Epidauros, though this is also inspired by the existence of the cult of Asklepios in both places.

There can be no doubt that Argive pretensions of the period of Pheidon inspired this myth-making, which could be promoted by the local epic. In similar fashion the mythical history of Corinth was developed by the Bacchiad poet Eumelos. If the claim could be asserted that Argos had once dominated the eastern Peloponnese then it could also be asserted that with the expansion of Sparta she has lost ground. The claim to restore what had been lost and impose discipline on the perioecic towns of the Argolid could be the issue which brought Pheidon support against the Argive aristocracy, and the reason for the propaganda-mythology concerned with the heritage of Temenos.

The crux is the date of Pheidon. According to Pausanias (seldom a dependable authority): 'The people of Pisa brought disaster on themselves by their enmity to the Eleans, and by seeking to wrest the presidency of the [Olympic] games from the latter. For in the eighth Olympiad [748 BC] they called in the Argive Pheidon, the most high-handed of Greek tyrants, and held the games jointly with him.'[23]

It has frequently been felt that in the eighth century the Olympic Games were hardly of such moment as to invite the attention of Pheidon, just as the idea of an Olympic truce so early has been rejected for the same reason. On the other hand, whatever the date accepted, it is hard to believe that Pheidon's excursion across the Peloponnese was merely to help the Pisatans in the celebration of the games. An attractive suggestion is that his plan was to distract the Eleans from aiding the Spartans against southern Lakonia and Helos. An eighth-century Pheidon could also be connected with internal troubles at Corinth around the time of the colonization of Syracuse, as aggressor against that city in support of certain of the Bacchiad nobility. A late writer mentions the death of a Pheidon when giving aid to his friends at Corinth. This could be Pheidon of Argos. On the other hand it could be the other Pheidon, of Corinth, mentioned by Aristotle as 'one of the earliest legislators [who] held that the numbers of family plots [? *oikoi*] and the numbers of citizens should be kept equal to one another . . .', [24] which sounds like some sort of involvement in a politico-economic issue such as might have arisen at the time of the fall of the Bacchiads or before. Finally it *might* be suggested that a dynamic figure such as Pheidon in the eighth century might take an interest in colonization through a satellite Megara, though there is little or no archaeological evidence for such a theory (see Chapter 5).

Despite the attractions of placing Pheidon in the eighth century, it involves an excessive manipulation of chronology to make a place for him in the line of the Argive kingship at the necessary period. Such a dating also means that a feeble kingship follows at a time when Argos seems to be the leading power in the Peloponnese, that is, in the first half of the seventh century when Sparta was involved in the troubles of the Second Messenian War. There is, it is true, no stated association of Pheidon with the battle of Hysiai (see Chapter 7), and it must be admitted that the date of the battle is not clearly established as 669 BC. None the less Pheidon seems a more likely victor than one of his undistinguished successors in the kingship. The battle, it may be suggested, was the result of an ill-judged invasion of Argos, arising from a confusion of policy at Sparta. It was followed by· a retaliatory excursion of the Argives into the western Peloponnese in support of the Messenians. The celebration of the Olympic Games in 668 BC by Pheidon in concert with the Pisatans can be regarded as incidental to the main purpose. If Strabo is correct in his statement that the Eleans presided over the first twenty-six Olympic festivals, but that from Olympiad 26 (of 676 BC) to the fall of Pisa the Pisatans were presidents, the games of 668 BC were not unofficial or irregular. It was none the less a unique occasion, representing the high point of Argive power in the Peloponnese.

Aristotle in his observations on tyranny distinguishes between the type of tyrant represented by Pheidon, 'those who started as kings and ended as tyrants', and another category 'drawn from the populace and the masses to serve as their protectors against the notables, and to prevent them from suffering any injustice from that class'. [25] He goes on to point out the characteristics, in his opinion, of this category: the quest for wealth as the prop of power; fear of the 'masses', and their disarming and dispersion in the country (or their concentration for better supervision); hostility to the 'notables' as the most likely source of opposition, resulting in attempts to ruin them or drive them into exile; the 'lopping-off' of the pre-eminent and the removal of men of spirit; the forbidding of all forms of association, such as common meals and clubs. Aristotle in the *Politics* cites a considerable number of examples of this type, some of them tyrannies in the modern sense of the word. A textbook example of tyranny, as Aristotle describes it, is afforded by the Athenian Pisistratids (to be discussed in Chapter 8). Like other Greeks he was well aware that some notable achievements were to the credit of this hated form of rule. For this reason he displays a particular interest in tyranny, stating at some length the reasons for its dissolution, and (because of its potential for the development of the *polis*) the ways by which it might be preserved: by moderation and restraint, by good administration, attention to religious ceremonial and the conciliation of as large a measure of support as possible – in fact an assimilation of tyranny to kingship to attain a state of 'half-goodness'.

Aristotle is here influenced by the observation that while most tyrannies were relatively short-lived, some were more enduring, and some too displayed a resemblance to the traditional kingship and arose as a reaction against extreme aristocracy. Those that lasted displayed some good qualities:

The tyranny of longest duration was that of Orthagoras and his descendants at Sikyon, which lasted a century. The reason for its permanence was the moderation of their behaviour towards their subjects, and their general obedience to rules of law: Kleisthenes was too much of a soldier to be despised, and the dynasty generally courted the favour of its subjects by the attentions it paid them. . . . The second tyranny in point of length was that of the family of Kypselos at Corinth, which lasted seventy-three years and a half: Kypselos himself was tyrant for thirty years, Periander for forty years and a half, and Psammetichos, the son of Gordias, for three. The causes of this long duration were the same as at Sikyon: Kypselos courted the favour of his subjects, and dispensed with a guard during the whole of his reign. Periander proved himself a soldier, if he also proved a despot. The third tyranny in point of length was that of the family of Peisistratos at Athens; but this was not continuous. Peisistratos was expelled twice during the course of his reign and was only tyrant for seventeen years in a period of thirty-three: his sons between them ruled for eighteen years, and the whole reign of the family was thus confined to a period of thirty-five years.[26]

For Aristotle Periander was the problem: he has to admit that 'many of the characteristics [of the repressive tyrant] are supposed to have been originally instituted by Periander of Corinth',[27] yet he survived for a very long time, and his period was a brilliant one for Corinth.

The tyrants of Sikyon began with Orthagoras, whose father was Andreas, cook and attendant, so the story went, to a Delphic embassy from Sikyon: an example, therefore, of the tyrant of lowly origins. The approximate dates of the succession are: Orthagoras *c.* 655/4 to *c.* 648/7 BC; Myron I *c.* 648/7 to *c.* 608/7 BC (in 648 BC he won the chariot race at Olympia, and dedicated a bronze model which Pausanias calls 'a chamber'; it cannot have been the later Sikyonian Treasury); Myron II *c.* 608/7 to *c.* 600 BC; Kleisthenes, the outstanding figure of the dynasty, *c.* 600 BC to some uncertain date after 570 BC and before 556/5 BC, when his successor Aischines was expelled. Kleisthenes clearly played an important part in Greek affairs and struck the Greek imagination (see Chapter 8). The rest seem a shadowy lot of whom the later Greeks knew little (Strabo follows Aristotle in commenting on the long duration of the dynasty and its 'reasonableness').

It is difficult to think of the Orthagorids before Kleisthenes as representing anything but a reassertion of kingship. The source of the support for these mild tyrants will be debated later. Here it may be pointed out that before the city was moved inland in the Hellenistic period and established on a lofty ridge, it was located on the sea, but overshadowing Corinth prevented Sikyon from gaining importance in this sphere. To judge from modern conditions it was undoubtedly fertile (unlike Corinth). Like Corinth it was noted for its craftsmen who practised 'painting and the moulding of clay and all such craft'. Thus there were peasants and craftsmen. There may also have been some dependent class of serfs. There were certainly the non-Dorian and Dorian elements, later a division to be exploited by Kleisthenes. Unless his anti-Dorian behaviour is grossly exaggerated, the Dorians must have been in a minority. According to Strabo the original inhabitants were 'Ionians' and the territory was called Aigialeia, 'the shore', giving the name Aigialeis to the non-Dorian Kleisthenic tribe. It was presumably in this pre-Dorian period that the Greeks would have placed the subordination of Sikyon to Polybos of Corinth.

In contrast the Greeks knew or thought they knew a great deal about the tyrants of Corinth. The history of early Corinth was probably elaborated in the epic and its dynasties of early kings sound more artificial than most. The epic poet Eumelos of Corinth was himself a member of the eighth-century Corinthian aristocracy. The Dorizing of Corinth was effected by Aletes, son-in-law of Temenos, and thus the city was associated with the A give 'heritage', but with a certain independence marked in the myth by the estrangement from the other Temenid kin. Five generations on from Aletes came Bacchias, who was followed by another five generations of rulers until Telestas was murdered and replaced by an annual *prytanis*, a change from life-kingship to annual 'presidency'. In the *Iliad* Corinth is 'rich', the description also used by Thucydides, who, in his account of the importance of early Corinth, is as much describing the achievement of the Bacchiad aristocracy as of the following tyranny. It has been seen already that in the eighth century

Corinth rose to prosperity and high artistic achievement, as the pottery, outstanding in technique and artistry, shows and continued to show in the seventh century. Under the Bacchiads took place the expansion of Corinthian interests in the west, and at the eastern end of the Gulf of Corinth, at the expense of Megara. In general at this early period Corinth was anti-Argive, though as indicated already in connection with Pheidon it is possible to argue an intervention by him in the affairs of Corinth at the time of the foundation of Syracuse, in support of a pro-Argive faction. All of this depends on the placing of Pheidon in the eighth century. Since he is better placed in the first half of the seventh century, as suggested earlier, he might be identified with the Pheidon who was killed at Corinth 'bringing help to his friends' at the time of the final fall of the Bacchiads and not in the earlier internal strife. In either case it would be surprising if Corinth were not an object of Pheidon's ambitions when the aristocracy was becoming unpopular.

It must be stressed that the Corinthian Bacchiad aristocracy served the city well, but this did not prevent its expulsion. One factor in its downfall may have been a non-Dorian ('Aeolian') element in Corinth, suggested by the connection with Sisyphos (founder of the second line of mythical kings). A source of weakness may also have been a Heraclid clan hostile to the main body of the Bacchiads, to which Archias, the founder of Syracuse, and Chersikrates of Kerkyra belonged. The whole of this clan did not leave in the troubles of the eighth century, since Phalios, founder of Epidamnos, came from Corinth at the invitation of the Corcyreans, and *that* in the heyday of the tyranny. It is, however, unwise to make too much of the hostility of Corinth and Kerkyra on this score (including the sea battle of 664 BC), since there are no indications of enmity between Syracuse and Corinth.

Another possible factor in the downfall of the Bacchiads was the suggested intervention of Pheidon; elsewhere and at other times tyrants seek to aid others to obtain the same position. The founder of the Corinthian tyranny who expelled the Bacchiads (but not necessarily the whole aristocracy) was Kypselos. It is unfortunate that the dates of the dynasty are in doubt. Three different sets of dates have been suggested: 657–584 BC, 622–549 BC or 614–541 BC. If Pheidon is involved the earliest set must be chosen. Other indications of date are: that a daughter of Kypselos married Teisandros, the Athenian Philaid, father of Kypselos and grandfather of Miltiades the Elder; that Periander was associated with Thrasyboulos of Miletos and Alyattes of Lydia, and also acted as arbitrator between Mytilene and Athens in the affair of Sigeion. All these leave too much margin for close dating. The uncertainty has to be accepted.

Kypselos was the son of Eetion, descended from Kaineus the Lapith (and so pre-Dorian?) or from Melas of Gonoussa, who joined the Dorians under Aletes and was suffered to stay in Corinth despite the warning of an oracle. Eetion married Labda, daughter of the Bacchiad Amphion, whom no Bacchiad would marry because of her lameness. Their son was Kypselos – not, therefore, of lowly birth – in whom were fulfilled two oracles, one addressed to Eetion and another older one threatening the downfall of the Bacchiads. Herodotus gives the story with its strong folk-tale element, telling how Labda saved her child from Bacchiad emissaries sent to kill him, by concealing him in a chest or corn-measure (*kypsele*), which, it was believed, gave the child its name. The story continued that when Kypselos came to manhood he was again the subject of a Delphic oracle which hailed him as king (*basileus*) of Corinth, and promised the same office to his children, but not to his grandchildren. Here in the Kypselos story the oracle is represented as encouraging tyranny. The *post eventum* knowledge that Kypselos' son Periander was succeeded by his nephew would indicate a date in the sixth century or later for the confection of the story, which is not without its interest in the matter of the relation of Delphi and tyrants.

Thus encouraged, Kypselos expelled the Bacchiads, some of whom went to Kerkyra. One of them, Demaratos, made his way to Etruria and, possibly with Corinthian craftsmen, settled at Tarquinii. A late source, deriving from Ephoros, adds the details that Kypselos, thanks to his office of *polemarch* or military commander (a detail derived from an early list?), won over the people – how precisely is not explained – and killed a Bacchiad Hippokleides or Patrokleides, who held some sort of office as 'king' (*basileus*), which need not mean that office in its fullest sense, but a residual function, perhaps religious. The action against the Bacchiads (with outside help?) may account for his ambivalent reputation, of severity followed by later mildness, since he dispensed with a bodyguard: in Aristotle's terms, therefore, a king rather than a tyrant. Kypselos' son and successor was regarded as a typical tyrant, originator, according to Aristotle, of the less laudable ways of keeping down opposition, or of some of them. In Herodotus, as in the case of Kypselos, so too in that of Periander, a certain amount of semi-folk tale gathered about him to illustrate his wickedness and ultimately to demonstrate that crime doesn't pay: the brutal killing of his wife; the steps taken to provide her with clothing in the spirit world; the alienation of his younger son Lykophron on account of his mother's killing; the part played in that alienation by the grandfather, Prokles, tyrant of Epidauros, and his consequent removal by Periander; Lykophron's ejection from home, and exile in Kerkyra; Periander's desperate efforts to secure his return to be his successor, even to offering to take his son's place in Kerkyra and leave the field clear in Corinth; the resultant murder of Lykophron and the taking of three hundred hostage children of leading Kerkyreans in revenge and their dispatch to Alyattes of Lydia to be made eunuchs; their rescue by the Samians through a quaint strategem, and the consequent hostility of Corinth and Samos. So, for all his efforts, it was his brother Gorgios' son, Psammetichos, who succeeded him for a brief space. This was a horrific story of the sort beloved of Herodotus, suitable pabulum for the Greek disposition to moralize, reaching its ultimate absurdity in Diogenes Laertius' account of Periander in the third century AD, making him, as one of the 'seven sages', the reformed criminal uttering platitudes on tyranny which clearly echo Aristotle.

It was, none the less, impossible to deny that Periander, despite his reputation of being a 'bad' tyrant, had done much to promote the greatness of Corinth. He avoided an excessive taking of sides in the struggles of his times, being a friend (if the stories are true) of Thrasyboulos of Miletos and also of Alyattes of Lydia, his opponent. He maintained friendly relations with the Egyptian rulers of the Twenty-sixth Dynasty; in Greece possibly with Eretria, and with Athens, as the arbitrator between Athens and Mytilene over Sigeion. The eastern connection is perhaps reflected in the increased exports of Corinthian pottery in this direction in the last decades of the seventh century.

Like the aristocracy at an early date, the Corinthian tyrants were distinguished by their activity in the West, a sphere where the Kerkyreans were also active, as indicated by the foundation of Epidamnos on the mainland. Periander probably exploited the favourable position of Corinth by the creation of the *diolkos*, a track on which small ships could be conveyed across the isthmus as an alternative to transshipment from one Corinthian port to the other. In addition other bases were required for the provisioning of ships and the protection of trade routes, to deny facilities to enemies or potential enemies and provide them for those who frequented her home port and traded in her mart. The Kypselid tyrants found colonies very useful, and it seems clear that from the Adriatic coast they were anxious to penetrate into the barbarous hinterland. The Corinthian bronzes found at Trebenischte near Lake Ochrid may indicate such penetration, on a route which led from Kerkyrean Epidamnos and Corinthian Apollonia (a foundation of Periander) through the territory of Lyncestis (which later claimed a connection with the Bacchiads) to the northern Aegean, the Roman Via Egnatia. At the end of this route were eastern Macedonia and Chalkidike, where there was planted the Corinthian colony of Potidaia, which retained close links with the mother city. It is generally believed that Periander founded it around 600 BC.

Corinth had been active in the eastern Mediterranean for a long time, as the presence of her pottery shows, along with the oriental-seeming cult of Aphrodite and possibly her perfume trade. It can be argued that even in the eighth century she was interested in the Black Sea approaches and the sea itself. The epic poet Eumelos dealt with Aietes, ruler of Kolchis,

Medea his daughter and Jason the Argonaut, associating all three closely with Corinth. He may also have called one of the Muses Borysthenis (from Borysthenes, the Greek name for the Dnieper). However this may be, nothing came of it as far as can be judged. On the other hand the foundation of Potidaia in Chalkidike is a well-established reality and a unique effort of Corinth in an area where it is puzzling that she did not attempt more. The reasons for its foundation are unclear. There were other better sites than Potidaia as an eastern terminal of the trans-Balkan route. Population pressure is unlikely in view of the western foundations of the dynasty. There is a temptation to think it was founded in connection with the Macedonian supplies of silver worked by the inland native tribes. If so, it was not for the minting of Corinthian coins, since these first appeared much later (though the exact date is uncertain). Some kind of a case *could* be made out that Corinth succeeded Argos as overlord of Aegina, or as partner with the latter state now engaging in trade with Egypt, a good market for bar silver. It may incidentally be pointed out that there is no evidence for trade rivalry between Aegina and Corinth. East–west trade meant the crossing of the isthmus, through either Megarian or Corinthian territory, with the rival places of resort on the eastern side being Aegina and Athens. So the actual or potential rivalries were between Corinth and Megara and between Athens and Aegina. There can be no doubt of the interest of Corinth in her own trade and the general exploitation of traffic through the isthmus. The main direction was west: Kypselos founded Leukas, Sollion, Anaktorion, Chalkis (interestingly named) and Ambrakia, and Periander was the founder of Apollonia. Whether the award by Periander, as arbitrator, of Sigeion on the Hellespont to Athens has any commercial significance it is impossible to say.

The isthmus position of Corinth and her trade gave her the wealth she could not obtain from a relatively infertile land. Significantly also, it was said that craftsmen were 'least despised at Corinth'. In the late seventh century and in the first half of the sixth there was mass-production of pottery decorated with animal friezes and a narrative style with inscriptions explaining the scenes from mythology. Some of the decoration, of grotesque dancing figures or confronted 'griffin-birds', is tasteless in the extreme and slipshod. Gradually the black-figure style of Athens overtook the Corinthian in quality and quantity, but technically good pots with linear and floral decoration continued to be exported, or at any rate produced, into the fifth century. There was a change of fashion among such customers as the Etruscans: the animal-frieze style was going out everywhere, and the Athenians did the figure style better. There may have been other factors: changes of fashion or taste in relation to the contents of the closed vases; the replacement of clay by metal for table equipment and by alabaster for perfume containers. Certainly the

Corinthians were distinguished bronze-workers. The wealth and skills of Corinth under the tyrants are indicated by the gold Zeus dedicated at Olympia by Kypselos (and perhaps by the Boston gold bowl), by the treasury at Delphi, and by that splendid creation the 'Chest of Kypselos' in cedar wood, with figures in gold and ivory, representing mythological scenes. Enough survives from the seventh century in wood and ivory (and in gold bands) to indicate the possibility of such a work of art at that time, but not earlier than the later seventh century; it could certainly not have been an heirloom in the family of Eetion, or early enough to have inscriptions by the eighth-century epic poet Eumelos.

It is tolerably clear that for the Classical Greeks the seventh-century tyrant Pheidon and the Kypselids (extending into the sixth) were of extreme interest. So was the sixth-century Orthagorid Kleisthenes, to be considered in Chapter 8. There were others also, mainly later, but it would be tedious to enumerate them all. Three more may be mentioned: first Thrasyboulos of Miletos, linked in tradition with Periander, and the doughty opponent of the Lydian kings Sadyattes and Alyattes (pp. 150–1).

Relatively little is known of Thrasyboulos to match the importance of Miletos, chief exponent of Euxine colonization, and bastion, in her own interests rather than on behalf of all the Asia Minor Greeks, against the power of Lydia. Aristotle explains his tyranny as 'due to his holding the office of *prytanis* which carried a number of important prerogatives'.[28] It will be recalled that the term was associated with the Bacchiads also. A certain folk-tale element is present in the story of the cornfield and the 'lopping' of the pre-eminent ears of corn, and in the story of the way in which he tricked the emissaries of Alyattes when Miletos was under siege. His dates are not easy to determine. He is made the contemporary of the Lydians Sadyattes and Alyattes and of Periander. Diogenes Laertius makes him a contemporary of the Milesian philosopher Thales, and in turn makes Thales a contemporary of Croesus, the successor of Alyattes. A long reign is thus inferred. An obscure reference in Plutarch of uncertain value mentions at Miletos 'tyrants associated with Thoas and Damasenor', who were expelled and replaced by oligarchic associations with the names Ploutis and Xeiromacha (? guilds). It sounds like a late and ill-conceived effort to explain the term 'Aeinautai' (certainly some kind of guild) at Miletos, and gives no indication of date or relationship of the tyrants in question to Thrasyboulos. The tradition is altogether too thin for such an important-seeming figure.

Of very considerable interest for a number of reasons is the tyrant of Megara, Theagenes. In terms of chronology he is again a problem. He is credited with the construction of a fountain (in effect a water supply) at Megara. In the sixth century (as it is generally assumed) one Eupalinos of Megara was the builder of an underground aqueduct at Samos. It is a remarkable piece of engineering skill to be seen still in the hill behind the site of the Samian Heraion. Some historians have accordingly been disposed to suggest the same man as builder of the Megarian water supply, which involves bringing Theagenes also into the sixth century. Theagenes, however, was said in the Attic tradition to be the father-in-law of Kylon, the young aristocrat and Olympic victor who with some of his contemporaries and with the aid of troops from his father-in-law attempted but failed to set himself up as tyrant in Athens, an important episode of early Athenian history to be discussed in Chapter 7. If Theagenes has to be moved down, so must Kylon, with disastrous results for the historical narrative. In effect there seem to be good grounds for placing Kylon in the thirties (or twenties) of the seventh century, and consequently Theagenes also. He is thus placed between the earlier Megarian activity at Kalchedon (684 BC) and Byzantium (667 BC) and the hostilities which arose between Megara and Athens as a result of the conspiracy of Kylon and the contest for Salamis. It would be useful to place him with greater accuracy, but the renewed excavation of the fountain at Megara is unlikely to contribute much.

Theagenes, according to Aristotle, was one of that category of tyrants who maintained a bodyguard, and presumably from this source came the assistance sent to Kylon. Of exceptional interest is the story also given by Aristotle: that Theagenes made his way to the tyranny 'after slaughtering the herds of the rich, finding them grazing along the river'.[29] In the same passage Theagenes is bracketed with Peisistratos of Athens, who likewise won confidence by hostility to the rich, in his case by opposition to the 'Men of the Plain'. The characteristic of both was the stirring up of hostility (the sense of *polemikoi* here). Here also it is suggested that favourable circumstances for the appearance of tyrants were small communities of scattered peasants busy with their own affairs. The particular interest of the Theagenes story is the cattle slaughter. Was there a conflict of interest between peasant cultivation and the cattle-raising of the wealthy: the cattle driving out the cultivator? As in the case of some other tyrants too little is known of Theagenes, and of whether he had successors, and how their fall, or his, led to subsequent events in Megara: a short period of moderation, which is placed immediately after the expulsion of Theagenes, followed by excesses of the *demos*, the plundering of the rich (as being the creditors of the poor), their expulsion into exile, and finally their return by force and the establishment of an oligarchy. These were perhaps the circumstances in which there took place that association of the noble-born and the 'base' rich which is lamented by Theognis. There are, however, grave problems of chronology.

Finally it is worth mentioning the 'Pisatan tyranny' of Pantaleon and his sons Damophon and Pyrrhos established in southern Elis. The story was that they ruled 'Pisa' and exercised presidency of the games, either for an extended period in the second half of the seventh century and in the first quarter of the sixth, or Pantaleon in Olympiad 34 (644 BC) only. According to Strabo the Pisatans under Pantaleon aided the Messenians, in concert with the Argives and Arcadians, against Sparta in the Second Messenian War, which is to be associated with Pheidon and his intervention in Olympia in 668 BC. The 'Pisatan' dynasty had therefore come into being at quite an early date and continued its hostility to the Eleans over three reigns, until Damophon was finally put down by them in a war in which the 'Pisatans' were supported by other small communities of southern Elis. It has been argued that in fact there was no true community of 'Pisa', which was a figment of fourth-century Arcadian propaganda. In the final war the 'Pisatans' had the support of two communities in Triphylia south of Elis. Another one, Dyspontion, claimed foundation by Dysponteus, son of Oinomaos of Olympia, very much pre-conquest. In effect the 'Pisatans', and Pantaleon and his sons, represented a pre-conquest faction, opposed to the 'Dorized' Eleans of northern Elis, for whom the control of the games was a point of dispute. There can be little to suggest a 'tyranny'; Pantaleon himself is called 'king' (*basileus*).

Reserved for Chapter 8 is a consideration of a third type, as Aristotle believed, of personal rule: the *aisymneteia*. The word appears in Homer as a description of supervisors at a musical performance, drawn from or acting on behalf of the people (*demioi*); much later it is the name, appearing in inscriptions, for a regular magistracy. It may be a word of foreign origin, or it may derive from *aisa*, 'lot' or 'portion', and so an *aisymnetes* is an 'apportioner', standing between two or more sets of claimants. One is immediately reminded of Solon. Aristotle, however, describes the function as something resembling but distinct from kingship and tyranny: 'an elective form of tyranny'. He cites as an example not Solon but Pittakos of Mytilene, 'elected . . . to deal with the attacks of the exiles commanded by Antimenidas and the lyric poet Alkaios'.[30]

The background of Pittakos is of exceptional interest, as it is set in the period of the Lesbian poets Sappho and Alkaios, at the turn from the seventh to the sixth century. There was a period of disorder in some of the Asia Minor states arising from the pretensions and misbehaviour of noble clans claiming descent from city-founders, such as the Penthilidai at Mytilene, the Basilidai at Ephesos and Erythrai and the Neleidai at Miletos; some of them were, no doubt, the horse-owners mentioned by Aristotle. Against them another element of the populace reacted in Mytilene, choosing Pittakos as leader, and being lucky that he did not seek to turn himself into an orthodox tyrant.

It is reasonable to suppose that what has been well described as 'the violent and empty-headed politics' of Alkaios and many of his like was an indication of the ultimate decay of the aristocratic tradition. This appears in the poems of Kallinos of Ephesos and Tyrtaios of Sparta, appealing for a display of warlike and selfless citizen behaviour, and in the contemptuous attitudes of Archilochos. There was also among the nobles an unwillingness to recognize a changing world, while the 'hoplite spirit', as it might be called, of the *polis* had not fully come into being. In Athens Solon came to the fore in a similar but so far less violent situation of aristocratic irresponsibility. He had in common with Pittakos that he was *chosen* by what must have been a considerable element comprising among others sensible aristocrats in the citizen community, tired of internal strife and fearful of worse. To Solon was committed the *politeia*, an internationally vague term. He is called not *Aisymnetes* but *Diallaktes* ('reconciler') and archon, occupying therefore in the latter capacity a regular office. Plutarch calls him 'reconciler and lawgiver'. Both Solon and Pittakos seem to have been of aristocratic origins (despite what Alkaios says of Pittakos), but belonging to the *Mesoi* as far as their economic status was concerned. The rule of Pittakos was longer and tougher, involving the use of force, but they both withdrew, when in their opinion they had done what was necessary, and did not seek to prolong their authority.

It is in general a confused picture. It is easier to see why aristocracies were vulnerable and contained the seeds of destruction within themselves than to explain their replacement by individual rulers, whether *basileis* or *tyrannoi*. It is, incidentally, pointless to lay stress on the differences at an early date between these two terms; both could be self-made men, usurpers of a throne or of prerogatives, like Gyges of Lydia. The full idea of the tyrant was developed only much later. Their main characteristic was that they made a break in a tradition. They overthrew the hereditary nobility in their own state, though they were not averse to alliances with aristocrats in other states. If the hereditary nobility recovered something of their power later they would for the future be seen for what they were, self-made men too, no longer 'the best' (*aristoi*) with that intangible *arete*, but just 'the few', an exclusiveness of power and wealth, which disappeared when wealth was lost, so that it became possible for them to be joined by others, in conditions of greater social mobility both upwards and downwards. It was, on the whole a good thing. The point has already been made (p. 113) that a proverb which must date from the introduction of the Aeginetan coinage signalizes the triumph of money over the moral virtues. It will be seen in Chapter 7 (p. 175) that the proverb 'Money is the Man. No poor man at all is noble or held in honour' goes back to Alkaios at the beginning of the sixth century, and was put by him in the mouth of a Spartan. This belief perhaps arose from envy. Some of the ancient nobility in the sixth (and early fifth?) century, still treasuring its quality of 'the best', could not understand that the world had changed.

They were dismayed that wealth gave power not only to the 'right' people but also to others. What was worse, some of the 'right' people, 'the noble and the best', were tempted to associate themselves with the 'base' in their quest for wealth. This is the theme, it may be repeated, of Theognis, deploring the influx of wealth and the decline of 'birth' and writing of the confusion of the 'good' and the 'bad', terms uniting social and moral and economic judgements. As he puts it: 'The good man scruples not to wed the low-born daughter of a low-born man, if he provide much wealth. Nor yet does a woman hate to be the bed-fellow of a low-born man, if he be rich, but she desires a wealthy husband instead of one well-born. For wealth they hold in honour, and the well-born weds the daughter of a low-born father, and the low-born the daughter of a noble. Thus wealth confounds our stock.'[31]

This misconception of eugenics has appeared since; and to quite recent times this intermarriage, when the mechanics of the process are clear enough, was called 'marrying into trade'. For the period under consideration the identity of these so-called base-born but wealthy people presents a major problem. It is difficult to believe that they were a figment of the aristocratic imagination. They certainly were not just craftsmen of a lesser sort, though these were the objects of aristocratic contempt at all times. They could *just* be middle-class farmers who had prospered more than their social superiors. It might even be thought, looking at them from another angle, that they were erstwhile *aristoi* who had fallen from grace and turned to trade, forgetting the ancestral *arete*. In that case they might be 'base' but not 'base-born'. There is a tendency to be influenced by the ideas of the Classical period, when the *emporos* or seagoing merchant was not so ill thought of as the *kapelos* or petty market-trader, but was not highly respected. At an earlier period a man might travel to see the world as well as trade, which in effect meant taking a cargo to cover expenses. Hesiod, counselling his farmer 'to hang his rudder in the smoke' except under pressure of necessity, infers that cultivators might trade by sea directly and not through a middleman. The identification of this 'trading class' is a problem, especially in view of the temptation to connect them with the tyranny, particularly at Corinth, and to go even further and suggest that as non-landowners they did not possess full citizen rights despite their wealth, and so looked to an anti-aristocratic ruler to help them.

The growth of wealth is not to be exaggerated, but it has to be admitted. It is apparent in the literary sources, and demonstrated by the increase in works of major art and architecture at the end of the seventh century. The introduction of electrum coinage (if not silver) in the latter part of the same century made available a means of evaluation and exchange, and facilitated the accumulation and transport of wealth. It also had other effects. Economic oppression and distress seem to increase or appear for the first time side by side with coinage (not necessarily coinage issued by the state so affected). It is easy to see why. The power, mobility and influence of a rustic or city nobility would be greatly increased if they could turn the natural products and labour of a peasantry into money. The more they could rack-rent the peasantry in question and force them into serfdom, the better for them, if not for the community as a whole. It could be argued that those higher in the economic scale might see the same fate impending. It should be added that even before the development of coinage, gold, silver and electrum in the form of bullion or ornaments and plate could be accumulated.

The existence of trade is equally certain: from the literary sources, as, for example, in Hesiod's *Works and Days*; and from the archaeological evidence of the colonial foundations and other sites; and from contacts within Greece proper. In the nature of things trade by land was limited by the difficulties of travel and the primitive means of transport. Travel by sea was easier, but ships were small, and it is difficult to judge to what extent a middleman was needed to accumulate cargo. We are painfully ignorant of the way in which crafts and industry (if the word is properly used at all) were organized. Traffic by sea could take place only for part of the year; and while it might conflict with civil and military citizen duties, it would not necessarily do so with cultivation and the pursuit of crafts. The real issue, from the economic standpoint, is the relationship of trader to producer, whether of natural commodities or of manufactured goods. The production, at any rate of natural commodities – grain, olives, wine or timber – is inseparably connected with the land, and it is reasonable to expect close links here between production and trade, carried on by the same or related persons. How else did the trader obtain his commodities or his capital? On the other hand the political aspect of this, the status of the trader and his citizen rights, is in no way peculiar to his particular class. It was not the ownership of land as a basis of citizenship, or the possession of citizenship which mattered, but the degree to which the individual had a voice in the government of the *polis* under an aristocracy.

If a trading class played no particular or special part in supporting tyrants as champions of their rights, there is the alternative of the hoplite army to be considered. The tyranny was, indeed, associated with military office or success. Kypselos might be an example of the former and Peisistratos of Athens and Kleisthenes of Sikyon (see pp. 203ff; 209ff) of the latter.

The assessment of the hoplite army and its political significance is not easy. The *hoplon* or large shield of bronze-faced leather, or just of leather with a bronze blazon, was different from the Attic Geometric 'Dipylon' shield (a version of the figure-of-eight type?), which can hardly have been an effective protection against missiles, and from the small 'targe' with its central handle clearly intended for single combat with swords. The hoplite equipment ultimately consisted of a crested helmet, two-piece breastplate, with a *mitra* or semicircular 'apron' beneath it, thigh pieces, greaves and ankle-guards, in addition to the great round shield with its blazon, which appears to have had no particular heraldic or group significance. The equipment need not have been so elaborate at the beginning. The helmet and cuirass from the Argive Panoply grave, *c.* 710–700 BC, are hoplite equipment, though the origins of such bronze work may lie in Central Europe (see p. 65) and of the helmet in the Near East. It looks expensive, and few can have owned such equipment so early. The hoplite sword would generally be of iron, but the making of iron armour was beyond Greek technology. Since a Greek soldier provided his own arms he had to be a man of some substance, at least a 'yeoman farmer', as it is commonly said.

For the technique of warfare the literary sources are something of a hotch-potch, or ambiguous. In the *Iliad* the great heroes, the named men, fight in the battle front in single combat, with the spear and on foot. The chariot is the refuge of the hard-pressed. There is something like a reference to massed chariots in the *Iliad*, and Nestor's battle line is composed of chariots and foot soldiers. Both may be anachronisms from the Bronze Age. In the *Iliad* also there are 'ranks' of heroes as well as of horses. Despite the circus act of *Iliad* xv, 679 (not in battle) there is little mention of horse-riding. It must therefore be assumed that cavalry, such as the famous cavalry of Kolophon, largely came in later. Its value, *if* the Greeks had no stirrups, must have been small except for reconnaissance, to throw foot soldiers into disorder, or to arrive fresh for a military engagement and get away quickly if necessary. It would have been a prestige symbol rather than an effective arm of warfare.

The aristocrat dismounted from his chariot or his horse and joined, as a *promachos*, or fighter in the front rank, with comrades who had neither chariot nor horse. The equipment described above, the panoply, ultimately suggested the hoplite *formation*, the advance in line shoulder to shoulder, presenting a serried line of shields in which the soldier tended to cover his unshielded right side by the shield of his comrade on the right, though he had to allow space to wield his weapons. Something like hoplite battles seem to be described here and there in the *Iliad*, but in a confused fashion. The formation appears most clearly on Corinthian pottery of the second half of the seventh century, as on the Chigi Jug. Is it so represented because it is something commonplace or something new? It is noteworthy that it does not appear on Attic pottery in succession to the files of shielded warriors of the late Geometric period. In a fragment of Kallinos of Ephesos (a slightly younger contemporary of Archilochos), who in the mid-seventh century writes of the troubles of Asia Minor, it is difficult to detect any suggestion of the hoplite formation. Kallinos' words sound like a description of single combats: 'Let each go forward straight, with spear raised and valiant heart behind his shield';[32] or again: 'In the eyes of his fellows he is like a tower for one, though being *one*, he performs deeds worthy of many.'[33] In Tyrtaios, contemporary of the Second Messenian War, there is some ambiguity. Some exhortations sound like references to single combat. When young men are summoned to fight 'abiding by each other' the phrase is ambiguous and seems to mean 'not leaving each other in the lurch', as the soldier does who is described as 'standing out of range of missiles'. It is in any case a stock phrase. There is, on the other hand, a clear reference to the large hoplite shield, Homerically 'bossed' (which is a convention from epic language). There seems also to be a reference to the panoply, the hoplite equipment, and a quite clear reference to 'the fence of hollow shields'. An interesting feature in Tyrtaios is the instruction to the light-armed soldiers (*gymnetes*) to 'hurl great boulders, crouching beneath the shields on this side and that': a combination of heavy troops with light, the latter wielding stones and darts.[34] The hoplite formation was one which depended on cohesion, and needed and fostered a comradeship of either kin or neighbours.

There is a natural tendency to connect Pheidon with the development of the hoplite army by way of the Argive Panoply grave, but in the oracle-proverb quoted earlier (p. 128) the Argives are 'linen-corseleted', a form of defensive armour which goes back to the late Bronze Age and is also represented by the corslet of the sixth-century Pharaoh Amasis. It is also natural to think of the Euboeans, but while they inhabited an island rich in cattle for leather, if the name is anything to go on, also in bronze, and are given credit for excellence in these, their title 'spear-famed' explains little in terms of battle tactics. It may be suggested that the Spartans were the true developers of the hoplite army, but over a considerable period, and it will be argued in Chapter 7 that this went side by side with the confrontation of kings and *gerousia* (council of elders) on one side with the assembly on the other. The Spartans should have credit for this, as for *probouleusis* also, but it is clear from the fact that they did not attain full success against Argos and Tegea until the sixth century, that the full development of the hoplite army did not take place until then.

It also developed elsewhere, as at Corinth, but again over a period of time, and it is to be noted that it must be the *early* stages which are to be connected with the tyranny. A better case can be made out for the hoplite army as a factor in the overthrow, in some Greek cities, of the aristocracy, than for the supposed 'trading class'. It might be suggested that in the seventh century, in certain *poleis*, there took place a breakdown of the closely knit clan or *genos* organization (largely through aristocratic misbehaviour and stupidity), so that a common interest ceased to exist between and unite nobles, *mesoi* and *aporoi* (see above) *de haut en bas*, comprising noble *promachoi*, the *mesoi* as rank-and-file foot soldiers of the better-armed sort, and light-armed *aporoi*, using darts and stones. Not only the poor but also the middle-class cultivators could feel themselves economically menaced by an ever more bigoted and rapacious aristocracy, bringing about a horizontal alignment against the *aristoi*, cutting across the clan structure. The ultimate in this development was the Kleisthenic constitution and army organization of Athens in the late sixth century.

It would be a mistake, however, to rest too heavily on the development of the hoplite army as an explanation of the tyranny. Every *polis*, there can be no doubt, had its local issues, which could be the subject of what Aristotle represents as demagogic activity on the part of the would-be tyrant against the ruling aristocracy. Unhappily the detailed information we command is totally inadequate for an independent judgement, and reliance has to be placed on Aristotle's generalizations and on an assortment of snippets from other sources.

An oddity is the association of tyranny at Sikyon and perhaps elsewhere with a form of 'racialism', taking the form of a championing of 'non-Dorians' against the 'Dorian' elements, as by Kleisthenes of Sikyon (p. 209–10), which must have rested ultimately on inter-state rivalries, between Sikyon and Argos. Other issues might be a demand for a redivision of land, or a written law code to replace the customary law administered by the aristocracy. We know little of the detail of events, or of events at all, in such regions as Thessaly, Boeotia and Euboea. As far as our knowledge goes tyranny did not appear in Arcadia and Elis, or else it lurked in milder form under the title of *basileus*. In the case of the latter two areas its absence might be explained by the retention of relatively primitive conditions and the absence of a concentration of population. Such a concentration might seem to encourage a more intensive political life and more opportunity for the discussion of grievances and the sharing of resentments. Aristotle, while asserting that tyranny was made more secure by the scattering of potential dissidents, also claimed that tyranny was facilitated in a state where a scattered country peasantry was intent on its own pursuits. If this was so Kylon, the would-be tyrant of Athens (pp. 185–6), did not find it so, and there can be no doubt that each case of the success or failure of a tyrant had its own particular circumstances.

The Greeks of Greece proper had, in the late eighth century and in the seventh, the experiences so far related in the present chapter. They were not subjected to invasion or attack from an external source: this had taken place earlier and was to come again later in the form of the Persians. They were not subjected to pressure from a near and powerful neighbour: this would come from Macedonia in the fourth century. And there were no barbarian nomad raids.

Because of their geographical position on the fringes of Anatolia the

Eastern Greeks, as they are frequently called, were exposed to these hazards on all three coasts, north, west and south. On the west they could be threatened by an alien power in the interior of western Asia Minor, and on at any rate the eastern portion of the southern coast by the great power of the Near and Middle East, the Assyrians; on the Euxine coast there was a danger of incursions by nomads from the region of the Caucasus and possibly from Thrace.

In the period under consideration the principal Greek cities of western Asia Minor were not directly affected by the military activities of the Assyrians or of the rulers of the Vannic kingdom (Urartu), which in any case by the earlier seventh century had been subordinated effectively to Assyria. The Phrygians acted as a buffer between the dominant power in eastern Anatolia and the Greeks on the western coast. There was not the direct contact which the Greeks of Cyprus and the eastern Mediterranean had with the Assyrians. And between the coastal Greeks and the Phrygians lay another people, the Lydians. The period under consideration saw the decline (not disappearance) of the kingdom of Phrygia, occasioned by the inroads of the nomadic Kimmerians who continued to devastate Asia Minor for a considerable period of time, and the rise of a powerful dynasty of Lydian rulers whose ambition from the beginning was to dominate the eastern Greeks.

The Phrygians occupied the area in west-central Anatolia of the middle and upper Sangarios (River Sakarya) and the great bend of the Halys (the River Kızıl Irmak). Somewhat further east they held some of the former Hittite sites (Alaca Hüyük, Boğazköy and Alişar). They had entered Asia Minor from the west (see pp. 37–8) and spoke an Indo-European language. By the eighth century BC they had attained a high level of material culture. There were two important sites, both in the upper valley of the Sangarios: Midas City (Midas-Şehri), so called from the traditionally named Tomb of Midas very near the site, and Gordion (Yassihüyük) west of Polatli. The Greeks knew the names of Phrygian kings, Gordios and Midas, the former associated with the celebrated knot cut by Alexander, and the latter with great wealth. The American excavation at Gordion, revealing the city-site with palace, houses, walls and gates, and the great royal chamber tomb built of logs beneath a huge mound, shows the high technical skill of the Phrygians in building, bronze work and wood inlay. The chamber tomb contains an especially important assemblage of material: cauldrons and fibulae of bronze, and furniture. The Phrygians' relationship with their eastern neighbours is well established. Under the names of Mushki and Tabal they had hostile contact with the Assyrians and friendly contact and alliance with the Urartians. Gordion lay on an overland trade route from eastern Anatolia, along which came the bronze work of Urartu. The Phrygians reached their highest point of political importance in the late eighth century under a King Midas, but a great disaster came from the appearance of the nomad Kimmerians (the Gimirrai of the Assyrians, the Gomer of the Old Testament).

Herodotus gives a muddled account of the Kimmerians, distinguishing them, probably wrongly, from the Scythians. According to him they were originally located in southern Russia and were displaced by the Scythians, who crossed the River Araxes (? the Volga) after being worsted by the Massagetai. Some (?) Scythians, he claims, missed their way in pursuit of the Kimmerians and entered Media, a confusion with a later nomad raid into north-western Persia. The Kimmerians, according to Herodotus, in defiance of geography, 'fled along the sea shore' (that is the southern coast of the Euxine) and some settled at Sinope the site of a Greek colony. It may be noted that *if* there were eighth-century Greek colonies in this area (Sinope and Trapezos) their destruction and subsequent refoundation could thus be accounted for.

It is more likely that a mass of nomads burst out of the steppe and were subsequently divided into three: one came through the Caucasus into eastern Asia Minor; another occupied southern Russia in the vicinity of the Crimea; and a third made their way eventually round the western side of the Euxine into Thrace, there picked up elements of the Thracian Treres and penetrated Asia Minor from the north-west. The horde which came through the Caucasus inflicted a defeat in 714 BC (in the reign of Sargon [722–705 BC] in Assyria) on Rusas I, King of Urartu, who committed suicide. Subsequently his successor, Rusas II, is found allied with the Kimmerians against Assyria under Esarhaddon (681–669 BC). At the end of the eighth century or early in the seventh the Kimmerians attacked Phrygia. The Phrygians were defeated and Gordion was sacked (as the excavations show). Later the Assyrian records of Esarhaddon mention the death by suicide of Mita of the Mushki. The death of Midas was also known to the later Greeks; it was dated by Eusebius-Jerome at 696 or 695 BC. The king who lay buried in the great grave mound at Gordion may have been this Midas. He was surrounded by a great wealth of bronze work but no gold. It has been suggested it was all used in an attempt to buy off the nomads. Subsequently Phrygia recovered culturally, but not as a great power. As far as the eastern depredations of the Kimmerians are concerned they were, under King Teushpa, defeated by Esarhaddon in 679.BC and thrown back from the Taurus. The effect of this defeat was to turn them westward again.

The prime purpose of this account is to discuss the relationship of the Phrygians with the eastern Greeks. The later Greeks knew of Midas 'of the golden touch', the first non-Greek to make an offering at Delphi. There was a tradition that he had married the daughter of Agamemnon, King of Kyme in Aeolis. The overland trade route certainly came west as far as the territory of Phrygia. To what extent there was contact further westwards with the eastern Greeks is a debatable point. Objects in bronze – cauldrons, libation bowls, fibulae and belt buckles – are certainly present in Greek centres, but there is the question of their date, of whether they came during or after the great days of Phrygia. As far as pottery is concerned the Phrygian–Greek relationship is quite obscure: it is somewhat difficult to believe in Phrygian influence on Aegean Island pottery of the end of the eighth century. It is equally debatable whether the Greeks supplied the Phrygians with the alphabet and mercenaries. The existence of an earlier version of the Persian Royal Road might not be disputed, passing through Phrygia, but in many respects the routes by way of Rhodes and Cyprus, or through Trapezos and the Euxine to eastern Anatolia, seem easier ways of contact with the Near East.

The decline of Phrygia was followed at no great distance in time by the rise of Lydia, which at the time of Phrygian greatness had probably been in the position of a vassal. The Lydians were an ancient people, as the Greeks believed (see p. 66), and they seem in fact to have possessed a continuous cultural tradition from the Late Bronze Age. The site of Sardis was occupied in the early Iron Age, and there are some indications of contact in the eighth century with the Greeks. The crucial event for Lydia and the eastern Greeks was the replacement of a Heraclid dynasty, which, it was claimed, went back to the end of the thirteenth century BC, by a usurper, in effect a *tyrannos*, which may be a Lydian word. Archilochos uses it (*tyrannis*) in a context where he refers to this usurper, Gyges. As Herodotus tells the story, Gyges (Assyrian 'Gugu'), son of Daskylos, came to the Lydian throne as the result of a quaint series of events involving Kandaules or Myrsilos, his predecessor, the last Heraclid king, and the latter's wife. The Mermnad dynasty thus established comprised five kings, all deeply involved with the eastern Greeks and eastern Asia Minor: Gyges, Ardys, Sadyattes, Alyattes and Kroisos, who in the mid-sixth century fell victim to the Persians.

The chronology of these rulers presents serious problems. Like the Spartan king list in Greece, the chronology of the Mermnad line forms the backbone of eastern Greek seventh-century and earlier sixth-century history. The dates of the succession of the Mermnad kings was in antiquity worked back from the defeat of Kroisos (Croesus) by the Persians, placed in either 548 BC or 546 BC. Unfortunately there are divergences between Herodotus and Eusebius, both in the total of years of the five kings (Herodotus: 170; Eusebius: 152) and in their individual reigns. Consequently Herodotus' figures give 716–678 BC for Gyges, and those of Eusebius give 670–664 BC. Since Archilochos mentions 'golden Gyges' (and the *tyrannis* also), and Herodotus believed them to be contemporary, the chronology of Gyges involves a great deal more than the history of Lydia. Fortunately there are oriental synchronisms – with the period of Assurbanipal (668–626 BC) – and it is tolerably clear that

Archilochos is to be placed about the middle of the seventh century, since he mentions the total eclipse, visible in Thasos, of 648 BC. It may be added that similar oriental material involving Kyros the Persian and Nabuna'id of Babylon help to determine the end-date of the reign of Kroisos (Croesus). A recent study concerned with this problem would suggest the following dates: Gyges, c. 680–652 BC; Ardys, 651 to 'before 613 BC'; Sadyattes, 'before 613 BC' to c. 607 BC; Alyattes, c. 607–560 BC; Kroisos, 560 BC–547 BC. A number of other dates are fitted into this framework, involving the Lydians, Assyrians, Kimmerians and Ionian Greek cities. In most cases the important matter is the order of events, rather than their exact dating.

On his seizure of power c. 680 BC Gyges, according to Herodotus, encountered violent opposition from the Lydians, and by agreement an appeal was made to Delphi, which recognized him as king but warned of vengeance in the fifth generation. It is hardly necessary to believe that the Lydians had so much regard for the oracle, or that Apollo foresaw the fate of Kroisos. Gyges' confirmation in the kingship must have been due to other reasons, but it was useful later propaganda both for his dynasty and for the oracle at Delphi, and served to explain the generous gifts to the oracle made by Gyges himself and after him by Alyattes and Kroisos. The date c. 680 BC for the coming to power of Gyges is a reasonable conjecture (taking account of better-dated subsequent events) based on a statement of Strabo that Abydos on the Troad side of the Hellespont was founded by Miletos with the permission of Gyges, 'for the region and the whole Troad was under his rule'.[35] The same, it has been suggested, may well be true of Daskyleion (possibly named after Gyges' father) and Kyzikos. They were both on the Propontis, and so, with Abydos, strategically placed in relation not only to the sea route to the Euxine but also to the crossing from Europe (Thrace). The date of the foundation of Kyzikos is given as 675 BC, and it is reasonable to believe that the other two belong to the same period, taken to be the early years of Gyges' rule. There are two difficulties: the implied rapid extension of Gyges' empire in the period 680–675 BC, unless the preceding Lydian dynasty had expanded north-westwards, and the reason why Gyges should thus promote the interests of the Ionian Greeks when subsequently, like his successors, he seemed set on damaging them. Leaving aside, as explanation, the changing whims of a semi-oriental potentate, it might be suggested he was concerned with the danger of nomad invasion from Europe rather than access to the Euxine, which he could secure by land.

Shortly afterwards Gyges and Lydia faced the same danger from the Kimmerians as had overtaken the Phrygians. Despite their defeat and repulse from the Taurus in 679 BC, by the Assyrians, or because of it, the Kimmerians turned west and made their first eruption into Lydia, sometime in the period 667–664 BC, which led to an appeal of Gyges for help to the Assyrians, which is recorded in the Annals of Assurbanipal. The Assyrian king records the appeal as from a would-be vassal, and states that from that time Gyges was victorious over the Kimmerians. Later, however, with more confidence in himself than conditions warranted, Gyges went back on his allegiance, as Assurbanipal records, and also sent help to Psammetichos in Egypt, c. 655 BC, in the form of Ionian and Carian mercenaries, probably 'the bronze men' of Herodotus; the Assyrian record also in fact mentions troops sent to Psammetichos. In the sequel, and, as Assurbanipal believed, in answer to his prayers to the gods of Assyria, Gyges suffered another attack from the Kimmerians and fell in battle c. 652 BC. Some time between the two Kimmerian invasions Gyges turned against the Ionian cities, attacking Miletos and Smyrna (from the latter of which he was stoutly repulsed, as it was afterwards remembered), and captured the lower town (asty) of Kolophon, thus beginning the Lydian pressure against the Ionian cities which continued until, after Kroisos, it was replaced by the successful aggression of the Persians.

Gyges was succeeded by his son Ardys in 651 BC, who again had to suffer nomad attack, this time by the Treres mentioned earlier. They were probably a mixed body, partly nomads and partly Thracians, including the Thracian tribe of that name. At an earlier date (?) they entered Asia Minor from the west, and now c. 645 BC sacked Sardis, except the citadel. Their earlier arrival in Asia Minor may account for the interest of Gyges in the Propontis. A section of the Treres appear to have settled at Antandros for one hundred years, according to Aristotle. Ardys is also credited with the capture of Priene and with campaigning against Miletos.

At some date before 613 BC Ardys was succeeded by Sadyattes, who pursued for six years a campaign against Miletos. After a short reign he was followed, c. 607 BC, by Alyattes (who may appear as Walwesh on Lydian electrum coins). The exact order of his campaigns, particularly involving the eastern Greek cities, is unclear. His policy (if clearly defined) must have been influenced by the fall of Nineveh. The fall of the Assyrian capital took place in 612 BC. It fell to the Medes under Kyaxares and their allies the Babylonians under Nabopolassar. There was also at much the same time an inroad of Scythians into the Middle East. The ultimate defeat of the Assyrians allowed Kyaxares to take over Urartu, and so become the immediate eastern neighbour of Lydia. There followed after an interval the war between the Lydians and Medes of 590–585 BC. It may be added that the ultimate result (after the 'Battle of the Eclipse') was an alliance of Media and Lydia, a fateful link between the Middle East and Anatolia. When, subsequently, the Medes fell victim to the Persians under Kyros, Kroisos, as ally of the Medes, fought the Persians, to his own ruin and that of the eastern Greeks.

The military operations of Alyattes should be placed in the following order: the five-year campaign which ended the 'Twelve-Year War' against Miletos under Thrasyboulos must come first (*c.* 607–602 BC); it was followed quickly by the invasion of Klazomenian territory (in which the Lydians suffered defeat) and by the siege and destruction of Smyrna (*c.* 602–600 BC). The operations against the Greek cities, it may be suggested, were intended to secure the Lydian rear against the Medes. Alyattes may have foreseen the possibility of a seduction by the Medes of the eastern Greeks in his rear, just as later Kyros the Persian attempted to win the support of the Greeks against Kroisos. Alyattes is also said to have 'driven the Kimmerians out of Asia'[36] (i.e. Asia Minor), a statement involving the question of their ultimate fate. It seems that this cannot refer to a major defeat of the nomads (under the Lygdamis of Strabo, called Dugdamme by Assurbanipal), which is to be placed between 637 BC and 626 BC, and therefore in the reign of Ardys. It can only refer, if correctly credited to Alyattes, to an expulsion of the Treres from Antandros, which should be placed in the seventies of the sixth century. The career of Alyattes after the destruction of Smyrna belongs to the sixth century, as does that of his successor Kroisos, under whom, according to Herodotus, the Ionian Greeks suffered unremitting harassment. He attacked Ephesos (and compelled the Ephesians to change the site of their city), and 'afterwards on some pretext or other he made war in turn upon every Ionian and Aeolian state, bringing forward where he could a substantial ground of complaint, where such failed him, advancing some poor excuse'.[37]

It was in such a world with such hazards that the Ionian and other eastern Greeks had to live, though they had their relations with the Aegean and old Greece also (see below on the excavation of Smyrna). It is not clear how soon their settlement of eastern Greece attained the form it had in the seventh century. As it has been seen in Chapter 4, the migration was a complex process, with some communities absorbing others or shifting their location, as in the episodes traditionally involving Ephesos, Kolophon and Smyrna. Or else communities were eliminated, as, for example, Melie. The Kolophon–Smyrna episode and the Meliac War involve particular difficulties, if these events are pushed back into the ninth century, taking with them the Panionion and the festival and league associated with it. On the one hand it is worth bearing in mind that in the mid-ninth century Smyrna built a new city wall on her landward site, which does not argue a feeling of security (but this *may* be because she did not succeed in entering the Panionion League). On the other hand there is the difficulty that the excavation at the Panionion seems to indicate a date *c.* 700 BC for the destruction of Melie and in consequence a temptation to associate the League with the rise of Lydia and the appearance of the Kimmerians. In effect, however, the idea of the Ionian cities standing together against an enemy is hardly convincing for the seventh century, or indeed later, as the events of the Ionian Revolt show in the first decade of the fifth century. This impression of Greek inter-state hostility rather than co-operation is given in succession by the episode of Smyrna, the hostilities in the period of the Lelantine War between Chios and Erythrai, Samos and Miletos, and by the suggestion that when attacked by Alyattes Miletos received no help from any Ionian city except Chios. There was also the internal political strife, particularly and clearly demonstrated at Mytilene in the poems of Alkaios. These may have arisen partly from the diversity of population in the eastern Greek cities: witness the Hittite–Lydian name Myrsilos for a political figure at Mytilene, and the strongly non-Greek cult of Artemis at Ephesos.

To these hostilities were added others, even more striking. In a war between Ephesos and Magnesia on the Maiandros in the mid-seventh century, Magnesia, 'having long been prosperous', was totally destroyed by the Treres, who seem to have been allies of the Ephesians. This may account for nomad-style objects found at the Ephesian Artemision. Thereupon the Magnesian territory was occupied by Miletos! This turmoil has somehow to be related to Propontic colonization (see p. 150) and that of the Black Sea, in relation to which Strabo comments on the great part played by Miletos. This activity belonged mainly to the latter part of the seventh century (establishment or re-establishment of Sinope *c*. 630 BC), but some foundations were earlier: Istros between 663 BC and 656 BC, with the appearance of Istrokles as the name of an Ionian potter around mid-century. It is to be suggested that a change took place between 684 BC, when the Megarians established Kalchedon on the Asiatic side of the Bosphoros to control a *land* route to the Black Sea (a clear example of an 'isthmus route'), and 667 BC, when Byzantium was founded not only to exploit the tunny-fishing but also to afford a port of call for ships. There is no reason to believe in Megarian blindness (as suggested by Herodotus and by a bogus oracle in Strabo), but rather in a change of circumstances, in part related to Milesian foundations at Abydos, Kyzikos and Daskyleion. This vigorous colonization shows the capacity of the Ionian Greeks to rise above their troubles in Asia Minor, and to seek an alternative to the unsafe or hostile mainland behind them. An interest in the Black Sea seems to be suggested by the references of Mimnermos of Kolophon (in the *Nanno*?) to Jason, the Golden Fleece, and the 'Streams of Ocean'.

The military struggles of the Greek cities one against another, and the attacks of Lydians and Kimmerians, echo in the pathetic fragments of elegiac and other verse composed in Asia Minor in the later seventh century. They give, despite their fragmentary character, a contemporary impression which could not otherwise be obtained. Kallinos of Ephesos around the mid-seventh century speaks of the Kimmerians, the Treres, the destruction of Sardis and the woes of Smyrna. In a four-line fragment he upbraids the sloth of the young men, who think they sit in peace 'while in fact war prevails over the whole land'.[38] There follows after a break another longer fragment, speaking of courage in the battle line and the glory of death in the field. If this is *not* a passage from the poetry of Tyrtaios, who urged on his youthful countrymen such sentiments in the Messenian Revolt (see Chapter 7), it shows exactly the same attitude. In like fashion Mimnermos tells of the fortunes of Smyrna, looking back, it would seem, to the noble heroes of the earlier attack on the city by Gyges, which was gallantly repulsed: 'Not his were such [feeble] effort and [poor] spirit, as I learn from my elders, who saw him driving in confusion the serried lines of Lydian cavalry on the Hermos plain. Never at all did Pallas Athene find fault in him, his bitter strength of valour when in the battle-front he would rush amid the press of bloody war, defying the sharp missiles of the enemy.'[39]

The purpose of this poetry was to stir up the men of Smyrna in particular, and to prepare them to resist the coming attack of Alyattes at the end of the seventh century. There must be a strong inclination to see both in this and in the words of Kallinos a suggestion that men of the present day have not the spirit of their fathers. This may indeed be a commonplace, useful when urging youth on to do its duty, as Tyrtaios did. On the other hand it is hard not to call to mind the other fragments of Mimnermos' poetry. He was regarded as 'sweet' by later admirers, and also 'clear' (the word here used *could* also mean 'shrill', or even 'whining'). He had, certainly, a charming command of descriptive language, as in telling of the Sun's nightly journey: 'For the Sun's lot is labour every day; nor ever has he or his horses rest, when rosy-fingered Dawn, leaving the Ocean, mounts into the sky. He is conveyed over the sea surge, skimming the water, in a wondrous bed, rich-wrought, forged by Hephaistos' hand of precious gold, upborne on wings, from the Hesperids to the Ethiop land, where team and chariot stand and wait till Eos early-born shall come. Then mounts Hyperion's son his chariot for another day.'[40]

Less attractively, he was, like other Greeks at times, much concerned with the brevity of the period of youth, beauty and love, and the inevitable onset of hideous old age. In the surviving fragments there is no mention of the *dignity* of the old man and the respect due to him: 'Zeus's gift of Immortality to Tithonos was worse than woeful death.'

These again, it has been suggested, are commonplaces of personal lyric, like his description of passion, paralleled also in Sappho. It must be always a matter of debate in these two elements of the poetry of Mimnermos how much is convention and how much a reflection of the spirit of the later seventh century as it prevailed among the eastern Greeks. On a literal interpretation it might be concluded that there was too little sense of citizen duty, morbid preoccupation and a lack of restraint in regard to the conventions: Mimnermos suggests the ignoring of the opinions of others and pleasing oneself. It may be noted that despair at man's impotence in the face of life's ills appears also in a poem of Semonides of Amorgos, who originally came from Samos.

It has sometimes been suggested that the Ionian Greeks (with their 'trailing robes') had time to cultivate their minds and indulge their emotions by reason of a more fertile soil and the services of a subordinated native population; that they were in advance, culturally, of the Greeks of mainland Greece, that they were a luxurious, plump and pudgy lot very different from the taut Dorians, and altogether unwarlike. The extreme conclusions seem unlikely: they resisted the Lydians gallantly at the time of Gyges. This was clearly remembered, in reference to Smyrna and Gyges, and Miletos and Alyattes. And Smyrna did resist Alyattes *c*. 600 BC, as the excavations show. On the other hand if the eastern Greeks of Ionia did indeed have greater leisure and facility for the pursuit of culture by reason of their more favourable economic circumstances, it is hard to believe that this was not offset by the troubles and turmoils among themselves, and those coming from their eastern neighbours, which would seem to be greater than anything facing their fellows west across the Aegean. In the same fashion, at first sight the conditions hardly seem propitious for any pre-eminent development in material culture. Judgement is difficult, since the evidence from western Asia Minor is inadequate, except in the case of Smyrna, the well-explored typical promontory town. As can be seen from the changes in pottery on the site, the original Aeolic foundation became thoroughly Ionian by the beginning of the eighth century, but according to Herodotus it failed to become a member of the Panionion. It acquired a new city wall by the mid-ninth century: too early, therefore, for an expectation of attack from a non-Greek source. The danger must have been from other Greek settlements. The eighth-century settlement was densely packed despite the remodelling and extension of the fortifications in the second half of the century. Contacts with other states are indicated by wine jars from Chios and possibly from Lesbos, oil jars from Attica and Dipylon-style Attic pottery; also by a good deal of Proto-Corinthian of around 700 BC. Then in the seventh century, *c*. 700 BC, there was an earthquake which ruined the fortifications. Oddly enough, despite the attack of Gyges, the Smyrnaeans do not appear to have restored their walls until the late seventh century (in the face of the threat from Alyattes?).

The excavators describe the seventh century at Smyrna as a period of great expansion, showing in domestic architecture 'a planned spaciousness' and a spreading of settlement off the promontory site to the neighbouring coast. There was an increase of amenity, including baths for domestic use. The standard of construction was high, and of particular interest are the unfinished temple and sacred enclosure. 'The new unfinished temple was designed with massive stone columns. The surviving fragments of the great capitals show handsomely carved frond and lotus designs of a complexity unique in Greek architecture. . . .'[41] Imports continued from other areas, including pottery from Corinth. On the other hand Smyrna sent out no colonies; it is therefore reasonable to suppose that it did not suffer from population pressure. It might be added here that given the fertility of Asia Minor's western coast, overpopulation was *not* the reason for colonization. Since Smyrna is probably better known through excavation than any other eastern Greek city it is natural that an attempt should be made to estimate its population, though comparative material is inadequate. It is thought that more than half the population in the seventh century lived outside the promontory city. An estimate of numbers speaks of one thousand families, making Smyrna a city of moderate size, inferior to Kyme in Aeolis and the large Ionian cities such as Erythrai, in some of which there was a much greater proportion of country-dwellers. The Smyrnaeans, it seems, in general lived tolerably well; the wealthy no doubt very well. Yet their well-being, if the historical account is to be believed, was precarious. Why did so many (and more in other cities) live outside the walls, which in any case were neglected until the late seventh century? Was it in the belief that it would be possible to come to terms with enemies, or that resistance was impossible, or because of a disinclination to be cramped and uncomfortable? Probably the experience of Smyrna and of other cities was the same: that ultimately there is no coming to terms with a great autocratic power. So Miletos and Smyrna eventually resisted, and the latter was destroyed by Alyattes.

It would be wrong to charge the Ionians with softness and cowardice, and the effects of luxury. In the next century Xenophanes of Kolophon (c. 565–470 BC) was to speak of the useless luxury learned from the Lydians, the purple robes and perfumes of a thousand citizens. In the seventh century external enmities and internal strife were far more likely to have harmed the eastern Greeks, who were disinclined to co-operate. Consequently they fell victims to Lydia, which might not have been an unmixed disadvantage if the Lydians had not been replaced by the Persians. Certainly some of their best achievements took place in the sixth century, under Lydia.

CHAPTER 7

# THE ABNORMAL STATES

Two of the city-states of early Greece stand apart, in the sense that the process of their development was or seems to have been different from that of the rest, which had certain experiences in common, for instance participation in colonization, expansion of trade, and tyranny as a form of government: the themes of Chapters 5 and 6. These two city-states were Sparta and Athens. They happened also to be the two greatest states of Classical Greece, representing that polarization in politics and culture commented on in an earlier chapter. It is possible that their apparent abnormality has been accentuated by this and by the poverty or obscurity of early sources. Both were the objects of particular study in Antiquity from the fifth century onwards. This interest was increased in the fourth century BC, in a period which saw the decline of both Sparta and Athens, and continued later under the Romans for cultural, moral and anti-quarian reasons.

This latter period produced Plutarch. He wrote in the first and second centuries AD and incorporated a good deal of the bric-à-brac of history in his *Moralia*. He also produced, for moral edification rather than for austere historical purposes, a series of *Parallel Lives* in which he dealt with important figures of Greek and Roman history in pairs, one Greek and one Roman, adding a comparison of the two. The groupings are interesting and significant for his own historical ideas. Among these are lives of Lykourgos, traditionally the ancient lawgiver of Sparta (for whom the Roman parallel was the mythical Numa), of Lysander and Agesilaos, prominent figures in the classical history of Sparta, and of Agis IV and Kleomenes III, who in the third century BC sought to restore what they believed to be the ancient way of life instituted by Lykourgos, from which Sparta had declined, in moral, social and military terms, in the fourth century BC. For the Romans of Plutarch's day the ancient regime of Sparta was largely of tourist interest: so the black broth was still made and the flogging of boys at the altar of Artemis Orthia continued, for the better contemplation of which a Roman-type theatre was erected. Plutarch claims that boys were still whipped to death in his own time. The local Spartans seem to have preserved a certain number of ancient practices of a less barbarous sort, but their interest in them can only have been piously antiquarian.

A great gulf of time lay between this period and early Sparta, and there was small likelihood in this late period of any tendentious interpretation of the past. On the other hand this possibility was certainly present at an earlier period: as in more or less contemporary sources relating to the attempted reforms of Agis IV and Kleomenes III, and in the earlier sources used by Plutarch for the history of Sparta. In these the nature, origins, development and effects of the Spartan way of life were themes to be argued about and viewed with strong partisanship. This is the case with Plato, and with Xenophon, the Athenian soldier and profound admirer of Sparta, who wrote a *Constitution of the Lacedaemonians*. There was always a danger that personal theories, prejudices and resentments (as in the *Old Oligarch*) might be propped on assertions about the remote past. Probably the most important source for later writers was the *Constitution of the Lacedaemonians* of the school of Aristotle, which now survives only in a limited number of fragments. The *Politics* of Aristotle also provides comment, mainly critical, and concerned with contemporary Sparta. Of the two great historians of the fifth century BC Herodotus discusses early Sparta in Book I of his *History*, and has a good deal to say on the subsequent development of the state, in that and later books. He is the one source (Pausanias being the other) for the Spartan King List, the backbone of early Greek chronology. Thucydides is more concerned with Classical Sparta as one of the two sides in the fifth-century confrontation which led to the Great Peloponnesian War. There are in addition a great many details drawn by later writers from earlier authors whose works have been lost: the source may be cited or is merely to be guessed at. The problem is to assess the reliability of such sources, and to locate the events they mention properly, in a chronological sense.

A particular problem arises in connection with Spartan activity in Messenia to the west of Mount Taygetos; namely the Spartan conquest of this area, and the suppression of a subsequent Messenian revolt. After the Messenians were restored with their capital at Messene in 370 BC by the Boeotians under Epaminondas, it was felt necessary to supply a systematic account of the early history of the state, including the story of the resistance of the Messenians to their Spartan masters. A good deal of this material was used by Pausanias in his account of Messenia. It incorporates a mass of romantic fiction, and the problem is to distinguish history from fiction, and details of the seventh-century insurrection from others which might belong in the fifth.

Here also there is a severe problem of chronology, coupled indirectly with the question of Lykourgos. Was he a real person like Solon, or a useful figment of the Spartan imagination? The Delphic oracle, it would appear, was uncertain whether to call him god or man, and Plutarch observes: 'There is so much uncertainty in the accounts which historians have left us of Lykourgos, the lawgiver of Sparta, that scarcely anything is asserted by one of them which is not called into question or contradicted by the rest.'[1] He was connected, as guardian of King Charillos, with an early portion of the Spartan King List. Aristotle was said to have claimed that the name of Lykourgos appeared on a bronze quoit, which associated him with the institution of the truce during the celebration of the Olympic Games. Central to the problem of Lykourgos and to the problem of the constitutional development of Sparta is the 'Great Rhetra' or enactment quoted by Plutarch and purporting to be a response delivered to Lykourgos by the Delphic oracle, but more likely to be a Spartan decree. The problems are: its date; how it was transmitted to later times (since it is claimed by Plutarch that the 'laws' of Lykourgos were not written down); how the terms used in this constitutional document are to be interpreted; and whether the so-called 'rider' was a later addition, as Plutarch thought it was, or part of the original enactment.

The obscurities of the 'Great Rhetra' and the ingenuity lavished on it by scholars serve to emphasize the limitations of anything like contemporary evidence for the eighth and seventh centuries at the least. Of great importance is the poet Tyrtaios, a Spartan who fought in the Messenian revolt. The fragments of his poem entitled *Eunomia* or 'Good Order' seem to refer to contemporary and earlier events, and he seems to paraphrase the Great Rhetra. The passages which have survived are of inestimable value, but they *are* fragments and have been subjected to a process of selection and a loss of context. The attitudes of Tyrtaios himself are not easy to elucidate.

Finally there is the question of archaeology. However abundant such evidence could be, many of the problems of early Sparta are not of the sort to be solved by its methods. In addition the exploration of Lakonia by excavation is a good deal less than satisfactory.

The very great part played by Athens in the history of Greece, and the fact that Athenian writers to a considerable extent 'captured' the historical tradition, meant that the material purporting to relate to early Athens was relatively large in quantity. The quality of some of it is another matter. A major issue in the Classical period was the development of the democracy, moderate and radical. This was always of interest, and for long (until Rome became master of Greece) it was a matter of partisan feeling and contention. In the fourth century there was the question, obviously much debated, of why Athens seemed to be in decline. How far was this due to the *demos*? At what point had the rot set in? And by reason of what constitutional changes? There was a tendency to look back, according to the political attitudes of the person concerned, from Pericles to Kleisthenes, or from Kleisthenes to Solon, or beyond Solon to a theoretical seventh-century constitution. In default of genuine contemporary evidence there could be an inclination to create it, as, for example, in the case of the supposed seventh-century 'Constitution of Drakon'. Obviously of great importance is the verse of the Athenian lawgiver Solon. The study of what survives of it is exposed to the hazard that ancient quotations from the *corpus* of Solon's writing could be selective, to fit the views of the writer using them. This is too easily forgotten in the modern study of Solon's work. This problem has to be borne in mind when we use as sources for earlier Athenian history the *Constitution of the Athenians* of the School of Aristotle (on which and other constitutions the *Politics* were based) and Plutarch's *Life of Solon*. And much remains wholly obscure, as will later be apparent.

Both of the works mentioned above are important sources. Plutarch's *Life of Theseus* (to which he gives as a parallel the *Life of Romulus*) is of dubious value. Even Plutarch himself observes: 'May I therefore succeed in purifying Fable, making her submit to reason and take on the semblance of History. But when she obstinately disdains to make herself credible, and refuses to admit any element of probability, I shall pray for kindly readers and such as receive with indulgence the tales of Antiquity.'[2] Plutarch, therefore, had his misgivings. The background of Theseus is the Heroic Age, before the siege of Troy, but the union of Attica with its centre at Athens, though a phenomenon credited to Theseus, belongs in effect to the Dark Age, and may descend to the seventh century. It would be difficult to extract anything of vital importance from the *Life of Theseus*, except the trivial elements it incorporates on the social organization of early Athens, of the sort which was the particular interest of the group of fourth-century writers, the Atthidographers, who concerned themselves particularly with local affairs of early Athens and questions of cult and social organization. The problem presents itself as to what source of information for early events and dates lay behind the narrative of these specialist writers, that of Herodotus and Thucydides, and their lesser forerunners, contemporaries and successors. Was there an Attic chronicle, an 'Atthis', possibly related to a list of yearly archons who gave their name to the year? As in the case of Sparta with the problems of the King List and the Olympic victors, so for Athens the question of the archon list arises: first for the life archons from Kodros, then the decennial archons purporting to fill the gap between the life archons and the institution of the annual archonship in the seventh century. There is then the question of how far the list of annual archons is to be depended on before the sixth century. It may also be pointed out that, as in the case of Sparta, so for Athens what seem to be important events, such as the curious war between Athens and Aegina, float unanchored within wide chronological limits.

Finally there is the question of archaeological evidence, which might at first sight seem free of subjective and tendentious interpretations. There are, none the less, occasions for subjective interpretation in the case of Athens, and problems of inadequate excavation in the case of Lakonia. In what follows the archaeological evidence is considered first, followed by the ancient tradition.

## SPARTA

The problem of the traditional 'Dorian invasion' has already been considered in some detail, as has its sequel, the settlement of the Peloponnese. It is important to distinguish this traditional account, based in Antiquity on geographical and linguistic phenomena, from the real pattern of events now to be examined.

The archaeological exploration of Lakonia is incomplete: sites revealed by topographical survey remain unexplored or only partially excavated. On the evidence available it is, none the less, clear that this area possessed flourishing centres in the Late Helladic III B. In the case of the immediate area of later Sparta little Late Helladic material has been found, and that not associated with structures. On the other hand two miles away at the site of the later shrine of Menelaos and Helen there was a considerable settlement; there was a Mycenaean shrine at Amyklai, the centre of the cult of Apollo Hyakinthios in the Archaic and Classical periods; and there is a large town site at Palaiopyrgia (south of Amyklai), probably to be associated with the Vapheio *tholos* tomb. There are other settlements to the south in the region of Helos. These centres seem to have been deserted at the end of Late Helladic III B or early Late Helladic III C, as a sequel to violent destruction by fire, to judge from the evidence of the Menelaion site. At Amyklai there is no clear continuity. The Proto-Geometric pottery particularly associated with this site (Amyklaian ware) has no link with the latest Mycenaean. The contents of tombs show the same break, but in the region of Monemvasia the tomb contents continue into Late Helladic III C, though apparently not beyond. It has been pointed out that this area is isolated from inland Lakonia, and that like Perati in eastern Attica in the same period it looked east towards the Aegean.

Lakonia, therefore, suffered from the same disaster which overtook other areas of Greece in the early twelfth century. It could be that it suffered depopulation to a considerable extent, but to establish this clearly a great deal more excavation will have to be carried out. What comes after the apparent break is represented in material terms by Proto-Geometric and Geometric pottery, and a limited number of other objects, such as the bronze spearheads from Amyklai. Proto-Geometric pottery has been found at Amyklai, and a limited amount at other sites, including Sparta. It is a very distinctive pottery with a peculiar shiny metallic glaze. It has many local characteristics unconnected with the earlier Mycenaean or with contemporary Attic or Argive; on the other hand it has one or two links in patterns with Attic Proto-Geometric, and others with the Proto-Geometric of the western Peloponnese. There are problems as to its date range. It is reasonable to suppose that its beginnings *could* go back to the eleventh century. At Amyklai it is stratified immediately beneath Late Geometric, and it has been suggested that it continued until the middle of the eighth century.

A picture is thus presented of an area long backward; not, on the present evidence using iron, largely isolated and showing no foreign imports. At some time in the long period covered by this Proto-Geometric pottery a penetration must be supposed into Lakonia of new 'Dorian' population elements, coming into a land thinly populated. By what route they came is uncertain: hardly by the Isthmus of Corinth. It is more likely that they came by way of Elis and through the Alpheios Valley, or by one of the routes to the north of it. They thus passed through Arcadia, of which the archaeological record is also imperfectly known. They must have been small bands of pastoralists who had finally to settle down as cultivators. Their ultimate origins were in the north-west, as in the tradition, and it has been suggested that they brought an Illyrian element in the Greek they spoke.

The archaeological record seems to suggest that it took a long period for these backward incomers, establishing themselves first in northern Lakonia, to multiply and expand, and so meet other expanding incomers into the Peloponnese, and whatever remnant there was of earlier inhabitants in Lakonia itself. That this was so seems to follow from the fact that the first cultural expansion was late. The Amyklaian Proto-Geometric, it has been seen, continued into the eighth century and was then followed by the equivalent of Late Geometric elsewhere, which in turn lasted into the seventh century. The development has thus been summed up by a recent writer: 'Laconia now emerges from her comparative isolation of earlier times. Although most of the Late Geometric shapes are found nowhere else in Greece, their decoration owes much to Argive and Corinthian Late Geometric, the Argive element being the stronger of the two';[3] this despite the fact that while Corinthian pottery was imported from 730 to 720 BC, no imports from Argos have so far appeared. This serves as a warning against conclusions too readily drawn from negative archaeological evidence. As far as exports are concerned there are some to Arcadia, over which area both Lakonia and Argos exerted influence, and there is a limited amount of Lakonian Geometric in southern Italy, found at Scoglio del Tonno, which is to be connected with the establishment of a Spartan colony at Taras in 706 BC.

In the whole question of material cultural development and links with the outside world the site of the shrine of Artemis Orthia at Sparta is of great importance. Apart from a limited amount of Proto-Geometric on the site (which may be no earlier than the middle of the eighth century) there is a thick deposit which contains in its lowest level the remains of a pebble pavement and the earliest altar. This deposit also contained a quantity of pottery, carvings in ivory and bone, bronzes, terracottas, seals and beads. The earliest pottery is the same Late Geometric which occurs at Amyklai and seems to continue from some time in the second half of the eighth century into the seventh. The earliest levels of the deposit at Artemis Orthia need not therefore be dated much earlier than the end of the eighth century, and so the earliest associated objects need not be earlier than this date. On the same basis the main series of ivories are not earlier than mid-seventh century. This is an important reassessment, since the excavators dated the earliest levels to the ninth century and gave a correspondingly early date to some of the associated objects, and dates which now seem too early to objects in the higher levels. It may be pointed out that dates as accurate as possible are necessary to fit the implications of the material objects found, and the integration of them into the general framework of Spartan cultural development: the importation of ivory for the carvings, and the part played by Lakonia in the orientalizing process; the dating of actual oriental objects found; the significance of the representation on Geometric pottery of dancers and musical instruments, and the appearance of musicians with harps and pipes among the lead figurines; not least the representation of the hoplite soldier in the same category of lead object. The general impression to be gained from the archaeological evidence is of an area long backward, and then showing a tardy development (and one inferior to Corinth and Argos, to judge from the ivories of Sparta compared with those of Perachora and the Argive Heraion) in the second half of the seventh century. It was not an area in the van of Archaic cultural development, and certainly not one prominent in the eighth century. It is against such a background that the wider social, constitutional and inter-state developments have to be considered.

A basic problem in the study of early Sparta concerns the tradition represented by the writers mentioned earlier. It is not certain when the idea of the unique character of the Spartan training and way of life and government first came into being, but it must have begun to develop in the second half of the sixth century, when Sparta gave an impression of stability in unstable times, and became leader of a Peloponnesian League, the opponent of tyrants and the Persians. The Persian War of 480–479 BC introduced the rivalry of Sparta and Athens, which was increased by the coming into being of the Delian League. The fall of pro-Spartan Kimon and the rise of Pericles introduced a domestic political attitude to Sparta both in the radical democrats of Athens and in their opponents, the conservatives and oligarchs of various shades of opinion. An important feature of the second half of the fifth century was the development of oligarchic political clubs and the establishment of bonds of sympathy between those holding anti-democratic views in Athens and the oligarchic elements in the city states of the Athenian Empire. The trend was intensified in the Great Peloponnesian War from 431 BC, and especially when the radical democracy seemed unfitted to conduct a war, and brought about a débâcle of the Syracusan expedition. The effect was the emergence of extreme oligarchs into the open to promote the reactionary revolution of the 'Four Hundred' in 411 BC. This was a failure, and the radical democracy was restored, only to lose the war against Sparta. There followed, with Spartan support, the short-lived oligarchic regime of the 'Thirty Tyrants'.

These political developments in Athens were attended by the promotion of ideas favouring 'orderly' and 'disciplined' Sparta, and condemning the vices of radical democratic Athens. One of the earliest examples of this type of thought (c. 431 BC or somewhat later) is the pamphlet included in the works of Xenophon, *The Constitution of the Athenians*, entitled by modern scholars *The Old Oligarch*. Its radical democratic counterpart is the praise of Athens in the funeral speech of 431 BC which Thucydides ascribes to Pericles. The same author incorporates in his account of the preliminaries and early stages of the Great Peloponnesian War other comments (some born of later hindsight) by representatives of either side on the strengths, weaknesses and vices of their opponents. These, and the pro-Spartan semi-philosophical doctrines, were developed by late fifth-century idealizers of Sparta such as Kritias the oligarch. They were taken up by early fourth-century writers and so passed to the historian Ephoros (as Strabo indicates), who expounded the theory associating the Spartan system and way of life with that of Crete, to explain the apparent similarities between the two. The doctrine was that the Cretan constitution handed down by Zeus to Rhadamanthos was intended to attain freedom (as the highest good) through unity (*homonoia*) and valour (*andreia*), secured by the friendships of youths and men and the common life of the youth groups (*agelai*) and the messes (*andreia*). These, it was claimed, the ancient lawgiver of Sparta, Lykourgos, took over from Crete. Thus primitive tribal institutions were ascribed to a lawgiver, and an idealized picture of Sparta was evolved, to impress men like Xenophon, though no one who lived in

the fourth century BC could overlook altogether the decline of contemporary Sparta and the malfunctioning of her constitution, as is clear
from Aristotle's observations in the *Politics*. The natural reaction was to
idealize a Sparta of long ago, as, for example, in support of the Hellenistic
reforming kings Agis IV and Kleomenes III. It was much easier, at a longer
distance of time, for Plutarch, with his picture of a Sparta universally
admired, to ignore what had gone wrong: 'The Lacedaemonians inspired
men not with a mere willingness, but with an absolute desire to be their
subjects',[4] *and*: 'They [the Greeks] had their eyes always fixed on the city
of Sparta itself, as the perfect model of good manners and wise
government.'[5]

The tradition thus developed gave the credit for this 'perfect model' to
the lawgiver Lykourgos, and had perforce to place its institution as far
back in Greek history as possible. Once the principle was accepted of this
*one* legislator, who, according to Herodotus and Xenophon, had received
from the Delphic oracle 'the entire system of laws', the problem was to
locate the lawgiver in time and explain the reason for his appearance and
reforms. There is clearly no certain tradition as to his date: as alternatives
it was placed in the remote period of the earliest kings of Sparta; or earlier
than the foundation of the Olympic Games (776 BC); or contemporary
with their foundation if his name, as Aristotle believed, appeared on the
quoit recording the Olympic truce. Alternatively his death was put 120
or 130 years before the institution of the Ephors and King Theopompos *c*. 700 BC. Thus Lykourgos in this case is to be placed *c*. 830 or 820
BC. As an alternative to this he was made guardian of King Charillos, *c*.
775–750 BC, or placed five hundred years back from Agis II (427–399),
the five hundred years of the 'greatness' of Sparta before the rot
occasioned by money set in. Another dating according to Pausanias was
that his legislation took place under Agesilaos I (*c*. 815–785 BC).

There was a conviction, therefore, that Lykourgos should be placed in
the ninth century or in the first half of the eighth, and so before the First
Messenian War, to be dated approximately to 743–724 BC or 735–716 BC,
and before such cultural development as is indicated by archaeology for
the end of the eighth century. It is the period in tradition of the earliest
Spartan expansion from northern Lakonia. It was believed that the pre-
Dorian inhabitants of Kynouria (the eastern Peloponnesian territory
disputed between Argos and Sparta) were expelled in the early ninth
century; the first hostilities with Argos took place in the first half of the
ninth century, at a time when, if Herodotus is to be believed, 'the whole
country as far as Cape Malea belonged to the Argives, and not only the
entire tract on the mainland but also Kythera and the other islands'.[6]
Then in the first half of the eighth century there took place the capture of
Pharis and Geronthrai (subsequently colonized) under the Spartan King
Teleklos (*c*. 760–740 BC) and the capture and subjection of Helos under

King Alkamenes (c. 740–700 BC). Thus the Spartans gained access to the sea (and may at this time have colonized Melos and Thera), expelled or subdued the original inhabitants of southern Lakonia, and probably settled Dorian kin there, later to become the *perioikoi* ('dwellers round' – free but not full citizens). In the same period (the earlier eighth century) the ancient settlement of Amyklai south of Sparta was reduced and became the fifth oba or village community of Sparta, the others being Limnai, Konooura, Messoa and Pitane. Throughout the period down to the first half of the seventh century hostilities appear to have continued with Argos. There were also attempts at penetration into Arcadia, including an unsuccessful expedition against Tegea under King Charillos (c. 775–750 BC).

It must be wondered how much of this expansion took place earlier than the first half of the eighth century in view of the meagre archaeological record. On the other hand it is clear that the latter part of the eighth century shows a cultural advance. It is not clear how far this advance owed anything to Spartan access to the sea. At some time the Spartans also moved west into Messenia over the mountain chain of Taygetos. Southern Messenia had already been settled by Dorian communities largely subordinated to Sparta. The new aggression was into northern Messenia, the Plain of Sthenyklaros. Its cause, it is reasonable to suppose, was population pressure at a time when other states suffering in the same way, or from internal political strife, resorted to colonization. The latter cause cannot be suggested in the case of the First Messenian War, since the enserfment or expulsion of the Messenians would not remove dissidents from within the Spartan state. The reason for the conquest, therefore, must have been a rapid increase in population not solved by expansion into southern Lakonia. It is unlikely that there was a conscious act of policy thus early, intended to produce a community of soldiers sustained by the labour of the Messenians and so freed from the necessity of working for their livelihood. It was believed to be a long war, and it may be guessed that it was fought at a fairly primitive level. It was dated (by Olympiads) to either 743–724 BC or 735–716 BC. Messenian victors appear in the third, fourth, seventh, eighth, tenth and eleventh Olympic festivals, but cease after the eleventh, that is, 735 BC. This may seem to confirm the second set of dates, which would also fit the tradition of the Partheniai (a name of uncertain meaning), described by Aristotle as the illegitimate sons of Spartan full citizens, irregularly begotten during the war. 'They conspired to vindicate their rights', and were sent to found the colony of Taras in southern Italy in 706 BC.

It should be noted that very early dates were suggested for the conquest of the Messenians, related to their liberation and re-establishment in their country by the Thebans and Epaminondas in 370 BC. This event, it was thought, took place either five hundred or four hundred years after the conquest, so the latter took place in 870 BC or in 770 BC. These dates sound like some kind of attempt to relate the war to Lykourgos, who was given similar dates. Pausanias seems to suggest another date, which from the context should apply to the conquest of Messenia, when he describes 'the Messenian War' as 'raging most hotly' in the reign of Polydoros, whose murder took place when the war was over and the Messenians were reduced to subjection. Polydoros' reign is to be dated to *c.* 700–665 BC, as the younger colleague of Theopompos (*c.* 720–675 BC) who terminated the conquest. The most commonly accepted dates, however, are either 743–724 BC or 735–716 BC: most probably the second, to judge from the disappearance of Messenian victors from the Olympic list. These dates have to be related to the second Messenian episode, the rising of the conquered Messenians against their Spartan masters, who treated them ruthlessly, as in the words of Tyrtaios: 'Like asses galled with heavy loads, to their masters bringing by doleful necessity half of all the fruit that the tilled land yields.'[7] As a contemporary and a Spartan he might be expected to know, but it is interesting to note that in the opinion of Plutarch the worst oppression of the helots began only with the great earthquake and near-disaster to the Spartan state which took place in the sixties of the fifth century. Tyrtaios was a contemporary of the revolt, and composed war songs and hortatory verse to encourage the Spartans in the struggle. He gives a more or less contemporary indication of the length of the interval between conquest and revolt, as well as of the duration of the campaign of conquest: '... to our King, the friend of the gods, Theopompos, through whom we took spacious Messene, Messene so good to plough and so good to plant, for which there fought ever unceasingly nineteen years, keeping an unfaltering heart, the Spearman fathers of our fathers, and in the twentieth year the foeman left his rich lands and fled from the great uplands of Ithome.'[8]

This quotation of Tyrtaios by Strabo relates the two wars by generations, and it is natural to expect a calculation in *years* based on the conventional longer and shorter generations of forty years and thirty-three (three generations to a century). The term of years had then to be related to a fixed point of time, probably the last Messenian victory at Olympia, to produce an Olympiad date. The revolt was placed in the thirty-eighth year after the capture of Ithome. If we take the date for this event as 716 BC, the revolt would begin in 678 BC, but Pausanias also gives its beginning as the fourth year of Olympiad 23 (685 BC), which looks like a calculation from something like 724 BC, and its end as the first year of Olympiad 28, which is 668 BC. Also, according to Pausanias the Messenians were restored in the third year of Olympiad 102, that is in 370 BC, 297 years after the capture of Eira, the centre of Messenian resistance, which would be in 667 BC.

A strong tradition therefore placed the revolt in the first half of the seventh century. It should be noted that just as the conquest was placed alternatively in the reign of Polydoros (*c.* 700–665 BC), so the revolt was also brought down to match, its beginning being set in the reign of Anaxandros (*c.* 640–615 BC) and its duration extended into the early sixth century, perhaps to explain Sparta's lack of success against Tegea in the late seventh century and the early sixth.

The revolt might reasonably be associated with other events in the Peloponnese discussed earlier.

In this second Messenian War the Argives, Arcadians and Pisatans were aligned against Sparta. In the first half of the seventh century the Argives inflicted a great defeat on the Spartans at Hysiai. As this place was within the borders of Argos, the defeat would seem to have been a sequel to Spartan aggression and perhaps a misjudgement by the Spartans of their military strength. The defeat must have had a disastrous effect on Spartan morale. Unhappily the date of the battle, commonly given as 669 BC, is ill established. It was certainly a bold venture for a state still involved with the Messenians. It may also be repeated that those who are unwilling to place Pheidon in the eighth century and his presidency of the Olympic Games in Olympiad 8 (748 BC) would date his expedition to Olympia to 668 BC (Olympiad 28), perhaps an intervention incidental to an effort to aid the Messenians and a sequel to the defeat of Hysiai, though Pheidon is not connected by name with that battle.

It may seem that chronological problems showing little prospect of final solution have here been excessively debated, but the conquest and the revolt (the First and Second Messenian Wars) are an integral part of the framework of events in the Peloponnese in the latter part of the eighth century and in the first half of the seventh. For Sparta the military events are also the background of constitutional developments which must be dated as firmly as possible. An important link between the two is the evolution of the hoplite army discussed in relation to Argos in Chapter 6, and the relations of an assembly based on such an army with the other elements in the constitution. There is also the problem of dating the Spartan 'system', the mode of training (the *agoge*) and way of life, including the organization of the land and of the army. If it was not the creation of one man at one time, when and why did various elements of it come into being or suffer modification?

The Classical Spartan machinery of government consisted first of the two kings. It is idle to speculate why there were two, and what their relationship might be with the three primitive 'Dorian' tribes or with the 'villages' (*obai*) which made up Spartan territory proper. They led the army in war, but apart from this appear to have enjoyed more honour than power, though from time to time in Sparta kings of exceptional ability could wield great influence. They had membership of the *gerousia*,

167

which apart from themselves consisted of twenty-eight men of sixty years of age or over who held office for life, were chosen by acclamation and seem to have been drawn from an 'aristocratic' element (in the traditional Greek sense) of the body of full citizens. There were five annual magistrates, the ephors or 'overseers', who were elected from the whole body of full citizens. In the course of the Classical period they became the pre-eminent authority, supervising the kings and the general working of the system. The *gerousia* seems at first sight far less important than the ephors, though it performed certain advisory and judicial functions. None the less continuity in office must have meant a greater *ultimate* influence than that of the ephors, who held office for one year only, however much a powerful personality among them could be dominant in his year. There were other lesser functionaries (not a part of the constitution) concerned with the organization of public life and the *agoge*, and a hierarchy of military officers involved in the complex system of the Spartan army, as described by Xenophon in his *Constitution of the Lacedaemonians*. Finally there was the assembly of all full citizens, the *homoioi* or 'equals'. They were distinguished from the *hypomeiones* or 'inferiors', who had for some reason fallen from the status of *homoioi*, or had never attained it, and the *neodamodeis* or 'new-enfranchised', who were of non-Spartan, possibly helot origins, but given Spartan citizenship. The citizenship of the *homoioi* depended on the successful completion of the *agoge*, election to a mess (the *syssition* or *andreion*), continued good conduct as a citizen-soldier and continued payment of dues in kind to the mess, with a small sum of money in addition. Spartan citizenship was, therefore, a form of club membership, serving a military purpose, since the messes were the smallest units, in effect, of the military system, an essential feature of the comradeship in arms which was retained in time of peace.

The messes and the full-time citizen army rested on the cultivation of land by the helots. In theory the land so cultivated was divided into nine thousand lots; an alternative idea was that there were six thousand originally, and that King Polydoros later added three thousand more. According to Plutarch the new-born Spartan child, on his approval by the elders as fit to survive, was granted one of these lots, from which was drawn on his behalf a half-share of the commodities produced by the helots attached to it. This looks like an over-simplified theory, though it may well have given rise to the idea of 'the ancient lots' which could not be alienated, though other property might be, even if this practice was frowned on. The main difficulties are these: as against the separate allotment to the new-born child there was the compulsion (ascribed to Lykourgos) on a Spartiate 'to leave his lot to his son entire', until the abatement of this rule by the ephor Epitadeus, which set in motion the alienation of land in the fourth century and the concentration of property in the hands of a limited number of individuals, particularly heiresses, though this may have applied to land other than the ancient lots. The question arises, if Plutarch is correct, as to whether each child of a Spartan family received one lot each, or was the father's lot divided among several sons, with consequent loss of income and status? Yet again, if there was a reduction in population in the fourth century, did not that mean more land available until 370 BC and the restoration of the Messenians? In general, theory seems much more simplified than practice can have been. One thing seems to emerge: from time to time from economic inequality political inequality appeared and consequent unrest, and this factor, clearly operating in the fourth century BC, is also to be looked for earlier.

The Spartan army was a complex organization of full Spartiates, *perioikoi* and attendant helots. In Xenophon's time it comprised six regiments (*morai*), each subdivided into two *lochoi* and a series of smaller units in which Spartiates and *perioikoi* were combined by reason of the decline of manpower in the fourth century. It was mustered by age groups, the number summoned to service, beginning with the younger men, being determined by the current military situation. It can be said that it was an army based on comradeship and the close relationships of the mess. This army organization probably came into being in the later fifth century BC. Earlier there was an army based on the *obai* or villages of Sparta, Pitane, Konooura, Messoa and Limnai, to which, as we have seen, Amyklai had been added after the campaign against that community. This army was organized by *lochoi*, which may or may not have corresponded with the *obai*, and while much is obscure the bond between soldiers who fought together could be one between neighbours, different therefore from the Kleisthenic army later in Athens. Earlier than the *obal* army there was the ancient tribal organization of the Dorians mentioned only by Tyrtaios, who addresses one of his exhortations to the Hylleis, Pamphyloi and Dymanes in a context which seems to relate to the revolt. The disappearance of the tribal army, which was a kinship army resembling the pre-Kleisthenic army in Athens, and like it incorporating an organization of brotherhoods or clans, and the reasons for its replacement by the *obal* organization, represent an important problem of early Spartan history.

It is very unlikely that the system was constructed as one whole at one time, a point already made in relation to the statement of Herodotus: 'Some report besides . . . that the Pythoness delivered him [Lykourgos] the entire system of laws.'[9] It was a system subject to modification from time to time, and, if it was such, efforts to connect it with a historical and datable Lykourgos have very little point. It suffices to see in what conditions he was believed to have operated, and what he was thought to have done, but it should not be believed that all the conditions prevailed at one time. It may be pointed out that Greek writers were not at all preoccupied by anachronisms: thus in defiance of facts which they must have known, he was made to banish gold and silver from the state – a fiction to contrast with the reality of Lysander's introduction of such money in the form of the booty of the Great Peloponnesian War. It may also be noticed that as a match for Solon he was made to abolish debts. According to Herodotus the Spartans until the time of Lykourgos were 'the worst governed people'. He appeared at a time of political and social stress, which led him to take action (as Plutarch claims in his *Life of Kleomenes*) by the nature of which he could be described as a re-volutionary. In this action he had thirty co-adjutors; two dropped out, to leave twenty-eight, matching, suspiciously enough, the number of the Spartan *gerousia*, who are described elsewhere by Plutarch as 'the chief aiders and assistants' in his plans. There are divergent views of Lykourgos expressed in different places: he is 'a bulwark against the insolence of the People'[10] from the standpoint of the kings; alternatively he represented a *restraint* on the kings through his institution of the *gerousia*. He was said by Herodotus to have established the ephors also. On the other hand Aristotle credited the ephorate to Theopompos as a mark of his moderation, bringing about the survival of the kingship; Plutarch thought the same, adducing the reason that 'the oligarchic element was *still* too strong and dominant'.[11] Add to all this the fact that Lykourgos was described as a son of Eunomos (the 'Man of Good Law') and given a son Eukosmos (the 'Man of Good Order'), and he is clearly seen to represent a hotch-potch of various ill-understood developments in which the supposed standing of kings, council and assembly are not unin-fluenced by the theory of the 'mixed constitution', a concept, of the late Greeks, in which the government of Sparta was seen finally to be a balance of these three elements. The balance was maintained, according to Aristotle, by their satisfaction with their rights: the kings because of their prerogatives; the 'upper classes' because of their access to the *gerousia* ('a reward for excellence'); and 'the people at large' because of their access to the ephorate.

In contrast to the figure of Lykourgos the Great Rhetra (p. 158) is worth careful consideration. It is quoted by Plutarch in his *Life of Lycurgus* and seemingly paraphrased by Tyrtaios in a poem with a political content. Despite the supposed ban on the writing down of Spartan laws it *could* be an early document, surviving like other Archaic documents from the seventh century on a bronze plate or on stone, and even from the late eighth. Had it been a late and spurious confection it would surely have been made easier of interpretation. As it is there are difficulties of terminology and corruption at important points, but there is a consider-able degree of agreement on its translation. The problem is the interpretation. A reasonable translation would run:

[The Spartan people] shall found a sanctuary of Zeus Syllanios and Athena Syllania, shall marshal the tribes [*phylai*] and *obai*, shall establish thirty men as a Council of Elders including the leaders [i.e. the kings], and shall, season after season, keep the festival of Apollo between Babyka and Knakion. These [the Council of Elders] shall bring proposals and withdraw; the *demos* shall have the right to criticize and the final voice. And if the *demos* formulates crookedly the elders and the leaders shall decline to accept that formulation.

Plutarch goes on to explain that the final element (the 'rider') was added later: '. . . because . . . the People by adding or omitting words distorted and perverted the sense of propositions, Kings Theopompos and Polydoros inserted into the Rhetra or Grand Covenant the following clause . . . that is to say, refuse ratification, and dismiss the People as depravers and perverters of their counsel'.[12] Of the kings mentioned Theopompos was the ruler credited with the institution of the ephorate; Polydoros was murdered *c.* 665 BC by one with the interesting name of Polemarchos, who despite his act had a tomb in Sparta. Pausanias adds: '. . . the Spartans honour King Polydoros so highly that his likeness is graved on the signet with which the magistrates seal everything which needs sealing.'[13] It may be noted from the same author that the repute of Polydoros was high in Sparta and throughout Greece and that he endeared himself 'by his mild and affable deportment and by a series of judgements in which he had tempered justice with mercy'.[14] Plutarch in his account of the 'rider' goes on to say that the kings succeeded in convincing the people that it was part of the original rhetra, and in support of this adduces the quotation, mentioned earlier, from Tyrtaios, which seems to be a paraphrase of the rhetra and also reproduces the sense of the rider. Plutarch's inference is that Tyrtaios was party to the deception: 'The god-honoured Kings shall begin deliberation, whose concern is the lovely city of Sparta, and the elder-born seniors; then the men of the people, making response to straight proposals, shall speak fair words and do everything just, and propose nothing crooked for this city. So victory and the ultimate decision shall attend the body of the People.'[15] Tyrtaios is the oldest authority for this document and seems to indicate that rhetra and rider were one. It is also a reasonable conclusion that this was an issue of his own time, that is, in general terms, of the period of the Messenian revolt in the first half of the seventh century.

The interpretation of the Rhetra is difficult. An attractive suggestion has been made that questions rather than proposals were to be introduced by the *gerousia* by way of discovering the attitude of the assembly, and when the assembly (the *gerousia* standing aside) had discussed the question, the *gerousia* in the light of this discussion would submit a proposal to a reconvened assembly for ratification, not for discussion. If the assembly was then troublesome it was dismissed and the proposal of the *gerousia* became law.

Despite the fact that the context in which Plutarch quotes the rhetra seems to be one concerned with the council *vis-à-vis* the kings, following the pattern of the early opposition of kingship and aristocracy, with the consequent diminution of the kingship, the actual terms of the rhetra represent rather a confrontation of the kings and the *gerousia* on the one side, with the assembly on the other, the assembly meeting at set times on the occasion of a religious festival. This confrontation must be between the aristocratic element of an early Greek state and the hoplite army: in constitutional terms between a steering (*probouleutic*) council and a theoretically sovereign assembly, and this at a date well before the arrangements made in Chios (as demonstrated by the famous stone column, the *kurbis*) or even by Solon in Athens (see Chapter 8).

As has been seen in Chapter 6, this hoplite army can hardly have developed before the seventh century. It is true that the celebrated Argive hoplite panoply grave seems to belong to the late eighth century, but a considerable period must intervene between the invention of the equipment and its widespread production, a period required also for the development of the technique of hoplite warfare (which could be based on either tribal kinship or village neighbourhood). There is a certain presumption that Pheidon of Argos, to be dated in the first half of the seventh century, was the first proponent (or among the first) of hoplite warfare. In the vase-painting of Corinth the hoplite battle line appears in the second half of the seventh century, to be connected probably with the appearance of the tyranny there. If, therefore, the Great Rhetra is correctly interpreted as such a confrontation, this cannot have taken place in the eighth century. There were undoubtedly stresses arising from the First Messenian War (witness the episode of the Partheniai), but the full development of the issue between the earlier aristocracy and the hoplite assembly came later, in the period of the revolt. The hortatory poems of Tyrtaios indicate the type of military organization, and that there was a crisis of morale in Sparta:

You are of the lineage of the invincible Herakles; so be of good cheer, not yet is the face of Zeus turned away. Fear not a multitude of men, nor flinch, but let every man hold his shield straight towards the fore-front, making life an object of enmity and the dark spirits of death equally dear as the rays of the sun. For you know the destroying deeds of lamentable Ares, and well have learned the disposition of woeful war; you have had, young men, company both with those who flee and those who pursue, and you have had a surfeit of both. Those who, standing shoulder to shoulder, go with a will into close quarters and the battle-front, of these are fewer slain; these save the people in the ranks behind. As for those that turn to fear, all their valour is lost; no man can tell in words each and all the ills that befall a man if he once come to dishonour. For a sore thing it is in dreadful warfare to pierce the midriff of a dying man, and disgraced is the dead that lies in the dust with a spear-point in his back. So let each man bite his lip and stay with firmly planted feet, covering with the belly of his broad shield thighs and legs below and breast and shoulders above; let him brandish the strong spear in his right hand, shake the fearsome crest upon his head; let him learn how to fight by doing doughty deeds, and not stand shield in hand beyond the missiles. Let every man close with the foe, and with his own spear or else with his sword, wound and take an enemy, and setting foot beside foot, pressing shield against shield, crest beside crest, helmet beside helmet, fight his adversary breast to breast with sword or long spear in hand.[16]

There is, indeed, in Tyrtaios an epic element in language, and a suggestion of man-to-man single combat. None the less it is tolerably clear here and in other fragments of his poems (including the one where reference is made to the Dorian tribes) that the hoplite type of warfare is involved, with its characteristic front of serried shields. It is also clear from his exhortations to be heroic and to stand and fight that some Spartans had failed to do this; that there had been flight as well as pursuit, and that there had been a preoccupation about whether Zeus 'had turned his face away' or not. A style of behaviour in battle and an attitude of mind so suggested are very different from that of the traditional Spartan as later conceived. Some had fled or avoided the mêlée. Some younger men had saved their lives while older men had died. And, it may also be noted, in one of the fragmentary poems of Tyrtaios there are presented the alternatives of honourable death in battle or loss of land resulting in want and exile. It is difficult to believe that this is merely a poetic commonplace. The Second Messenian War was quite certainly a hard struggle, with more at issue than the reduction of the Messenians.

That there were internal stresses is indicated by the murder of Polydoros, despite his reputation for mildness and justice. Some may have thought him insufficiently repressive in difficult times. The defeat of Hysiai (someone's mistaken policy, perhaps that of Polydoros) must have occasioned resentment and heart-searching. This was the age of Pheidon, when it was realistic to praise Argive warriors and Spartan women, but not Spartan warriors. There was a crisis of policy and of morale, and hostility between the Spartan aristocracy and the hoplite assembly, which produced the rhetra. This enactment took away in the 'rider' what it seemed to concede in the earlier clauses. If this was so, it does not really matter whether there was one enactment, or two separated by an interval. Plutarch, and no doubt others before him, thought it was quite unconvincing that a concession was made as to the sovereignty of the assembly and then withdrawn in the same enactment. Somehow, it was felt, it might be more convincing if there were two enactments. In fact it is to be doubted whether together or separately the rhetra and rider would be accepted by a militant assembly. Either the militancy was cowed, which is difficult to believe, or the assembly was won over by a concession.

It is to be recalled that Theopompos was credited with the creation or advancement of the ephorate. Did this yearly magistracy, which was said to have 'saved the kingship', represent the concession, giving the 'people' something for itself? In this connection the monthly exchange of oaths must be borne in mind: on the part of the kings, to rule according to the established laws of the State; and on the part of the ephors, to keep the kingship unshaken as long as the kings kept their oath. As Aristotle suggests, the outcome was a balance of rights and privileges.

There was also the question of the quality and organization of the army and the establishment of efficiency and good morale. It could be suggested that the exercises at the summer festival of the Gymnopaidiai represented an element of military training. The change from the tribal army to the *obal* army presents problems. It is generally agreed that a change in organization took place, but judgement is hampered by uncertainty as to the date of the change and the relationship of the *lochoi* or army divisions to the *obai* or 'villages' of Sparta. If the change is dated in the second half of the seventh century (it can hardly have taken place during the revolt) it is natural to assume a quest for greater efficiency and cohesion. If the tribal army was based on kinship and the brotherhood unit (as well as the mess) it is not unreasonable to assume social inequalities and also a dangerous tendency for kinsmen to fight side by side, preventing what was later claimed with pride: that any Spartan could fight side by side with any other. Integration and the elimination of special loyalties were, in the case of Kleisthenic Athens, attained by the creation of artificial tribes. It is hard to see why, in the *obal* army, locality was chosen instead. This is the most intractable problem relating to early Sparta, and one not likely to be solved until more is known of tribes and *phratriai* (brotherhoods), of the early relationship of tribes and *obai* outside the army, and the number of the latter.

In addition to army problems there appear to have been economic difficulties, manifested in an outcry for redistribution of the land. Aristotle in the *Politics* points out that internal political strife (*stasis*) can arise where some are very poor and others are rich, and most of all this happens in times of war. Here he quotes the Messenian War, meaning the revolt: 'This happened too in Sparta at the time of the Messenian War. This is clear from the poem of Tyrtaios entitled "Eunomia"; for certain men impoverished by the war demanded a redistribution of land.'[17] Pausanias may be referring to the same issue: 'The Lacedaemonians made a resolution, since they were engaging in cultivation for those in Eira [i.e. the Messenian stronghold] rather than for themselves, to leave Messenia and that portion of Laconia adjacent unsown as long as they were at war. And from this there was a shortage of corn in Sparta, and with the shortage political strife. For those who had their property in this region did not endure it to be uncultivated. For these Tyrtaios settled the differences.'[18] There is no way of checking whether Tyrtaios did anything of the sort. Possibly Pausanias is mistranslating *eunomia*, 'a state of good order', as 'fair shares [for all]'. Aristotle and Pausanias believed that this happened *in* the war, and presumed that some suffered more than others, perhaps falling from being *homoioi* to the status of *hypomeiones*, since they could not pay their mess dues. It is to be suggested that these men, by reason of the location of their lands, felt themselves vulnerable also in a future revolt, or by reason of resentful helot cultivators. Was the answer the establishment of the nine thousand lots (or some number of lots) in Laconia to be a surer basis of the system in an area more easily controlled, since it must be admitted that the coercion of the Messenian helots to keep up their production sounds a formidable task even for the Spartans?

However this may be, Sparta's economic problems took a long time to solve. Disparity of wealth was not easily removed, if it ever was, except in later theory. There was a proverb: 'Wealth makes The Man. No poor man at all is noble or held in honour.' This truism was reiterated in different circumstances and times by Theognis of Megara, but the proverb is also put by Alkaios of Lesbos, probably at the end of the seventh century, into the mouth of a Spartan. In like manner the lack of success against Tegea for a considerable period shows that a great deal had to be done to develop military strength in Sparta. Argos was not easily to be overtaken.

One question remains: how far did Sparta's military preoccupations affect her cultural development? In the graphic arts there was nothing of very high quality, to judge from the finds at the shrine of Artemis Orthia. Sparta was well behind Corinth. On the other hand such arts *were* pursued and advanced in quality in the sixth century, though this may have been due to the *perioikoi*. As literary evidence there is the fragmentary poetry of Alkman, who belongs to the second half of the seventh century. If he was from Sardis in Asia Minor he was another whom the Spartans drew from that area, like Terpander of Lesbos earlier and Bathykles of Magnesia later. It is significant that an alternative idea was that he was a Lakonian but 'by birth a slave': significant, since he speaks of elaborate jewelry, fine Lakonian wine, abundance of purple and fine clothes, poppy-seed cakes, drinking songs and the like. So the lyre is matched against the spear, in the words of Terpander. It would be difficult to prove beyond doubt that there was a degree of luxury (for some at any rate) in late seventh-century Sparta. The fragments are for the most part brief and the context unknown, but a love of life and beauty is very apparent, and there are indications that it continued in the sixth century.

Early Athens also seemed to diverge in important respects from the normal line of *polis* development. A number of aspects of the early state have already been considered: the condition of Attica in the Late Helladic III c down to 1050 BC, and in the following period, from this date to the beginning of what is called the full Geometric. This may conveniently be called the Proto-Geometric period (pp. 77–80). There is also the probable significance of burial practices as a means of determining the nature of the population in an area for which autochthony (the survival of an original population unchanged by immigration) was claimed; the place of Athens in heroic saga (pp. 54; 60) and particularly the coming of the Neleid Melanthos from Pylos to replace the line of Theseus and repel the 'Dorian' attack on Attica, which was also done in the next generation by his son Kodros; and the supposed participation of the inhabitants of Attica under Neleid leadership in the Ionian migration (pp. 60–1). Attica and Athens are involved in all the problems of Early Iron Age Greece, and outstandingly prominent in the archaeological sphere, so that it is clear that the tradition is not wholly a product of later Athenian propaganda.

Athens and Attica were involved in the decline of Greece at the end of the Bronze Age, and in the recovery thereafter, starting with the period marked by the development of the Proto-Geometric pottery style. There will always be a divergence of opinion on the magnitude of the part played by Athens, on the ways in which her artistic influence was transmitted elsewhere, and on the degree to which there were independent developments in other regions. There must also always be debate on the question of continuity from the Bronze Age, and the intrusion of new elements of the social structure of the state: tribes, phratries, clans (*gene*) and the like.

Athens was an outstanding centre of production of geometrically decorated pottery, which has such a large part in the study of Early Greece that the era of its prevalence is called the Geometric Period. The Geometric pottery of Athens and Attica has been closely and skilfully studied, and conclusions can be based on such a study ranging far beyond the purely ceramic. It is possible to conclude that in the period 900–850 BC for Athens and other Greek centres there was a lack of contact beyond that of immediate neighbours: a parochial period and one in which conditions in the eastern Mediterranean were unfavourable to an expansion of trade. In the half-century 850–800 BC there was an improvement of communication, in the eastern Mediterranean by the end of the century. Athens was a great centre of ceramic development, and also shows imports from the Levant and Cyprus. There is always the problem of estimating the original *volume* of such imports from what survives. In Attica itself there appears to have been a coastward movement which continued in the period 800–750 BC. This was the time when Attic exports of pottery abroad were at their highest point, well represented in Cyprus and the eastern Mediterranean. In Athens also this was the period of development of the Dipylon Cemetery, and also of country cemeteries, as at Anavysos. It should be noted that the archaeological material comes almost entirely from cemeteries, *not* from settlements. The Dipylon Cemetery at Athens gives its name to the painter of monumental amphorae and mixing bowls, the 'Dipylon Master', to be dated *c.* 760–750 BC. The period is characterized by the appearance of shoulder panels on large and small vases, with figures in angular silhouette. Very large pots like those produced by the Dipylon Master were used as grave markers and no doubt served in a cult of the dead. It has been pointed out that before 770 BC only twelve of these burials with large pots as markers are known, but in the next twenty years there are twenty. Conclusions of any sort would, however, be hazardous on such slender numerical grounds.

In this period, 800–750 BC, oriental imports are not particularly impressive, but there is some fine jewelry of native production under oriental influence, or perhaps made by immigrant oriental craftsmen (*cf* the case of Crete, p. 103). Again, however, in view of the limited amount surviving it is hazardous to regard this jewelry as clearly indicative of a wealthy aristocracy. Then in the period 750–700 BC there appear some curious phenomena: indications of a rise in Attic population and an increase in country centres; no official Attic colonization (*cf.* Argos) at a time when some states were very active; a decline in Attic exports and ceramic influence, and a Hellenizing, in the last quarter of the century, of the orientalizing style in jewelry apparent in the preceding period. This is clearly indicated by the replacement on gold headbands of naturalistic animals by stylized Geometric. Two quotations from the most recent and outstanding work on Greek Geometric pottery relevant to these periods may be set side by side. First, on the Dipylon grave monuments: 'These grave monuments . . . commemorate a generation of Athenians who had taken an energetic part in overseas commerce; in their day Athens was a prosperous maritime city which had been as active as any other Greek state in the revival of free communications with the Near East';[19] and, second, on the impression given by the period *c.* 750–700 BC: 'It appears then that during the late eighth century the men of Attica were contracting out of their enterprises abroad, and transforming themselves into a quiet, inward-looking people whose interests were in agriculture and no longer in commerce.'[20]

The fact that Athens did not officially take part in colonization would not exclude the possibility that she engaged in trade. There is the parallel of Aegina. It is also true that some sudden change in policy (or relatively sudden change) cannot be excluded: later on Athens was to turn from the land to the sea in a military sense at the time of the Persian invasion of Greece in 480 BC – just as striking a reversal of policy. The second of the two propositions is more objective. The first depends more on subjective judgement. It rests in part on the presence of Athenian pottery abroad. It is natural to suppose that at this early period a great number of merchants participated in trade: both Phoenicians and members of a variety of Greek states, including islanders and Corinthians. In similar fashion in the Classical period traders were a mixed lot, and the widespread presence of Attic pottery, both black-figured and red-figured, has never been taken to mean that the Athenians necessarily carried it to the regions where it has been found. Something has been said on the nature of early Greek trade in Chapter 6, and it may be repeated that there is nothing against the participation of an aristocracy in trade. Indeed a good deal is to be said for it in connection with silver, and olive oil, exported in the 'SOS amphorae', so called from the neck decoration.

The great issue, however, on which the first of the two statements quoted is based, is the interpretation of some of the pictures in silhouette to be seen on the great pots of the Dipylon period. These comprise, first, chariot and horseman processions, which may be suggested as epic scenes by the presence of prize tripods, though the horsemen hardly seem in place in such a context. There are warriors who bear the so-called Dipylon shield, vaguely resembling the Bronze Age figure-of-eight shield, which also appears associated with warrior figures in bronze. There are also processions of warriors with spears and round shields who *could* be hoplites. There are scenes, too, some of them very elaborate, of the lying-in-state (*ekthesis*) of what are clearly members of the aristocracy. As has been seen in an earlier chapter there are also some possible scenes from saga, but caution is needed in their interpretation. Most relevant in the present context, and for the theory under discussion, are the representations of ships (and shipwrecks) and sea battles, rather than peaceful mercantile activity (not easy to depict in any case). The argument must be agreed as cogent that these great monumental pots were produced on commission, not drawn from stock, so that the pictures of naval activity may well have had some particular connection with the interests and activities of the deceased. They cannot be accepted as incontrovertible evidence of trading. They are unlikely to represent an organized state fleet of any dimensions (see pp. 117–18, on the observations of Thucydides), but they could very well be inspired by privateering activities of aristocratic Attic individuals or families, protecting trade and traders useful to Athens, plundering where they could, and defending the coasts of Attica. The movement to the coast may have had a connection with this, since it was safer to live close to the sea than it had been.

This maritime interest seems well substantiated. It is harder to believe that these are epic sea battles. Athens was a member of the Amphiktyony of Kalaureia, an oddly assorted collection of states, the purpose of which, apart from the worship of Poseidon, it is difficult to see. Athens was not cited in antiquity as participating in the Lelantine War; nor was Aegina. This is surprising if Athens and Attica were so prominent in the maritime sphere. This interest in the sea certainly ceased by the late eighth century, and there is nothing to suggest such an interest clearly in the seventh. It is natural to seek a reason for this change of policy. One might be found in the series of events related (but not dated) by Herodotus, from which arose 'the ancient enmity' between Athens and Aegina, two relatively close neighbours across the Saronic Gulf. The story sounds childish enough. The relevant point here is that Epidauros was involved, and Aegina, the latter being subject to Epidauros, and Epidauros allied or subject to Argos. There took place an Athenian attack on Aegina, 'with one ship' according to the Athenians; 'with a large number' according to the Aeginetans. The sequel was a defeat and disgrace for Athens, and an embargo on the use of Attic pottery at the Aeginetan shrine of Damia and Auxesia round which the dispute centred.

Attic pottery has been found in Aegina from Middle Geometric I, but there is a total absence of Attic Late Geometric I *b* (750–735 BC), while Corinthian Late Geometric was imported in quantity. If this ceramic evidence is in any way significant, the embargo was imposed in the heyday of Athenian maritime activity. On the other hand imports were resumed in Late Geometric II (735–700 BC), and important seventh-century Proto-Attic pottery comes from Aegina. The ceramic evidence is not very satisfactory for dating. If the naval clash was a big one (to produce the Athenian 'retreat from the sea'), the account of Herodotus hardly bears this out. The episode is certainly a puzzle. It sounds like a confrontation between two neighbouring states of the sort apparent in the Lelantine War, and there is a temptation to see the hand of Pheidon of Argos behind Epidauros and Aegina, but the dates as indicated by the absence of pottery will not suit. It is just possible that the hostilities belong to the seventh century before the Aeginetans (building themselves ships) got away from the tutelage of Epidauros in the late seventh century. They may even have been associated with Megara in activity against Athens.

It will be seen, therefore, that this episode is hardly a satisfactory explanation for a change of Athenian policy. There is another possibility. According to Aristotle the life tenure of the archon (the ruling magistrate) was reduced to one of ten years in 752 BC. Earlier, after the self-sacrifice of Kodros (p. 60), who gave his life in battle to secure a victory for Athens, the kingship was abolished and replaced by a life magistracy in one family, with some form of accountability. The family was that of the Medontidai, 'the descendants of Medon'. The latter name means 'the ruler', and marks the story as fictitious, as does the fact that the family was not named after Kodros, his father, or Melanthos, his grandfather. It was in this succession of life archons that the reduction took place to a ten-year tenure of office, which is either a meaningless space-filler or conceals the introduction of some form of elective principle now if not earlier. In 712 BC the office was opened to all the nobility (*eupatridai*), and finally in 683 BC the archonship was reduced to one year and put into commission (see below). This is the Attic tradition, much concerned with names and lists. Like so much else involved with the government of early Athens, it is strongly redolent of formalizing invention. The reality could very well be simpler. The gradual attrition of the kingship may have been a long process, but the final stage in it could have come quickly by the reduction to a one-year office and the opening of it to all the nobility, as one operation. It might be suggested that this took place in the late eighth century, and resulted (perhaps as a result of internal strife) in a change of policy seemingly demonstrated by the material evidence (*if* it is correctly interpreted) for a reduction of trading and other maritime activity. But this is conjecture.

There are other problems which afflict the historian of early Athens. They are not made any easier of solution by the later material, more abundant than for other city states, made available by the Atthido-graphers of the fourth century BC, who based their observations on oral tradition or on an exercise of the imagination, sometimes politically biased. The increase in very recent years of archaeological knowledge has meant that information from this source has also to be taken into account, and it is often difficult to square the two.

Something has already been said in general terms on the social organization of early Attica, and it is now necessary to consider it in more detail. It must be assumed that the land of Attica was penetrated by incomers who brought in the Greek language or some component of it, to be added to a non-Greek language already spoken by a pre-existent population, the presence of which the Athenians admitted when they spoke of the Pelasgians. As has been seen already, at least western and and central Attica were affected by the troubles, decline, depopulation and undoubted strife which characterized the end of the Bronze Age, and produced the fragmentation of the Mycenaean kingdom of Attica. Some faint memories of those troubled days may lurk behind events named in the tradition: the coming of Ion, the division of Attica by Kekrops into twelve town-districts, the strife of the sons of Pandion, the wars between Athens and Eleusis, and the synoecism of Theseus, his ejection, the return of his family and its replacement by Melanthos. There are, on the other hand, also indications of some element of continuity from Bronze Age to Iron Age, and consequently some carry-over of social institutions might be expected.

The nice problem is how the social structure of the early Athenian state came into being, whether transmitted from the Bronze Age (Early, Middle or Late; Indo-European or non-Indo-European) or created in the Iron Age. In either case a matter of prime importance is the integration of incomers, such as the Pylians with Melanthos, or others mentioned in general terms by Thucydides: 'The most powerful victims of war or faction from the rest of Hellas took refuge with the Athenians as a safe retreat. . . .'[21] What in modern times would be called citizenship was not in Classical or earlier times based on the *polites* or citizen being a member of the *polis* simply. There were other institutions, some of them earlier than the *polis*, which made the citizen. There were four tribes, commonly called Ionian (because they appear in Asia Minor also in some cities), but better described as Attic. There has never been any agreement on the source of their odd names: Geleontes, Hopletes, Argadeis and Aigikoreis. They were never satisfactorily explained by the Athenians, who credited their institution to Ion and connected their names with those of his four sons. It is impossible to explain their origins. They can never have had a territorial and local significance, and must belong to a remote nomadic past. Even if they originally had some local significance this certainly did not survive, given the movements of population in Attica attested by archaeology.

Within this tribal framework the later writers placed other institutions uncertain as to date, and in some cases too formal in pattern to carry much conviction. These were, first, the division of each tribe into pre-Kleisthenic thirds or *trittyes*, numbering twelve in all. These, it was believed, were again divided into forty-eight *naukrariai*, headed by 'chiefs' or *naukraroi*, who were again presided over by *prytaneis*. This organization must be of late introduction into the tribal system, if indeed such a formal arrangement existed at all. The *naukrariai* sound like divisions of a naval levy system and so involve the whole problem of an early Athenian fleet. They are, however, generally accounted to be divisions of Attica for financial and administrative purposes: they controlled funds from some source or other and made payments. The *naukraroi* are given, by Aristotle, the same sort of duties as the *demarchoi* in the Kleisthenic organization of Attica. In Herodotus' account of the conspiracy of Kylon (an account which attempted to exculpate the Alkmeonidai and the archon Megakles), the 'presidents of the *naukraroi*' are given as the functionaries who exercised command of the local levies and overall authority (see below). This need not be taken too seriously. It is unlikely that the *naukrariai* were a very ancient institution. They possibly formed a relatively late system, of which the function was, in part, to organize ships drawn from private sources for naval purposes.

Two other institutions mentioned earlier (in Chapter 5) formed part of the structure of the Attic tribes, and were based on a theory of kinship.

These were the phratry (*phratria*) and *genos*, commonly translated as 'clan'. The former, by its etymology, *must* indicate original kinship, though later it certainly involved a much wider group, becoming the basis of citizenship and of legal procedures, as in Drakon's homicide law. The *genos* existed within the phratry, its etymology indicating (noble) birth. The members of a *genos* were called *gennetai*. They represented different economic and social levels in what has been described as a 'vertical' social structure. The *genos* was probably later than the phratry. The *genos* was a means of aristocratic dominance; the phratry an institution of much wider self-help. The *genos* was headed by a family group (*oikos*), which claimed to be 'noble', but it incorporated other levels of society: for the local administration of justice (in the days before the development of centralized government), the performance of local cult, and probably the organization of local levies (linked, possibly, with the *naukrariai*). The *genos* took its name from a mythical ancestor, and had a strong local attachment. The clan heads would claim to be 'the sons of noble fathers' (*eupatridai*). There was also a clan of this name. Later Athenians gave the name of *eupatridai* to the most exalted of the classes in the early Athenian state: the others were the *georgoi* (cultivators, though the *eupatridai* were also cultivators) and the *demiourgoi* or 'public craftsmen' (or 'those working on behalf of the community'), i.e. specialists who might include not only craftsmen but also traders (a problem of terminology which arises in the epic). It must be stressed that these three socio-economic classes, thus defined, are anything but satisfactory. The *eupatridai* to a very great extent must have derived their wealth from cultivation. It has also been inferred by some that they participated in trade and privateering, though the evidence is ambiguous, and it seems doubtful if there was any clear division between the pursuit of trading and cultivation.

As early as the period of Solon's reforms at the beginning of the sixth century and probably before, there were other socio-economic divisions. His *pentakosiomedimnoi*, 'five hundred measure men', were in some respects the equivalent of the *eupatridai*, but determined by wealth not birth, though this meant less of a difference then than later. The *hippeis*, the second income class in Solon's reformed system, would represent the cavalry of the early Athenian state. The third class, of *zeugitai*, must have existed in pre-Solonian Athens. If *zeugos* means a yoke of oxen, they were 'teamsters', farmers of moderate wealth. If the word means a set of armour, there is a temptation to see in them the hoplite element of the Athenian army, as distinct from the aristocratic cavalry. There were also the *thetes*. In the epic *thes* is a landless man who serves another; and the same was probably true of a later period. Apart from these free men and between the *thetes* and those of wholly servile status there were the *pelatai* of uncertain definition, who were later equated with the Latin *clientes*.

The diverse nature of these classes and the ambiguity of the terminology (sometimes poorly attested) make impossible a full solution of the problems relating to the basis of citizenship and the definition of the citizen body. It is generally assumed that there were a good many inhabitants of Attica excluded from the supervisory body, the 'boule' or 'council', from the assembly or *ekklesia*, the body 'summoned' to meet, of which the power to debate or innovate is quite uncertain, and from the executive magistracies. The chief of these, in the seventh century, formed a body of nine (?): the chief executive, the *archon eponymos*, so called since he gave his name to the current year; the war-leader or *polemarchos*; and the *archon basileus*, chief religious official in whom survived both the religious functions and the name (*basileus*) of the primitive king. There was a group of *thesmothetai*, eventually six in number. They may have been fewer at first. In the Classical period they acted, probably in an individual capacity, as judges. The *Constitution of Athens* claims that at first they acted as recorders of decisions taken by those exercising judicial functions, for future guidance. It is more likely that they gave decisions based on the customary law, and exercised other functions (with the three senior archons), as seems to appear from Thucydides' account of the suppression of the conspiracy of Kylon. There must have been decisions and rulings made by the archons in their various jurisdictions, by the *phylobasileis* or tribal 'kings', and by the *ephetai* (fifty-one in number), whom some scholars have regarded as forming the ancient council. There existed also a group of *kolakretai*, who were financial officials, dealing with the slender finances of the ancient state drawn from fines and confiscations. The element *kola* in their name, meaning 'ham', suggests that they were originally connected with sacrifices. In addition one or more officials had charge of the Treasury of Athena, which, in a primitive form, must have existed in the pre-Solonian period as a state 'bank' or reserve.

All these officials were drawn from the *aristoi (aristinden)*, the *eupatridai*, and were probably designated by the council, even if the assembly exercised some kind of *congé d'élire*. There is an indication in Thucydides' account of the conspiracy of Kylon that the *ekklesia* ('the Athenians') could give instructions to the archons: it is far from clear what this might mean. No constitutional document of a contemporary sort, resembling the seventh-century Great Rhetra at Sparta, or the well-known *kurbis* inscription found in Chios, exists to define the functions of the council (including the function of 'steering' [*probouleusis*]) or of the *ekklesia*. In the case of Athens also we have no indication in the seventh century of a confrontation on the lines of the Spartan (p. 171ff.). It is, indeed, difficult to identify those who might have confronted the council of *aristoi*. And here arises the problem of the basis of citizenship. It must be supposed that the development of the hoplite system took place in Attica as it did elsewhere (see pp. 142–5). The hoplite battle line does not appear on Attic seventh-century pottery (though single combats do), as it does on Corinthian pots (especially the Macmillan Aryballos [perfume vessel] and the Chigi jug). This is not, however, a particularly valid form of evidence, since the hoplite line does not appear on Argive pottery, despite the fact that Argos must have been an early exponent of this type of formation. None the less, if the *zeugitai* are interpreted as the possessors of a set of hoplite equipment, then hoplite soldiers did exist as part of the Athenian army, but for some reason they did not act as an element disruptive of aristocratic society. The reason may have been a greater strength in Attica of the vertical structure of the clan, but this is purely conjecture.

There is a good deal else in the organization of early Athenian society in which doubt and conjecture are prominent. In relation to the structure of the phratry, in addition to the *genos* there appear the terms *thiasos*, *orgeon* and *homogalaktes* (plural). A *thiasos* in general terms was an association of persons bound together by some activity, religious or cultural. In the structure of the phratry there were *thiasoi* (plural) of *orgeones*, and it is tolerably clear that the latter were those who celebrated religious rites (*orgia*). The *thiasoi* of *orgeones* were distinct within the phratry from the members of the *gene* (plural of *genos*), the *gennetai*. There is no indication of any local connection, though the periodic celebration of religious rites might seem to require it. Indeed the function of the phratry in recognizing the legitimately born children of Athenian citizens might seem to require knowledge relating to a locality. There are considerable problems here, as also in the functioning of the Kleisthenic *demes* in the same sphere. It is also to be noted that some phratries contained no *genos*. The *homogalaktes*, if the term is translated more or less literally, would be those 'who shared the same milk', which naturally suggests the relationship of foster-brothers, and in an aristocratic society the relationship of the 'noble' child, sharing the milk of his wet nurse with the latter's own offspring. A law of uncertain date, quoted in the fourth century BC, equates *gennetai* and *homogalaktes*, and names them side by side with the *orgeones* as legally entitled to be admitted to phratry membership. In Chapter 8 it will be seen that ingenious use has been made of the terms *thiasos* and *homogalaktes* to explain certain features of the Solonian crisis and the problem of the integration of incomers from elsewhere, which must have taken place in Attica as in other city-states.

The account of late eighth-century and seventh-century Athens as outlined above is intolerably confused and untidy, and it is to be suspected that Athenian institutions were in the same state. It is odd, also, that down to the thirties of the seventh century little is known of events in Athens and Attica, at a time when so much was happening elsewhere. Athens appears to be one of those happy states without a history: no confrontation of aristocracy and middle class; no economic pressures driving Athenians into official colonization; no real threat of tyranny for a long time. This threat, however, came at last. In the thirties, probably, of the seventh century a young Athenian noble called Kylon made an attempt at the tyranny. He was the son-in-law of the tyrant Theagenes in neighbouring Megara, and is called 'powerful' (*dynatos*) by Thucydides. He made the attempt aided by troops from Megara and by 'contemporaries' and friends, presumably young men of noble birth like himself. He had been an Olympic victor, and consequently when Apollo, consulted at Delphi, counselled him to make his attempt at the tyranny on 'the greatest festival of Zeus', he took this to be the Olympic festival, but he was wrong: Apollo really meant the local Attic festival of the Diasia. So Kylon paid the penalty suffered by those who misunderstood Apollo, or in reality Apollo's Delphic priests. His attempt failed. The canonical Olympic victor list placed Kylon's victory in the equivalent of 640 BC, and the local chronicle of Attica (the *Atthis*) put his conspiracy, and the year of the archon Megakles, involved in putting it down, in an Olympic year before the archonship of Aristaichmos in 621 BC (the year of Drakon's legislation). The conspiracy can thus be allotted to 632, 628 or 624 BC. Acceptance of one of these dates (as of others in the period) depends, of course, on the acceptance of the lists mentioned as valid for the later seventh and early sixth centuries.

Various details of the attempt are given by Herodotus, Thucydides and Plutarch (in his *Life of Solon*). Kylon succeeded in occupying the Acropolis, the centre of prestige in Athens as well as of defence after the departure of the last king. It was the centre of government. Possession of it might seem to carry the support of Athena. In reaction to the seizure the Athenians flocked in *en masse* from the country (where obviously the majority of them lived), and besieged the Acropolis. When they tired of the siege they committed the operation, as Thucydides asserts, to the nine archons with powers to take suitable action. Herodotus, on the other hand, claims that the charge was placed in the hands of 'the presidents of the *naukraroi*' (see above). Some of the besieged died of hunger and thirst. Kylon and his brother escaped. The rest, taking refuge on the altar of the goddess, surrendered on condition of a fair trial. Despite this they were taken away and slain. Plutarch adds the detail that some connected themselves by a thread to the sanctity of the ancient statue of the goddess, but the thread broke and they were killed at the altar of the Erinyes (Eumenides) on the way down from the Acropolis.

Thucydides makes it clear that the archons were responsible for the events in question, commenting that they possessed much authority at that time. He goes on to say that 'those to whom the siege was committed' killed the Kylonians and so acquired the taint of blood guilt (*enageis*) – he uses a plural and adds 'the clan connected with them'.[22] His reference is veiled and he does not directly name Megakles, the chief archon of the year, who must have taken the main responsibility, or the family of the Alkmeonidai to which he belonged. Herodotus expressed a contrary view, blaming the 'presidents of the *naukraroi*', while admitting that the charge of blood guilt was later brought against the Alkmeonidai, a version he may well have got from the adversaries of that family in his own time. As a sequel to the conspiracy internal strife appears to have arisen in Athens between the kinsmen of the murdered men and the Alkmeonidai and their supporters. The former at some time appear to have gained the upper hand, since the blood-guilty family was brought to trial before an aristocratic court and prosecuted by Myron of Phlya. The living were condemned to perpetual exile, the dead were dug up and their bones cast out beyond the frontiers of Attica. Plutarch, almost certainly in error, credits Solon with persuading the Alkmeonidai to stand trial: 'The remainder of the faction of Kylon grew strong again, and had continual quarrels with the family of Megakles; and now the quarrel being at its height, and the people divided, Solon being in reputation, interposed with the chiefest of the Athenians, and by entreaty and admonition persuaded the polluted to submit to a trial and the decision of three hundred noble citizens.'[23] The 'persuasion' does not sound very likely. Plutarch is equally incorrect when he suggests that at this juncture, in a war with Megara, the Athenians '*lost* Nisaia and Salamis *again*'. It is more likely that as a sequel to the conspiracy and the Megarian aid given to Kylon war arose between the two states, and Salamis, located between them, became a bone of contention for the *first* time. Plutarch also mentions that since Athens 'was disturbed with superstitious fears and strange appearances' as a result of pollution, they summoned Epimenides the Cretan, to purify the city, as the *Constitution of Athens* explains. It is likely, however, that this purification was carried out when the Alkmeonidai returned under Solon's amnesty at the beginning of the sixth century.

The next historical landmark for early Athens was the appearance of one Drakon (a name which in itself arouses suspicion), placed by the *Atthis* in the archonship of Aristaichmos, the equivalent of 621 BC. He belongs, therefore, to the period of troubles which followed after the Kylonian attempt at tyranny. He was believed to be a *thesmothetes*, and if he was, his concern was with the interpretation of the customary law. He was credited by later generations with a law code which dealt with homicide and a wider series of offences. These, it was believed, were in so many cases punished with death that his code was said to be written in blood. It need not be believed that there was anything like a full codification of the customary law before Solon; and the assertion that Drakon formulated a constitution is a figment of the fourth-century local historians. It must be suggested, however, that apart from the law on homicide (somehow connected with the blood guilt of the Alkmeonidai?)

he effected a much more severe formulation of the law of debt. This, it will be propounded in Chapter 8, was a deliberate attempt to dispossess those owning or renting land, on the part of the *aristoi*.

The Drakonian law on debt, the failure of harvests and the effects of raids on Attica as part of the war between Athens and Megara produced economic distress and grave injustice. In the *Constitution of Athens* it is said of the Athenians: 'Their constitution was in all other respects oligarchic and in particular the poor were enslaved to the rich, they themselves, their children and their wives.'[24] Altogether, Athens was awakened relatively suddenly to problems of which other states had been aware for some time. It is tolerably clear that at the turn from the seventh to the sixth century she was in a state of flux and transition, faced with crises to be solved in the sixth century only after a long period of strife.

# CHAPTER 8

# THE FOUNDATION OF
# CLASSICAL GREECE

The period under consideration in this chapter is characterized by developments which largely determined the form of Classical Greece. The first of these developments is linked with the final points made in Chapter 7: the appearance of a crisis in the affairs of Athens, to be resolved by Solon with only partial success. With this crisis is connected his establishment of what looks like the first formal Athenian constitution. The fact that in economic and social matters Solon was only partly successful meant a period of renewed faction and economic distress and the threat of a tyranny. From the faction strife emerged Peisistratos as a faction leader who eventually established himself as tyrant, not by a *coup d'état* or by political alliance (though he tried these means) but by the use of mercenaries. Strictly speaking his period of rule and that of his sons lie outside the scope of this book as defined in the Introduction, but it was through the Peisistratids that the foundations of Athenian political and cultural greatness were laid, and so something must be said of this achievement.

In the same period the Spartans began to reap the benefits of the changes made in the seventh century, and the strengthening of their hold on Messenia. Success was at last won, in the military sphere, against Argos, which none the less maintained her independence and importance in the Peloponnese even if Argive warriors were no longer superior to Spartan. Sparta also, at some uncertain date, gained the mastery over her Arcadian neighbour Tegea. Here the Spartans adopted a new policy: not one of reduction and enserfment (as in the case of the Messenians) but one of alliance, and the granting to the Tegeans of an honoured place in the battle line. This was the beginning of a period of leadership and responsibility exercised by the Spartans as champions of the Greeks, not just of the Dorians: a claim symbolized by the story of the bones of Orestes (p. 208). Sparta, in offering alliance and non-aggression in return for non-intervention on the part of her neighbours if the helots rose in revolt, was acting from self-interest, but she was also concerned with dangers from disorder within Greek states afflicted with decaying tyranny, and from the Persians, who could only benefit in their advance from such instability.

The third factor of great importance for the future of the Greeks concerned Asia Minor. Whatever had been the effects of Lydian aggression in the seventh century, the Asia Minor Greeks appear to have prospered in the first half of the sixth, particularly in the period of Kroisos. A change came when the eastern neighbours of Lydia, the Medes, succumbed to Persian attack, followed by the fall of Lydia itself. The result was the subjection of the eastern Greeks, and ultimately those of the mainland found this great oriental power dangerously close.

There are other important elements in the story of the first half of the sixth century: the continuance of tyranny, most strikingly represented by Kleisthenes of Sikyon, and its suppression; the internal strife of factions illustrated by events in Lesbos. Of exceptional interest for its possible relation to the policy of the Delphic priesthood, and as a portent of the future part to be played by Athens in the affairs of Greece, is the First Sacred War. It was followed by the development of the moral force of the oracle of Apollo. In terms of the graphic arts and architecture the first half of the sixth century is a great period of achievement. In the economic sphere there is the gradual appearance of coinage.


THE ATHENIAN CRISIS

The Aristotelian *Constitution of Athens*, as it has been preserved in the papyrus, lacks the earliest portion of the work, and starts in mid-sentence with a reference to Myron of Phlya and the aristocratic commission which judged and condemned the slayers of the Kylonians (pp. 185–6). After a reference to the purification of the state by Epimenides the Cretan, the writer continues with a description of the political and economic state of Attica:

After these events it came to pass that the nobles [*gnorimoi*] and the commons [*plethos*] were at variance for a considerable time. For the state was oligarchic in all other respects, and in particular the poor were in bondage to the rich, themselves, their children and their wives. They were called dependents [*pelatai*] and sixth-partners [*hektemoroi*], since at this rent they worked the fields of the rich. The whole earth was in the possession of a few. And if they failed to pay the rent they were liable to seizure, themselves and their children. Loans were, for all of them, secured by the person of the debtor, until the time of Solon, who first became the protector of the People. Enslavement was the harshest and most bitter feature of the system for the mass of the people, but they were resentful at the other aspects of it, since they had no share, so to speak, in its working.[1]

The writer goes on to describe the 'ancient constitution' before Drakon, when the basis of government lay with the noble and wealthy, at this time the same people (*aristinden kai ploutinden*). He deals with the evolution of the offices of the nine archons, adding that they decided cases on their own authority (*autoteleis*). The Council of the Areiopagos he describes as having the function of preserving the laws, and 'administering most aspects of government and, the most important, duly correcting and punishing the disorderly'.[2] He then describes the supposed constitution of Drakon, which rested, he claims, on 'those who provided their own arms' (*hopla*): a hoplite constitution, therefore, in which governmental functions are elaborately organized and allotted on a property basis valued in monetary terms. This constitution prevailed, the writer claims, at the time when Solon was called to perform special functions as 'reconciler and archon': 'Such being the organization [*taxis*] within the constitution, and the Many being enslaved to the Few, the People [*Demos*] rose against the Nobles. When the political strife [*stasis*] was severe and for a long time the two parties were lined up against each other, they chose by common consent Solon as reconciler and archon and committed the constitution into his hands. . . .'[3]

Whatever Drakon may have done in the matter of a reinterpretation of the customary law relating to homicide, debt or the like, no time needs to be wasted on the supposed Drakonian constitution, which finds no support in the later part of the Aristotelian work, and must be an interpolation, a figment of fourth-century political theory, based on the oligarchic attitudes taken at the time of the anti-democratic revolution of 411 BC. The point has been well made: 'The Constitution described betrays the thought of a particular party; the reformers of this school advocated their policy by maintaining that it really would restore Athens to the condition in which it was before the democratic changes began. Many, as we know, looked on Solon as the originator of the changes which they deplored. They would then recommend a constitution of this kind by saying it was like that which prevailed in Athens before the time of Solon.'[4]

Hence the interpolation; but it is unnecessary to reject all the details: while the money evaluation of property qualifications is a gross anachronism, and the 'constitution' is a hoplite one in the broadest sense only, the supervisory functions of the Areiopagos Council can be accepted, along with the existence in the pre-Solonian period of *zeugitai* and *hippeis* (but not of *pentakosiomedimnoi*, a commodity assessment of income introduced by Solon), of loans secured on the person and of a monopoly of land control by a limited body of citizens.

Aristotle sums up the achievement of Solon thus:

Solon is held, by one school of thought, to have been a good law-giver who may be credited with a triple achievement. He swept away an oligarchy which was far too absolute; he emancipated the people from serfdom, and he instituted that 'ancestral democracy' under which the constitution was so admirably tempered – with the Council of the Areiopagos standing for oligarchy, the method of electing the executive magistrates for aristocracy, and the system of popular courts. In actual fact, however, it would appear that two of these elements – the Council and the method of electing the executive magistrates – existed before his time and were simply continued by him. But he certainly introduced the principle of democracy by making membership of the law courts open to every citizen; and that is the reason why he is blamed by some of his critics, who argue that he really destroyed the other elements by making these popular law-courts, with their members appointed by lot, supreme in every case.[5]

In this account of 'Aristotle' there are to be noted the emancipation from serfdom, the reduction of an oppressive oligarchy and its replacement by the 'ancestral democracy', rather like the constitution of Sparta, described as a mixed constitution, which is what Aristotle means by 'tempered', though the kingly element is lacking and a rather slender distinction is made between an oligarchic and an aristocratic element. Also very considerable emphasis is laid on the popular courts. In fact this 'ancestral democracy' is as much or nearly as much an artificial construction of a later day (the end of the fifth century when the radical democracy was discredited by the disasters of the Peloponnesian War) as the supposed constitution of Drakon.

The reality was different, but it is possible to start from two linked issues: the economic oppression of a considerable element of the population of Attica and their lack of any say in the administration of the state affairs. The economic oppression is variously defined, in the *Constitution of Athens* and in the fragments of Solon's verse (the usual means of communication before the development of prose), quoted in the *Constitution* and elsewhere, including Plutarch's *Life of Solon*. Two forms of economic oppression are mentioned: enslavement in a rather vague sense, which might include a form of serfdom, and more specifically the sale *abroad* of some who had contracted debts secured on their person, which indicates true enslavement; others remained in Attica and cultivated the land of the oppressive Few. These are the *hektemoroi* or *pelatai* named in the *Constitution*. As described in this passage they are made to sound like serfs working land owned by their masters: a form of 'share-cropping' known in other times and places. They were not labourers for wages. These were the *thetes*, between whom and their employers no legal bond existed, since they were wholly free men who could be turned off when they were not wanted. And the *hektemoroi* were not slaves (*douloi*). Later, at any rate, an Athenian could not be enslaved to an Athenian; slaves possessed by an Athenian would have to be of non-Athenian origin. The *hektemoroi* were something between: debtors who paid a part of their cultivated produce to their creditors. This could be just enough or unjust; it depended on the amount, as in the case of modern income tax. Most scholars believe one-sixth to be oppressive enough; others, including some very distinguished names, have suggested five-sixths. The amount must surely depend on the purpose and scruples of the creditor. These *hektemoroi* cultivated land. As the *Constitution* puts it, 'They worked the fields of the rich.'

This land, it must be suggested, was not the absolute property of the rich in question. Aside from the whole problem of group ownership it is to be noted that the *Constitution* twice uses a phrase which indicates control rather than possession (*usus* not *possessio*). Solon, in his comment on the situation and his attempt to deal with it, speaks of the 'enslavement' of the earth, and of the existence of marker stones (often wrongly called mortgage stones), which indicated a debt encumbrance on the land, of some sort. Since, however, debts were secured on the *person*, the land could not be pledged, nor taken in amortization of a debt. This is the natural conclusion from the idea of group ownership (by clan or *oikos*), in turn confirmed by the securing of debts *on the person*. The suggestion has indeed been made that there were two kinds of land tenure: group holding and individual holding, with the further conclusion that debt-involvement concerned in the first type produced the *hektemoroi*, who could pledge their persons only in the form of their labour, and would not be sold into slavery, since their labour would thus be lost (and slaves, it might be suggested, could not be used to replace them on group-held land). On the other hand indebtedness of those who held individual land could be covered by seizure of their land and the sale of their persons, if this was necessary to cover the debt. To sustain this theory the ingenious suggestion has to be made that incomers were involved. Some of these, as individuals under the name of *homogalaktes* (interpreted as 'sharers in a feast', see above, p. 184) were integrated into the *gene* and presumably shared in the group land. Others as members of *thiasoi* of *orgeones* (see p. 184) were incorporated in the phratries and had no *genos* connection. It is then further suggested that these had developed for themselves cultivated land from the wild (mainly the hillsides), or came in at a time when Attica was less thickly populated than later.

The theory has the merit of seeming to deal sensibly with the problem of the integration of incomers (in the social and economic, but not necessarily the political sense), and with the apparently different fates of two classes of debtors: serfdom for the *hektemoroi*, and sale abroad for others as slaves. There are objections: serfdom and enslavement could be consecutive stages applying to clan cultivators of group land as much as to others who were absolute possessors. The main objection is that the acquisition of land individually owned meant a form of 'enclosure'. It is certainly true that land previously uncultivated *could* be developed.

Th is reason to believe this happened under Peisistratos later. Would it, effect, happen earlier, when marginal land and hillsides, in some measure common land, were needed for the grazing of goats and the gathering of fuel? It seems better to reject this distinction in land tenure: to regard all land as group-held, by *gennetai* or *non-gennetai*, and to accept that the *hektemor* who could not carry out his obligations could be, with his family, sold abroad as a slave, with the agreement of his clan head, though this need not *necessarily* happen.

Something has been said in Chapter 7 of the possible development of the socio-economic situation in Athens. Political tension manifested itself as a result of the conspiracy of Kylon and the subsequent war with Megara, accompanied for obscure reasons by economic troubles, which are stressed in the poems of Solon. In them appear oppressors and the impoverished and exploited oppressed. Factions thus polarized do not come to any sort of terms, but to blows. There must, therefore, have been a substantial third party. It is very unlikely that the two extremes and the middle matched in any way the three factions which the *Constitution* places later, coming after Solon's reforms, but which Plutarch places before the reforms. The latter seems to perceive the importance of a third party when he describes the faction of the Shore as standing 'for a mixed government and so hindering either of the other parties from prevailing',[6] and when he mentions the combination together of 'the greatest number and bravest'[7]. Such a party need not be composed entirely of the economic *mesoi*; it could contain moderate *eupatridai*; nor need it be composed of trading interests (as sometimes there is a temptation to believe), since the crisis covered all aspects of the economy and its structure.

The direct causes of the crisis, which, if it looks sudden in terms of the historical perspective, need not be so in terms of years (developing, say, in a decade), were economic, and clearly understood by the ancient authorities as such, stressing as they do a state of indebtedness. The debts were incurred by those whose income margin was always slender, or who had suffered economic attrition over a period. The debt was incurred by borrowing commodities when the borrower's own production was inadequate, as seed corn and other necessities for agricultural production. It is not easy to see that at this early date rash speculation in trade or inefficient pursuit of crafts could come into question, but this *might* have been so. Such indebtedness could be produced by natural disasters (lack of rain or too much at the wrong time, or disease) which even in highly developed economies can rapidly produce a crisis situation. The point has already been made on several occasions that the organization of land tenure is obscure: it is useful to assume that there was rented land, and the practice of share-cropping. In such a situation again there could be a falling behind in rent payments or crop production, occasioned by the same causes. It is unlikely that the more avaricious

*eupatridai* (and Solon castigates the rich for their avarice) would overlook advantages to be gained from such a situation (aided possibly by Drakon's arrangements): the reduction of the number of mouths consuming natural products, by the sale of debtors abroad; the extortion of more labour from serfs, attended by a reduction in their consumption. The ultimate effect would be an artificially increased surplus which could be sold abroad, though it must be admitted that this would involve a tolerably developed money economy, which, numismatically, it is difficult to establish. Indeed it must sometimes be felt that the economic argument for the existence of a money economy at this time should override the rather negative numismatic arguments. It is easy to see the advantages of wealth thus acquired (if not in coin, then in electrum, gold and silver bullion), for bribes, hire of mercenaries and in general for transportability of wealth.

How far the question of property succession through the eldest son or, alternatively, the division of land for independent cultivation by all the sons caused economic difficulties, it is impossible to say; the same is true of land fragmentation by the provision of dowries, though here the question arises whether family-held land could be used for this purpose (was this the reason for the exaction of a surety for the return of a dowry?). There are many problems, but Solon makes it clear that the land was encumbered and that the encumbrance was signified by marker stones, which he removed, he claims, and so set the land free. He thus sums up his achievement in righting wrongs. It is not easy to translate and retain the flavour of this famous passage:

To these my purposes, as time will show, black Earth would bear me witness, the best and greatest mother of the Olympian Gods. I removed from her the marker-stones emplanted; thus, enslaved aforetime, she is now set free. Many sold abroad to slavery I brought back to Athens, their god-built native land, and others too who under debt-compulsion fled into exile, as wanderers in many places, forgetting the Attic tongue. Still others, here at home, in shameful serfdom, trembling at their masters' whims I set free. These things I did and carried through as promised, by arbitrary action, joining together force and justice both. I wrote ordinances for base and good alike, fitting straight justice to each man. Another man, taking the goad as I did, had he been of ill intent and covetous disposition, would not have held the people in restraint. Had I indeed desired what once the oppressors pleased, or what again the oppressed would fain devise against them, then this city had been widowed of many men. Wherefore, putting forth my resolution against all opponents, I turned at bay, a wolf amid the pack of hounds.[8]

One of Solon's poems seems to be complete; the rest are fragments, though the one translated above could also be complete. It must be supposed that the writer (or writers) of the *Constitution of Athens*, and Plutarch and others in later antiquity, had a fuller collection, but it seems

unlikely that any vital issue has been overlooked. One long poem has a generally moralizing tone in keeping with the common gnomic character of the early elegiac poets. It expresses Solon's own attitude to life and its activities: what is ordained no chance portent and no sacrifice will avert; the 'gifts' of the gods are inescapable. Another deals with the ages of man; one or two short fragments speak of youth and youthful love; the rest, apart from certain pieces addressed to individuals such as Mimnermos and Philokypros, are concerned with Athens and its fortunes. They must vary in date: they refer to Salamis, to the temptation to tyranny and the danger of its emergence; to the faults of the people on either side, oppressors and oppressed; to *dysnomie* (lawlessness) and *eunomie* (good order), neither sacred nor profane property being immune; to the risk of civil war; to his own attitudes, as a reformer, to either side; to the action he took to avert disaster and to achieve a balance of justice. He also makes clear the reactions his reforms evoked: misunderstanding, contempt (that he did not exploit the situation to his own advantage) and resentment that he had not favoured one side, particularly that of the oppressed, to whom he gave, as he claims, as much as was good for them. It is clear that he had no high regard for either extreme: indeed he stood between them, 'like a boundary stone between the battle lines': 'I gave, on the one hand, to the Demos as much privilege as suffices, neither robbing them of esteem nor giving it in excess. On the other hand I contrived that they who had the power and admiration through their wealth should suffer nothing unseemly. I took my stand, holding my strong shield over both, and suffered neither side to gain an unjust victory.'[9]

The practical details of economic and political reforms are nowhere mentioned in the poems surviving, except that on one occasion he does distinguish the three basic forms of employment – trade, agriculture, crafts – and mentions in addition singer, seer and physician. There is also an obscure reference to the 'many-treed land', cultivated for a year. On the other hand the details of the action taken by Solon are to be found in the *Constitution of Athens*, in Plutarch's *Life of Solon* and in a great variety of late writers. The material varies very greatly in quality. As an early and outstanding figure in the history of Athens Solon attracted to his name acts and enactments which may not have been his, but which fitted his reputation and the general tradition concerning his work. It should be noted also that the background was not easily understood by later writers, and so they may have erred in the interpretation of detail. Equally Solon himself may not fully have understood the likely effects of his reforms, and so it is risky to interpret his intentions from the results.

In the *Constitution of Athens* Solon's reforms are placed in order: the cancellation of debts (*seisachtheia*) and the prohibition of loans involving the pledging of the person of the borrower, followed by the code of laws and, in the third place (though this is not clear from the text), by the

increase of measures (from the Pheidonian), and of weights and of the standard coin (*nomisma*). The law code or separate once-for-all enactments (as later in the case of the Kleisthenic constitution) established citizen rights and duties within a framework of income classes, and defined the functions of magistrates and the governmental bodies. The accounts of both the *Constitution* and of Plutarch lack clarity and involve endless problems. Thus *all* debts, public and private, were cancelled; and there was, indeed, a story that Solon revealed the intended cancellation to some of the *gnorimoi* and they raised loans and combined to purchase 'much land'; and some even claimed that Solon himself participated. (It is to be noted that specific names are mentioned.) As part of the cancellation of debts the encumbrance on land, indicated by the marker stones, was removed, as Solon himself infers. A necessary corollary was the bringing back to Attica of those sold abroad, an action also mentioned by Solon.

There are many difficulties: the sharp practice named in the story above infers a money economy and the possibility that land could be acquired by sale; the means used for the recovery of those sold abroad is not made clear; the Archaic state would possess little in the way of funds. An equally difficult problem is what became of the land delivered of its debt encumbrance. Did it return, or its use return, to the family group or individual owner, *if* indeed there were individual owners? There was, it is generally agreed, no redistribution of land (*gēs anadasmos*), to the chagrin of the impoverished. There is also a suggestion that erstwhile creditors suffered loss by the cancellation of debts, so the land 'freed' did not pass into their possession. There is, it may be added, a suggestion that there was a limit imposed on land-holding. It is far from clear that Solon reinstated the dispossessed; as it is also unclear what the legal status of land was from this time forward. Was it now or at some later date completely or relatively freely disposable?

The *Constitution* mentions, as part of the organization of the State, the division of citizens into four income classes, determined by 'dry' and 'wet' measures (*medimnos* and *metretes*), that is of cereals, wine and oil. How such produce as fruit, including grapes, figs and olives, came into this system is quite unclear. The point has already been made that three categories of citizen probably existed before Solon's reform: *hippeis*, *zeugitai* and *thetes*, though their rights and privileges were probably ill-defined. The *Constitution* regards all four classes as being in existence earlier, including the 'five hundred measure men', and thus infers that the income classes existed before his reforms. This is unlikely. The 'five hundred-measure men' obtained this number of measures or more from their own property; the *hippeis* three hundred or more; the *zeugitai* two hundred or more (it is interesting to note that the *Constitution* can offer no explanation of the name); and the *thetes* below two hundred. Among these income classes

were apportioned citizen rights and administrative duties: 'The [other] administrative functions he allotted to the five hundred measure men, *hippeis* and *zeugitai*: the nine archons, the stewards, the *poletai*, the Eleven and the *kolakretai*; to each in keeping with the size of their assessment, so he allotted the office, but to those of the thetic assessment he gave only a part in the Assembly and the Courts.'[10] That is, the *thetes* were integrated into the citizen body, and their status was clearly defined. This participation in the work of the assembly included the election of the state officials (the method adopted being, at any rate for the archons, preliminary election and then reduction of the elected to the number required by lot-drawing). The reference in the passage quoted above to 'the Courts' refers to the later practice whereby a proportion of the assembly was constituted as a judicial body (the *heliaia*). It is unlikely that in Solon's time there was more than the right of appeal to this body from official decisions. In the *Politics* Aristotle expresses the general principle that 'he who enjoys the right of sharing in deliberative or judicial office ... attains thereby the status of a citizen of his state'.[11] Earlier he observes: '... the citizen ... is best defined by the one criterion, "a man who shares in the administration of justice and in the holding of office".'[12] More specifically in reference to Athens: 'Solon himself would seem to have given the people only the necessary minimum of power. He gave them simply the rights of electing the magistrates and calling them to account.'[13]

This (however defined in practice) represented a great step forward for the majority of those who were now full citizens. It is reasonable to assume that all the inhabitants of Attica, excluding minors, women, slaves and resident aliens, had these rights. Office, on the other hand, was restricted; so was membership of the Areiopagos council, which was recruited from ex-archons and given the general supervision over the State and its laws. Solon is also credited with a new steering (*probouleutic*) council of four hundred members to prepare business for the assembly, but some have doubted its existence on the grounds that the relatively primitive State would have little complicated business which could not be dealt with by the archons. In any case the economic and social status of its members (one hundred recruited from each of the four Attic tribes) is unknown, but the *thetes* are not likely to have been included.

It has been seen earlier that the *Constitution of Athens* mentions among Solon's reforms the 'increase' of measures and weights, and of the standard coin (*nomisma*). In this connection some nice problems arise, which are directly or indirectly bound up with the idea of a money economy. The question of the introduction of coinage has already been approached in Chapter 6. It *could* be that by Solon's time the silver coinage of Aegina had been established and was circulating in Attica. It is frequently assumed that the words of the *Constitution*, '... the mina formerly having the weight of seventy *drachmai* was filled up to [the number of] one hundred',[14] means a decrease in weight of the *drachma*. According to the fourth-century Attic local historian Androtion, '. . . he made the *mina* one hundred *drachmai*, being formerly seventy-three',[15] which Androtion explained as an arrangement to pay debts in a reduced coinage as an alternative to an outright cancellation. The reason given is a nonsense, but it has been noted that the change would accurately represent the difference in weight between the Aeginetic and the 'Euboic' *drachma*, which was the basis of the later Attic standard. The *Constitution* adds: 'The primitive type of coin was the two-drachma piece',[16] and then mentions the change effected in the talent-mina weight system. The basic assumptions are: the circulation in Attica of Aeginetan coins in and before Solon's time, or the existence of Attic didrachms originally of Aeginetic weight, replaced by didrachms of Euboic weight. An attempt to find such coins by ascribing to Attica didrachms of Aeginetic weight bearing the type of an amphora and connecting these with other amphora-type didrachms of Euboic weight (in the 'heraldic' series) must be totally rejected. Far more important in the present context is the assumption of a money economy, both in Plutarch and in certain elements of Solon's law code indicating payments in coin and also loans, at a time when it is not certain even that Aeginetan coinage had come into use.

There is also the problem of the income classes. They seem to have continued in some way to exist in use into the fourth century BC, though affected by the decline in the value of money, so that even a member of the class of five hundred measure men could be a poor man. The use of wet and dry measures would seem to indicate an economy existing before the introduction of coined money, though it is difficult to believe that a notional money equivalent of the measure was not introduced fairly soon. In any case assessment would have been difficult enough, with differences of value of wine, oil and grain, both barley and wheat, and possibly other commodities, and market fluctuations from year to year. The story of Athemion, son of Diphilos, ostensibly supported by an Acropolis inscription recording that he rose from *thes* to *hippeus*, would infer periodic reassessment, and the possibility of movement from one income class to another, which would certainly be brought about also by a decline, as time passed, in the value (in terms of goods and services) of the drachma. It would be hard to resist the suggestion that the division into income classes was a later fiction, if it were not for the name *pentakosiomedimnoi*. It can only be said that the assessment of status by wealth in the form of income is an understandable alternative to that by birth, but how it was carried out is a puzzle of the first order.

Solon codified and no doubt amplified the customary law. The *Constitution* represented him as carrying out a revision, repealing the 'laws' of Dracon except those concerned with homicide, which he left untouched. The new code was inscribed on *axones*, apparently four-sided wooden tablets revolving in frames. Another term, *kyrbeis*, also appears, which may be an alternative term for *axones*. The name suggests a pillar form, and it was believed in antiquity that the *kyrbeis* recorded the regulations for ritual and sacrifices. These legal inscriptions are variously described as set up in the market-place, council chamber, *prytaneion* (town hall) or *Stoa Basileios* (the Royal Stoa). It is of the essence of codified and written laws that they should be set up in a public place, so that they were available for consultation by all who could read the archaic *boustrophedon* text (with lines alternately written from left to right and from right to left). This is preferable to the suggestion that they were placed by Solon on the Acropolis, and brought down to the market-place in the sixties of the fifth century by the radical Ephialtes. Fragments of the wooden *axones* were preserved in the *prytaneion* in the time of Plutarch. A not unimportant point is the length of time they survived intact, since this issue must involve the genuine tradition of the text. A point between 200 BC and 50 BC has been argued as the date of their disappearance as an effective record. They are certainly quoted down to the fourth century BC, but it is possible that there were later copyings of the original. A crucial point in the history of the text would be either the revolution of the 'Four Hundred' in 411 BC, followed by the recodification of 409–408 BC, or the regime of the Thirty Tyrants in 404 BC (who are said to have modified one at least of Solon's laws), and the recodification which took place from 403 BC at the restoration of the democracy.

A wide range of offences, obligations and relationships is covered by the fragments of the code preserved in ancient authors. In some cases money penalties presuppose, as noted above, a money economy. The code dealt with physical violence, including various types of homicide; offences against property, and the award of damages; verbal injuries, including slandering of the dead; intervention in hindrance of judicial self-help; witnesses; avoidance of military service; rights of trial and prosecution on behalf of a third party; questions of morals (including pederasty); relations within the family (the rights of children, adoption, the position of heiresses) and with neighbours and their boundaries, including rights connected with access to water and even the gathering of animal manure. It must be supposed that the code formed the basis for the functioning of the magistracies, and in a surviving fragment at least the *naukraroi* are mentioned as financial officials. Some elements of the code are of exceptional interest. As early as Herodotus it was believed that Solon had taken a law from the Egyptians requiring a declaration of the source of livelihood, which must mean a statement of income. A similar preoccupation, no doubt, with this aspect of Solon's arrangements led Plutarch to suggest that in the income assessments a sheep or a *drachma* was the equivalent of a *medimnos*. More explicitly it was believed, in connection with the rewards for killing wolves and cubs, that an ox represented five *drachmai* and a sheep one, the prices indicated by Demetrios Phaleron. Plutarch goes on to say that choice victims might be valued many times higher, 'but they too are cheap compared with the present'. Even Plutarch recognized the principle of the decline in the value of money.

Various problems of inheritance were dealt with. It was enacted that inheritance and succession should take place through the relations of the father or the father's mother, and failing such relations an outsider might inherit. So Plutarch says: 'Formerly it was not permitted, and the property and the house had to remain in the clan [*genos*], but Solon permitted a man if he had no children to give his property to whom he wished.'[17] This, if correct, was the first step in the freeing of property from group organization and ownership. That land could now be bought and sold would seem to follow from the statement of Aristotle that a limit was imposed on the amount of land which might be acquired. There were other economic measures: a ban on exports except the products of the olive – intended to check the export of grain or replace its cultivation by that of the more valuable olive tree, which was well suited to the stony land of Attica; the encouragement of the practice of crafts to deal with unemployment ('one who has not taught his son a craft cannot claim maintenance from him'); and for a similar purpose the promotion of the immigration of craftsmen, who were offered citizenship. It is clear from the pottery of the late seventh and early sixth centuries that in the case of this craft immigrant potters and vase painters came in some numbers from Corinth. No limit was imposed on usury, but the pledging of the person was forbidden.

It is to be noted that an amnesty was granted to all who had suffered *atimia* (loss of citizen rights) before the archonship of Solon, especially to those who had been debtors. Those, however, were excluded 'who suffered exile after condemnation either by the Court of the Areiopagos or the Ephetai or the Prytaneion, by the tribal kings, for murder or [other slaying] or attempted tyranny.' Yet, seemingly in defiance of this formulation reported by Plutarch, the blood-guilty Alkmeonidai returned with their clan head Alkmeon, who commanded the Athenian forces in the First Sacred War (see below).

There was much else which is hinted at in late authors and lexicographers of varying reliability, such as the sumptuary laws regulating marriages and funerals and trade in perfume (for use in the lying-in-state?). These might be directed against the luxury and display of great families, and the same might be true of the regulation of the festival calendar. On the other hand the rights of organizations and associations were secured, as appears from a Latin legal source: 'If a deme or members of a phratry or *orgeones* or members of a clan or of a dining club or burial club or members of a *thiasos* or an association for privateering or trade make a mutual arrangement, this shall stand if it is not contrary to state regulations.'[18] The passage shows the numerous corporate bodies existing at this early date. It might also be taken to show that Solon, even if he wished to do so, could do little about the existing social structure.

A detached view of Solon must see him not as a philanthropist sentimentally disposed to the poor and oppressed, but as one determined to rectify the injustice done to debtors, and equally to condemn the attitudes of either extreme, the exploited as well as the exploiters. He understood that the economy of Athens must be manipulated; that both sides must suffer in the process, and that while the poorer element of the population was to be delivered from oppression, it must equally be made to stand on its own feet. There was to be no uneconomic redistribution of the land in small plots. It was rather to be developed by those who could raise loans but with unrestricted interest. The poor majority could be wage-earners following agricultural and pastoral pursuits or engaging in crafts. In the category of cultivation the olive was to be the staple product. Each man had rights as a citizen secured to him.

Within the limits of what he could do Solon's plans were good and just. As he put it: 'I held my strong shield about both sides.'[19] In the exercise of justice he pleased no one, probably not even those who supported him initially. He formalized the constitution of Athens and the rules of citizenship, codified the law and did his best for the economy of Attica. On the other hand it seems very clear that he had insufficient support to carry out any thoroughgoing reform of the social structure of locality, clan and tribe. So the old order remained, with serious consequences in view of an ambitious and disgruntled upper class and dissatisfied poor.

When Solon had completed his reforms, which can hardly have been carried out in one year of the archonship, he exacted, so it was said, an oath that his enactments would be observed for ten years. Then he set out on his travels. He returned, the story was, to find that things had gone wrong again or were tending to cause trouble. The power of locally influential families had not been broken. Their faction strife is highlighted by the two cases of *anarchia*, when a chief archon could not be elected. This happened after Solon's reforms and during his absence. Almost immediately after his return a dangerous tendency was illustrated by the example of Damasias: elected archon one year, continuing in office a second year and forcibly expelled in the third. He was followed by a curious coalition of representatives, so the *Constitution* says, of *eupatrids*, *agroikoi* and *demiourgoi*. The *agroikoi* can reasonably be identified as countrymen, the *demiourgoi* possibly as craftsmen (and so townsmen?), in which case Solon's action had caused them to grow in importance. When

Solon in a surviving fragment of his poem warns of the danger of tyranny he may have Damasias in mind as a symptom. His young kinsman Peisistratos must have been a youth on Solon's return, and it was a matter of hindsight if later Athenians saw in Solon's words a reference to a danger of tyranny from that quarter. Indeed significant contact of the two is as unlikely to have taken place as between Solon and Lydian Kroisos.

The *Constitution of Athens* (and at an earlier date Herodotus and at a later date Plutarch) speaks of three factions in Attica. First the *pedieis*, the 'party of the Plain', interpreted as the area of land between the sea, Parnes, Pentelikon and Hymettos and including Athens. This was a sought-after territory in which were located the seats and shrines of the most ancient (as they claimed) families of Attica, apart from those connected with Eleusis. The second was the 'party of the Shore', the *paralioi*, who could hardly be interpreted as the inhabitants of the whole long ribbon of Attic coast. They were, rather, the inhabitants of the Paralia, an area of south-eastern and southern Attica characterized by considerable fertility in vines and olives, and in modern times by important discoveries of what are obviously clan or family burial places and probably shrines. Thus there have been made at Vari finds of splendid seventh- and sixth-century Attic black-figure pottery, and of superb examples of Archaic sculpture, from the last decade of the seventh century, such as the Sounion *kouros* (youth), and into the sixth, such as the Berlin standing goddess, and a number of other statues of youths (and maidens) of outstanding quality, from clan centres. They also represent a considerable degree of wealth able to command such high artistic skill.

It is clear that the development, noted earlier, of rural settlement in Attica in the eighth century continued into the seventh and sixth, and indeed, as Thucydides makes clear, into the Classical period. For the 'Plain' and the Paralia a disparity of economic or social interest is difficult to conceive, though local rivalries can certainly be accepted. The third faction, the *hyperakrioi* or *diakrioi*, is not easily explained. Who were the 'men beyond the heights', or the 'men in the heights'? It is not difficult to conceive of the *akra* as the mountain faces descending to the plain, like the descending face of Parnes. Something of the sort is preferable to some connection with the 'corn line' and the area above it. Given the localized definition of the other two 'faction' areas, it could be suggested that the *hyperakria* or the *diakria* (to coin these words) might be the area of north-eastern Attica, with an extension south along the east coast. In part this might be conceived as a rather remote and depressed area of less fertile and desirable land with a high proportion of grazing and scrub, to which the term *eschatia* was applied. It has been from time to time suggested that this was the region of crofters and shepherds, which is arguable. Given this, a formal pattern could be constructed: the 'Plain' representing the nobility; the 'Shore' (taken literally) comprised of 'merchants and fishermen', and the 'Hill' (admittedly a later formation) representing the underprivileged and poverty-stricken element. Something has already been said in Chapter 7 on the interrelationship of social and economic organization. No rational account of Attica under these aspects would substantiate any such formal pattern.

It could be argued that if the 'factions' corresponded to areas of Attica this was the penultimate stage in the development of the *polis*-territory from what had once been a much fragmented area. In other words there were still those who believed that regions were more important than a centralized Attica. In such a case, it is to be noted, the *paralia* must be taken as south-eastern and southern Attica, and the protagonists or antagonists of centralization must be represented by influential families in these areas. A later, manifestly artificial tradition (based on hindsight) emerged to name faction leaders: Lykourgos, the Eteoboutad, as leader of the 'party of the Plain', Megakles, the Alkmeonid, as leader of the 'Shore' and Peisistratos, probably related to the east-coast family of the Philaidai, as leader of the 'Hill' party. This appearance of named individuals is to be compared with a similar phenomenon appearing earlier in the traditional account of Solon and his 'friends': Konon, Kleinias and Hipponikos. The stress is on individuals rather than on abstract tendencies in the development of Attica. It is difficult to avoid the impression that this period in Athens was characterized by the appearance of local 'dynasts', who were would-be tyrants (in a period in which tyranny was not wholly discredited). To be a tyrant was clearly the intent of Damasias; earlier it was expected of Solon; and it became a reality with Peisistratos.

The account in the *Constitution of Athens* of the events which led to the tyranny of Peisistratos is one confused by certain ambiguities. Did the discontent which brought him for the first time (and very briefly) to the tyranny arise from the reforms of Solon or from a repetition of an economic crisis which Solon's reforms failed to prevent? The *Constitution* assumes that apart from the strife of factions, noble families and individuals there were economic and other troubles: the discontent of those who had been freed of their debt bondage but found no relief of their poverty – or it might be that these were men of the next generation who found themselves equally distressed; and the apprehensions of men, whether of inferior pre-Solonian citizen status or those who had been brought in from other states to promote the craft development of Athens, who felt no confidence that the status given them by Solon would stand. As the *Constitution* points out, their apprehensions were justified during the reaction after the fall of the tyranny. Whether the creditors who suffered at the cancellation could also be involved after such a period of time is a moot point.

It is tolerably certain that Peisistratos, like his rivals, was the leader of a very heterogeneous faction, which clearly emerges from the story of his career. As the *Constitution* describes it (it is interesting to note that there is no Plutarch's *Life* of Peisistratos) his first attempt was a *coup d'état*: described in the terms of later political theorists as a clash between rival groups, followed by the granting by the assembly (through his partisan Aristion) of a bodyguard of 'club-bearers', which was followed by a seizure of the Acropolis. It is a story of great naivety. The element relating to the assembly fails to carry conviction; the body of strong-arm men sounds convincing enough; they had appeared in other Greek cities as a feature of the strife of noble factions. Peisistratos miscalculated his strength, and a combination of opposing factions resulted in his repulse back to the country. The sequel appears to demonstrate most clearly the 'dynastic' would-be tyrant trend in Athens at this time. This was a coalition, as it is represented, with Megakles the Alkmeonid, and the marriage of Peisistratos (he a man already with grown-up sons) to Megakles' daughter. The idea was that if Megakles himself could not be tyrant at least a grandchild might be: but no such offspring materialized and a quarrel ensued. So out into exile, this time out of Attica, went Peisistratos, to Macedonia and northern Greece, whence with the benevolence of a number of Greek states he returned back by force with mercenaries hired with the resources of gold and silver drawn from Thrace, which area was a close interest of Athens down into the Classical period. Peisistratos landed at Marathon, and seems to have been unopposed until he advanced to the strategic passageway between Pentelikon and Hymettos. There at Pallene he fought and defeated his opponents. It is obvious that the aristocracy of Attica and the people were divided and weakened, and so Peisistratos triumphed. This would be around 547 BC, one of the decisive dates of Archaic Greek history.

In terms of material culture Athens made outstanding progress based on the achievement of the seventh century. To the first half of the sixth century belongs a good deal of the Archaic sculpture of lively and colourful character which decorated various early structures on the Acropolis, including a temple of Athena. The quality of the sculpture which as cult statues or dedications and as grave monuments adorned country centres outside Athens is very striking and an index of the wealth of a country-based aristocracy. An outstanding style of pottery decoration also characterized Athens, from the earliest orderly black-figure of the Nessos Painter onwards. In its earlier stages it shows the undoubted influence of the Corinthian style, but very soon far outdistanced it in quality. The Attic miniature and monumental styles of black-figure appear not only in Attica (as in the seventh century) but, as the sixth century progresses, to an ever-increasing degree abroad in the Mediterranean and particularly in the West, beginning in Etruria.

With this ever-spreading presence of Attic pottery – the indestructible survivor, it must be assumed, of other exports – is linked the problem of Athenian interest in overseas trade. The evidence of the pottery makes clear that merchants frequented the mart of Athens. Among other commodities, it is certain that olive oil attracted the trader, exported in the 'SOS' amphorae (so called from the neck pattern). It does not follow that Athenians were the carriers of such trade, which may have included silver from early mining in the Laurion region.

The Athenian policy in relation to foreign trade has largely to be conjectured. Hostility to her neighbours Aegina and Megara and the repeated preoccupation with Salamis need not have any connection with trade; the same is true of Athens' first emergence into the wider world of Greek affairs through her involvement in the First Sacred War. Solon's ban on the export of natural products except the olive *might* indicate a shortage of corn and a consequent concern for its importation, in which case likely sources were the northern Aegean and Black Sea areas. The Athenian tyrants had an interest in Thrace and some position there until the advance into Europe of the Persians. They could draw corn from this area, as well as timber and precious metals. Peisistratos certainly displayed an interest in the Hellespontine approach to the Black Sea. While the settlement of Miltiades the Elder in the Thracian Chersonese (the Gallipoli Peninsula) may have been a matter of acquiescence only, Peisistratos established his illegitimate son Hegesistratos in Sigeion on the southern shore of the Hellespont. This operation of the tyrant was regarded as a reoccupation of the area in question, which had earlier been an objective of the Athenians. The tradition was that around the turn of the century the Athenians and Mytileneans fought a campaign for Sigeion in which the Athenian commander Phrynon was killed by the Mytilenean Pittakos, the opponent of the lyric poet of Lesbos Alkaios in the political struggles in the island. The poet was also involved in the Sigeion campaign, and like Archilochos at an earlier date abandoned his shield in flight. This was subsequently dedicated by the Athenians in the temple of Athena at Sigeion. The success of Pittakos, attained after earlier reverses, led to his election by the *demos* of Mytilene to the special office of *aisymnetes* (pp. 139–40), and thus the Sigeion War forms a link between Mytilene in the throes of faction strife, and Athens poised on the brink of the same.

It must be agreed that, whatever happened subsequently under Peisistratos, a campaign was fought by Athens at this early date and so far from her home territory. The shield of Alkaios looks like a piece of evidence to perpetuate the memory of the campaign. It would also appear from fragments of Alkaios' poetry and of a commentary on them that he referred to the Sigeion campaign, to the exploit of Pittakos and Phrynon, and possibly to the arbitration of Periander of Corinth, who awarded Sigeion to the Athenians, but the nearby Achilleion to Mytilene. Subsequently the tradition concerning this curious campaign may have been garbled, but the poetry of Alkaios (though partisan) must have provided a contemporary source of information.

The Athenian commander Phrynon was known as an Olympic victor in 636–635 BC, and tradition held that Pittakos killed him in 607–606 BC. The campaign is therefore relatively firmly fixed at the end of the seventh century, in the period of Solon, at much the same time as the struggle over Salamis, but before the involvement of Athens in the First Sacred War. It is clearly not a projection backwards in time from the period of the tyranny.

The essential point of interest is that it seems to be well established that Athens did engage in this distant campaign, the objective of which is quite unclear. It is difficult to accept the idea that imports of corn to Attica had to be secured. In any case this was not the way to secure this purpose, which would have to be obtained by trade treaties. A more convincing suggestion is that an effort was being made to exploit the passage of shipping through a notoriously difficult sea way from the Aegean to the Euxine, since wind and current made necessary halts in the passage of ships, which would have to be made at such points as Sigeion. It is not too difficult to think of Solon and his associates learning a lesson from Corinth, which under Periander established at this period the *diolkos*, a device rather like a railway track on which vehicles could transport small vessels across the isthmus. For Athens some kind of control at the Hellespont could be supplemented by a land route across Attica from north-east to south-west, bypassing Sounion. There was still the problem of Aeginetan and Megarian hostility for which there was only a military solution. It is also to be noted that Athens could not yet reap fully the advantages of Sigeion, since Periander awarded nearby Achilleion to Mytilene. The acquisition was none the less the first step in Athens' emergence from her seventh-century seclusion.

## SPARTA AND THE PELOPONNESE

It has been seen in Chapter 7 that Sparta faced a crisis involving a revolt of her Messenian serfs. It is to be placed fairly early in the seventh century and it may be called the 'Tyrtaios War' by reason of the participation in it of the elegiac poet of that name, the fragments of whose poetry hint at wider issues than just a hard-fought and long drawn-out campaign (the subject later of romantic embellishment) against the Messenians.

The removal of internal stresses and the consolidation of a new social and military system required a considerable period of time. It meant that

Spartan military power long remained weak, as is indicated by the failure to attain military success in Arcadia. The Arcadians under the leadership of the king of Orchomenos had taken the side of the Messenians in their revolt. In the process of the resistance to Sparta the village organization of south-eastern Arcadia, Sparta's nearest neighbours, was, already in the seventh century, consolidated into the *polis* of Tegea. Later came a similar consolidation to form Mantinea, and later again, in resistance to the growth of the Eleans in the sixth century, the development of Heraia in western Arcadia. Tradition related that the Spartans were deceived by a Delphic oracle into invading the territory of Tegea with the aim of its subjection. The result was a Spartan defeat and humiliation. It seems clear that Spartan military strength took some time to build up. It might also be suggested that around 600 BC there was renewed trouble with the Messenian helots, if events which some would place earlier and some later (in the fifth century) are in effect to be located at this time at the turn from the seventh to the sixth century. If so, it was demonstrated to the Spartans that they could not engage in aggression abroad and maintain a firm hold on Messenia. At this juncture also there was undoubtedly trouble with Argos, not yet reduced to second place in the Peloponnese. It has indeed been suggested that some of the expansion of Spartan control over the south-eastern Peloponnese including Kythera, generally ascribed to a much earlier period (the eighth century), in fact took place in the period around 600 BC.

Such was the position of Sparta in the earlier decades of the sixth century, during which two great names figured in the history of the Peloponnese: Periander of Corinth and Kleisthenes of Sikyon. It was a period marked also by a military campaign of great significance: the war of the Amphiktyonic League of Anthela, ostensibly in protection of Apollo's oracular shrine of Delphi against Krisa near the coast below. Sparta, too much engaged in affairs nearer home, had no part in this campaign. Her non-participation can hardly have been due to the part played in the war by Kleisthenes of Sikyon, since the anti-Dorian attitude of the latter was directed against Argos, the foe of Sparta. Whatever the reason, Sparta later stood high in the favour of Delphi.

The success of Spartan reorganization manifested itself in the sixth century first in the battle fought over the disputed territory of Thyreatis, the famous Battle of the Champions, to be placed (since Kroisos took account of it in seeking Greek allies against the Persians) somewhere in the middle of the sixth century. It marked a certain decline of Argos – not very great since the Argives remained redoubtable opponents of Sparta – and an increasing military influence of Sparta: Spartan warriors were now coming to the fore, to replace those of Argos. The history of Sparta in the earlier sixth century included the names of the kings who ultimately won success against the Tegeans. They were Anaxandridas and Ariston, in whose time (somewhere around 560 BC) 'a favourable war was fought with Tegea', partly to be accounted for by a decline in Arcadian cohesion (marked by the decline of the royal house of Orchomenos) and the development from a village system of the *polis* of Tegea. It is to be suspected that *polis*-development meant increased strife and consequent weakness, and an absence of an earlier unity under the rulers of Orchomenos. The defeat of Tegea meant some gain of territory for Sparta: Karyai, Oion and Phylake, earlier part of Tegea, are later to be found as Lakonian subordinate communities. This apart, the defeat of Tegea was followed by an arrangement. There was no subjugation of the Arcadian city, but an agreement and an alliance with the admission of Tegea into an honoured place in the Spartan battle line.

In this fashion, and through a probable alliance of Sparta and Elis, the foundations were laid of a series of alliances, later formalized under the leadership of Sparta, which had by mid-century acquired the reputation of being the leader of the Greeks: a leadership symbolized for Herodotus by the gift of a famous linen corselet from Pharaoh Amasis of Egypt, and by a great bronze mixing-bowl.sent by the Spartans to Kroisos of Lydia. That both were stolen by the piratical Samians served to demonstrate into what a complex and difficult wider world the Spartans were entering, like the contemporary Athenians.

According to the tradition the success of Sparta against Tegea was due to the recovery of the bones of Orestes, pre-Dorian son of Agamemnon, from Tegea (or possibly from Orestheion). A reasonable interpretation of the story is that from policy the Spartans were developing a claim to represent the interests of the Greeks and even the non-Dorians, a Hellenic responsibility, it might be said. The same was the sense of the reply of King Kleomenes of Sparta to the priestess of Athena who sought to bar his entry to the Acropolis of Athens: 'I am not a Dorian but an Achaean',[20] converted into positive action when, at the complaint of the Athenians, he intervened in Aegina to remove the pro-Persian Aeginetans.

At much the same time as the kingship of Anaxandridas there was the ephorate of Chilon, the date of whose office is to be placed between 560 BC and 556 BC. He was regarded as one of the great names of Spartan history, and credited with a part in the full development of the 'Constitution' of Lykourgos. He was also associated with the policy of Sparta directed against tyranny. In a late papyrus it is recorded: 'Chilon the Lakedai-monian, having become ephor and general, and Anaxandridas put down the tyrannies among the Greeks.'[21] A list of tyrannies so put down, mainly in an indirect fashion, is given by Plutarch and by a commentary on the fourth-century orator Aeschines. They include Hippias at Athens and Aischines at Sikyon, and in fact the list extends far beyond the probable lifetime of Chilon and Anaxandridas. The basic reason for the anti-tyrant policy of Sparta was the realization that this was an unstable form of government, which generally, on its fall, was replaced by some form of oligarchy, acceptable to Sparta as relatively stable if not ideal. The relations of some tyrants with Persia might seem to jeopardize the safety of the Greeks. This was true of the Peisistratidai in Athens; and in the case of Athens also the tyrants might be rated as pro-Argive. It is, however, difficult to discover a universal rule.

## THE GREEK TYRANNY AND ITS DECLINE

The decline of tyranny, which it became the policy of Sparta to promote, was a lengthy process, and the sixth century was in fact marked by outstanding examples of this form of government. In Asia Minor Thrasyboulos of Miletos successfully resisted the attacks of Lydia under Alyattes, a twelve-year war ending c. 602 BC in a treaty. The early sixth century also saw the continuance of the tyranny of Periander of Corinth, the friend of the Milesian tyrant and the arbitrator between Athens and Mytilene. There is no doubt that Corinth and Miletos were closely associated commercially as part of the continuing development of a trade nexus between East and West, between the Aegean and the eastern Mediterranean and Egypt, the Adriatic and Italy and Sicily. Further west there was the Phokaian foundation of Massilia c. 600 BC and trade into Gaul. In this Corinth exploited her isthmus position between the Aegean and the Gulf of Corinth and constructed the *diolkos* (p. 135). The trade connections can be seen from the widespread distribution of Corinthian pottery in the animal and figure styles down to the middle of the sixth century, but already overshadowed in some measure by Attic, destined to replace it as the dominant fabric. At some time also, possibly towards the middle of the sixth century, Corinth issued its own coinage with the figure of Pegasos and the letter *koppa*, later joined on the reverse by the head of Athena.

Periander (see Chapter 6 above) was seen as a leading figure in early Greece, and the promoter of Corinthian greatness. He also came to represent (justly or not) some of the worst aspects of tyranny; he was also, incongruously enough, numbered with Solon and Chilon among the 'seven sages' of Greece. With his death the tyranny at Corinth effectively came to an end, since his nephew Psammetichos was murdered after a brief reign, and the Kypselids were replaced by an oligarchic form of government.

The other outstanding tyrant of the earlier sixth century was Kleisthenes of Sikyon. Following on the relatively innocuous regime of the earlier Orthagorids Sikyon attained its great days under Kleisthenes, as a leading city on the Gulf of Corinth, the rival of Corinth. Kleisthenes represented a resurgence in his city of an anti-Dorian element. If it was intended as a gesture of Hellenic significance it was not well conceived, and could not match the Spartan claim to represent non-Dorian as well as Dorian. Basically, however, it was a reaction against Argos and was centred on Adrastos, the mythical Argive hero, the object of cult in Sikyon. Kleisthenes' crude and childish mode of procedure has frequently been commented on: importing Melanippos from Thebes to drive out Adrastos, discontinuing the recitation of the Homeric poems, renaming in opprobrious terms the three Dorian tribes of Sikyon and giving pre-eminence to the fourth non-Dorian tribe of the Aigialeis. It does not sound a particularly well-conceived policy, at a time when unity, not division, was being sought in Greece. Anti-Argive should mean pro-Spartan, but it is not clear what the relations of Sparta and Sikyon were.

Kleisthenes reigned as tyrant for some thirty years (c. 600 to 570 BC) and two events were associated with his name. The one was the semi-folktale suitor competition for the hand of his daughter Agariste, in which, tradition related, a number of aristocratic suitors from various Greek states assembled at Sikyon to be feasted and to undergo tests. As Herodotus puts it: 'So all the Greeks who were proud of their own merit or of their country flocked to Sikyon as suitors; and Kleisthenes had a foot-course and a wrestling-ground made ready, to try their powers.'[22] The suitors came from Sybaris and Siris in southern Italy, from Epidamnos, Aetolia, Argos, Arcadia, Elis, Athens, Eretria, Krannon and the Molossoi. It would be difficult to discover a pattern in this. It fits the geographical location of Sikyon that mainland Greece and the west were represented, while the Aegean and Asia Minor were not. Corinth is conspicuous by its absence, but Herodotus records that Kleisthenes' favourite was Hippokleides, son of Teisandros, 'by family akin to the Kypselidai of Corinth'. It would be rash to regard this as implying that there was no rivalry between Corinth and Sikyon. In the sequel Megakles of the Alkmeonidai, son of Alkmeon who had returned from exile under Solon, obtained the hand of Agariste, since Hippokleides disgusted Kleisthenes by his behaviour. The pair produced the statesman Kleisthenes of Athens, and Pericles was descended from them.

This was the kind of episode beloved of Herodotus more than a century later. A great deal which might be of contemporary significance and not just artistic embellishment escaped Herodotus and escapes modern scholars. Some details were no doubt related by the Alkmeonidai, who were the contemporaries of Herodotus; it is to be wondered what was said of Hippokleides by members of the clan of the Philaidai to which he belonged. Whatever his disgrace at Sikyon, in 566–565 BC he was chief archon at Athens, and played a part in the development of the Panathenaic festival. What is clearly significant is the nexus of inter-state relations built up in this period between *polis* aristocracies and tyrannies, and sometimes with outside powers. Thus in the seventh century there was the marriage connection between the Athenian Kylon and Theagenes of Megara, while the wife of Periander of Corinth was Melissa, daughter of Prokles of Epidauros and of Eristheneia of the royal house of Arcadia. Herodotus mentions the connection of the Philaidai and the Kypselidai; a Kypselos was an early sixth-century archon of Athens. Periander's nephew and successor was Psammetichos, bearing the name of three Egyptian kings of the Twenty-sixth Dynasty. Alkmeon of Athens was associated with the royal house of Lydia, and a surviving Attic epitaph records an Athenian noble called Kroisos who died in battle. The outcome of the marriage contest at Sikyon was the link between Kleisthenes and Megakles of the Alkmeonidai; later there was another between Athens and Argos, through the marriage of Peisistratos and the Argive Timonassa. There were no doubt others which played a part in the alignments of the sixth century, but they did not include Sparta.

Kleisthenes was also involved in an important event of the early sixth century, the First Sacred War, which was fought in the first decade (?) of the sixth century over Delphi. It is an episode in the wider world of Greek affairs and in the development of the Greek people, politically and spiritually. From the seventh century onwards Delphi developed as the centre of an oracle of Apollo, which replaced one of Ge (Earth). The story was that though Apollo was Lord of Lykia, Maionia and Miletos and ruler over 'wave-girt Delos' he sought a place in Greece, and, coming to 'rocky Pytho', he slew the dragon of Ge and established there his priesthood of Cretans (who hailed him in chorus as Paion, 'The Healer') and his temple, associated in the *Hymn to the Pythian Apollo* with the names of Trophonios and Agamedes. The process of the displacement of Ge by Apollo may well have been a long one, but it was largely completed when the sacred enclosure (*temenos*) was reorganized after the destruction of the early temple in 548 BC.

Unlike the sanctuary of Olympia in the western Peloponnese, associated with the names of Herakles, Hera and Zeus, Delphi did not have from the beginning a tradition of athletic and other contests, but as the centre of an oracle of Apollo it had a greater importance than earlier Olympia, with its predominantly Peloponnesian and western connections. It must be remembered that there were other oracular centres, as that of Apollo himself at the shrine of the Branchidai near Miletos, and that of Zeus, of ancient standing, at Dodona in Epeiros. The connection of the early Delphic oracle with colonization, especially the colonization of Sicily, may have been a retrospective claim based on the later distinction of the oracle. On the other hand the archaeological evidence indicates a development running parallel with the rise of Corinth, and so going back to the eighth century. The finds of pottery at Delphi would seem to reflect the importance of the Corinthian connection, and the ancient treasury of Corinth appears to have housed important early dedications. The tyrants of Corinth, as seen earlier, had reason to be grateful to Apollo. The seventh-century temple, presumably that credited to Trophonios and Agamedes, seems to have been, even thus early, an important structure. There was a gradual accumulation of dedications by Greeks and non-Greeks, and numerous 'treasuries' were constructed to house them, ultimately representing states as far apart as Knidos in the eastern Aegean and Massilia in the far west. The importance also of Delphi as a commemoration and prestige centre is underlined by the ever-increasing series of monuments of other types recording in particular military victories. They did not always contribute to inter-state amity.

These developments could not fail to make Delphi an object of interest to those Greek powers who would like to control the oracle – and it is unlikely that many really believed that the voice of the Pythia was the voice of a god – and the Delphic riches. Relating or purporting to relate to this early period there existed a series of oracles delivered by the god exploiting ambiguity of language or of factual detail. Some might be genuine; most, it is to be suspected, were later confections based on hindsight. None the less they reflect certain convictions later held concerning the attitudes of the oracle: it encouraged tyranny (Kypselos and Kylon); it deceived Sparta on the prospect of victory over Tegea; at some time in the reign of Kleisthenes of Sikyon, in relation to his anti-Argive policy, it was abusively hostile to him: 'Adrastos is the Sikyonians' king; but thou art only a robber.' It must be borne in mind that the concept in later times of the earlier oracle and its ways could not fail to be influenced by Delphic policy from the late sixth century onwards: the corrupt influence of the Athenian Alkmeonidai in exile at Delphi, intended to win Spartan support for their restoration and the ejection of Hippias; the shifting and shifty policy of Delphi at the time of the Persian invasion of 480 BC and later.

Parallel, it would seem, to the growth in the importance of Delphi, there were developments in northern and central Greece, south of Macedonia where a dynasty precariously ruled claiming origins in the Heroic Age. In what is assumed to be the seventh century there drew together in and south of the Peneios Valley the cantons of Pelasgiotis, Histiaiotis, Phthiotis and Thessaliotis, the first impulse perhaps coming from the latter area, since the resulting combination was called the confederacy of the Thessalians. The traditional leader in this development was Aleuas the Red of Larissa. The association of cantons was presided over by a *tagos* (commander) elected for life. Through this development the Thessalians were able to dominate an assemblage of central Greek communities: Phokis, Doris, Lokris, Malis, the Ainianes,

Dolopes, Achaioi (not to be confused with the Peloponnesian), Magnetes, Perrhaiboi, Euboeans and Boeotians. They were a motley collection, some backward culturally and politically. A uniting agency, under the Thessalians led (?) by the Aleuadai of Larissa, was an association called an *amphiktyonia* represented by a council of deputies (*amphiktyones*). The word originally meant 'those who dwell as near-neighbours'. There were other such associations, for instance at Onchestos in Boeotia and at Kalaureia in the north-eastern Peloponnese, but the one under consideration became the amphiktyonia *par excellence*. Its representatives met at the temple of Demeter at Anthela, in the 'gates' (*pylai*) to central Greece near Thermopylai. It is to be noted that the association played a considerable part in the development of the concept of the Hellenes, originally a name for the inhabitants of a region in southern Thessaly. The Thessalians, it would seem, exerted pressure southwards to the Corinthian Gulf for a considerable period until their failure against Boeotia at Keressos *c.* 570 BC and against Phokis at Hyampolis, but their southward interests continued, witness the cavalry aid sent to Hippias of Athens when he was first attacked by Sparta.

The greatest enterprise of the Thessalians and their allies, under the leadership of Eurylochus the Aleuad of Larissa, was concerned with Delphi. With them were associated forces from Athens under Alkmeon (lately returned from exile) and from Kleisthenes of Sikyon, who seems to have played a leading part in the operation. This campaign, called the First Sacred War, was ostensibly directed against Krisa (Kirrha), a community in the plain below Delphi, since, it was said, the Krisaians harassed and preyed on the pilgrims landing from the sea to visit the oracle of Apollo. Krisa was taken and destroyed and the plain (to remain uncultivated) was devoted to Apollo. Amphictyonic votes were given to Athens (representing the Ionians?) and to 'the Dorians of the Peloponnese', by which the council was given a more fully Hellenic character.

This most interesting early example of inter-state co-operation presents some problems, particularly the involvement of Athens (with Alkmeon as commander and Solon – some said – as advisor) and of Kleisthenes of Sikyon. A simple explanation of the aims of the Thessalians would be that they had not hitherto exercised any control over Delphi; this had been in the hands of Krisa. The war was part of the southward push of the Thessalians, to put the finishing touches to the league. For Athens and Sikyon there was the prestige of participation and, very likely, they had been promised the votes as a reward for their services. Certainly the suggestion is hardly acceptable that Krisa was a trade rival of Sikyon and that this, in part at any rate, accounted for the involvement of Kleisthenes. This can hardly have been so. For east–west trade Sikyon and Krisa were too near the isthmus to be effective rivals of Corinth; for north–south trade Krisa and Sikyon could be complementary, but again both compared poorly with Corinth. A better reason could be that the war was in effect directed against Delphi itself and its priesthood, in reaction to the policy indicated by the oracular responses mentioned above. If this is so, hindsight inserted into the *Hymn to the Pythian Apollo* the warning of the god to his Delphic priesthood at their installation: 'Guard you my temple and receive the tribes of men that gather to this place, and especially show mortal man my will, and do you keep righteousness in your heart. But if any shall be disobedient and pay no heed to my warning, or if there shall be any idle word or deed and outrage as is common among mortal men, then other men shall be your masters and with a strong hand shall make you subjects for ever.'[23]

It has already been pointed out that the attitude of the oracle was anything but satisfactory later, as in 480 BC, at the time of the Persian invasion, when the Thessalian Aleuadai of Larissa were favourably disposed to the invaders. The same may have been true earlier, for reasons unknown, under the dominion of Krisa. Whatever the truth of such a suggestion Delphi did find itself under 'other masters' in the form of the Amphictyonic Council augmented by Athenian and Dorian representatives, and now probably for the first time meeting at Delphi as well as at Anthela.

Thus began a period which saw a great increase in the importance of festivals, and especially in the prestige of the Olympic Games as an occasion for the meeting of the Greeks and that close integration of religion, literary and athletic culture and politics which made Greek civilization. In 586/5 BC the Pythian Games were founded to develop side by side with the Olympic Games; they were to be the two great national festivals of Greece and the Greeks outside the homeland. To them were added the games at Nemea and at the Isthmus. In 585 BC Kleisthenes won the chariot race at Delphi (as he did at Olympia in 576 BC, repeating the victory of an earlier Orthagorid, Myron I, in 648 BC). These events marked the height of his fame, and in 575 BC took place the marriage of his daughter Agariste. His victorious chariot was later preserved at Delphi under a form of *baldacchino*, the 'Sikyonian *monopteros*' decorated with archaic sculpture and to be dated *c.* 560 BC. It would be interesting to know when he adopted his anti-Dorian policy at home: if after the end of the Sacred War, then the opprobrious address to him from the oracle would seem to indicate he did not remain in favour at Delphi after the construction of the old tholos by him *c.* 580 BC. It is tempting to place his anti-Dorian anti-Argive policy after the marriage of Agariste in 575 BC. It is suggested that he died *c.* 570 BC, to be succeeded by Aischines, possibly his son, who figures on the list of tyrants whose fall was promoted by Sparta, but the fact that the opprobrious Dorian tribal names were not abolished till much later seems to indicate that the non-Dorian element, the Aigialeis, remained strong.

The oracle and the priesthood may have slipped back into their old ways with some rapidity, but there was a conviction in Antiquity that Delphi also played a more elevated role in sixth-century Greece, as the promoter of moral principles, of law and order, and of sweetness, wisdom and light. This development of the concept of Apollo is a very manifest one. Earlier, as in *Iliad* i, he is a remorseless and dread deity with his death-dealing arrows at Troy, very far from being 'The Healer'. In *Iliad* xxiv he is the god who urges mercy, and the concept develops of a god of light, reason and restraint. In the Homeric *Hymn to the Pythian Apollo* (of the sixth century, and almost certainly of a date after the war) the 'lovely resonant note' of his lyre replaces 'the dread clang' of his bow in *Iliad* i. As the eventual exponent of music, joy, order and restraint, who could be better to counsel lawgivers, clear away pollutions, interpret ancient customs or be the patron of the 'Seven Sages'? It is with this aspect of Apollo that there is associated the familiar Delphic maxims of 'Nothing too much' and 'Know Thyself'.

The development in the concept of Apollo was the measure of the strivings in the same direction of his Greek worshippers, in which it is painfully clear that the theory outran the practice, just as Apollo retained deplorable characteristics which troubled some of the later Greeks. None the less the striving was there, it might be said: a quest for justice by Solon; later a quest for moderation on the part of the Spartans (and Chilon was one of the Seven Sages); a seeking after a rational explanation of the universe on the part of the Milesian philosophers; some concern with purification, and efforts to replace or supplement the Olympian religion with something more personal. The problem really is whether in some of these Delphi inspired the Greeks or reflected contemporary developments. Whatever the answer might be, the first half of the sixth century saw notable progress in matters of the mind and spirit, parallel to conspicuous achievements in literature and art: in poetry with the choral lyric, in vase-painting with the great excellence of Attic black-figure; and in sculpture and architecture on a large scale. All the developments so apparent in the second half of the century and in the early fifth are firmly rooted in the period before 550 BC.

### THE EASTERN GREEKS AND LYDIA;
### THE SOUTHERN AND WESTERN MEDITERRANEAN;
### THE PERSIANS

It has been seen in Chapter 6 that the Greeks of western Asia Minor were overshadowed and reduced by the power of Lydia under Alyattes. He came to the throne *c.* 607 BC and continued the campaign conducted by his father Sadyattes against Miletos under the tyrant Thrasyboulos, which was terminated by a treaty *c*. 602 BC after a period of hostilities totalling twelve years. Other cities of the eastern Greeks fared worse; Smyrna was besieged, captured and destroyed. It has already been suggested (p. 151) that Alyattes was influenced by events on his eastern borders, and was in effect securing his rear by dealing with the Greeks.

Events of the utmost importance had taken place in eastern Anatolia and the Middle East. In the earlier seventh century the Assyrians had directed their attention to the eastern Mediterranean and eastern Anatolia, making contact with the Phrygians and Lydians through Urartu, and claiming a Lydian king as a vassal. The last of the great kings of Assyria, Ashurbanipal (the Sardanapallos of the Greeks), died in 626 BC. Assyria had exhausted herself in wide-ranging campaigns, and was vulnerable to attack from the Scythians of the steppe, who between 628 and 626 BC staged a great raid to the borders of Egypt, from which Assyria never recovered. Other enemies were the Kurds of the region of Mannai south-east of Lake Urmia, and further south-east (in the region of Hamadan) the Medes, under a notable ruler whom the Greeks called Kyaxares.

On the death of Ashurbanipal Babylonia broke away from Assyria and took its own place, side by side with the Medes, under the leadership of Nabopolassar (625–604 BC). Both combined together to destroy Nineveh and the remaining feeble power of Assyria in 612 BC. The former Assyrian territories were divided. Nabopolassar occupied southern Assyria and northern Mesopotamia, and Kyaxares the territory further to the north. Necho of Egypt (609–593 BC), son of Psamatik (Psammetichos) I of the Twenty-sixth Dynasty, took advantage of the destruction of 'Assyria to seize Syria and Palestine, but he was defeated at the Battle of Carchemish in 605 BC by Nebuchadrezzar, the son and successor (604–562 BC) of Nabopolassar, and driven back into Egypt. There followed the Babylonian intervention in Palestine, which ended in the destruction of Jerusalem in 586 BC and the Captivity.

At some point, it may be noted, between 601 BC and 586 BC Antimenidas, the brother of the Lesbian poet Alkaios, served as a mercenary in Palestine, which for the poet represented 'the ends of the earth'. Antimenidas cannot have been the solitary example of a Greek mercenary at this time in these regions. Others certainly served with Necho. It must be a matter of debate how much they understood of these events. The same would apply *a fortiori* for their kinsmen in Greece and western Asia Minor. On the other hand Alyattes must have been greatly preoccupied by this basic reorganization of the Middle East. It was inevitable that the Medes under a ruler like Kyaxares would move westwards, absorbing Urartu and whatever else they could secure, and it is unnecessary to quote a semi-folk-tale from Herodotus to account for the hostilities between the Medes and Lydia. A long, evenly matched struggle took place, beginning in 591 BC and ending in a battle terminated by an eclipse of the sun (the 'Battle of the Eclipse'), probably in 585 BC (according to Herodotus foretold by Thales of Miletos). There followed an agreement whereby (in the words of Herodotus) Alyattes should give his daughter Aryenis in marriage to Astyages, the son of Kyaxares. In this way there was peace between Lydia and her eastern neighbour, inherited *c.* 560 BC from Alyattes by his son, Kroisos. The latter, the last member of the Mermnad dynasty, remorselessly continued the Lydian pressure on the Greek cities. The words of Herodotus may usefully be quoted again:

Of the Greek cities Ephesos was the first he attacked. The Ephesians, when he laid siege to the place, dedicated their city to Artemis by stretching a rope from the town wall to the temple of the goddess, which was distant from the ancient city, then besieged by Kroisos, a space of seven furlongs. They were, as I have said, the first Greeks whom he attacked. Afterwards, on some pretext or other he made war in turn upon every Ionian and Aiolian state, bringing forward, where he could, a substantial ground of complaint; where such failed him, advancing some poor excuse. . . . In this way he made himself master of all the Greek cities in Asia and forced them to become his tributaries. . . . Kroisos afterwards, in the course of many years, brought under his sway almost all the nations to the west of the Halys. The Lycians and Cilicians [Kilikes] alone continued free; all the other tribes he reduced and held in subjection. They were the following: the Lydians, Phrygians, Mysians, Mariandynians, Chalybians, Paphlagonians, Thynians and Bithynians, Thracians, Carians, Ionians, Dorians, Aiolians and Pamphylians.[24]

This was an extensive kingdom comparable to the later Pergamene realm, and incorporating peoples of very different cultural development. In keeping with Kroisos' admiration for Delphi and the Greeks it is difficult to reject the idea that the Asia Minor Greeks had a 'special relationship' with the Lydian ruler. There is every reason for believing that they prospered economically in relation to this large hinterland. Their achievements in the arts and literature were the equal of those of mainland Greece. They drew intellectual advantage from contact with their neighbours, but they did not suffer from the more stifling aspects of oriental culture. The development of rationalism, the quest for an alternative to the *Theogony* of Hesiod, as represented by Thales, Anaximander and Anaximenes at Miletos, belongs to the period under consideration, and the later developments in the west such as those represented by Pythagoras at Kroton, and Xenophanes of Kolophon who went to Zankle and Katana, are firmly rooted in it and in Asia Minor. The eastern Greeks had also presented an unedifying spectacle of internal political strife, nowhere more apparent than in the Lesbos of Sappho and Alkaios, but it was followed there by the reaction of the *demos* (the people in general, *not* the 'lower orders') and the election of Pittakos as *aisymnetes*: the triumph of communal reason over aristocratic bigotry. The history of events in Lesbos, pieced together from the fragments of the poetry of Alkaios, shows the vain struggle of an aristocracy, it has been said 'against the tide of history'. The loud and bellicose cries of Alkaois are as significant in this connection as the laments of Theognis in mainland Greece. On the other hand, the celebrated constitutional inscription from Chios, to be dated somewhere in the period 575–550 BC, represents a significant development also, with its 'people's council' (*demosie bole*), fifty elected men from each tribe. Political progress was certainly made.

An important component in the international scene of the first half of the sixth century was northern Africa, and particularly Egypt under the Twenty-sixth Dynasty, founded by Psamatik (Psammetichos) I, *c.* 663–609 BC. From being a minor figure and a vassal of the Assyrians he made himself an independent ruler of Upper and Lower Egypt with the aid of Greek and Carian mercenaries sent by Gyges of Lydia (p. 150). It was through these that the Greeks made their first acquaintance with the ancient land and its wonders, and possibly through an early trading station of the Milesians (Milesion Teichos). Towards the end of his reign the Greek trading centre of Naukratis was founded (*c.* 615–610 BC). There were also garrisons of mercenaries, in which connection Herodotus mentions Stratopeda ('the Camps').

The pattern of the earlier settlement of the Greeks, both mercenaries and others, is obscured through inadequate evidence on the location of these camps and of Daphnai (possibly Tell Defenneh). There may at first have been other settlements of Greeks in the Nile Delta. Psamatik I was followed by Necho, whose activities in Palestine–Syria, with Nebuchad-rezzar as his opponent, have been mentioned already (p. 216), and he in turn by Psamatik II, who carried out an expedition up the Nile into Nubia, with eastern Greek mercenaries who scratched their names on one of the colossi at Abu Simbel. The successor of this relatively minor ruler was Hophra (Apries), 588–567 BC, whose ill-judgement caused him to clash in Palestine with Nebuchadrezzar (which ended in the destruction of Jerusalem) and involved him in a disastrous campaign against the Greeks of Kyrene, while his reliance on foreign mercenaries provoked a rebellion on the part of the native Egyptians. The result was ultimately the murder of Apries and the establishment as pharaoh of Amasis or Aahmes (596/8–525 BC). He thus came to power when Media and Babylonia were still powerful and lived to see the Medes replaced, and the end in 556 BC of the dynasty of Nabopolassar, followed by the last ruler of Babylon, the antiquarian Nabuna'id (Nabonidos). Ultimately Amasis, too, had to rely on mercenaries, but in such a way as to avoid arousing Egyptian nationalist resentment against the foreigners. To effect this he may have concentrated Greek traders at Naukratis and removed the mercenaries to Sais (Memphis) to be his bodyguard. He annexed Cyprus and married a wife, Ladike from Kyrene.

In Kyrene to the west of Egypt a Dorian Greek colony had been founded in the later seventh century in a region famous for its sheep and the medicinal *silphium* plant, which became the symbol of Kyrene and later appeared on its coins. It was ruled by a dynasty of kings named Battos or Arkesilas, one of whom (Arkesilas II?) appears on a famous Lakonian cup formerly, like other examples of the fabric, called Cyrenaic. From Kyrene westwards other settlements, Barke, Euhesperides and Taucheira, were founded, in effect encroaching on the gap between Kyrene and the Carthaginian sphere in northern Africa. Thus there was a dynasty favouring the Greeks in Egypt and a Greek dynasty, in effect, in Kyrene, the southern arm of the Greek expansion towards the middle Mediterranean, parallel to the consolidation of the Greek colonies in Sicily and Italy. There was a further expansion into the western Mediterranean to the coasts of Gaul and Spain, where as yet the Carthaginians and Etruscans had not combined to exclude the Greeks. So Massilia was founded *c*. 600 BC by the Phokaians of Asia Minor.

As at the destruction of Nineveh in 612 BC, so again at mid-century the Middle East experienced in relation to its power structure another change of even greater moment than the fall of Assyria. To the east of Elam and south-east of the area occupied by the Medes there had been established at an early date another Indo-European-speaking people in the region later called Persis. The events of the seventh century gave the opportunity for the development of the power of the Persians, beginning historically with the establishment *c*. 650 BC of Achaimenes (Hakhamanish) as ruler of the area of later Persis, and founder of a dynasty. His successor Chishpish, whom the later Greeks called Teispes, established himself in Elam, profiting from its weakness and from the decline of Assyria. A district of Elam was called Anshan, and from Teispes onwards members of the dynasty were called 'the Great King, King of Anshan'. Susa became their capital, and the authority of these rulers was extended into north-eastern Iran, into Parthia and Hyrcania.

The rise of the Persians was therefore one of the by-products of the Middle Eastern crisis of the late seventh century and its sequel, though the Persians could not yet contest the power of the Medes and of Babylon. This came at mid-sixth century. On the death of Nebuchadrezzar Babylon declined. Astyages may not have seemed to possess the vigour of his father Kyaxares, and according to Herodotus had a reputation for cruelty. So Kyros (Kurush) II, commonly called 'Cyrus the Great', who was great-great-grandson of Achaimenes (and second cousin of Hystaspes [Vishtaspa], ruler of Parthia and Hyrcania, and father of Dareios I), attacked Astyages and deposed him in 550 BC. As the Medes and Persians were so closely related this made little difference in the territories formerly controlled by the Medes (Kyros established his capital at Pasargadai), but a new dynasty now exercised authority up to the Halys boundary of the empire of Kroisos. The latter failed to estimate rightly the power and energy of Kyros. The oracle of Delphi, when consulted, knew not what advice to give, and so gave the ambiguous response that Kroisos, if he attacked Kyros 'would destroy a great kingdom'. Ostensibly to avenge his brother-in-law Astyages, but in reality, it may be suspected, to recover the territories east of the Halys, Kroisos invaded Cappadocia, and consequently suffered a reverse at the Battle of Pteria (547 BC). This was followed by a lightning winter campaign by Kyros, which captured Sardis and the person of Kroisos: a train of events on which the Greeks could base a number of moral lessons. Thus the shadow of Persia replaced that of Lydia over the eastern Greeks. They had been invited by Kyros to abandon the Lydian side. They refused to do so, not, it may be suggested, out of loyalty to Kroisos, but because they underestimated Kyros and knew too little of the Persians. Consequently the sequel to the fall of Lydia was their reduction by Harpagos, Kyros' supporter and commander, except for Miletos, which came to terms. So another basic change overtook the Near East and Anatolia.

The events which followed do not strictly fall within the compass of this book, but form a suitable epilogue to this final chapter. The points have already been made of the emergence of Sparta as a leader in Greece, and the developing importance of Athens under the tyranny, so that when the threat of Persia ultimately came to Greece these two states were the leaders in resistance and the chief powers of Greece thereafter. There is no way of knowing whether at his final accession to power (probably in 547 BC) Peisistratos understood the significance of events in Asia Minor, but it must be noted that he retook Sigeion and held it, presumably by the goodwill of the Persians. Later the Peisistratidai looked to Persia, and Hippias found a refuge at the Persian court. The Spartans were too late to aid Kroisos (who had sought and received their alliance, as he had that of Amasis previously, and of Babylon). In any case they had no strength to send effective aid to him at such a distance, or subsequently to the Asia Minor Greeks. These appealed to Sparta through an envoy richly dressed and long-winded, but (perhaps for this reason) got no effective support. The Spartans contented themselves with sending a rebuke to Kyros; an envoy, Lakrines, was sent 'to prohibit Kyros in the name of the Lakedaimonians from offering molestation to any city of Greece, since they would not allow it'.[25] This serves only to show their total ignorance of Persian power and military skill. Later, it can be argued, they saw the danger from Persian aggression and from those states of Greece, such as Athens under the tyranny, and of Aegina at the time of Marathon, which for a variety of reasons leaned to Persia. It is doubtful, however, if they really saw the danger earlier, or perceived the situation clearly which existed after the defeat of Kroisos. The bulwark of Lydia had disappeared; the Greek cities of Asia Minor were reduced and the Persians were at the Aegean; Babylon was in decline and unable to defend the eastern Mediterranean coasts (it was in fact reduced by the Persians in 538 BC). The only substantial opponent of the Persians, but not strong enough to take the initiative, and forced to wait on events, was Amasis of Egypt, who is found concentrating his mercenaries, cultivating Delphi and the Greeks, especially the Spartans, and allying himself with Polykrates of Samos. All of which was inadequate, and there was at this juncture no effective resistance to Persia. Subsequent events showed the weakness of Egypt, and the inability of the eastern Greeks to resist when they revolted. It was to be sixty years before resistance was shown to be possible, by men whose spirit was very different from that of the eastern Greeks.

One of the more striking aspects of the events of the mid-sixth century concerns these same Greeks. They had prospered under the dominion of Kroisos, materially and culturally. After the defeat of Lydia it is difficult to avoid the impression that the virtue went out of them and that they received a mortal blow to their morale, which led to the suggestion of Bias of Priene that they should migrate to Sardinia. Some, indeed, did retire: some of the Phokaians went off to Alalia in Corsica, and some of the inhabitants of Teos to Abdera in Thrace. Individuals also left Asia Minor: the poet Anakreon went to Athens, and the philosopher Xenophanes of Kolophon to Sicily. It is tolerably clear also that artists left. This dispersion was good for Greece and the West. It meant, however, in the case of communities, the loss to Asia Minor of the more enterprising and resolute citizens, in the case of departing artists and literary figures, a loss to eastern Greek culture. As to the factors causing a loss of morale, there must certainly have been a recognition of the geographical vulnerability of the eastern Greek cities in relation to their eastern neighbour, which promised nothing but continuing subservience. It is just possible that the Ionian Greeks feared that the Persians would, in matters of trade, favour the Phoenicians, who were to be the main source of their navy. There was also the loss, it must be presumed, after the conquest of Egypt by Cambyses II, of a privileged position, for the Greeks, in that country.

Adverse economic trends, however, can hardly have manifested themselves so rapidly or have produced so profound an effect. The real operative factors, it may be suggested, were two. First, the overwhelming effectiveness of Persian siege operations, skill in which the Medes and Persians had acquired from the Assyrians, the experts in siege warfare, as their historical reliefs show. Herodotus thus describes the campaigns of Harpagos: 'Appointed by Kyros to conduct the war in these parts, he entered Ionia and took the cities by means of mounds. Forcing the enemy to shut themselves up within their defences, he heaped mounds of earth against their walls, and thus carried the towns.'[26] The second factor was an alienation of rulers and ruled which never existed between Greeks and Lydians, who had much in common. Whether or not the early Persians, inhabiting a country of fine horses and good men, enjoyed a primitive simplicity 'practising the bow and speaking the truth', they held even after the orientalization certain principles which caused them to regard the Greeks with contempt: witness the reply of Kyros to the Spartans (which also showed how little the Persians knew of the Spartans!) : 'I have never yet been afraid of any men who have a set place in the middle of the city, where they come together and cheat each other and forswear themselves.'[27] It took a relatively long time for the Persians to learn the qualities of the Greeks (and their teachers were the Spartans and Athenians) and a very much longer time for the Greeks to learn those of the Persians by way of Alexander the Great.

From this time forward the Asia Minor Greeks present something of a depressing spectacle, and the future was to mainland Greece.

# REFERENCES AND NOTES

The references are to quoted matter only: the notes have been reduced to the absolute minimum of quoted observations (see the Preface).

INTRODUCTION

1  George Grote, *A History of Greece*, (1846), p. vii.
2  Id., *op. cit.*, p. vii.
3  Id., *op. cit.*, pp. viii–ix.
4  Id., *op. cit.*, p. v.

CHAPTER 1: THE GEOGRAPHICAL BACKGROUND

1  Hesiod, *Works and Days*, 646–9, trans. H.G. Evelyn-White, (Loeb C.L. 1950).
2  Archilochos, frag. 12; trans. R.J.H. M.L. West, *Iambi et Elegi Graeci*, 1 (Oxford 1971).
3  Hesiod, *op. cit.*, 663–70.
4  Id., *op. cit.*, 678–81.
5  Sophocles, *Antigone*, trans. R. Jebb, 332 ff.
6  Homer, *Iliad*, III, 10, trans. R.J.H.
7  Aeschylus, *Agamemnon*, 495, trans. R.G.H.
8  Archilochos, frags. 21, 22; trans. R.J.H. West, *op. cit.*

CHAPTER 2: CRETE AND THE GREEKS

1  *Odyssey*, XIX, 172, trans. R.J.H.
2  *Iliad*, XVIII, 590, trans. R.J.H.
3  Pausanias, IX, 40, 2, trans. R.J.H.
4  Diodorus Siculus, IV, 61, trans. R.J.H.
5  Odyssey, XI, 321, trans. R.J.H.
6  Plutarch, *Life of Theseus* 21 (25), in *Plutarch' Lives. The Dryden Plutarch*, revised by A.H. Clough, Everyman's Library no. 407, 1. (London 1929).
7  Thucydides, 1, 4, trans. Richard Crawley, Everyman's Library no. 455 (London 1926).

CHAPTER 3 : PREHISTORIC GREECE

1   M. Ventris and J. Chadwick, *Documents in Mycenaean Greek*, 2nd ed. (Cambridge 1973), p. 396.

2   J.L. Caskey, *Cambridge Ancient History*[2], fasc. 24 (1964) *passim*; see also fasc. 45 (1966), 14–15, *The Early Bronze Age*, not included in a consolidated 3rd ed.

3   C.W. Blegen, *Cambridge Ancient History* [2], fasc. 1; also Blegen, *Troy*, Ancient Peoples and Places series (London 1963), pp. 147ff. For the important Troy VI, see also the consolidated volume *Cambridge Ancient History*[3], pp. 683–5.

4   Grote, *op. cit.*, p. vii.

5   Thucydides, I, 10.

6   D. Page, *History and the Homeric Iliad* (California 1959), pp. 6, 25 (n. 12).

7   *Iliad*, II, 579–80.

8   *Odyssey*, VI, 298, trans. Butcher and Lang (London 1922).

9   Herodotus, V, 59, trans. G. Rawlinson, Everyman's Library (London 1912).

10  Pausanias, II, 4, trans. R.J.H.

11  Thucydides, I, 12.

12  Pausanias II, 18–19, trans. J.G. Frazer.


CHAPTER 4 : OBSCURITY AND RECOVERY

1   Hesiod, *op. cit.*, 156–60.

2   Id., *op. cit.*, 161–79.

3   Thucydides, I, 12.

4   N. Sanders, in *The European Community in Later Prehistory (Studies in honour of C.F.C. Hawkes)*, ed. J. Boardman, M.A. Brown and T.G.E. Powell (London 1971), p. 23.

5   Id., *op. cit.*, p. 25.

6   Pausanias, VII, 2, 8, trans. Frazer.

7   Pausanias, VII, 2, 5, trans. Frazer.

8   Strabo, XIV, 1, 6 (634–5,) trans. Loeb C.L.

9   Pausanias, VII, 3, 5, trans Frazer.

10  Pausanias, VII, 3, 5, trans. Frazer.

11  Pausanias, VII, 2, 1, trans. Frazer.

12  Pausanias, VII, 2, 8, trans. Frazer.

13  Strabo, XIII, 1, 59 (611), trans. Loeb C.L.

14  Iasos: see *Archaeological Reports for 1970–71* (Hellenic Society, London, 1971), pp. 46–7.

15  Thucydides, I, 12, 4.

16  On Naxos and the site of Grotta, see see V.R.d'A. Desborough. *The Last Mycenaeans* (Oxford 1964), p. 149; see also Desborough, *Protogeometric Pottery* (Oxford 1952), p. 213.

17  *Odyssey*, VI, 262 ff., trans. Butcher and Lang.


CHAPTER 5 : EXPANSION AND INNOVATION

1   D. Page, *Sappho and Alcaeus* (Oxford 1955), p. 223.

2   *Odyssey*, IX, 106ff., trans. Butcher and Lang.
3   Herodotus, IV, 152.
4   Herodotus, IV, 47–57.
5   Herodotus, IV, 13.
6   Thucydides, II, 1.
7   Herodotus, II, 43.


CHAPTER 6: THE BEGINNING OF CONSOLIDATION: TYRANTS AND
HOPLITES

1   Herodotus, II, 135.
2   Id., VI, 127.
3   Strabo, VII, 3, 33 (358).
4   *Etymologicum Magnum*, s.v. 'obeliskos'.
5   J.N. Coldstream, *Greek Geometric Pottery* (London 1968), p. 359.
6   Thucydides, I, 13ff.
7   Thucydides, I, 15, trans. Crawley and Hopper.
8   Thucydides, I, 17, trans. Hopper.
9   Aristotle, *Politics*, 1279 b 6, trans. E. Barker, *The Politics of Aristotle* (Oxford 1946).
10  *Op. cit.*, 1285 a 30.
11  *Op. cit.*, 1310 b 7–31.
12  *Op. cit.*, 1289 b 33–40.
13  Archilochos, frag. 3; West, *op. cit.*, ch. 1, n. 3, trans. R.J.H.
13a An odd phenomenon is the dispute of Chalkis and Andros over Akanthos, Plutarch, *QG* 298 a–b.
14  Herodotus, II, 152, trans. G. Rawlinson.
15  Archilochos, frag. 1, ref. as in 13 above, trans. R.J.H.
16  Pausanias, VIII, 27, 1, trans. Frazer.
17  Id., VII, 17, 1.
18  Id., II, 19, 2.
19  *Palatine Anthology*, XIV, 73, trans. Paton, in *The Greek Anthology* (Loeb C.L.). See A. Andrewes, *The Greek Tyrants* (London 1960), p. 39.
20  Aristotle, *Politics*, 1310 b 18.
21  Ephoros in Strabo, VII, 3, 33 (358), trans. Loeb C.L.
22  The Temenion: Pausanias, II, 38, 1.
23  Pausanias, VI, 22, 2, trans. Frazer.
24  Aristotle, *Politics*, 1265 b 12.
25  *Op. cit.*, 1310 b 12.
26  *Op. cit.*, 1315 b 11.
27  *Op. cit.*, 1313 a 36.
28  *Op. cit.*, 1305 a 16. Thrasyboulos is not mentioned by name.
29  *Op. cit.*, 1305 a 24.
30  *Op. cit.*, 1285 a 35.

31 West, *Iambi et Elegi Graeci*, I, *Theognidea*, *185–90*. See pp. 172–3 for West's observations on the problems of disentangling the various elements in this assemblage of verse.

32 Kallinos, frag. 1, 9–11, trans. R.J.H.; West, *Iambi et Elegi Graeci*, 11.

33 *Loc. cit.*, 20–21, trans. R.J.H.

34 Tyrtaios, frag. 11, 35, trans. R.J.H.; West, *op. cit.*

35 Strabo, XIII, 1, 22 (590), trans. Loeb C.L.

36 Herodotus, 1, 16, trans. R.J.H.

37 Herodotus, 1, 26, trans. G. Rawlinson.

38 Kallinos, frag. 1, 1–4, trans. R.J.H.; West, *op. cit.*

39 Mimnermos, frag. 14, trans. R.J.H.; West, *op. cit.*

40 Mimnermos, frag. 12, trans. R.J.H.; West, *op. cit.*

41 See J.M. Cook, *The Greeks in Ionia and the East* (London 1962), chapter VI.

CHAPTER 7:   THE ABNORMAL STATES

1 Plutarch, *Life of Lycurgus*, *The Dryden Plutarch*, revised by A.H. Clough, Everyman's Library no. 407 (London 1929), 1.

2 Plutarch, *Life of Theseus*, 1, trans. Clough and Hopper.

3 Coldstream, *op. cit.*, p. 215.

4 Plutarch, *Life of Lycurgus*, XXX.

5 *Ibid.*

6 Herodotus, 1, 82, 2, trans. Rawlinson.

7 Tyrtaios, frag. 6 (in Pausanias, 11, 14, 4–5), trans. R.J.H.; West, *op. cit.*, 11.

8 Tyrtaios, frag. 5 (in Strabo, VI, 3, 3 (279), trans. R.J.H.; West, *op. cit.*

9 Herodotus, 1, 65–8, trans. Rawlinson.

10 Plutarch, *Life of Lycurgus*, V for the attitude of the kings and the effect of the *gerousia*.

11 Plutarch, *Life of Lycurgus*, VII.

12 *Id.*, VI.

13 Pausanias, III, 3, 2; III, 11, 10, trans. Frazer.

14 *Id.*, III, 3, 2.

15 Tyrtaios, frag. 4 (in Plutarch, Life of Lycurgus, VI); West, *op. cit.*, 11.

16 Tyrtaios, frag. 11 (in Stobaeus IV, 9, 16), trans. R.J.H.; West, *op. cit.*

17 Aristotle, *Politics*, 1306 b 36.

18 Pausanias, IV, 18, 2–3, trans. Frazer.

19 Coldstream, *op. cit.*, p. 351.

20 *Ibid.*, p. 361.

21 Thucydides, 1, 2.

22 Thucydides, 1, 126, 11–12.

23 Plutarch, *Life of Solon*, XII, Everyman ed., see 1 above.

24 Aristotle, *Constitution of Athens*, 11, trans. R.J.H.; ed. J.E. Sandys, (London 1912).

CHAPTER 8:   THE FOUNDATION OF CLASSICAL GREECE

1 Aristotle, *Constitution of Athens*, 11.

2   *Op. cit.*, III, 6.

3   *Op. cit.*, III, 5, 1–2.

4   *Op cit.*, Sandys's notes to Chapter 4, and Headlam's comment, p. 18.

5   Aristotle, *Politics*, 1273 b 36–1274 a 5.

6   Plutarch, *Life of Solon*, XIII.

7   *Ibid.*

8   Solon, frag. 36 in *Constitution of Athens*, 12, 4ff; West, *op. cit.*, II (trans. R.J.H.).

9   Solon, frag. 5 in *Constitution of Athens*, 11, 2–12, 1; West, *op. cit.*

10  Aristotle, *Constitution of Athens*, VII, 3.

11  Aristotle, *Politics*, 1275 b 17.

12  *Op. cit.*, 1275 a 22.

13  *Op. cit.*, 1274 a 15.

14  Aristotle, *Constitution of Athens*, X.

15  Androtion in Plutarch, *Life of Solon*, 15, trans. R.J.H.

16  Aristotle, *Constitution of Athens*, X, 2–7.

17  Plutarch, *Life of Solon*, XXI.

18  *Digest*, XVII, 22, 4; A. Martina, *Solon. Testimonia Veterum* (Rome 1968), p. 342a, trans. R.J.H.

19  Solon, frag. 5, 5 (West) in *Constitution of Athens*, 11.

20  Herodotus, V, 72, 3.

21  *Rylands Papyri*, 18, trans. F. E. Adcock, Cambridge Ancient History[1], IV, 74; Plutarch, *de malignitate Herodoti*, 21; *Schol. ad Aeschinem*, II, 77.

22  Herodotus, VI, 126, 3.

23  *Hymn to the Pythian Apollo*, 538–44, trans. H.G. Evelyn-White.

24  Herodotus, I, 26–8.

25  *Id.*, I, 152.

26  *Id.*, I, 162.

27  *Id.*, I, 153.

# BIBLIOGRAPHY

## ABBREVIATIONS

AA   *Archäologischer Anzeiger* (Berlin)

AAA   *Athens Annals of Archaeology* (Athens)

AARP   *Art and Archaeology Research Papers* (London)

AD   *Archaiologikon Deltion* (n.s. from vol. 16 = Athens, 1960)

AJA   *American Journal of Archaeology* (Princeton, USA)

Ant.   *Antiquity* (Cambridge)

Ant.J.   *The Antiquaries Journal* (London)

AR   *Archaeological Reports*. Society of Hellenic Studies and the British School at Athens (London)

AS   *Anatolian Studies*. British Institute at Ankara (London)

BAMA   *Bronze Age Migrations in the Aegean* (London, 1973)

BICS   *Bulletin of the Institute of Classical Studies* (London)

BPI   *Bolletino di Paletnologia Italiana* (Rome)

BSA   *Annual of the British School of Archaeology in Athens* (London)

CAH   *Cambridge Ancient History*, vol. 1, 2nd ed., vol. 2, 2nd ed. (fascicules); vol. 2, part 1 revised = 3rd ed. (1973)

ECLP   *The European Community in Later Prehistory*, Boardman, J., Brown, M.A., Powell, T.G.E. (Hawkes Festschrift) (London, 1971)

JHS   *The Journal of Hellenic Studies* (London)

JNES   *The Journal of Near Eastern Studies* (Chicago)

MH   *Museum Helveticum* (Basel)

PBSR   *Papers of the British School at Rome* (London)

PP   *Parola del Passato* (Naples)

PPS   *Proceedings of the Prehistoric Society* (London)

SMA   *Studies in Mediterranean Archaeology* (Lund)

# THE GEOGRAPHICAL BACKGROUND

For general coverage, see: N.G.L. Hammond, *History of Greece*, 2nd ed. (Oxford, 1967), pp. 1–18; more extensive, M. Cary, *The Geographical Background of Greek and Roman History* (Oxford, 1949), bibliography pp. 314ff.; useful is J.O. Thompson, *History of Ancient Geography* (Cambridge, 1948), bibliography pp. 392–4. Highly technical and detailed in terms of geology and physical geography, A. Philippsen, *Griechische Landschaften* (Frankfurt, 1950–9). A.A.M. van der Heyden and H.H. Scullard, *Atlas of the Ancient World* (London, 1959), might be found useful for the simplified maps.

The following deal with important points:

Birmingham, J.M., *AS* 11 (1961), pp. 185–95 (route across Anatolia).
Bryson, R.A., Lamb, H.H. and Donley, D.L., 'Drought and the Decline of Mycenae', *Antiquity* 48 (1974), pp. 46–50 (good references).
Cook, R.M., *Historia* 11 (1962), pp. 113–14 (colonization).
Graham, A.J., *BICS* 5 (1958), pp. 25–39 and refs. there (penetration of the Black Sea).
Graham, A.J., *JHS* 91 (1971), pp. 35ff. (colonization).

# CRETE IN MYTHOLOGY

(a) GENERAL:

Hooker, J.T., 'Homer and the Late Minoan Crete', *JHS* 89 (1969), pp. 60ff.
Huxley, G.L., 'The Minoans in Greek Sources.', *BICS* 16 (1969), pp. 165–6. Proceedings of first conference of the British Assoc. for Mycenean Studies held in London, 24–25 September 1968.

(b) THE LABYRINTH:

On coins of Knossos: *B.M. Guide to the Principal Coins of the Greeks* (London, 1932), pl. 5.40 and pl. 24.54.
Gallavoti, C., 'Labyrinthos', *PP* 54 (1957), pp. 161–76.
Heller, J.H., 'A Labyrinth from Pylos', *AJA* 65 (1961), pp. 57–62.
Ladendorf, H., 'Das Labyrinth in Antike und neuen Zeit', *AA* (1963), pp. 761ff.
Lissi Caronna, E., 'Labirinti', *Atti e Memorie della Società Magna Grecia* (Tivoli, 1970–1).

(c) MINOS AND DAIDALOS:

Dunbabin, T.J., 'Minos and Daidalos in Sicily', *PBSR* 16 (1948), pp. 1–18.

(d) THE 'TOMB OF MINOS':
The 'Temple Tomb' at Knossos: J.D.S. Pendlebury, *A Handbook to the Palace of Minos*, 2nd ed. (London, 1935), pp. 58–9.
The 'Tomb of Minos' in Sicily: see M. Guido, *Sicily: An Archaeological Guide* (London, 1967). Review by A.M. Small, *Ant.J.* 48 (1968), p. 318.

(e) THE MINOAN THALASSOCRACY:
C.J. Starr, *Historia* 3 (1954–5), pp. 282–91.
Ships: From Gazi in Crete, representation on a clay coffin of a large ship with a triangular sail, *AR* (1970–1), p. 31. Others from other sites, as on seals and sealings. There are now the Theran naval battle frescoes. *Thera* vi (Athens, 1974), pls 7 and 9.

(f) 'ATLANTIS':
Galanopoulos, A.G., and Bacon, E., *Atlantis: The Truth Behind the Legend* (London, 1969).
See *Colston Papers* 18 (London, 1965), pp. 440–50, especially pp. 444–50 for the question of Thera-type disaster in Near Eastern records. The dates do not fit very well.

# GREECE AND THE AEGEAN (EXCLUDING CRETE) IN THE BRONZE AGE

(a) SUBSTANTIAL WORKS OF WIDE IMPORT:
Blegen, C.W. *et al.*, *The Palace of Nestor at Pylos*, i, ii (Princeton, 1966, 1969).
Buchholz, H.-G., and Karageorghis, V., *Prehistoric Greece and Cyprus* (London, 1973). Bibliography pp. 176–84.
Desborough, V.d'A., *The Last Mycenaeans and their Successors* (Oxford, 1964).
Finley, M.I., ed., *Early Greece: The Bronze and Archaic Ages* (London, 1970).
Marinatos, S. and Hirmer, M., *Crete and Mycenae* (London, 1960).
Matz, F., *Kreta, Mykenä, Troja* (Stuttgart, 1956).
Mylonas, G.E., *Ancient Mycenae* (London, 1957).
Mylonas, G.E., *Mycenae and the Mycenaean Age* (Princeton, 1966).
Piggott, Stuart, ed., *The Dawn of Civilisation* (London, 1961). M.S.F. Hood on 'The Aegean'.
Renfrew, Colin, *The Emergence of Civilisation* (London, 1972). Excellent bibliography pp. 551–75.
Severyns, A., *Grèce et Proche-Orient avant Homère* (Brussels, 1960).
Skoufopoulos, N.C., 'Mycenaean Citadels', *SMA* 22 (1971).
Taylour, Lord William, *The Mycenaeans* (London, 1964).
Vermeule, E., *Greece in the Bronze Age* (Chicago, 1964). With detailed bibliography pp. 351ff. and chapter notes.

Wace, A.J.B., *Mycenae* (Princeton, 1949).

(b) INVASIONS, INDO-EUROPEANS, THE EARLY AND MIDDLE BRONZE:

Caskey, J. L., 'Greece and the Aegean Islands in the Middle Bronze Age', *CAH*, 2nd ed., ch. 45 (1966) = *CAH*, 3rd ed., vol. 2, part I, pp. 117–40.

Caskey, J.L., 'Greece, Crete and the Aegean Islands in the Early Bronze Age', *CAH*, 2nd ed., ch. 24 (1964).

Crossland, R.A., 'Immigrants from the North', *CAH*, 2nd ed., ch. 60 (1967).

Crossland, R.A., 'Recent Re-appraisal of Evidence for the Chronology of the Differentiation of Indo-Europeans', *AARP*, pp. 24–35.

Crossland, R. A., and Birchall, A., eds., *Bronze Age Migrations in the Aegean* (London, 1973).

Georgiev, V. I., 'La Grèce et les Indo-Europcans', *AARP*, pp. 24–35.

Hampl, Franz, 'Die Chronologie der Einwanderung der griechischen Stämme und das Problem der Nationalität der Träger der mykenischen Kultur', *MH* 17 (1960), pp. 57–86.

Howell, R.J., 'The Origins of the Middle Helladic Culture', *BAMA*, p. 73ff.

Lloyd, S. and Mellaart, J., *Beycesultan* i, ii (London, 1962).

Mellaart, J., 'The End of the Bronze Age in Anatolia and the Aegean', *AJA* 62 (1958), p. 21ff.

Palmer, L. R., *Achaeans and Indo-Europeans* (Oxford, 1955).

Popham, M. and Sackett, L.H., *Excavations at Lefkandi, Euboea, 1964–66: Preliminary Report* (London, 1968), ch. 9.

Schachermeyr, F., 'Vor-Indo-Europäische Substrate und Indo-Europäische Zuwanderungen in der griechisch-anatolischen Frühzeit', *AARP*, pp. 10–14.

Stubbings, F.H., 'The Rise of Mycenaean Civilisation', *CAH*, 3rd ed., vol. 2, part I, pp. 627–58.

Tritsch, F.J., 'Minyans and Luvians', *AARP*, pp. 42–5.

(c) THE LINEAR A AND B SCRIPTS:

Chadwick, J., *The Decipherment of Linear B* (Cambridge, 1960).

Dow, S. and Chadwick, J., 'The Linear Scripts and the Tablets as Historical Documents', *CAH*, 2nd ed. (1971), chapter XIII.

Palmer, L.R., *The Interpretation of Mycenaean Greek Texts* (Oxford, 1963). With extensive bibliography.

Palmer, L.R., *Mycenaeans and Minoans* (London, 1961).

Pope, M., 'Aegean Writing and Linear A', *SMA* 8 (1954), pp. 1–16.

Ventris, M. and Chadwick, J., *Documents in Mycenaean Greek*, 2nd ed. (Cambridge, 1973). See especially p. 396: M. Pope on the relation of Linear A and Linear B.

(d) THE PREHISTORY OF THE GREEK LANGUAGE:

Chadwick, J., 'The Prehistory of the Greek Language', *CAH*, 2nd ed., ch. XXXIX.

Wyatt, F. Jr., 'Greek Dialectology and Greek Prehistory', *AARP*, pp. 18–22.

*'Substrate' elements:*

Hainsworth, J.B., 'Some Observations on the Indo-European place-names of Greece', *AARP*, pp. 39–42.

Hester, D.A., 'Recent Developments in Mediterranean "substrate" Studies', *Minos* 9 (1963), pp. 219–35.

Levin, S., 'Greek with Substrate', *Kadmos* 11, pp. 129–39.

Note the ideas of M.S.F. Hood implicit in the title of his book. *The Home of the Heroes, The Aegean before the Greeks.*

Phenomena, or 'A Jargon'–What is the Difference?

(e) GREECE AND THE EAST MEDITERRANEAN:

Cadogan, J., 'Mycenaean Trade', *BICS*, Mycenaean Seminar 1968–9, pp. 152–4.

Faure, Paul, 'Toponymes Créto-Mycéniens dans une liste d'Amenophis III', *Kadmos* 7, pp. 138–9.

Hankey, V., on Beth Shan, *AJA* 70 (1966), pp. 169–71.

Hankey, V., 'Mycenaean Pottery in the Middle East: Notes on finds since 1951', *BSA* 62 (1967), p. 107ff.

Hankey, V., 'Mycenaean Trade with the South-eastern Mediterranean', *Mélanges de l'Universite St Joseph* 46 (Beirut, 1970–1), p. 9ff.

Merrillees, R.S., 'Aegean Bronze Age relations with Egypt', *AJA* 76 (1972), pp. 281–94.

Smith, W.S., *Interconnections in the Ancient Near East* (Yale, 1965).

Stubbings, F., 'The Expansion of Mycenaean Civilisation', *CAH*, 2nd ed. (1964), ch. 26.

Stubbings, F., *Mycenaean Pottery from the Levant* (Cambridge, 1951).

See also below, on the Sea Peoples, and the forthcoming proceedings of the Sheffield Conference on the Sea Peoples.

(f) GREECE AND THE WEST:

Branigan, K., 'Prehistoric Relations between Italy and the Aegean', *BPI* n.s. 17 (1966), pp. 97–109.

Renfrew, C. and Whitehouse, R., 'The Copper Age of Peninsular Italy and the Aegean', *BSA* 69 (1974), pp. 343–90.

Renfrew, C., 'Wessex without Mycenae', *BSA* 63 (1968), p. 277ff.

Taylour, Lord William, *Mycenaean Pottery in Italy and Adjacent Areas* (Cambridge, 1958).

Faïence beads:

McKerrell, H., *PPS* 38 (1972), p. 286ff.

Newton, R.J. and Renfrew, C., 'British Faïence beads reconsidered', *Ant.* 44 (1970), pp. 199–206.

(g) THE SEA PEOPLES:

Barnett, R.D., 'The Sea Peoples', *CAH*, 2nd ed. (1969), ch. 68, bibliography.

De Vaux, R., 'La Phénicie et les Peuples de la Mer', *Mélanges de l'Université St Joseph* 45 (Beirut, 1969), pp. 481–98.

Kardara, C.P., 'The Peoples of the Land and of the Sea', *AAA* iii, pp. 440–54.

Kimming, W., 'Seevölkerbewegung und Urnenfelder-Kultur', *Studien aus Alt-Europa* 1 (Cologne, 1964), pp. 220–83.

Nelson, H.H., 'The Naval Battle pictured at Medinet Habu', *JNES* ii, pp. 40–55.

Nibbi, A., 'The Identification of the Sea People', *BAMA* pp. 203ff.

Sandars, Nancy K., 'From Bronze Age to Iron Age: A Sequel to a Sequel', *ECLP*, pp. 3–29, esp. pp. 23–4.

Schachermeyr, F., '"Hörnerhelme" und "Federkronen" als Kopfbedeckungen bei den Seevölkern der Ägyptischen Reliefs', *Ugaritica* v, pp. 451–9.

(h) THE AḪḪIJAVA PROBLEM:

Huxley, J.L., *Achaeans and Hittites* (Queen's University, Belfast, 1964).

Page, D.L., *History and the Homeric Iliad* (Berkeley, 1959), pp. 1–40.

(i) THE MYCENAEANS AND THE HOMERIC POEMS:

Page, D.L., *History and the Homeric Iliad* (Berkeley, 1959), pp. 118–77.

(j) HORSES, HORSE-RIDING, CHARIOTS:

Hood, M.S.F., 'A Mycenaean Cavalryman', *BSA* 48, pp. 84–93.

Littauer, M.A., 'The Military Use of the Chariot in the Aegean in the Late Bronze Age', *AJA* 76 (1972), pp. 145–57.

Powell, T.G.E., 'The Introduction of Horse-riding to Temperate Europe', *PPS* 37 (1971), pp. 1–14.

(k) ARMS AND ARMOUR:

Catling, H.W., 'A bronze plate from a scale-corselet found at Mycenae', *AA* 85 (1970), pp. 441–9.

Lorimer, H.L., *Homer and the Monuments* (London, 1950).

Sandars, N.K., 'From Bronze Age to Iron Age: A Sequel to a Sequel', *ECLP*, pp. 3–29, *passim*.

Snodgrass, A.M., 'The First European Body-armour', *ECLP*, pp. 33–50.

Snodgrass, A.M., 'The Linear B Arms and Armour Tablets', *Kadmos* 7, pp. 96–110. See p. 97 for Dendra armour and later form.

THE EARLY GREEKS

Allusions to Mycenaean military equipment are made in the following:
Greenhalgh, P.A.L., *Early Greek Warfare* (Cambridge, 1973).
Snodgrass, A.M., *Early Greek Armour and Weapons* (Edinburgh, 1964).

(1) TECHNICAL MATTERS:
Catling, H.W., Richards, E.E. and Blin-Stoyle, A.E., 'Correlations
between Composition and Provenance of Mycenaean and Minoan
pottery', *BSA* 58 (1963), p. 94ff.
Catling, H.W., *et al.*, 'Spectographic Analysis of Mycenaean and Minoan
Pottery', *Archaeometry* 4 (1961), pp. 31–8.
Catling, H.W. and Millett, A., 'A Study in the Composition Patterns of
Mycenaean Pictorial Pottery from Cyprus', *BSA* 60 (1965), p. 212ff.
Catling, H.W. and Millett, A., 'A Study of the Inscribed Stirrup-Jars from
Thebes', *Archaeometry* 8 (1965), pp. 3–85.
Du Plat Taylor, J., ed., *Marine Archaeology* (London, 1965): G.F. Bass on the
Cape Gelidonya wreck, p. 119ff.

(m) SITES OF PARTICULAR RELEVANCE (RECENT DISCOVERIES):

i. *Lefkandi* (Euboea);
Popham, M. and Sackett, L.H., *Excavations at Lefkandi, Euboea, 1964–66:
Preliminary Report* (1968).

ii. *Lefkas* (the graves):
J.L. Caskey, *CAH*, 2nd ed. (1964), I, ch. xxvi (a) pp. 23–4.
J.L. Caskey, *CAH*, 2nd ed. (1966), II, ch. iv (a), pp. 14–15.
N.J.L. Hammond, *ECLP*, pp. 104–12.
N.J.L. Hammond, *BSA* 62 (1967), pp. 77–105.
N.J.L. Hammond, *BSA* 69 (1974), pp. 127–42.
K. Branigan, *BSA* 70 (1975), 37–49.

iii. *Marathon-Vrana:*
Marinatos, S., *ECLP*, pp. 184–90.
Marinatos, S., *ECLP ibid.* (chariot users).

iv. *Miletus:*
'Die Ausgrabungen beim Athena-tempel in Milet 1957', *Istanbuler Mit-
teilungen* 9/10 (1959–60), pp. 1ff.

v. *Messenia, Mycenaean Sites:*
*AD* 16.(1960), pls. 91ff., 98–9; chron. 112–19.
*AD* 17 (1960–1), pls. 106–10.
*AAA*, iii, pp. 125–36 (Cretan masons' marks at Peristeria).

vi. *Mycenae:*
Sanctuary area: *AR* (1972–3), p. 13.
Mylonas, J.E., *The Cult Center of Mycenae* (Athens, 1972).

234

Taylour, Lord William, 'Mycenae 1968', *Ant.* 43 (1969), pp. 91–7.
Taylour, Lord William, 'New Light on Mycenaean Religion', *Ant.* 44 (1970), pp. 270–80.

vii. *Nichoria, Messenia:*
McDonald, W. and Rapp, J., *The Minnesota Messenia Expedition* (Minnesota, 1972).

viii. *Delos:*
'Etudes deliennes', *BCH*, Suppl. I (1973), pp. 415ff. (on the Artemision Ivories).

ix. *Troy:*
Blegen, C.W., *Troy* (London, 1963).

x. *Kythera:*
Coldstream, J.N. and Huxley, J.L., eds., *Kythera. Excavations and Studies* (London, 1972).

xi. *Tiryns:*
Passages to springs, *AA*, (1963–4), p. 8; excavation of the lower town, *AAA* 4, pp. 398–406; *AAA* 7 (1974), p. 15ff. (note Linear B tablets and continuity from LH III B to Geometric); *AA* (1967), pp. 92–101.

## OBSCURITY AND RECONSTRUCTION

Alin, Per, 'Das Ende der mykenischen Fundstätten auf dem griechischen Festland', *SMA*, i (Lund, 1962).
Broneer, O., 'The Cyclopean Wall on the Isthmus of Corinth and its bearing on Late Bronze Chronology', *Hesperia* 37 (1968), pp. 346–62.
Desborough, V.R.d'A., *The Greek Dark Ages* (London, 1972).
Desborough, V.R.d'A., *The Last Mycenaeans and their Successors* (Oxford, 1964).
Desborough, V.R.d'A., *Protogeometric Pottery* (Oxford, 1952).
Sakellariou, Michel B., *La Migration grecque en Ionie* (Athens, 1958).
Snodgrass, A.M., *The Dark Ages of Greece* (Edinburgh, 1971). Good notes.
Huxley, G.L., *The Early Ionians* (London, 1966).

## EXPANSION AND INNOVATION

Boardman, J., *The Greeks Overseas* (London, 1964).
Coldstream, J.N., *Greek Geometric Pottery* (London, 1968).
Cook, J.M., *The Greeks in Ionia and the East* (London, 1962).
Dunbabin, T.J., *The Greeks and their Eastern Neighbours* (London, 1957).

Dunbabin, T.J., *The Western Greeks* (Oxford, 1948).
Jeffrey, L.H., *The Local Scripts of Archaic Greece* (Oxford, 1961).
Seltman, C., *Greek Coins*, 2nd ed. (London, 1955).
Kraay, C.M. and Max Hirmer, *Greek Coins* (London, 1966).

## THE BEGINNING OF CONSOLIDATION:
## HOPLITES AND TYRANTS

For useful and readily accessible illustrations, see G.M.A. Richter, *A Handbook of Greek Art* (London, 1959) and J.C. Stobart, *The Glory that was Greece*, 4th ed. (London, 1964).
Andrewes, A., *The Greek Tyrants* (London, 1960).
Berve, H., *Die Tyrannis bei den Griechen* (Munich, 1967).
Greenhalgh, P.A.L., *Early Greek Warfare* (Cambridge, 1973).
Starr, C.J., *The Origins of Greek Civilisation* (London, 1962).
Snodgrass, A.M., *Early Greek Armour and Weapons* (Edinburgh, 1964).

## THE ABNORMAL STATES

(a) SPARTA:
Boardman, J., 'Artemis Orthia, Chronology', *BSA* 58 (1963), p. 1ff.
Boer, W. den, *Laconian Studies* (Amsterdam, 1954).
Chrimes, K.M.T., *Ancient Sparta* (Manchester, 1949).
Dawkins, R.M. *et al.*, *The Sanctuary of Artemis Orthia at Sparta* (London, 1929).
Forrest, W.J., *A History of Sparta 950–192 BC* (London, 1968).
Huxley, J.L., *Early Sparta* (London, 1962).
Jones, A.H.M., *Sparta* (Oxford, 1967).
Kiechle, F., *Lakonien und Sparta* (Munich, 1963).
Michell, H., *Sparta* (Cambridge, 1952).

(b) ATHENS:
Andrewes, A., *The Greek Tyrants* (London, 1960).
Jacoby, F., *Atthis* (Oxford, 1949).
See below in relation to Solon.

## SOLON AND ATHENS;
## SPARTA AND THE PELOPONNESE

(a) SOLON AND RELATED QUESTIONS:
Berve, H., *Die Tyrannis bei den Griechen* (Munich, 1967).

Ehrenberg, V., *From Solon to Socrates* (London, 1968).

Forrest, J., on the First Sacred War, *BCH* 80 (1956), pp. 33–52.

Jacoby, F., *Atthis* (Oxford, 1949).

   Martina, Antonius, *Solon, Testimonia*, with notes (Rome, 1968).

Parke, H.W., *Greek Oracles* (London, 1967).

Ruschenbusch, E., *Solonos Nomoi, Historia*, Einzelschrift 9 (Wiesbadan, 1966).

(b)  ATTIC SCULPTURE:

   The better known examples in G.M.A. Richter, *Kouroi* (London, 1960); *Korai* (London, 1968); the latest Kouros and Kore (possibly the Phrasikleia known from an inscription) from Merenda, *AR* (1972–3), pp. 6–7. G.M.A. Richter, *The Archaic Gravestones of Attica* (London, 1961).

(c)  INSCRIPTIONS:

   Jeffrey, L.H., *BSA* 57 (1962), pp. 115–53.

(d)  RECENT PUBLICATION:

   Jeffrey, L.H., *Archaic Greece. The City-States* c. *700–500 B.C.* (London, 1976).

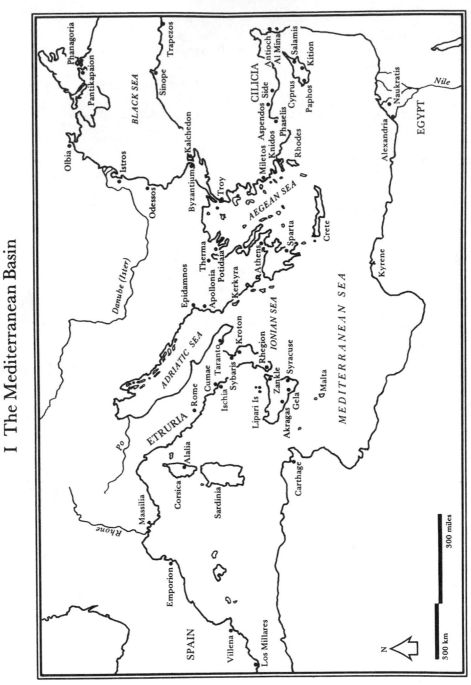

I The Mediterranean Basin

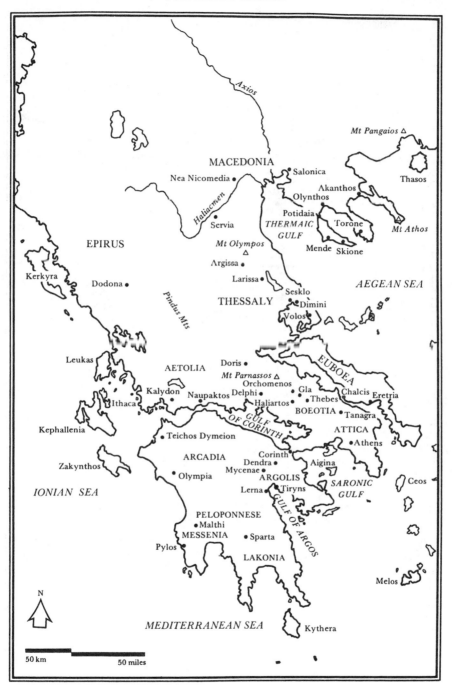

*Axios*

*Mt Pangaios* △

MACEDONIA

Nea Nicomedia •   • Salonica

Thasos

Akanthos

Olynthos

*Haliacmen*

• Servia   Potidaia

THERMAIC   Torone

GULF   • *Mt Athos* △

EPIRUS   *Mt Olympos*   Mende   Skione

△

Kerkyra   *Argissa* •

Dodona •   Larissa •   *AEGEAN SEA*

Seslko

*Pindus Mts*   THESSALY   Dimini

Volos

Leukas   Doris •   *EUBOEA*

AETOLIA   *Mt Parnassos* △

Kalydon   Orchomenos

Naupaktos   Delphi •   • Gla   Chalcis

Ithaca   • Haliartos   • Thebes   Eretria

BOEOTIA   • Tanagra

Kephallenia   • Teichos Dymeion   ATTICA

ARCADIA   Corinth   • Athens

Zakynthos   Dendra •

• Olympia   Mycenae •   Aigina   Ceos

*IONIAN SEA*   ARGOLIS   *SARONIC*

Lerna •   Tiryns   *GULF*

PELOPONNESE

• Malthi   *GULF OF ARGOS*

MESSENIA   • Sparta

Pylos •   LAKONIA

Melos

N

*MEDITERRANEAN SEA*   Kythera

50 km

50 miles

## II Greece

BLACK SEA

Photolivos

Mt Pangaios △   ● Abdera

THRACE

Thasos

Byzantium

Kalchedon

● Ainos

Samothrace

THRACIAN SEA

Imbros

Sestos

Kyzikos

● Abydos

Lemnos   ● Poliochni   ● Sigeum

TROAS

Scyros

AEGEAN SEA

Lesbos   ● Thermi

AEOLIS

● Kyme

Phokaia

Chios   ● Erythrai

Smyrna

IONIA

● Teos

Kolophon ●

● Ephesus

Andros

Samos

△ Mt Mykale

Ceos

Tenos

Icaria

● Priene

● Miletus

CARIA

● Delos

CYCLADES   Naxos

Paros

Halicarnassus

Amorgos

Siphnos

Kos   Knidos

Melos

Thera

Rhodes

LYKIAN SEA

N

CRETAN SEA

Karpathos

50 km        50 miles

III  The Eastern Aegean and Western Asia Minor

240

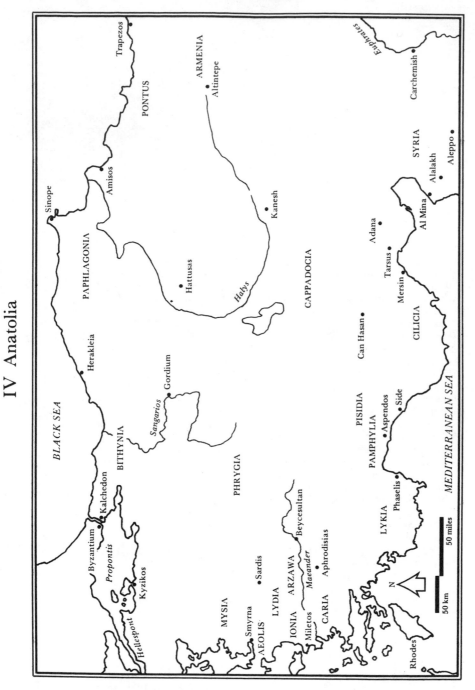

IV Anatolia

# INDEX

Abantes, 70, 73
Abaris, 97
Abdera, 92, 93, 124, 221
Abu Simbel, 107, 218
Abydos, 124, 149, 152
Achaea, Achaeans, 2, 38, 53, 54, 56, 60, 64, 72, 91, 124
Achaean dialect, 58
Achaimenes (Hakhamanish), 219
'Achaioi', 53, 54, 213
Achaios, 54
Acheloos Valley, 1
Achilleion, 206
Achilles, 11, 40, 42, 45, 49, 101
Achilles, Shield of, 110
Adana, 6, 69
Adrastos, King of Argos, 43, 48, 210, 212
Adriatic, 4, 58, 209
Aegean, 1, 3, 4, 5; Carians, 72; dialects, 55, 58; Dorian invasion, 59; Early Bronze culture, 19; lack of Late Helladic destruction, 38; trade routes, 103
Aegina, 19, 9c; Argos dominates, 128, 136; Athenian pottery found in, 115; campaigns against Athens, 62, 123, 179, 205; coinage, 111, 113–14; and Egypt, 125; fortifications, 25; shrine of Damia and Auxesia, 179; trade rivalry with Athens, 136
Aeolian dialect, 54
Aeolian Islands, 14
Aeolic dialect, 58, 59
Aeolis, 58, 69, 70, 95–6
Aeschines, 208
Aeschylus, 49; *Oresteia*, 40
Aetolia, 1, 44, 57, 58, 59, 210
Africa, 92, 124, 218, 219
Agamedes, 212

Agamemnon, 10, 27, 32, 40–1, 42, 45, 46, 49, 50, 129, 147,
Agamemnon cult, 48
Agariste, 111, 210, 214
Agesilaos I, King of Sparta, 156, 164
Aghia Irini, 24, 25, 33, 36
Aghios Kosmas, 19
Agis II, King of Sparta, 164
Agis IV, King of Sparta, 156, 157, 164
Agrinion, 1
Ahab, King, 102
Ahhiya, 42–3, 78, 79
Aietes, 97, 135–6
Aigaiai, 70
Aigeus, 12
Aigialeis, 132, 210, 214
Aigikoreis, 181
Aigiroessa, 70
Aigyptos, 27
Ainianes, 212
Ainos, 92, 124
Aiolos, 54
Aipytos, 60
Aischines, 132, 208, 214 (see Aeschines)
Aithon, 10
Ajax, 47, 49–50, 128
Akanthos, 92, 124
Akarnania, 1, 58
Akastos, 71
Akragas, 13, 91, 120
Al Mina (Poseideion), 103, 105, 115
Alaca Hüyük, 26, 146
Alalia, 92, 221
Albania, 20, 67
Aletes, 129, 132, 134
Aleuadai of Larissa, 213, 214
Aleuas the Red of Larissa, 212
Alexander the Great, 146, 222

THE EARLY GREEKS

Theron, 13
Theseus, 12–14, 32, 41, 44–8, 60, 71, 159, 176, 180
Thessalians, confederacy of, 212–13
Thessaliotis, 212
Thessalos the Heraclid, 74, 129
Thessaly: archaeology, 22, 23, 33; dialect, 58, 59; Dorian invasion, 54, 59; Dryopians, 57; fortifications, 38; Lelantine War, 122; pottery, 77, 80; *tholos* tombs, 30; trade routes, 1–2
Thiaki, 5, 44, 87, 90
'Thirty Tyrants', 163
Thoas, 55, 137
*tholos* tombs, 24, 28–30, 32, 48, 49, 79
Thorikos, 30
Thrace, 1, 84; archaeology, 18, 19; Greek colonization, 5, 72, 86, 92–3, 124, 125–6; inhabitants of Teos migrate to, 221; language, 17; nomadic invasions, 147, 150; supports Peisistratos, 204; trade with Athens, 205
Thrakides, 72
Thrasyboulos of Miletos, 133, 135, 137, 151, 209, 216
Thrasymedes, 51
Thucydides, 41, 42, 68, 70, 78, 124; on Athens, 79, 159, 163, 181, 183, 185–6, 202; on Carians, 72; on Corinth, 132; on Dorian invasion, 56, 59, 60; on early Greek settlers, 76; on Herakles, 44; *History*, 69, 116–17, 118–19, 120; on the Lelantine War, 122, 123; on Minos, 14; on the Return of the Herakleidai, 50; on the Sicilian Expedition, 89; on Sparta, 157; on the Trojan War, 43, 54; on war between Athens and Sparta, 106
Thyrea, 127, 129
Thyreatis, 207
Tigris River, 7
Timonassa, 211
Timphrestos, Mount, 59
Tiryns, 23, 40, 48, 127; access to springs, 38; destruction, 38; fortifications, 63; fortress palace, 19, 31, 32, 33; and Herakles, 44; *megara*, 46; wall-paintings, 34, 35
Tisamenos, 50–1, 57, 60
Tjekker, 66
Tlepolemos, 74, 129
Tomi, 96
Torone, 121, 126
trade, 142, 209; Athens, 136, 177–8, 205; trade routes, 1–7, 102–3
Trapezos (Trabzon, Trebizond), 6, 7, 94,

102, 123, 147, 148
Trebenischte, 135
Treres, 147, 15, 151, 152, 153
Trikkala, 1
Triopion, 70
Triphylia, 2, 57, 60, 139
Tris Langadas, 44
Troizen, 128
Trojan War, 9–10, 13, 28, 40–3, 49, 52, 68, 69
Trophonios, 212
Troy: destruction and rebuilding, 18, 37, 66; Early Bronze culture, 19; *megaron* structures, 22; pottery remains, 66–7
Turkey, 1, 6
Tursha, 58, 66, 67
'Twelve-Year War', 151
Tydeus, 43
Tyndareos, 51
tyranny, development of, 118–20, 126, 130–5, 137–41, 145, 189, 209–10; Athens, 120, 138, 185–6, 203–4, 208–9; Solon on, 202; and Sparta, 208–9
Tyrrhenian Sea, 91
Tyrrhenians, 66
Tyrsenoi, 58
Tyrtaios of Sparta, 140, 144, 153, 166, 169, 170, 171, 172–3, 206; *Eunomia*, 158, 174–5
'Tyrtaios War', 206

Ugarit, 26
Urartu, 7, 94, 98–100, 102, 146, 150, 216
Urmia, Lake, 98–9, 216
Urnfield culture, 65
Uruk period, 23
Üsküdar, 93

Van, Lake, 94, 98, 99, 102
Vannic kingdom, *see* Urartu
Vapheio, 29–30, 32, 44, 160
Vardar Valley, 1
Vardaroftsa, 65
Vari, 104, 202
Velia, 92
Vergina, 65
Verria, 7
Via Egnatia, 135
Vitruvius, 75, 76
Vrana, 20

wall-paintings, Mycenaean, 34, 35
warfare, 117, 118–23, 172–4; naval warfare, 117, 118, 123; *see also* hoplite army
'Warrior Vase', 39

256